Soviet Cinema

Directors and Films

compiled by

Alexander S. Birkos

Archon Books   1976

Library of Congress Cataloging in Publication Data

Birkos, Alexander S.
    Soviet cinema.

        Bibliography: p.
        1. Moving-picture producers and directors—Russia—
Biography. 2. Moving-pictures—Russia—Catalogs.
I. Title.
PN1998.A2B56   791.43'0233'0922   76-7082
ISBN 0-208-01581-7

For my brother,

JOHN (VANYA),

whose own steel was finely tempered in the forges of many
worldly universities during his trek along the road to life.

CONTENTS

ILLUSTRATIONS

PREFACE

This work stems from a life-long interest in Soviet films that
started when my parents took me as a youngster to see my first Russian
movie, *Chapayev*. My appreciation of film as a social-political mirror
was broadened while I was a student in the Russian Language Division
of the U.S. Army Language School. It is my hope that this volume,
which started as an avocational interest, will be helpful to film enthusiasts who want to know a bit more about Soviet films and film-makers.
As such the book is intended largely as a beginning reference for the
general movie goer.

The focus is on the period 1918-75 and this work is divided into
two major divisions. The first is a listing of directors who were active in
that period and the second is a list of Soviet films released during that
time. My objective has been broad comprehensiveness rather than ex-
haustive all-inclusiveness. I have included all films where it was possible
to trace down the date of release and name of director. Some of the
films are merely listed where I have been unable to locate information
about them or have not personally seen them.

I would be grateful to hear from any reader regarding omissions
or errors that might have inadvertently occurred during the compilation
of this work.

Several people helped during the compilation of this book and
without their assistance it might never have been finished. Mrs. Virginia
Mulica and Mrs. Twila Oakes of Mount Shasta City Library, and
Mrs. Thora Leoni and her staff of Siskiyou County Library receive my
gratitude for their inexhaustible cheerfulness while processing mountains of inter-library loan requests. Miss Mary Corliss, Stills Archivist of
The Museum of Modern Art; Mrs. Michelle Snapes, Chief Stills Officer
of the British Film Institute; and the staffs of Artkino Pictures, Inc. and
the Pacific Film Archive were most gracious in answering queries about

films and photographs. To two of my relatives, Lawrence and Dolores Hayes, goes my heartfelt thanks for help in ways too numerous to cite here. Finally, my gratitude to my wife, Laura, who always understood the why of my "mental absences" during this and other projects.

Alexander S. Birkos
Mount Shasta, California

INTRODUCTION

In the years since Stalin's death in 1953, Soviet directors have steadily increased the annual output of films, from an all-time low of five feature films in 1952 to an annual average of 135 today, not including documentaries, shorts and cartoons. Some films have been good and some bad, much as is the case in other countries. To a greater degree than in other countries the Soviet director has always been held accountable for the failure or success, artistically or politically, of his films. Censorship of films goes back to tsarist times and is not unique to the Soviet era, but there are definite signs that it has relaxed greatly since the strangling harshness of Stalin's last years. Controversial and daring films continue to be released and, despite revisions, offer us a good glimpse of changing Soviet life styles. Films on historical subjects, too, are showing fresher and more revealing views about the past. The new generation of Soviet film-makers has shown itself to possess as much talent as its predecessors and has received ample critical acclaim and its fair share of prizes at international film festivals. The Soviet film industry has never had such good times as the 1960s and 1970s, and Soviet audiences have not forsaken the silver screen for television as have their counterparts in the West.

The films of the directors who are listed in this book bear witness to the changes that have taken place in the USSR since 1918. Soviet motion pictures provide the filmgoer with entertainment, and with a good deal of insight as to how the Soviets view their own society and the world around them. It is true that Soviet films are political, but what film, in the final analysis, is not? D. W. Griffith's classic *Birth of a Nation* is an excellent presentation of the pro-Southern point of view about the American Civil War and its aftermath. The films of any country will reflect the views and values of that country, as most film critics now generally agree.

However, Soviet films can be enjoyed for themselves alone and much of their artistry would be lost if we looked at them only as political documents. The vivid scenes of the clash between the tsar's soldiers and the revolutionary masses on the Odessa steps in *Battleship Potemkin* are still a highpoint in the editing of film as done by Eisenstein. The deep emotions of an elderly woman who finally begins to see the futility and cruelty in her life gave Pudovkin's *Mother* far more dramatic value than its political statement, and show us why Pudovkin is considered a virtuoso of silent film art. In the last two years Vasili Shukshin's *The Red Snowball Tree* (or *Red Berry*) has evoked much critical admiration for its lyrical and compassionate treatment of an ex-convict who fails to overcome his past. And in comedies, too, Soviet films can be enjoyed for the sake of having a good laugh over stories like Eldar Ryazanov's *Carnival Night.* The enjoyment of any particular film is deepened when the viewer also understands some of the historical forces that operated at the time it was made.

The halcyon days for Soviet film-makers extended from 1918 through 1928. While the country and millions of people endured the hardships of the Russian Civil War, famine, economic devastation, and bitter social struggle, young, eager film-makers, many only in their teens, came forth to launch the Golden Age of Soviet cinema. Never were directors to enjoy so much freedom in matters of form, style, and theme, and, above all, the freedom to depict society as they saw it. The legitimacy of film as an art form was established at this time, when Lenin said that cinema was the most important of all the arts for Communists. In one simple utterance Lenin had uplifted the stature of film while simultaneously tieing its fate to the will of the Party. It might also be added that Soviet cinema is at the fate of the man who controls the Party. Under Lenin, who was cosmopolitan, intellectually inclined, and well travelled, Soviet films attained their peak in abstract symbolism. Under Stalin, the provincial, suspicious underground revolutionary, Soviet films descended to bland "socialist realism" and were devoid of witty satire.

From the very beginning 'education' was given higher priority than 'art' in film work when the Soviet film industry was officially established as the Cinema Section of the State Commissariat of Education in 1917. This choice of priority was not altogether bad because of the low educational level of the population, which partially explains why Soviet audiences were not fond of some of the abstract films of Eisenstein and Dovzhenko in the 1920s. In early 1918 Lenin extricated the country from further involvement in World War I and the Bolsheviks found themselves seriously challenged by the Whites and Allied foreign intervention. The film industry was then torn apart by the large scale flight of hundreds of experienced directors and actors. Much equipment and film stock was either taken out of the country or destroyed and thus exacerbated the problems that confronted Soviet cinema in its first years. Only a few directors from the tsarist era remained behind after the October Revolution, but the artistic vacuum was quickly filled by young people who were eager to make films despite the difficulties of the times.

The films of 1918-21 were mostly short, and graphically crude, propaganda film pamphlets *(agitki)* which were made to support the Bolshevik cause during the Civil War. Travelling cinemas, the so-called "agit-trains", went everywhere with these quickly and cheaply produced short films in order to educate and agitate both troops and civilians. While often short on dramatic art and technically crude, the *agitki* served well both as propaganda and as on-the-job training for future directors of theatrical, documentary, newsreel, and popular science-educational films. A few feature-length theatrical films were made during these years, *Polikushka* and *Sickle and Hammer* among them, but the shortage of film deterred many efforts. When Alexander Razumni attempted to adapt Gorki's novel *Mother* for the screen in 1920 the effort resulted in an episodic structure that could only be considered a transition or prelude to future feature films.

With Bolshevik victory in 1921 the young Soviet state, still a diplomatic outcast on the foreign scene, wrestled with the postwar problems of the country while the film industry began to experiment with form, style, and content. The recent experiences of the October Revolution and Civil War became a recurring theme on Soviet screens in such films as *Battleship Potemkin, The End of St. Petersburg, October,* and *Little Red Devils* (or *Red Imps*). The revolutionary theme has never ceased to provide rich material for film-makers. The victory of the peasant and industrial worker over the aristocracy and middle classes spelled the end of bourgeois values, styles and themes where film-makers were concerned. From 1921 to early 1928, revolutionary and abstract films in the lean, sharp manner of Eisenstein and Pudovkin more and more became the favorites of the critics while older traditionalists like Gardin and Protazanov who could not or would not free themselves of the old romanticist, drawing room repertory came in for increasingly heavy attack. In these years Eisenstein, Pudovkin, and Dovzhenko made an indelible imprint on film art and editing that was to influence film-makers around the world. Yet men like Gardin and Protazanov claimed large audiences because they were able to win the hearts of their viewers with ample doses of romance, which is today given due credit by Soviet film historians. The two styles were, however, able to co-exist in these years of the New Economic Policy and offered movie-goers a wide range of film art.

In order to breathe new life into the devastated economy, the Communist Party took a doctrinal step backwards and allowed the existence of some private enterprise and foreign economic investment. The nationalization of the economy was slowed down in 1921-27 and the remnants of the old bourgeois middle class were tolerated a while longer. The whole period was one characterized by transition, socially, economically, politically, and artistically. Film became a conscious mirror of Soviet life and experience, when the revolutionary mass was glorified in *Battleship Potemkin* and social problems arising from housing shortages could be laughed at in *Bed and Sofa.* The expansion of the film industry was given impetus in these years by no less a person than Stalin.

As Commissar of Nationalities Stalin helped to facilitate the establishment of national film studios as early as April 1921, when he supported the addition of a cinema section to the Georgian Commissariat of Education. By 1925 film studios had been established in Belorussia, Armenia, Georgia, Azerbaidzhan, and Uzbekistan while the film industry of the Ukraine was undergoing exciting development. These republican studios provided a richer, multi-national flavor for Soviet films while also broadening the potential for multi-national Party propaganda. They have continued to be an important part of the film scene to this day and have produced some remarkable works which in the eyes of many critics have challenged the long-held preeminence of the Moscow and Leningrad studios.

The freedom of Soviet cinema in the 1920s was chiefly due to the lack of a single dominant political policy. From 1924 to 1928 the Party was split between the followers of Trotsky and those of Stalin. Party differences over foreign policy carried over into films. At times the West was a target of satire, as in the classic *The Extraordinary Adventures of Mr. West in the Land of the Bolsheviks.* At other times hostility towards the West was sharper as in *Miss Mend, Candidate for President,* and *New Babylon.* There was still belief that the proletariat in the West would rise to overthrow the capitalists, an idea that faded by the early 1930s when Stalin decided to concentrate all energies on developing socialism in one country, the USSR.

Although the USSR was still not widely recognized on a diplomatic level until the 1930s, Soviet films were increasingly exhibited abroad after the success and acclaim of Eisenstein's *Battleship Potemkin* in 1925. The export of films was important for the film industry as a means of accumulating badly needed foreign currency in order to purchase needed film stock and equipment. It was not until 1940 that the Soviets became self-sufficient in the manufacture of film stock and equipment.

Socially, the NEP period was characterized by a struggle between old and new beliefs. Atheism, backed by the full support of the Party, was making a determined assault against the church as mirrored in films such as *Cross and Mauser, Behind Convent Walls*, and the satirical *Bad Trouble*. Sexual customs were changing and the role of women in Soviet society were treated in ample measure in *Bed and Sofa, The Parisian Cobbler*, and *The Peasant Women of Ryazan*. Free love was openly tolerated in the 1920s, but more traditional family relationships and morality were encouraged from the 1930s. The fact that women had gained a new role in society was reflected within the industry itself which saw the rise of women directors in the 1920s beginning with Olga Preobrazhenskaya and Esther Shub and later continuing with women like Vera Stroyeva, Yulia Solntseva, Irina Poplavskaya, and Larissa Shepitko. Women were no longer the mere handservants of men after the October Revolution and countless films dealt with this theme well over three decades before the rise of the women's liberation movement in the West.

Beginning in the 1920s Soviet films probed and examined the status of women in tsarist society, and those made in the Central Asian republics were especially strong in portraying the grim, unenviable lot of women prior to 1917. The films of the 1920s revealed how the Revolution was a necessary force for the social liberation of women. By the 1930s the emphasis shifted to showing women taking their rightful place along side men in all areas of Soviet society, a classic example being *Member of the Government*. In the war years of 1941-45 women were seen not only as loving mothers and wives, but as active and heroic defenders of the motherland in *The Rainbow, Mashenka*, and *She Defends Her Country* among others. Since the 1950s the Soviet woman is depicted as a modern person of the time, seeking love and, very often, professional fulfillment while wrestling with personal emotions and needs. With each passing decade the differences between her and her Western sister have become much blurred and perhaps thus supporting the notion among many political and social observers that Soviet and Western societies are converging rather than diverging.

The New Economic Policy ended in 1928 which coincided with Stalin's victory over his chief opponent Trotsky. The Golden Age of cinema ended as private enterprise was swamped by an intense campaign of nationalization of industry and collectivization of agriculture with the start of the First Five-Year Plan (1928-32). The revolutionary fervor, youthful exuberance, and stylistic innovation of film-makers were dampened by the resolutions of the All-Union Communist Conference on Cinema Affairs in March 1928. The Conference, echoing the resolutions of the earlier Fifteenth Party Congress, called for more attention to the social needs of Soviet society, in other words supporting the Party in its programs and policies. The handwriting on the wall as to future developments was clear to some and a new exodus of directors and actors took place, including Fedor Ozep, Boris Glagolin, Anna Sten, Alexander Granovski, and Ivan Koval-Samborski. This second emigration however was rapidly offset by the arrival of the second generation of directors and actors fresh from the state film schools at Moscow and Leningrad.

From 1929 on there was less innovation and symbolism, which now came under attack as "formalism." Emphasis was to be on "socialist realism" which meant more naturalistic presentation, a clearer statement of theme, and, above all else, a positive view of Soviet life and aims. The film-maker had to interpret life within the framework of socialist needs and ideology. Party goals were emphasized and supported in all theatrical films. Documentary directors, too, came under criticism for being overly passive where propaganda was concerned. In early 1930 the Central Committee of the Communist Party urged documentarists to become more actively involved in the social life of the country by reflecting state policies in their work.

Throughout the 1930s the Party took greater control over the film industry and tighter censorship was firmly established. Under Boris Shumyatski the cinema was treated as little more than an industrial enterprise. There was now less individualistic virtuosity by directors as compared to the 1920s. This was the period of Eisenstein's inactivity. Films were now more distinctly Bolshevik and militant in tone. The work of the national minority studios was more closely scrutinized for even the slightest hint of nationalism; this development coincided with Stalin's purging and reorganizing of the Ukrainian Communist Party. The tight censorship was one reason why film production fell off as compared to the 1920s.

The years from 1929 to 1941 witnessed intensive heavy industrialization at the expense of the light consumer industry, the collectivization of agriculture and its resistance on the part of the well-to-do peasants *(kulaks)*; famine in the wake of wholesale slaughter of livestock by the *kulaks*; the modernization of the armed forces; the development of the Soviet Far East and Far North; the Sovietization of society; and the great purges. Stalin's determination to make Soviet Russia strong was accompanied by social turmoil. Individual needs and desires had to be sacrificed for the greater good of the country as a whole. In films the individual paled in importance compared to the collective group, as can be seen in *The Brave Seven, Party Card,* and *Aerograd* among other films. From the 1930s through the early 1950s films stressed the notion that community (Party and country) interests were all important and had to take precedence over those of individuals. In contrast to this often repeated theme the films since 1953 have concentrated more on individuals and how the community can help them. The vast domestic changes of the 1930s were accompanied by new foreign developments which were also reflected in the theatrical films of the time.

Hitler's rise to power in 1933 and the subsequent crushing of the German Communist Party were serious political setbacks for Stalin. Hitler's Germany was looked upon as a serious threat to the USSR and Stalin moved to improve relations with the West. In the Far East, Japan's expansion into China and Manchuria posed a danger to the security of the USSR. *The Deserter* and *Aerograd* illustrate the new foreign threats. The latter film in fact gave rise to what is called the "border" genre of Soviet film in the 1930s. Many works of that time dealt with the heroic feats of border troops in an unceasing battle against saboteurs and spies along the Soviet-Polish and Soviet-Chinese frontiers. "Border" films almost seemed to be the order of the day by their sheer quantity and, while few matched Dovzhenko's *Aerograd* in visual appeal and drama, they enjoyed popularity with Soviet audiences because of their adventurous and suspenseful content. This type of film continues to be produced even now though in fewer numbers than in its heyday of the Thirties. During this decade the hostility towards the United States, France, and England lessened appreciably, although anti-capitalist dramas continued to be filmed. As new themes made their appearance on Soviet screens so too did technical advances.

For a few years the Soviet film industry lagged behind the sound and color film advances in the West. Sound came into films, and then only on an experimental basis, in 1930, but it was not until 1935 that the production of silent movies ended. The delay was primarily because of shortages in equipment, which first had been imported from Germany on a small scale in 1929, and because officials wanted to await the results of the work of P. G. Tager in Moscow and A. F. Shorin in Leningrad. At this time, too, Eisenstein urged his fellow film-makers to go slowly in utilizing the new medium. What he cautioned against was using sound haphazardly for its own novel sake rather than as an artistic or dramatic enhancement of the visual aspects of film art. The delay in using sound provided the Soviets with a positive advance in that they bypassed the troublesome sound-on-disc technique in favor of the more satisfactory sound-on-film process. Also, the Soviets succeeded in utilizing sound in a more artistic manner than did their Western counterparts who initially did not take the time to study the full potential of sound as a dramatic counterpoint to the visual image. On the other hand not all Soviet directors were successful in their initial use of sound, Pudovkin being a case in point. His first sound film, *A Simple Case*, became his first failure and at least one contemporary, Mikhail Romm, felt that Pudovkin's sound films were not as good as his silent works.

Color films did not appear in the USSR until 1936, again only experimentally. This almost hesitant beginning in the use of color occurred at a time when the technical quality of Soviet film was showing marked improvement. Compared to the preceding decade, the films of the Thirties were noticeably more pleasing in tonal quality and by 1940 were as good as Western films. In the field of color photography the Soviets were held up by the outbreak of war which made further development almost nil because of other pressing priorities. Only after 1945, following the acquisition of the German Agfacolor process, did Soviet color films come into their own. On the other hand the Soviets made substantial progress in the field of stereoscopic, three-dimensional films. As early as 1940, with the film *Concert*, Soviet audiences could view a 3-D film without using special glasses which put the USSR well ahead of 3-D developments in the West.

The 1930s saw the decline of satire in favor of innocuous musical comedies, though many, like *Jazz Comedy* and *Musical Story*, were to please audiences and critics for many years. Comedy in general became blander and lacked the satirical punch of the 1920 film era; in fact comedy did not really revive until the mid-1950s with the appearance of *Firm Friends* and *Carnival Night*. Contemporary subjects received intensive scrutiny and usually upheld the current Party line. Socially, films reflected a more puritan approach to morals as Soviet life in general was depicted in highly idealistic terms as in films like *Lace*, *Song of the First Girl*, and *The Earth Thirsts*.

The great purges reached their climax in 1937 and coincided with the beginnings of the film hagiography of Stalin. This trend continued until his death in 1953. Mikhail Romm's two great films, *Lenin in October* (1937) and *Lenin in 1918* (1938), while giving due, reverent attention to Lenin, portrayed Stalin as the helpmate, adviser, and true political heir of Lenin. The theme was again repeated after 1945 in *The Vow* and *Unforgettable 1919*. Historical evidence, however, has shown that Stalin was frequently in opposition to Lenin, who in the last year of his life repudiated Stalin in a secret testament. In films since the mid-1950s Stalin takes on a sinister look which in some films is done subtly through lighting and make-up.

Hitler's ascendancy to power in Germany in 1933 and his subsequent diplomatic victories worried Stalin, who energetically pushed a campaign for collective security on the international scene. The anti-Nazi policy in the late 1930s was mirrored in three films that are still considered by many critics to be the best of the anti-Nazi films made anywhere: *The Oppenheim Family, Professor Mamlock,* and *Swamp Soldiers*. Patriotism and anti-German feeling were evident in Eisenstein's costly classic *Alexander Nevski*. This policy continued until the summer of 1939 when England and France proved unable to form a firm defensive pact with the USSR. A main stumbling block was the Polish Government, which steadfastly refused to grant transit rights to Soviet forces in case of German attack. Polish leaders feared Stalin more than Hitler, whom they felt they could contain. Stalin then performed his momentous about face and signed the Nazi-Soviet Nonaggression Pact in August 1939, thus freeing Hitler of anxieties about a two-front war in his campaign against Poland. Aside from its political impact, the treaty had a negative impact on the film industry because of the decline in the export and exhibition of Soviet films abroad. Then, too, Stalin's annexation of eastern Poland, the Baltic states, and the unpopular war with Finland did little to enhance the USSR's prestige abroad. Although Stalin's moves were made to strengthen the Soviet strategic position in case of war with Germany by extending the Soviet frontiers westward, they were largely wasted. Stalin gave little freedom to what was left of the purge-ravaged professional officer corps in defense matters because he wanted to avoid giving any provocation at all to Hitler, despite overwhelming evidence in early 1941 that the Nazi leader was preparing to attack.

With the German invasion on June 22, 1941 the entire energies and resources of the USSR were committed to defeating the enemy. World War II, like Lenin, the October Revolution, and the Civil War, has since become an often recurring theme in the Soviet cinema. As late as 1975 film-makers continued to produce a large number of theatrical and documentary films about the war in sharp contrast to Western film-makers. Soviet films during the war concentrated on national patriotism rather than unstinting loyalty to Party doctrine. There was however no lessening of the idea that the Communist Party would eventually lead the Soviet people to ultimate victory. Censorship was relaxed and anti-religious propaganda stopped as Stalin made peace with the Orthodox Church so that it would lend its support to the war effort. The great patriotic deeds of tsarist military and naval leaders were commemorated not only in military decorations but in films like *Suvorov* and *Kutuzov in 1812.* The production of anti-capitalist films came to an abrupt halt and one that was released, *The Dream,* proved a total failure.

In the first months of war, in the wake of staggering defeats and Stalin's colossal blunder at Kiev which resulted in the loss of over 500,000 Soviet troops, film studios were evacuated eastwards into the interior of the USSR. The physical dislocation of the film industry interrupted production of many feature films during the war and for some years after. High priority during the first two years of war was given to newsreels and documentaries. Because of shortages of equipment and studio space, the film industry produced short, dramatic and morale boosting films under the so-called *Fighting Film Albums* (or *Victory Will Be Ours*) series. The sole aim of these featurettes or medleys was to contribute in a positive sense to the war effort. These medleys were shown and produced on a near monthly basis from July 1941 through July 1942, and a few proved so popular that many were expanded into feature film length.

The main themes in feature films were heroism in combat, native patriotism, devotion to duty, and the cruelty of the enemy. Surprisingly most film historians, Soviet and Western, agree on the wartime films that they admire. Without exception these are grim and angry films about life behind enemy lines or under Nazi occupation. The uncompromising harshness of *Zoya, She Defends Her Country, Girl No. 217,* and *The Rainbow* best typify what the war meant to the average Soviet citizen during the life and death struggle. That the struggle was in doubt and life grim for the Soviets can be seen in the absence of musicals or musical comedies (unlike the situation with American and British films) until late 1943. Only with the appearance of *At 6 P.M. After the War,* a light musical and wartime romance, did audiences feel that victory was not far off. The films of 1941-45 are noteworthy for the near absence of Stalin and the lack of any attempt to explain the reasons for the unpreparedness for war in 1941.

When the guns ceased their thundering in 1945 the USSR and its film industry entered the second Stalinist or Cold War period that was to last until 1953. At home, four years of war had wrought unimagineable human suffering, bloodshed, and economic devastation, the true extent of which was not to be known in the West for several years. The war, too, gave rise to an active, armed anti-Communist resistance in the Ukraine and Baltic republics that was to last until well into the mid-1950s. By some estimates at least 20 million Soviet citizens were killed in the Great Patriotic War of 1941-45. Thousands of ex-prisoners of war and wartime deportees returned to the USSR where Stalin had them executed or sent to labor camps as traitors. The problems facing the returning war veterans and ex-POWs were not given much treatment in Soviet cinema until several years after Stalin's death as reflected in *Destiny of a Man, Silence, Clear Sky, Wings,* and *Belorussian Station.*

After 1946 the West was again depicted in films as an enemy against a political background in which Eastern Europe became Communist and the West sought to help the economic recovery of Western Europe through the Marshall Plan. The defection of Yugoslavia from the Stalinist camp in 1948 insured that Soviet films about Tito and the wartime partisan movement were withdrawn from exhibition in the USSR. The Cold War became a favorite theme among Soviet and Western film-makers.

Stalin again returned to Soviet screens as a larger than life, monumental figure. In *The Vow* (1946) he was again seen as the true and only political heir of Lenin. In the *Battle of Stalingrad* (1949) and *Fall of Berlin* (1950) he is the architect of Soviet victory while generals like Zhukov are his mere mortal executives. In these films, as in the 1930s, we see Stalin in firm and incontestable control of the political and military scene.

The Soviet film industry suffered a sharp quantitative decline in the release of feature films between 1946 and 1952. While twenty-seven films were released in 1947, only seven came out in 1951. A year after Stalin's death the number of feature films that were released totalled thirty-eight. Production suffered because of lingering wartime damage to film studios and Stalinist repression. A postwar purge was in full swing until 1953. Films were either banned outright or delayed because of revision. Scriptwriters were either reluctant to submit their work to interminable censorship or feared the consequences of criticism. Directors like Eisenstein, Leonid Lukov, Pudovkin, Gerasimov, Kozintsev, Trauberg, and Donskoi were subjected to bitter cirticism for "cosmopolitanism," in other words ignoring positive aspects of the Russian cultural heritage within the context of the Cold War. Films had to be patriotic and anti-Western, much in the same way that Hollywood began churning out anti-Communist films under the whiplash of McCarthyism.

Thematically, Soviet films of 1946-53 focused on the Cold War conflict, patriotic biographic treatments of great Russian personalities, or sterile idealizations of contemporary life. Few of the films had anything like deep emotional conflict among characters. No film depicting the true postwar conditions of Soviet life was released and the most celebrated case in this respect was the second part of Lukov's *Great Life,* which was not released until 1958 and in an highly edited version. The banning of the second part of Eisenstein's *Ivan the Terrible* was another blow that stifled creativity in the cinema of the late Forties. Eisenstein was criticized for giving an unfavorable view of Russia's past as presented in the film's portrayal of the first great tsar. Many critics are still fond of speculating whether Stalin saw too close a parallel between himself and Ivan in part II. Whereas in the first part Ivan struggled against the evil that surrounded him in his court, by the second part he became the epitome of evil itself. Eisenstein had wanted to present the psychological development of a historical figure as he saw it. In the event the film was not released until ten years after the director's death and must be seen if an understanding of the character of Ivan is to be gained in relation to the first part.

As in the 1930s, the individual and his needs were subjugated to those of the Party and the need for massive reconstruction of the war-torn country and economy. Once more Soviet citizens had to sacrifice consumer needs in order to repair factories and plants. By the time Stalin died in 1953 the Soviet economy had largely recovered from the devastation of war.

Since 1953 life in the Soviet Union has steadily improved from an economic point of view despite the still lingering housing shortages. The film industry however was not to undergo large scale expansion and modernization until the late 1960s, but Soviet films began showing new life and spirit in no less than a year after Stalin's demise. Kalatozov's *Firm Friends* (1954) marked the return of satire to screens, a trend which continues even now. Ryazanov's *Carnival Night* (1957) was a refreshing musical comedy which subtly introduced the notion that Soviet youth was not content to follow the ways of older generations. When Khrushchev denounced Stalin in 1956 he ushered in a new period of political, social, and economic life within the USSR and Eastern Europe. Despite the suppression of the Hungarian revolt in 1956 and the Czechoslovakian reform movement in 1968, Soviet films have reflected more humanism and concern for the individual. Negative aspects of Soviet life are, if cautiously, being revealed and dealt with as in *The Red Snowball Tree* (1974) which deals with a former criminal's attempt to find a place for himself in an uncaring society. The alienation of youth was examined by Khutsiev in *I Am Twenty* (1964). Soviet film-makers continue to probe the relationship of the individual to the collective group and the social responsibilities of each towards the other.

The 1960s and 1970s gave rise to a strong urge to examine the problems of contemporary society. In Gerasimov's *By the Lake* (1969) the contest between industrial needs and environmental protection reflects a problem that is universal and not merely limited to the capitalistic West. Soviet recent history is probed and found not always favorable as in Okeyev's *Bow To The Fire* (1970), Stolper's *The Living And The Dead* (1964), and Nakhapetov's *With You And Without You* (1973).

The post-1953 renascence of the Soviet cinema, despite continuing censorship, does not appear to be over. The new generation of directors has given a new view about Soviet society which appears less revolutionary and monumental, and more humanistically inclined. At a time of East-West detente, Soviet films have reflected changing economic and social currents in the USSR that indicate a steady convergence between capitalism and communism in the economic and social spheres. In recent years the Soviet film industry has embarked on more co-productions with capitalist countries, a trend that augurs well for international understanding and cooperation.

Since 1918 Soviet films have offered us a dynamic mirror of Soviet life and thought, but they should not only be looked at in a political perspective. Soviet film artists, like those of other countries, present a view of man's existence and his attempts to come to terms with the world around him. Man's struggle to improve his life forms the essential framework for the director and his artistic endeavors.

SOVIET CINEMA

FILM DIRECTORS

ABULADZE, Tengiz. b. 1924. Georgian.

First entered theatrical work as a student of acting at the Tbilisi State Theatrical Institute, 1943-46, simultaneously with Revaz Chkeidze. A few years later Abuladze, again with Chkeidze, entered Moscow's Higher State Institute of Cinematography where both men studied under Sergei Yutkevich. After graduating in 1953 Abuladze made a few short documentaries before teaming up with his friend Chkeidze to make *Magdana's Donkey* (1956). With this work the two men scored a success that marked them as directors to watch in the rising second wave of Soviet filmmakers. The film has been lauded by Soviet and Western critics as a landmark in revitalizing Georgian cinema and a beginning of the renascence of Soviet film.

After *Magdana's Donkey* Abuladze went on as an independent director and achieved another critical and popular triumph with *Grandma, Iliko, Illarion, and Me* (1963). While his films are firmly based on Georgian backgrounds they have universal themes that make them widely appealing.

Films: *Magdana's Donkey* (1956, with Revaz Chkeidze), *Somebody Else's Children* (1959), *Grandma, Iliko, Illarion, and Me* (1963), *The Prayer* (1968), *Molba* (1973).

AIMANOV, Shaken. b. 1914. Kazakh, actor and director.

Regarded as a pioneer in the Kazakh film industry, Aimanov began his acting career in the theater in 1933 before entering film work in 1940. All his films have a strong national flavor which may explain his relative lack of recognition in the West. He is credited with the light, deft touch of comedy that is characteristic in many Caucasian and Central Asian directors.

Films (as director): *Poem of Love* (1954), *Daughter of the Steppes* (1955), *We Live Here* (1957), *Our Splendid Doctor* (1958), *Crossroad* (1963), *Wings of A Song* (1966), *Land of Our Fathers* (1967), *The End of The Ataman* (1970).

ALEXANDROV, Grigori Vasilievich (real name: **Marmorenko**). b. 1903. Actor and director.

From the age of 9 Alexandrov worked around theaters in his native Ekaterinburg. In 1918 he studied in the production course of the

Workers' and Peasants' Theater. During the Civil War Alexandrov worked with a travelling theater on the Western front and served briefly as a film censor. After demobilization he went to Moscow in 1922 and enrolled as a student at the Proletkult Theater where he met and began a long association with Sergei Eisenstein.

Alexandrov made his acting debut in Eisenstein's short film *Glumov's Diary*. In *Strike* and *Battleship Potemkin* he served as an actor and assistant director. Eisenstein then promoted him to associate director for *October* and the much delayed and troubled *The Old and The New*. In the spring of 1929 Alexandrov was present at the meeting between Eisenstein and Stalin in which the latter made known his dissatisfaction with *The Old and The New*. Following last minute revisions on the film, Alexandrov accompanied Eisenstein and Eduard Tisse on their trip through Europe, Hollywood and Mexico. While in Paris Alexandrov made his debut as a director on the short musical *Romance Sentimentale*, which had been first offered to Eisenstein who refused it. After the abortive and troubled *Que Viva Mexico!*, the two men returned to the USSR in 1932. From this time on Alexandrov drew away from Eisenstein who was having difficulties with Boris Shumyatski, the then head of the Soviet film industry.

Alexandrov's first independent Soviet work was the short documentary *Internationale*. He then accepted the assignment for one of the first musical comedies, *Jazz Comedy*, which Eisenstein refused to do. Despite criticism that the film was hurried, it proved a popular success and earned Alexandrov the Order of the Red Banner of Labor. In January 1935 he received the Order of the Red Star, an award that was several degrees higher than the one given to Eisenstein at the same ceremony.

His next musical comedies, *Circus* and *Volga-Volga*, were highly popular and Alexandrov acted in both and collaborated in writing the scripts. During this period he married Lyubov Orlova, his leading actress. His next musical, *Bright Road*, proved successful, though Western reactions are mixed. With this film Alexandrov reached the zenith of his directing career. Whatever else might be said about his later films, Alexandrov had firmly established and refined the musical comedy as a genre of the Soviet film.

During World War II Alexandrov took over as director of Mosfilm Studio from Eisenstein who concentrated on filming *Ivan the Terrible*. He also served as a member of the editorial board of the highly successful

Fighting Film Albums series and of the Art Council of the Committee for Cinema Affairs which resolved film production problems during the war.

His first postwar film, *Spring*, was again a light comedy which saw Lyubov Orlova and the venerable actor Nikolai Cherkasov in the leading roles. Whatever the reason, the film did not do well. Like many another director at the time, he next made what now appears like an obligatory bow to Cold War anti-Americanism with *Meeting On the Elbe*. With *The Composer Glinka* Alexandrov achieved, if only for a time, a well-received success that had the earmarks of a strong comeback. He once more showed his skill and confidence with a musical theme. His success was short-lived as his next films have been barely noticed. *Lenin in Switzerland*, his last film, which was made to commemorate the fiftieth anniversary of the Russian Revolution proved unsuccessful.

Films (as director): *Romance Sentimentale* (1931), *Internationale* (1933), *Jazz Comedy* (1934), *Circus* (1936), *Report by Comrade Stalin* (1937), *Volga-Volga* (1938), *Bright Road* (or *Tanya*, 1940), *One Family* (1943), *People of The Caspian* (1944), *Spring* (1946), *Meeting On The Elbe* (1949), *The Composer Glinka* (1952), *From Man To Man* (1958), *Russian Souvenir* (1960), *Lenin in Switzerland* (1966).

[See also: **Alexandrov, Grigori.** "Potemkin and After," *Films and Filming*, 1957 (April), vol. 3, no. 7, p. 10.]

ALOV, Alexander. b. 1923. Russian.

Alov's career has been exclusively associated with that of Vladimir Naumov. Both attended the Higher State Institute of Cinematography in Moscow, where they were students of Igor Savchenko and graduated in 1951. When Savchenko began his *Taras Shevchenko* he took them on as assistant directors. They completed the film when Savchenko died suddenly. In their collaboration, Alov and Naumov have enjoyed much critical success beginning with *Pavel Korchagin* and again with *Peace To The Newcomer*, a moving, emotional drama about World War II. With their last film, *The Flight*, they once again scored an international success, and domestic controversy, with a film that portrayed honestly and sympathetically the plight and destiny of Russian emigres following the 1917 October Revolution. Together they have produced works that are not only bold, but underscored by strong emotional byplay, brisk action, and well developed characters.

Films: *Restless Youth* (1954), *Pavel Korchagin* (1957), *The Wind* (1959), *Peace To The Newcomer* (1961), *The Coin* (1963, made for Soviet television), *A Bad Joke* (1969), *The Flight* (1971).

ARNSHTAM, Lev. b. 1905, Dnepropetrovsk, Ukraine.

Originally Arnshtam embarked on a musical career and studied at the Leningrad Conservatory. In 1924 he joined the art theater of Meyerhold and worked there as a musician until 1927. He then went into film work as an assistant to Sergei Yutkevich on *The Golden Mountain* (1931), which was followed by work as sound director on *Alone* and scenarist-assistant director for *Counterplan*. Arnshtam had the benefit of absorbing the lessons learned in using sound during its transition into Soviet films, thus avoiding some of the problems that other directors had. After co-directing the travel documentary, *Ankara, Heart of Turkey*, went on to make his first independent film, *Girl Friends*, on which he had the supervisory assistance of Yutkevich. The film was a warm, idealistic story about the Russian Civil War in which Arnshtam avoided slipping into sentimentality. His next work, *Friends*, was also popular and established him as a rising, promising *regisseur*. Resounding, international acclaim was given to *Zoya*, now acknowledged as Arnshtam's best work. This was a highly impressionistic treatment about the 18-year old heroine who was captured and executed by the Germans. Despite the depiction of brutality and the tragic fate of the girl, *Zoya* is still a poetic film that makes no compromises to gain teary sympathy. In 1946 Arnshtam received a Stalin Prize for this film.

Arnshtam's *Glinka* (1947) was well received in its time and awarded the Stalin Prize. In retrospect the film appears to have a heavy nationalistic tone which is not surprising in view of the pro-patriotic policy of the time. The film, despite a good musical score, has since been overshadowed by Alexandrov's *The Composer Glinka*.

In 1950 Arnshtam began work on an anti-American scenario, *The Warmongers*, which would have been one of the most virulent Cold War films. For reasons still unclear the film never went into production. From this time on Arnshtam's career never again attained the same brilliance it had with *Zoya*. *Romeo and Juliet* was a colorful film ballet that might have marked a comeback had it not been for the unsuccessful *The Lesson of History*. Arnshtam is now retired.

Films: *Ankara, Heart of Turkey* (1934, with Yutkevich), *Girl Friends* (1936), *Friends* (1938), *Film Notes on Battles 1 and 2* (1941, with Kozintsev), *Zoya* (1944), *Glinka* (1947), *Romeo and Juliet* (1955), *The Lesson of History* (1957).

ATAMANOV, Lev (real name: **Atamanian**). b. 1905. Armenian.
Director of cartoon films and a student of Lev Kuleshov.

Films: *Tale of A White Calf* (1933, with V. Suteev), *A Dog and A Cat* (1938), *The Priest and The Goat* (1941), *The Magic Carpet* (1947), *The Snow Queen* (1957), *The Key* (1961), *The Bench* (1968).

BALLYUZEK, Vladimir. 1881-1957. Azerbaidzhanian.
First studied art before going into film work. After the October Revolution Ballyuzek remained in Russia and provided stimulus to the Azerbaidzhanian cinema with his first Soviet film in which the cast was composed entirely of native actors. *The Legend of the Maiden's Tower* proved moderately successful because of the exotic setting and legendary theme appeared natural for Ballyuzek's traditional, romanticist style. His romantic manner however seems to have interfered when he tried a revolutionary theme in *Hamburg*, which was also greatly overshadowed by Eisenstein's more powerful *Battleship Potemkin*. In his last film Ballyuzek again attempted his hand at a contemporary theme through satire, but the result was only moderately successful. At a time when revolutionary and innovative films were in favor his work proved too traditional and tame.

Films: *The Legend of the Maiden's Tower* (1924), *Hamburg* (1926), *The Gentleman and the Rooster* (1929).

BARNET, Boris. 1902-65. Actor and director.
First studied painting at the Moscow school of fine arts. In 1918 Barnet volunteered for the Red Army and after military service in the Civil War drifted into professional boxing. He then joined Lev Kuleshov's workshop as a student. Barnet acted in several films and most notably in *The Extraordinary Adventures of Mr. West In The Land of The Bolsheviks* and *The Living Corpse*.
Barnet made his first film as co-director with Fedor Ozep. *Miss*

Mend, one of the so-called Red detective thrillers, proved quite popular especially for its light touch. His debut as an independent filmmaker was marked by *Girl With A Hat Box,* which featured Anna Sten and proved immensely successful as a witty satire on the NEP period. The film exhibited a subtle blending of the comic with some semi-tragic elements that were so often associated with Charles Chaplin. Barnet reluctantly accepted the assignment for his next film, *Moscow in October,* which was one of a series that were to commemorate the tenth anniversary of the October Revolution. The film proved unsuccessful and included some poorly edited sequences that reflected Barnet's lack of interest in grand historical themes. He was again successful with *The House On Trubnaya Square,* a satire about tangled relationships and remnants of bourgeois society in contemporary Moscow. Some critics, however, found it too satirical, pointing up the fact that satire could pose problems for filmmakers.

In *Okraina* [The Borderlands] Barnet once again showed his skill in blending tragic and comic elements in a story about divided loyalties in a Russian community at the time of World War I and the Revolution. Barnet apparently missed the subtle shifts in Party ideology of the time because he was criticized for inaccurately portraying Russian life. From this time on Barnet's career declined, despite his being awarded the title of Honored Artist of the Republic in 1935. He never again made a serious attempt at satire. Barnet was one of the first directors to use color in film with his *By The Bluest of Seas.* After World War II he received good notices for *Feat of A Scout* and *Annushka,* but both were small ripples in what was once a bright film career. Most Soviet film historians now see him as a master of satire who had a poetic sense of the tragicomic. For reasons unknown Barnet committed suicide in 1965.

Films (as director): *Miss Mend* (1926, with Fedor Ozep), *Girl With A Hat Box* (1927), *Moscow in October* (1927), *The House On Trubnaya Square* (1928), *Thaw* (1931), *Okraina* (1933), *By The Bluest of Seas* (1936, with S. Mardanov), *The Old Jockey* (1940, banned for many years), *Manhood* (1941), *A Priceless Head* (1942), *One Night* (1945), *Feat of A Scout* (1948), *Pages of A Life* (1948, with Alexander Macheret), *Bountiful Summer* (1951), *The Poet, Wrestler and Clown* (1957, with Konstantin Yudin), *Annushka* (1959), *Alenka* (1961), *Whistle Stop* (1963).

[See also: Kusimna, E. "A Tribute to Boris Barnet," *Film Comment,* 1968 (Fall), vol. 5, no. 1, p. 33.]

BATALOV, Alexei. b. 1928. Russian. Actor and director.

Born in a theatrical family, Batalov is the nephew of the famous film actor Nikolai Batalov. He had his first acting role in the wartime film *Zoya* (1944). In 1950 he graduated the Moscow Art Theater Studio and joined the Soviet Army Theater with which he was active until 1953. He returned to film acting with *A Big Family* (1954) and has been featured in such films as *The Rumyantsev Case, Mother* (in which he took the same role as had his uncle in Pudovkin's silent film), *The Cranes Are Flying, My Dear Man, The Lady With The Little Dog, Nine Days of One Year,* and *A Day of Happiness.*

Batalov made his directing debut with *The Overcoat,* a remake of the Kozintsev and Trauberg work. Critics, Soviet and foreign, applauded the film and especially for the way Batalov successfully caputred the FEKS manner of the original. His following films did not repeat his first triumph.

Films (as director): *The Overcoat* (1960), *The Three Fat Men* (1966, with Iosif Shapiro).

BEGALIN, Mazhit. b. 1922.

Films: *Song of Manshuk* (1971).

BEK-NAZAROV, Amo Ivanovich. 1892-1963. Armenian. Actor and director.

Bek-Nazarov's role as the leading pioneer of Armenian cinema was officially recognized after his death by renaming Armenfilm Studios in his honor. He worked as an actor in Russian cinema from 1916 and was employed by the Khanzhonkov studio. As an actor he was usually cast in heroic-lover type roles. His early work as a filmmaker was heavily influenced, and marred by, the melodramatic romanticism that was so strongly entrenched in Russian films prior to the October Revolution.

After the Bolsheviks came to power, Bek-Nazarov elected to remain in the country and returned to the Caucasus where he took an active part in developing the Georgian, Azerbaidzhanian, and Armenian cinemas. After completing an acting role in Perestiani's *Arsen Georgiashvili* he made his first Georgian film, *In the Pillory.* This work enjoyed a modicum of success and was an attempt to depict local depotism of the tsarist era. However, the film still reflected the romanticism of the pre-1917 era and was made in an exotic manner. He followed this with a feature role in Shengelaya's *Gyulli*.

In the early 1920's Bek-Nazarov, along with G. Gogotidze, took on an administrative post with Goskinprom-Gruziya, the new Georgian film industry. He devoted a good deal of attention to expanding the distribution and exhibition outlets of Georgian films in European Russia, which brought more critical attention to the work of Georgian directors and helped to develop the export of Georgian films outside the Soviet Union.

After the Armenian film industry was officially established in 1923, Bek-Nazarov was invited to make the first dramatic or art feature film in Armenia. *Namus*, released in 1926, marked a turning point for Bek-Nazarov's career. In this work he overcame the traditionally-expected focus on the exotic and adventurous elements of Caucasian life and concentrated on the harsh realities of life in Armenia, his native land. The film enjoyed a good deal of success because of its social consciousness. Later he deepened his probings into Caucasian life with *Khas-push*, in which he focused on events in order to symbolize the action of masses rather than on individuals. *Khas-push* is now thought to be a reflection of Eisenstein's influence on Bek-Nazarov.

His two best works are *Pepo* and *David Bek*, which reflect Bek-Nazarov's full maturation as a filmmaker who was conscious of social and political elements of the stories he brought to the screen. In January 1935 he received the Order of the Red Star in recognition of his services to Armenian film and for *Pepo*. He was one of the few pre-revolutionary film artists that succceeded in breaking out of the confines of melodramatic romanticism. His work is still little known in the West and appears to be in need of further assessment.

Films (as director): *In the Pillory* (1924), *Lost Treasures* (1924), *Namus* (1926), *Shor and Shorshor* (1926), *Zare* (1926), *Khas-push* (1927), *Natella* (1928), *House On A Volcano* (1928), *Sevil* (1929), *Pepo* (1935), *Zangezur* (1938), *David Bek* (1943), *Girl Of The Ararat Valley* (1950).

BOGIN, Mikhail. b. 1936. Russian.

Graduated the Moscow film institute in 1965. His diploma film, *The Two*, was made in Riga and judged good enough for general exhibition.

Films: *The Two* (1965), *A Ballad of Love* (1966), *Sozya* (1967).

BONDARCHUK, Sergei. b. 1920. Actor and director.

One of the most admired and best known of Soviet actor-directors who came to the forefront of the so-called "second wave" after World War II. Bondarchuk made his acting debut during the war with a front-line Soviet Army theatrical ensemble. After 1945 he entered the Moscow film institute and studied under Sergei Gerasimov, under whose direction he made his film acting debut in *The Young Guard*.

As an actor Bondarchuk appears at his best in roles calling for compassionate bravura as in *Destiny Of A Man*, which earned him a Lenin Prize, and *Seryozha*. As Pierre in *War and Peace*, Bondarchuk seems lost in the gigantic scale of that colorful, long extravaganza. In 1960 he became the first Soviet film actor since the 1930s to take a role in a foreign film, the Italian *Era notte a Roma*, and later in the Yugoslav *Battle of the Neretva*. His acting credits include *The Young Guard, Story of a Real Man, Cavalier of the Gold Star, Taras Shevchenko, Admiral Ushakov, The Grasshopper, Othello, Unfinished Story, Destiny of a Man, Uncle Vanya, War and Peace,* and *They Fought For Their Motherland*.

Bondarchuk's directorial debut was marked by controversy and excitement when *Destiny of a Man* was released. The film took the grand prize at the Moscow Film Festival for its warm treatment of a Soviet prisoner of war who tries to build a new life after the war. The theme represented a remarkable breakthrough in Soviet films for treating a subject that would have been unthinkable in Stalin's time. The film was an artistic, political, and social triumph that encouraged more reexaminations of recent Soviet history on film.

In *War and Peace* and *Waterloo* Bondarchuk chose grand historical themes. While he was faithful to Tolstoi, *War and Peace* tended to be tedious by its sheer length. In *They Fought For Their Motherland* Bondarchuk chose the theme of World War II and was able to recapture his old warmth, barvura, and compassion. The film attempts to find reasons for human courage in the face of overwhelming odds.

Films (as director): *Destiny of a Man* (1959), *War and Peace* (1964), *Waterloo* (1970), *They Fought For Their Motherland* (1975).

[See also: Gillett, J. "Thinking Big," *Sight and Sound,* 1970 (Summer), vol. 39, no. 3, p. 135.]

Sergei Bondarchuk in *Destiny Of A Man*. (Artkino Pictures)

BRUMBERG, Valentina (b. 1899) and **Zenayeda** (b. 1900).

The Brumberg sisters graduated the Institute of Fine Arts in 1925 and have been associated with Soyuzmultfilm Studios as animators and cartoon directors since the 1920s. Their early films are little known and they seem to have been largely overshadowed by Ivanov-Vano, Khitruk, and Ptushko until the 1960s.

Films (partial list): *Great Troubles* (1961), *Three Fat Men* (1963), *The Brave Little Tailor* (1964), *An Hour Until The Meeting* (1965), *Golden Stepmother* (1966), *The Little Time Machine* (1967), *The Capricious Princess* (1969).

BYKOV, Rolan. b. 1929. Russian. Actor and director.

First studied acting at the Shchukin theater school in 1951. After a few years on stage Bykov returned to formal training at the Moscow Youth Theater, 1958-60. As a director he has concentrated on themes dealing with young people. His latest film is one of the most lavish he has done.

Films (as director): *Seven Nursemaids* (1962), *The Lost Summer* (1963, with Orlov), *Dr. Ai Bolit* (1967), *The Telegram* (1972), *Automobile, Violin, and The Dog Blob* (1975).

CHARDYNIN, Pyotr. 1878-1934. Russian.

Along with Yevgeni Bauer, Vladimir Gardin, and Yakov Protazanov, Chardynin was one of the most productive of the prerevolutionary film-makers, but unfortunately his work has gone largely unnoticed in the West. In 1910 he made his first film, *The Queen of Spades*, for the eminent producer Khanzhonkov and met with instant approval by critics and audiences. During World War I, in an effort to raise money for the Russian war effort, Chardynin proposed a bold, epic film based on Tolstoi's *Fruits of Enlightenment.* Moreover, Chardynin suggested that the venture be a cooperative undertaking by all the Russian studios, a notion that was unusual for that time. Although he generated a good deal of interest in the idea nothing came of it.

For a time during the Civil War he made a few short *agitkis* for the Bolsheviks, but does not appear to have been deeply committed to the new political system. In 1922 Chardynin agreed to be the head of the fledgling Soviet Ukrainian film industry, VUFKU (All-Ukrainian Photo-Cinema Administration), thus pioneering the making of Ukrainian films. After a brief time Chardynin emigrated to Latvia and after a few months, for reasons still unclear, returned to the USSR and VUFKU. From this time on he became very energetic in developing Ukrainian cinema by creating opportunities for young, unknown filmmakers, among the most famous of whom was Alexander Dovzhenko. It was under Chardynin that the Ukrainian film industry had its own monthly magazine, rather *avant-garde*, which promoted discussion of film theory.

Chardynin's films reflected the prerevolutionary, traditional style, but proved popular on the whole. His works were readily comprehensible to the filmgoer. The leading Ukrainian actor, Amvrosi Buchma, later pointed out that Chardynin worked tirelessly to get the very best he could from his actors. Buchma considered Chardynin his teacher and under whose direction he gave a memorable performance in *Taras Shevchenko*.

His most acclaimed films are *Taras Shevchenko* and *Ukraziya*. In these two works Chardynin seemed to have caught the revolutionary spirit that was prevalent in Soviet cinema at the time and succeeded, if temporarily, in breaking away from his usual traditional style.

Films: *The Queen of Spades* (1910), *The Kreutzer Sonata* (1911), *Workers' Quarters* (1912), *Accession of the Romanov Dynasty* (1913), *Chrysanthemums* (1914), *Woman of Tomorrow* (1914), *Flood* (1915), *Love of A State Councillor* (1915), *Natasha Rostova* (1915), *The Venetian Stocking* (1915), *Story of Seven Who Were Hanged* (1920), *Master of The Black Cliffs* (1923), *Candidate for President* (1924), *Magnetic Anomaly* (1924), *General From The Other World* (1925), *Taras Shevchenko* (1925), *Little Taras* (1926), *Taras Tryasilo* (1926), *Ukraziya* (1926), *Cherevichki* (1927), *Behind Convent Walls* (1928).

CHIAURELI, Mikhail. b. 1894. Georgian. Actor and director.

As a young man Chiaureli studied sculpture before he went into acting in Georgian films. He made his debut in Ivan Perestiani's *Arsen Georgiashvili*. Ironically Chiaureli as a director made a sound version of this film, *Arsen*, in which Perestiani took an acting role. Chiaureli also took the role of Dato in Perestiani's *Fortress of Suram*. Through the years Chiaureli was to alternate between acting and directing.

In 1928 he was able to direct his first, short film, *In the Last Hour*, which is now remembered only by Soviet film historians. It was a political Civil War story that suffered from a poor script. It was *First Lieutenant Streshnev*, co-directed with Yefim Dzigan, which is usually considered to be Chiaureli's debut as a director. The film enjoyed some success and dealt with a theme, the political maturation of a man who joins the Bolshevik cause during the Civil War, which by then was becoming usual fare for Soviet audiences. In his next two films, *Saba* and *Out Of The Way!*, continued his strong interest in themes that dealt with the social and political aspects of contemporary Georgian life. Both of these works were satirical attacks on old Georgian traditions that blocked the movement of social progress and thus reflected the sharpening social struggles in the USSR of the late 1920s and early 1930s. Despite his steadily increasing successes and growing technical skill, Chiaureli seriously considered leaving filmmaking because of the poor state of the art. It was after sound had been fully established and mastered in filmmaking that Chiaureli enjoyed bigger success with his his films.

After receiving the prestigious Order of Lenin in 1935, Chiaureli received more critical attention for his *Arsen, The Last Masquerade,* and *The Great Glow,* the last of which was the beginning of his Stalin films. In *The Vow* and the two-part, lavishly budgeted *The Fall of Berlin* Chiaureli reached the heights in the politicization of film art by idolizing a living political leader. In both these works Stalin emerges as a monumental, god-like figure and the eminent film historian Jay Leyda has written that few perhaps could have done it so well as did Chiaureli in direction and Gelovani in acting. Although Chiaureli was later to find himself in a controversy because of these films, he exhibited a good sense of drama coupled with skill in handling extravagant stories.

Following Stalin's death Chiaureli made only two more films and seems to have all but vanished from view. Perhaps unfairly many commentators have focused their attention on Chiaureli's Stalin films without examining the entire body of his work as a director. From a technical sense he was almost without peer and did have a sense of drama, even in *The Vow* Chiaureli heightened dramatic impact despite a small rearrangement of historical fact in the scene where Stalin takes his vow to Lenin at the mausoleum instead of at Lenin's bier. Since 1960 little has been heard of him.

Sergo Zakariadze in *A Soldier's Father*, Revaz Chkeidze. (Artkino Pictures)

Films (as director): *In The Last Hour* (1928), *First Lieutenant Streshnev* (1928, with Yefim Dzigan), *Saba* (1929), *Out Of The Way!* (1931), *Arsen* (1937), *The Last Masquerade* (1937), *The Great Glow* (1938), *Georgi Saakadze* (1943), *The Vow* (1946), *The Fall of Berlin* (1950), *Unforgettable 1919* (1952), *Otar's Widow* (1958), *Story Of A Girl* (1960).

CHKEIDZE, Revaz [Rezo]. b. 1924. Georgian.

Along with fellow Georgian Tengiz Abuladze, Chkeidze studied acting at the Tbilisi State Theatrical Institute, 1943-46, before entering the state film school in Moscow. While at the film school he studied under Sergei Yutkevich and Mikhail Romm, and graduated 1953. Following his co-direction of *Magdana's Donkey*, Chkeidze went on to direct films independently. Like Abuladze, Chkeidze is today acknowledged as one of the forerunners in the post-Stalin renascence of Soviet film, especially of Georgia. His best, and most widely acclaimed, film is *A Soldier's Father*, which earned for the venerable actor Sergo Zakariadze the prize for best male performance at the 1965 Moscow Film Festival. *Our Youth*, Chkeidze's last film, was partly autobiographical.

Films: *Magdana's Donkey* (1956, with Tengiz Abuladze), *Our Yard* (1957), *A Soldier's Father* (1965), *Our Youth* (1970).

CHUKHRAI, Grigori. b. 1921, Melitopol. Ukrainian.

Entered the State Institute of Cinematography in 1939, but his studies were interrupted by his mobilization into the Soviet Army after the German invasion in June 1941. During the war Chukhrai served with the airborne forces, participated in the Battle of Stalingrad and received a battlefield commission. It is known that he was twice very badly wounded. After 1945 Chukhrai once more entered the Moscow film school where he studied under Sergei Yutkevich and Mikhail Romm, graduating in 1951. For the next two years he worked as Romm's assistant in filming *Admiral Ushakov*.

His debut as an independent director brought him much national attention with his remake of *The Forty-First*. Foreign observers, while liking Chukhrai's colorful version of the classic story of a romance between a Red girl commander and her captive White officer, regarded

Yakov Protazanov's 1928 silent version the better of the two, especially for its deeper impact. Whatever the judgement may have been on his first film, Chukhrai scored an even bigger triumph with his much acclaimed *Ballad Of A Soldier*. Of this poignant, moving wartime drama, Chukhrai was later to say that he intended it as a tribute to his generation which marched off to war straight from the school classroom.

If Sergei Bondarchuk succeeded in opening the screen to a story about a former Soviet prisoner of war told in warm and compassionate terms, then Chukhrai broadened and deepened that theme in his sensational *Clear Sky* which revealed the political and social discrimination that met returning Soviet prisoners of war during Stalin's lifetime. Perhaps more for its social importance than for artistic or acting achievement the film took the grand prize at the 1961 Moscow Film Festival. Since the release of *Destiny Of A Man* and *Clear Sky,* other directors have followed Bondarchuk and Chukhrai in exploring the postwar life of Soviet veterans.

Chukhrai's last film was an impressionistic and slightly autobiographical look at the Battle of Stalingrad.

Films: *The Forty-First* (1956), *Ballad Of A Soldier* (1959), *Clear Sky* (1961), *There Was An Old Man And An Old Woman* (1964), *Memory* (1970).

[See also: Chukhrai, G. "Keeping The Old On Their Toes," *Films and Filming,* 1962 (October), vol. 9, no. 1, p. 26. Herlinghaus, H. "A Talk With Grigori Chukhrai," *Film Culture,* 1962 (Fall), vol. 26, p. 34.]

DANELIYA, Georgi. b. 1930. Georgian.

After spending two years as an architect Daneliya decided to embark upon a career in filmmaking. He entered the directors' workshop at Mosfilm studio in 1958 and graduated in 1960. During his last year as a student he collaborated with fellow student Igor Talankin on their joint diploma film, *There Are Also People,* which was released for general exhibition. After graduation Daneliya again teamed up with Talankin to make the much admired *Seryozha,* which was later judged by Soviet film historian Pisarevski as one of the notable 100 films of Soviet cinema.

Since *Seryozha,* Daneliya has been an independent director and received international attention for his light, humorous view of contemporary Moscow youth in *Walking Around Moscow*. Like many another Georgian filmmaker, Daneliya has exhibited a penchant for and skill in making satirical comedy, a film genre that long was dormant during Stalin's regime.

Films: *There Are Also People* (1960, with Igor Talankin), *Seryozha* (1960, with Igor Talankin), *The Way To The Wharf* (1962), *Walking Around Moscow* (1964), *Thirty-three* (1965), *Don't Grieve [Cheer Up!]* (1969).

DERBENEV, Vadim. b. 1934. Russian.
Attended the film school in Moscow where he specialized in cinematography and graduated in 1957. Derbenev has been active as a cinematographer and independent director at the Moldafilm Studio. His last film received much critical success, but little has been heard of him in recent years.

Films (as director): *Journey Into April* (1963), *The Dream Knight* (1964), *The Last Month of Autumn* (1965).

DONSKOI, Mark Semyonovich. b. 1901 in Odessa, Ukraine.
As a young boy Donskoi exhibited a flair and interest in drama and writing. With other school friends he put on short dramatic skits in a kind of neighborhood theater for other children, from which stems his lifelong interest in themes dealing with young people. At 14 he collaborated with two friends to publish a collection of short stories entitled *Three Authors*. In late adolescence and early adulthood Donskoi first studied medicine, then psychiatry, and finally law at which he practiced for a short time. He also seriously studied piano and even today is regarded as an excellent pianist.

During the Civil War Donskoi served in the Red Army and became a prisoner of the Whites, like Ermler, for almost a year. His observations of his captors and of his fellow prisoners formed the basis of several stories which were published as an anthology entitled *The Prisoners* in 1925. After his demobilization Donskoi, after flirting with the idea of becoming a boxer, went to Moscow and there decided to enter film work. For a time he studied under Eisenstein and concentrated on script writing.

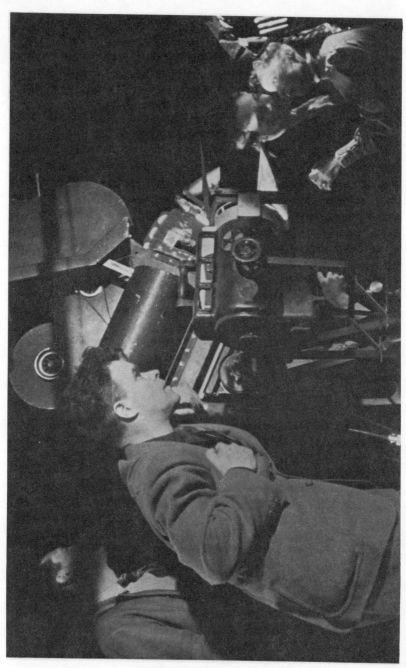

Mark Donskoi on the set of *The Country Teacher*. (British Film Institute)

In 1926 he joined Belgoskino studios, which were then located in Leningrad because of inadequate material and energy resources in Minsk. He worked first as a scenarist, writing the script for and acting in *The Prostitute*, directed by Oleg Freilikh. Donskoi then wrote the script for *The Last Stronghold* before making his debut as a director.

Donskoi's first critical success came with *The Value of Man* which he co-directed with M. Averbakh. The film dealt with the loose morals and coarse behavior of the Soviet Communist Youth, the Komsomol, which at the time was a notable social problem. In this work Donskoi wanted to show that, following the social disruption of the Civil War, young people basically wanted to behave like human, civilized beings. In theme the film was similar to Ermler's *The Parisian Cobbler*, which still overshadows Donskoi's work. His stature as a director was assured when he undertook to co-direct with Averbakh *In The Big City*. The film focused on the life of a poet who goes to the Moscow of the NEP period and slowly loses his talent and strength of character in the face of the corrupt, false values of an industrialized, urban society. This was a theme which came out in Donskoi's films frequently and which was the foundation of his later masterpiece.

Alien Shore and *Fire* did not repeat his earlier success and Donskoi for a time was on the verge of leaving film work. Had it not been for the encouragement of Sergei Yutkevich during this time the Soviet cinema might well have lost one of its most inspired directors. Donskoi, at Yutkevich's urging, undertook to make *Song About Happiness* in collaboration with Vladimir Legoshin. This was Donskoi's first big film and proved popular. The direction of the child actors by Donskoi and Legoshin was natural and brilliant, and both men thereafter were regarded as peerless in working with youngsters. Undoubtedly both men benefitted from having Yutkevich as general supervisor on the film. In 1935 Donskoi directed the Russian dubbing of *The Invisible Man* and then went to work on his magnum opus.

With *The Maxim Gorki Trilogy* (1938-40) Donskoi achieved the full promise of his bright talents. The acclaim accorded to this work has been repeated by critics and film historians over and over. In his later works Donskoi was frequently close in attaining the same success as with this work but never to surpass it. While engaged in production of *The Childhood of Maxim Gorki, Out In The World*, and *My Universities*, Donskoi formalized the principles of directing child actors that he had first developed in *Song About Happiness*. The *Trilogy* is still regarded as a near classic in the direction of youngsters. In this work Donskoi faithfully reflected the tone and mood of Gorki's autobiographical stories, and more importantly reflected the full capacities for human courage in the face of suffering and degradation. It is a rich and dynamic film achievement that still stands as an artistic tribute to the human spirit.

Donskoi's next two films, although popular, seem to have been lost in the brilliance of the *Trilogy*. He was not to enjoy another big, internationally acclaimed film until his second wartime feature-length work. Early in the Soviet-German war, when the USSR was still on the defensive, Donskoi made a selective adaptation of N.A. Ostrovski's Civil War novel, *How The Steel Was Tempered*. From Ostrovski's work Donskoi chose only those aspects that seemed relevant for Soviet war audiences. The film was popular but postwar critics seem fond of comparing it, perhaps unfairly, to Alov and Naumov's *Pavel Korchagin* which is a fuller and more extensive film treatment of Ostrovski's novel. It was with his next work that Donskoi again came to international limelight.

The Rainbow, released in 1944, was made after Donskoi had spent a good deal of time in observing German prisoners of war in order to give a strong, true portrait of the then enemy. This is Donskoi's angriest film and made at a time when the Soviets were recapturing their territory from the invaders. Even now the film does not seem dated or a virulent product of war because of the way in which the focal point of attention is on courage in the face of unyielding brutality. Donskoi, like Arnshtam in his *Zoya*, concentrated on those elements of man that are ennobling and appealing, unlike Romm's *Girl No. 217* which stressed harshness.

In the last year of war Donskoi joined the Communist Party and made *The Unconquered*. His third wartime feature film came off second best when compared to *The Rainbow*. After 1945 Donskoi's career declined, especially following the criticism and suppression of *Alitet Goes To The Hills* (1950). The film was a satire that proved not to the liking nor the amusement of Stalin who had parts of it destroyed. Not until three years after Stalin's death did Donskoi once more recapture attention with his *Mother*. This was the third Soviet film based on Gorki's novel. Alexander Razumni's effort of 1920 is all but forgotten. Donskoi is credited for his professional workmanlike result, but pride of place belongs to Pudovkin's 1926 film. A decade was to pass before

Donskoi reclaimed anything like his old international prestige that had followed in the wake of *The Maxim Gorki Trilogy* and *The Rainbow.*

A Mother's Devotion and *Heart Of A Mother,* both released in 1966, were pleasant and attractive surprises for foreign critics. The films depicted Lenin's early years and focused on the life of the great Bolshevik's mother. These are warm, lyrical and poetic stories that are remarkably free of Leninist hagiography.

When Donskoi began work on his latest film, *Chaliapin,* he achieved a dream that he had had since 1938, the year that the famous Russian singer died. The story seems to be a natural one for Donskoi as it deals with a man who is alienated from people while struggling with the problems of an emigre's life. The theme of the work, like Alov and Naumov's *The Flight,* deals with the problem of exile for a Russian and has deep implications at a time when many Russians have recently been forced into exile.

Donskoi is one of the great Soviet directors whose work has reflected a warm sense of the human condition and have exhibited a mastery in handling mood and atmosphere.

Films (as director): *Life* (1927), *The Value of Man* (1928, with M. Averbakh), *The Fop* (1929), *In The Big City* (1929, with M. Averbakh), *Alien Shore* (1930), *Fire* (1930), *Song About Happiness* (1934, with Vladimir Legoshin), *The Maxim Gorki Trilogy: The Childhood of Maxim Gorki* (1938), *Out In The World* (1939), *My Universities* (1940), *Brother Of A Hero* (1940), *Children Of The Soviet Arctic* (1941), *Beacon* (1942, featurette), *How The Steel Was Tempered* (1942), *The Rainbow* (1944), *The Unconquered* (1945), *Country Schoolteacher* (1948), *Alitet Goes To The Hills* (1950, banned), *Sporting Honor* (1951), *Mother* (1956), *At A High Cost* (1957), *Foma Gordeev* (1959), *Hello Children* (1962), *A Mother's Devotion* (1966), *Heart Of A Mother* (1966), *Chaliapin* (1972).

[See also: Cervoni, Albert. *Marc Donskoi.* Paris: Editions Seghers, 1966. Gillett, J. "Mark Donskoi: Filmography," *Focus on Film,* 1970 (March-April), no. 1, p. 10.]

DOVLATIAN, Frunze. b. 1927. Armenian.

Films: *Hello, It's Me* (1965).

DOVZHENKO, Alexander Petrovich. 1894-1956. Ukrainian, of peasant origin.

In recent years Dovzhenko's works have received increased attention and have been regularly revived in the programs of film societies and museums. He might well be considered the film poet laureate of the Ukraine. After his death the Kiev Studios were renamed in his honor as the greatest of the Ukrainian directors. Dovzhenko is now acknowledged as one of the giants, along with Eisenstein, Pudovkin, and Kuleshov, in the history of Soviet film.

After his service with the Red Army in the Civil War Dovzhenko worked for a time in the Ukrainian Commissariat of Education, having studied to be a teacher prior to World War I. However his restless spirit soon made him give up teaching for consular work in Soviet missions in Poland and Germany. In 1923 he returned to Kharkov and worked as a cartoonist for newspapers. Whenever time allowed Dovzhenko seriously studied painting and many of his drawings were published in *Kino*, the Ukrainian monthly film magazine. Eisenstein's *Strike* appears to have made a deep impression on Dovzhenko who was also being influenced by the articles in *Kino* which proclaimed film as the one true art form. Impetuously Doyzhenko quit his work and went to Odessa where, without any formal training or experience in filmmaking, he started on a new career at what was then considered a ripe old age of 32.

Dovzhenko's first film script, *Vasya The Reformer,* a short comedy, was quickly accepted by the officials of Odessa Studios and he was commissioned to direct it. The film proved successful and he was commissioned to make another comedy, *The Little Fruits of Love,* the script for which was written in less than five days. For his next work Dovzhenko turned to a different genre, mystery. *The Diplomatic Pouch,* an espionage thriller, proved very popular with Soviet audiences because detective and suspense serials had been popular in Russia even before 1917. With three successful films to his credit, VUFKU officials now expressed further confidence in him by giving approval for his first big, important film *Zvenigora.* This work proved that Dovzhenko had a great reservoir of natural, artistic talent, but for a time after its completion his future seemed uncertain.

Zvenigora was a work of complex symbolism spanning hundreds of years of Ukrainian history and folklore. When the VUFKU officials saw the finished film they were as confused by the surrealistic images as Dovzhenko thought general audiences might be. It was not a film that was easy to understand. The studio administrators then requested Eisenstein and Pudovkin to preview the film before they would approve its release. The two directors were enthusiastic about what they saw, impressed by the intellectual thrust of the work. Audiences, however, were only lukewarm to *Zvenigora* and Dovzhenko took the lesson to heart. With his next work, *Arsenal*, Dovzhenko employed less symbolism and more romanticism. Soviet historians see the work as marking him a leader of the so-called romantic wing of socialist realism.

In *Earth* Dovzhenko produced a film that has withstood the test of time and is certainly one of his best. More lyrical and less symbolic than its two immediate predecessors, *Earth* shows how poetic its director was. Peasant life in the Ukraine is ennobled, revealing Dovzhenko's deep emotional attachment to his native land and heritage. The film did not fully compliment the drive for agricultural collectivization which explains why the Party did not entirely like it. Later Dovzhenko was to feel more intensely the sting of official displeasure. At the time, too, Dovzhenko married Yulia Solntseva who was to be his most loyal companion and collaborator.

Dovzhenko next proposed a project about the Nobile tragedy but was turned down and instead requested to make another film about contemporary Ukrainian life and industrialization. He agreed to it enthusiastically, but *Ivan*, his first sound film did not repeat his earlier successes. Moreover, the Party was not overjoyed in the way that Dovzhenko depicted the good and the bad aspects of contemporary life. Critics, film historians, and audiences have always liked his next film better than *Ivan*.

The year 1935 was a high water mark in Dovzhenko's life. In January he was awarded the prestigious Order of Lenin and everyone liked *Aerograd* when it was released later that year. For Dovzhenko the film symbolized the thrust of the Soviet future — the opening and development of the Soviet Far East. The work was rich in its images of the Siberian landscape and had a strong story line about loyalty to the state taking precedence over any individual. Despite its strong political content Dovzhenko handled the material well without sinking to bald propaganda. The film was admired by the Party and even Pudovkin was impressed by it. The Ukrainian's career then took a fateful turn for the worst when Stalin asked him to undertake a new project.

After seeing *Chapayev* and declaring it the greatest film ever made, the Soviet leader requested Dovzhenko to make a film about the legendary Ukrainian Civil War commander Shchors. Although he agreed to do it Dovzhenko was certainly not enthusiastic about it and *Shchors* was a long time in the making. Not only was Dovzhenko under Stalin's watchful eye and prodding, but he must certainly have felt the pressures that were building up in Soviet society as a result of the purges that were ravaging the country. Moreover, the films of Ukrainian directors were closely scrutinized for even the least hint of Ukrainian nationalism or separatism and suffered accordingly. Faced with such an environment it is no wonder Dovzhenko took years to make *Shchors*.

To avoid any possible criticism over the issue of nationalism, Dovzhenko created new characters around the figure of Shchors and slightly altered the known historical facts. With the central character Dovzhenko was never happy and in the end Shchors comes out as a near monumental deity. At one point Dovzhenko became so dissatisfied with the script that he changed it after half had been filmed. Still the finished work is still largely admired for the way Dovzhenko treated and portrayed many of the characters, and the photography was beautiful if imposing and monumental. Shchors, to be sure, lacks the human warmth and occasional humor that one remembers about Chapayev. Stalin never liked the film which had such a drain on Dovzhenko. Several years were to pass before Dovzhenko actively directed another film.

Liberation, released in 1940, was largely made under Yulia Solntseva's direction with Dovzhenko taking the role of overall supervisor. The work, which gave a lyrical, pro-Soviet view of the reannexation of the Western Ukraine to the USSR, seems to have been made for political purposes only.

Dovzhenko had barely taken over as artistic head of the Kiev Studios when war broke out in June 1941. When the Red Army retreated from the Ukraine Dovzhenko left Kiev and served for a time as editor of frontline newspapers and pamphlets. Dovzhenko's father was killed during the Nazi occupation but his mother was to survive the war and see him return to Kiev in 1944.

During much of 1942 and 1943 Dovzhenko spent time while in Moscow in writing stories and one novel, *Victory.* The three feature-length documentaries, *Battle for the Ukraine* (1943), *The Kharkov Trial* (1945), and *Victory In The Ukraine* (1945), while often credited to him were actually directed by Yulia Solntseva but with Dovzhenko as supervisor. The films go beyond normal reportage and are marked by lyrical images that are so characteristic of the photography of Dovzhenko's films.

After the war, and once more in Kiev, Dovzhenko wrote a stage play about the life of the Russian naturalist Ivan Michurin. He was urged to make it into a film but was reluctant to do so as the experience of *Shchors* was still fresh in mind. In the end Dovzhenko accepted the assignment and the film was first entitled *Life In Bloom* and later *Michurin*. Filming began in 1946 and whatever apprehension Dovzhenko had originally events were to show he had been right. The film was not finished and released until 1949. *Michurin* was an unlucky film for Dovzhenko as it coincided with Zhdanov's campaign of cultural repression. The first version was severely criticized and had to be re-made to make it more patriotic and more in keeping with the theories of the self-styled botanist T.D. Lysenko, who was high in Stalin's favor. The reediting of *Michurin* was done largely without Dovzhenko's participation which was reflected in the film's uneveness.

Dovzhenko's new low point coincided with the nadir of Soviet cinema during the last few years of Stalin's life. Sometime in 1950 he wrote the scenario for what must have been an obligatory chore, but *Farewell, America,* an anti-American Cold War story was never filmed.

In his last few years of life, Dovzhenko still had his old energies and wrote several scripts all of which dealt with the Ukraine. One,*Poem About The Sea,* was finished and filming was to have begun on the day he died. Solntseva carried the project through and also finished two of his other works, *The Enchanted Desna* and *Story Of The Flaming Years.*

While he was alive Dovzhenko said that the cinema was the art of people and that the filmmaker himself had to be knowledgeable about the life he was portraying. How well Dovzhenko succeeded in bringing life to the screen is perhaps best summed up by Ivor Montagu who called him 'Poet of Life Eternal.'

Films: *Vasya The Reformer* (1926), *The Little Fruits Of Love* (1926), *The Diplomatic Pouch* (1927), *Zvenigora* (1927), *Arsenal* (1929), *Earth* (1930), *Ivan* (1932), *Aerograd* (1935), *Shchors* (1939), *Liberation* (1940), *Battle For The Ukraine* (1943, supervisor), *The Kharkov Trial* (1945, supervisor), *Victory In The Ukraine* (1945), *Michurin* (1949, with Yulia Solntseva).

[See also: Amengual, Barthelemy. *Dovjenko.* Paris: Editions Seghers,

1970. Leyda, Jay. "An Index To The Creative Work of Alexander Dovzhenko," *Sight and Sound*, 1947, special supplement. Montagu, Ivor. "Dovzhenko — Poet of Life Eternal," *Sight and Sound* (1957) (Summer, vol. 27, no. 1, p. 44. Schnitzer, Jean and Luda. *Dovjenko.* Paris: Edition Universitaires, 1966.]

DZIGAN, Yefim. b. 1898. Georgian.

After demobilization from the Red Army in 1922 Dzigan enrolled as a student in Boris Chaikovski's workshop. Later he worked as Pudovkin's assistant on *Mechanics Of The Brain.* For a time he was associated with Belgoskino studios before he decided to return to his native Georgia, where his career first bloomed as a director.

After the success of his collaboration with Chiaureli on *First Lieutenant Streshnev,* Dzigan was given his first independent film assignment, *God Of War* (1929). This work, anti-religious in theme, brought Dzigan a good deal of critical, positive attention for its symbolism in which the cross is united with the machine gun. The film was moderately popular with audiences, was one of the better Soviet antireligious films, and helped to revive a lagging Georgian film industry. Dzigan then returned to Belgoskino for his next two films.

The Trial Must Continue and *Woman* proved quite popular at the time as they dealt with the increased social status of women in Soviet society. The first emphasized the legal equality and rights of women while the second focused on equal job opportunities for women in mechanized agriculture. Dzigan's works, viewed as forerunners for the more popular and better known *Member of the Government,* have not been given much notice by Western observers. It was with his next film that Dzigan's career glowed brightly and is always considered his best, although some observers differ as to the degree of credit that should be given its director.

Dzigan collaborated on the script of *We Are From Kronstadt* with Vsevolod Vishnevski, who in fact adapted the script from his novel *An Optimistic Tragedy.* The film, which centered around the Bolshevik defense of Petrograd in 1919, was made at Mosfilm and still enjoys high repute by Soviet and foreign commentators and audiences. It was one of the great Soviet films of the 1930s and Dzigan's career reached its highest point of success. Never again did Dzigan make a film that equaled it and this would support the idea that credit should go mostly

to Vishnevski for the achievement of *We Are From Kronstadt.*
Vishnevski's novel and play were revived with much success twenty-six
years later by Samson Samsonov's *An Optimistic Tragedy* which was a
prize winner at the 1963 Cannes Film Festival.

Dzigan and Vishnevski attempted to repeat their success and collaborated once more on a film script for *First Cavalry Army.* This
proved to be unlucky and the work was halted by officials without explanation. Eisenstein, too, had been discouraged from a film project on
the same subject. The history of the First Cavalry Army was politically
sensitive and controversial.

The last three films that Dzigan made brought him little attention
and are almost forgotten. The last two were politically safe films,
Dzhambul dealt with the poet who was so fond of Stalin while *Prologue*
was based on a period of Lenin's life, neither however created much of
a critical stir.

Films: *First Lieutenant Streshnev* (1928, with Mikhail Chiaureli), *God
Of War* (1929), *The Trial Must Continue* (1931), *Woman* (1932), *We
Are From Kronstadt* (1936), *Cine-Concert for the 25th Anniversary of
the Red Army* (1943, with Sergei Gerasimov and Mikhail Kalatozov),
Dzhambul (1952), *Prologue* (1956).

EGGERT, Konstantin. 1883-1936? Actor and director.

One of the few Soviet film-makers known to have perished during
the purges of the 1930s. Eggert began his film career prior to the
Revolution and decided to remain in the country after 1917. Early in
the 1920s he joined Mezhrabpom-Rus, where he was active as an actor
and later as a director. His most remembered role was that of Tuskub
the Martian in *Aelita.*

As a director Eggert enjoyed a good measure of commercial success, but failed to satisfy Party critics. He seemed to have been indiffer-
ent or naive about Soviet politics where films were concerned. In his
first film, *Marriage of the Bear* which he co-directed with Vladimir
Gardin, he was taken to task for the film's strong focus on bourgeois
decadence. The experience marked him thereafter for he was, along
with Yakov Protazanov and Cheslav Sabinski, barred for a time from
directing in the late 1920s. In his last two films Eggert lavishly over-
spent his budgets, although he was not the only Soviet director to have
ever done so. In his last film, *Gobseck,* Eggert changed the script several

times in the midst of production in an attempt to stay within the Party line. Despite the great cost of the film, the work proved to be a fiasco as Eggert failed to blend Communist ideology with Balzac's story. Some time in 1936 Eggert was arrested and disappeared.

Films (as director): *Marriage of the Bear* (1926, with Vladimir Gardin), *House of Ice* (1928), *The Lame Nobleman* (1928), *Harbor of Storms* (1933), *Gobseck* (1935).

EISENSTEIN, Sergei Mikhailovich. 1898-1948. Director and film theoretician.

Few film-makers have been so studied or discussed as Eisenstein, one of the four giants of Soviet cinema. The small number of films that he made is miniscule when compared to the influence he exerted on world cinema in his own lifetime.

Eisenstein was born in Riga of a middle class, Jewish family. As a young boy he frequently went to the movies, accompanied by his governess. In his later years he admitted that he did not suffer from want while growing up and his later commitment to the Bolshevik cause was largely intellectual and not emotional. Prior to the Civil War he studied at Petrograd's Institute of Civil Engineering. After serving with the Red Army as an engineer and later as a set designer for a theatrical troupe, Eisenstein went to Moscow after demobilization in 1920. He fully intended to study Japanese art, but the theater was too strong an attraction.

In Moscow Eisenstein studied under Vsevolod Meyerhold along with Sergei Yutkevich and joined the Central Proletkult Theater. It was while producing the play *Enough Simplicity in Every Wise Man* that Eisenstein made his first, short film. *Glumov's Diary* was an eccentric and surrealistic film interlude in the play. While preparing the film Dziga Vertov was assigned to assist Eisenstein. After a few days Vertov left in disgust and with the firm belief that Eisenstein and his group were complete failures. Although the film was far from being a smash hit it did provide Eisenstein with experience and with material for study. In the same year he published the first of his theoretical writings, "Montage of Attractions," in which he stressed the importance of film editing.

With *Strike* in 1925, Eisenstein became firmly established as a director. The work's influence on other Soviet film-makers cannot be

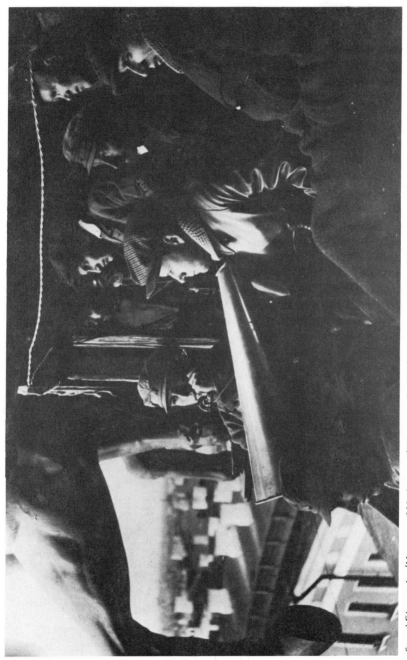

overemphasized. The work not only brought the Russian Revolution to the screen but revolutionized the cinema and was the laboratory for Eisenstein's later works. His next feature film brought him world acclaim.

With Eduard Tisse and Grigori Alexandrov, Eisenstein accepted the assignment for the film *1905* which was to commemorate the 1905 Revolution. Originally the mutiny on the battleship *Potemkin* was to be only a part of a large, epic film, but the more that Eisenstein became involved in the project the more he decided that the mutiny represented the essential spirit of the events of 1905. In *Battleship Potemkin* Eisenstein fulfilled many of his editing theories in which the viewer is set on a straight visual collision with maggoty meat and the Odessa steps sequence. For the first time the masses represented the true hero and the film was a mirror of the Russian revolutionary movement. At first the film created little sensation in the USSR and it was not until after its warm reception in Berlin that the Soviets gave *Potemkin* and its director proper attention. Both film and director have withstood the test of time and endless analysis.

After *Potemkin* Eisenstein set to work on a film that was to reflect official policies on Russian agriculture. *The General Line,* as it was first entitled, was started in 1926 and not completed until 1929. The film was plagued by delays when Eisenstein had to work on *October.* When he returned to the work much revision of the film and script were necessary because of changing policies. Eisenstein also began, for the first time, to edit and structure the film for emotional impact as a result of criticism that *October* was too intellectual, i.e. "formalism." When the film was finally released in 1929 as *The Old And The New* it failed to satisfy Party critics or Stalin. The film lacked the emotional impact that was to be found later in Dovzhenko's *Earth* and Ermler's *Peasants.*

While still engaged in editing *The Old And The New,* Eisenstein became the artistic head of the State Institute of Cinematography in Moscow and undertook an extensive revision of the curriculum. In his seminar in 1928 were two students who were to enjoy a brief flash of international fame for *Chapayev,* Sergei and Georgi Vasiliev.

In the late 1920s world cinema was stirred and reformed by a new technical innovation, sound. Film-makers in the West rushed to make use of it, often with laughable results. The potential of sound was not lost on Eisenstein who, along with Alexandrov and Pudovkin, issued a manifesto on sound. The three men cautioned against the over

Sergei Eisenstein on location for *The Old And The New.*
(Museum of Modern Art/Film Stills Archive)

hasty use of this new technical advance lest all the artistic achievements thus far attained in silent films be wiped out. Sound had to be studied carefully and its use be applied as an extension of the film art. How much effect the manifesto had on Soviet directors is not really known, but Soviet film-makers were slow in using sound as the necessary equipment was in very short supply in the USSR.

In August 1929, Eisenstein went abroad in company with Alexandrov and Tisse. His primary objective in making the trip was to study Western film developments as well as to study capitalism first hand for a projected film on Marx's *Capital*, which was never realized. In Hollywood Eisenstein contracted to do two film scripts, neither of which was filmed. Although he was the darling of Soviet cinema at the time, Hollywood society was scandalized by some of his eccentric mannerisms and neither was sorry when he left for Mexico.

Eisenstein's stay in Mexico was to result in a bitter disappointment for him and lasted throughout his remaining years. With financial support from the Upton Sinclairs, Eisenstein began work on *Que Viva Mexico!*, an epic film about Mexican history and life. Before it was completed funds were exhausted and a sharp dispute erupted between Eisenstein and Sinclair over the control and disposition of the work. Although Sinclair had promised that Eisenstein would edit the film he seized the work. There are reports that Sinclair's seizure was abetted by Boris Shumyatski who was Eisenstein's nemesis for several years. Despite repeated attempts, Eisenstein was never able to get control of the film and later parts of it were released as *Thunder Over Mexico, Eisenstein in Mexico,* and *Time in the Sun.* As late as the 1960s Girgori Alexandrov attempted to get the film and complete Eisenstein's work but failed.

Eisenstein returned to Moscow in April 1932 and resumed his teaching at the state film school at a time when Stalin was ascending in power. Soviet cinema was becoming more institutionalized under the anti-Semitic Boris Shumyatski. Although Eisenstein proposed several film projects his career and creativity were kept effectively checked by the head of the film industry. How low Eisenstein had descended in official favor was gallingly made evident at a public ceremony in 1935 when he was awarded the low ranking title of Honored Art Worker. Nevertheless, in the spring of 1935 he finally received approval for *Bezhin Meadow*, a story set against Russian rural society based on Turgenev's *Pages From a Huntsman's Notebook*. The film was two years in the making before it was halted by Shumyatski in March 1937. The picture was made in two versions because of delays caused by Eisenstein's falling ill twice during production. The first version came under criticism and had to be started afresh. The second version fared no better because of changes in state policies regarding agriculture and religion. Eisenstein once more was attacked for his formalism. In fact, throughout his career, Eisenstein never failed to receive some criticism for the intellectual thrust of his works. One always had to think when looking at an Eisenstein film and Stalin himself was distrustful of sophisticated intellect. However, Stalin had a hand in reviving Eisenstein's faltering career and encouraged the film-maker to undertake *Alexander Nevski*, originally entitled *Rus*.

Nevski was begun in late 1937 and Eisenstein finished it in the fall of 1938, several months ahead of schedule. To save time, but at great cost, the famous Battle on the Ice was filmed in the sweltering heat of mid-July and crushed glass and sand were used for snow. The film, while not entirely free of some carping, was a huge commercial success and certainly satisfying from a patriotic, anti-German point of view following the Nazi takeover of the Sudetenland. The work was one of the most deliberately structured of all Eisenstein's films. Even today the operatic-like character of the film is much admired, with the medieval-like mood being well maintained throughout the work. The musical score, the product of Eisenstein's close collaboration with Prokofiev, is still considered a remarkable piece of work that enhances the medieval flavor of the film. Eisenstein's career rebounded with *Nevski* and he belatedly received a justly deserved Order of Lenin in February 1939 as recognition of meritorious service to the state.

After a brief period on an abortive film project about the building of the Ferghana Canal Eisenstein took over as artistic supervisor of Mosfilm Studio, then as now the largest in the USSR. In mid-June 1941 he left Mosfilm to begin work on his last and grandest film, *Ivan the Terrible*. Actual production did not start until April 1943 because of the problems resulting from the dislocation of film studios in the face of the German invasion.

Ivan the Terrible became not only an epic film in itself but a reflection of Soviet wartime determination to achieve a work of national pride, similar to the contemporary British film *Henry V*. In a film that was lavish in budget and resources in the midst of a war, Eisenstein succeeded in portraying all facets of Ivan IV, good and bad. Whether or not Eisenstein wanted to make allegorical allusions to Stalin will never be known despite endless debate about this point. The film was originally planned as a trilogy, but only parts I and II were completed. Throughout the film was carefully planned and controlled in contrast to Eisenstein's spontaneous innovation in his earlier works. The medieval grandeur and haunting, dark atmosphere that surrounded Ivan IV is evoked and maintained by excellent camera work, musical scoring, the physical poses of the actors, and in the rhythm of the dialog. *Ivan the Terrible* probes deeply into the character of the first autocrat of Russia and shows the steady deterioration of a man constantly threatened by treachery.

The showing and release of Part I was a great triumph for Eisenstein, who received the then coveted Stalin Prize in February 1946. Then, following a heart attack, Eisenstein suffered disgrace after the official previewing of Part II. This part was less than flattering to the Russian tsar and critics attacked the director for erroneous interpretations of Ivan's character. After convalescing Eisenstein decided to make an effort to finish the project. In the spring of 1947 he was able to meet personally with Stalin in company with Nikolai Cherkasov, the lead actor. The talks resulted in Eisenstein's receiving approval to continue on with Part III and combine it with the less objectionable portions of Part II. The plan never materialized as Eisenstein, while in the midst of editing Part II, suffered a second, fatal heart attack and died on February 11, 1948. Part II was only released ten years later to much acclaim.

At the time of his death Eisenstein left unfinished a history of film and a theoretical article on the dramatic use of color in films. During his lifetime Eisenstein achieved a scale of international success that very few directors have ever attained. His work reflected the great potential of film as an art form.

Films: *Glumov's Diary* (1924), *Strike* (1925), *Battleship Potemkin* (1925), *October* (1927), *The Old And The New* (1929), *Que Viva Mexico!* (1931, uncompleted and never released in original form), *Bezhin Meadow* (1936-37, uncompleted and banned, parts of film destroyed during World War II and remaining portions were edited and released as a static film in 1967 under supervision of Sergei Yutkevich), *Alexander Nevski* (1938), *Ivan the Terrible* (Part I-1945, Part II-1958).

[See also: Eisenstein, Sergei. *The Complete Films of Eisenstein.* With

unpublished essay by Eisenstein. New York: E.P. Dutton, 1974.
_____. *Film Essays, with a Lecture.* New York: Praeger, 1970.
_____. *Film Form.* New York: Meridian Books, 1957.
_____. *The Film Sense.* New York: Harcourt, Brace and Co., 1942.
_____. *Ivan the Terrible.* New York: Simon and Schuster, 1962.
_____. *Notes of a Film Director.* London: Laurence and Wishart, 1959.
_____. *Potemkin.* New York: Simon and Schuster, 1968.
_____. *Que Viva Mexico!* London: Vision Press, 1952.
Gottesman, Ronald, and Harry Gelduld. *The Making and Unmaking of 'Que Viva Mexico!'.* Bloomington: Indiana State U. Press, 1970.
Kuleshov, Lev. "A Critique of Eisenstein's Films," *Film Journal,* 1972 (Fall/Winter), vol. 1, no. 3/4, p. 31.
Leyda, Jay. "Eisenstein's Bezhin Meadow," *Sight and Sound,* 1959 (Spring), vol. 28, no. 2, p. 74.
Montagu, Ivor. *With Eisenstein in Hollywood.* New York: International Publications, 1969.
Moussinac, Leon. *Sergei Eisenstein.* New York: Grove Press, 1960.
Nizhny, Vladimir. *Lessons With Eisenstein.* New York: Hill and Wang, 1969.
Seton, Marie. *Sergei Eisenstein: A Biography.* New York: Grove Press, 1960.]

EKK, Nikolai. b. 1902.

After graduating from the State Institute of Cinematography in 1928, Ekk was assigned to make a culture film about the leather trade, *How And How Not To Do It.* Despite its subject matter, the film was well received by critics and Ekk was considered to have much promise as a film director. The prophecy held good on his next, full length feature film, *The Road to Life.*

Ekk's film dealt with the problem of Soviet adolescent delinquents and Civil War orphans who were then roaming Soviet streets with impunity. *The Road to Life* focused on the rehabilitation of young delinquents at a time when the Soviet educational system was turning away from gross permissiveness to more discipline. In order to prepare the material, Ekk himself spent a year in studying Soviet youth and the educational process of the time. The film was also the first true Soviet sound film, having been conceived, written, and filmed as such. When it was released *The Road to Life* was an instant success artistically and socially. Even today Soviet and foreign critics agree in their admiration of the film. Ekk was propelled to the zenith of his career for *The Road to Life* and afterwards never quite measured up to the prophecy made about him.

Nightingale, Littel Nightingale, the first Soviet color feature film, proved a critical flop and Ekk had to drop his plans for two sequels to the work. For a time Ekk planned to film *Hamlet,* but the project never went into production.

Ekk's last two films, both made at the Kiev Studios, received lukewarm receptions and have gone largely unnoticed. After *May Night* Ekk became inactive and little is known about his activities. In the 1950s Ekk reedited *The Road to Life* with an updated sound track and the film enjoyed another period of popular revival. Ekk's masterpiece is so good even today that it has been reproduced on 16mm film for non-theatrical showings.

Films: *How And How Not To Do It* (1929), *The Road to Life* (1931), *Nightingale, Little Nightingale* (1936), *Sorochinski Fair* (1939), *May Night* (1941).

ERMLER, Friedrich Markovich. 1898-1969. Born in Latvia.

The film artist as social observer and critic perhaps best defines Ermler's achievement in film-making.

As a young boy Ermler became fascinated by movies and like Donskoi organized backyard skits with his friends. During the Civil War he joined the Red Army and became a member of the Communist Party in 1919. While fighting on the Northern front he was captured by the Whites and badly tortured.

After demobilization Ermler enrolled in the Leningrad film technicum in 1923 and one story about him claims he showed up for his first class with his Mauser still strapped to his side. At first he intended to study acting, but switched his concentration to directing. While still only a student Ermler organized his own workshop, the

Friedrich Ermler (Museum of Modern Art/Film Stills Archive)

Cinema Experimental Workshop (KEM). Ermler's group planned and staged film plays but was unable to do any actual shooting because of the lack of film stock. The objective of KEM, which was laid down in a manifesto written by Ermler, was the creation of a new revolutionary cinema based on material gleaned from society and its problems. While Ermler had some affinity with the FEKS group of Kozintsev and Trauberg in the area of content, he did not become eccentric or innovative in form or style.

The theme of man's moral rejuvenation as a result of social interaction crops up again and again in Ermler's films. This may explain why Soviet film historians have usually admired Ermler's works. His strong interest in psychology is reflected in the depth of character portrayal and conflict in his films. Despite his strong dedication to the Communist Party, Ermler had warm, sympathetic people in his films and not idealized stereotypes. Although one can easily see where Ermler's sympathies lay in his films he never lost sight of the dramatic contours of his material.

Ermler made his first, short, film in 1924 after persuading state health officials to sponsor a culture film on public health and medicine. *Skarlatina* was moderately successful and proved that the young director had some ability in film-making.

For his first full length feature film, Ermler collaborated with Eduard Ioganson on *Children of the Storm*, a rather simple story about a young Komsomol detective. The film proved commercially successful with Soviet audiences, who have always enjoyed mystery thrillers. His career was now well launched, but it was his next film that put him in the rank of noteworthy Soviet film-makers of the 1920s and also reflected the lessons of montage that he had assimilated after seeing Eisenstein's *Strike*.

Katka's Reinette Apples dealt with the moral and social rebirth of Soviet man during the cynical times of the NEP period following the Russian Civil War, a theme Ermler was quite fond of and repeated in his silent films. The opening scenes of the city streets and their haunting like atmosphere remind one of the expressionism in German films of the time. In time the streets take on a catalytic character of their own, forming the main arena for the interaction of the characters as they struggle to find their way to a new and uplifting way of life. Fedor Nikitin, who played Vadka with his crushed hat and tie askew, gave a warm, moving performance as the man who comes to Katka's aid. The excellence of Nikitin's acting was such that Ermler used him time and again in his films. *Katka's Reinette Apples* still remains as one of the finest Soviet films of the 1920s and stands as a kind of social document about Soviet urban society in that time.

In *House on the Ice* Ermler chose a story about the defense of Petrograd in 1919 in which he himself had participated. Moral problems once again formed the main theme of this work which became a success. Again Nikitin gave a fine performance.

Ermler's last two silent films were popular, commercially successful, and were highly admired by critics as they are now. *The Parisian Cobbler* brought Ermler even more stature in the eyes of critics for his almost fearless revelation of the bad morals of the Komsomols, which at the time had reached scandalous proportions. Nikitin, playing the part of the deaf mute cobbler Kirik, scored another triumph as the non-Party man who helps a young, pregnant, unwed woman whose condition is the result of an affair with an amoral Komsomol. The film, politically sensitive, was another triumph as Party officials gave it their blessing at a time when a campaign was begun to clean up the Communist Youth organization. In the same year Ermler attended a professional conference on film matters and boldly criticized the lack of technical qualifications among some of the Komsomols who were then going into film work.

Fragment of an Empire, Ermler's last silent film, is considered, at least by Soviet commentators, as a model of realism and social criticism. The story dealt with an amnesia victim who regains his memory during the 1920s and is astonished at the social progress that has been attained in contrast to the tsarist era. The film had a strong social-political message which never overshadows the dramatic structure of the work. When Ermler was editing the film he is known to have consulted Eisenstein, who made several suggestions which were incorporated in the finished work. With the release of this film Ermler's career was bright, but almost came to an end during the early 1930s.

With the coming of sound Ermler commenced work on a film project that was to have been entitled *Song.* For reasons not clear he abandoned the project and was on the verge of leaving the cinema. It appears that Ermler suffered from a loss of self-confidence in his own talents despite his many successful films. As in the case of Donskoi, Sergei Yutkevich proved instrumental in keeping Ermler in film work by asking him to co-direct *Counterplan.* This apparently gave Ermler the boost he needed to overcome his depression and go on to another period of success.

Counterplan, made with a limited sound track, dealt with the struggle between old and new social forces during the First Five-Year Plan. The theme was one Ermler was to repeat in his next, independent film. It was during the production of Counterplan that Ermler struck up a friendship with Sergei Kirov, who provided technical assistance and advice for the film. This meeting between the two men was to have a fateful twist a few years later. The good reception that met the release of the film showed that Ermler was still in good form and he then went to live on a collective farm for a year to gather material for his next work.

The difficulties of Soviet peasant life during Stalin's drive to collectivize agriculture in the 1930s are depicted in Peasants with harsh intensity. Murder, treachery, and bitter kulak resistance come through with a frankness that makes the film one of the boldest of its time. Yet, unlike Eisenstein's The Old And The New and Dovzhenko's Earth, one is never in doubt as to where the director's sympathies lie, on the side of collectivization. The film had a strong emotional impact on Soviet audiences and was also liked by the Party so much that Ermler received the Order of Lenin.

In the same year that Peasants was released Ermler travelled to New York and Hollywood as part of a Soviet delegation headed by Boris Shumyatski. The aim of this trip was to publicize Soviet films and increase their distribution. According to the historian Jay Leyda the delegation received less than a warm welcome and achieved little for their efforts.

After his return to the USSR Ermler was assigned to direct Great Citizen, a synthetic story based on the life of the recently assassinated Sergei Kirov, who had headed the Leningrad Party organization. Although the details of Kirov's murder are still murky but evidence that exists points responsibility at Stalin. Kirov's death and the subsequent purges made the film one of the most sensitive in Soviet film history. Ermler appears to have been a natural choice because of his friendship with Kirov and his known dedication to the Party. A lesser hand might well have produced a piece of political hack work, but not so with Ermler.

Work hardly began on the two-part film when delays were experienced when some of the cast were reluctant or refused to take politically odious roles. Next Ermler had to stop work because of obstruction by studio officials and Party bureaucrats who disputed the ending of the scenario. The circumstances of Kirov's death were in doubt even then and a six-month delay resulted over the dispute about the script. Only after the arrest of the Party officials and some of the studio personnel was production resumed. The two parts of the film were released in 1938 and 1939. Today the film is highly regarded for the realistic portrayal of characters in such a way that the film's justification for the purges is muted. The ideology in the film appears more subtle than in *Peasants* and the work is one of Ermler's best. Historically the film offers a good glimpse of Soviet political life and inner Party politics of the 1930s.

In 1940 Ermler was appointed artistic head of Lenfilm Studio, a post he was to hold for several years. With the outbreak of war Ermler supervised the evacuation of the Studio to the interior and it was not until 1943 that his first wartime film was released.

Highly patriotic in tone, *She Defends Her Country* was popular with Soviet audiences as well as in the United States, where it was exhibited with an English-language sound track. Ermler received a Stalin Prize for the film. The film today seems dated and tends to pale when compared with Donskoi's *The Rainbow* or Arnshtam's *Zoya*. The work also does not stand up well when compared to Ermler's second film of the war.

The Great Turning Point, originally entitled *General of the Army*, had its inspiration in the Battle of Stalingrad. Ermler spent almost two years in interviewing several of the Soviet generals who participated in the battle and most notably General Vatutin. As a result of Vatutin's criticism Ermler recast the scenario in story and theme. Production started in 1944 after Ermler and his staff returned to Lenfilm Studios. Filming proceeded on alternate days against the backdrop of wartorn Leningrad. On days when he was not shooting Ermler labored side by side with other studio workers in restoring the damaged Lenfilm Studios. Moviegoers and critics were pleased by *The Great Turning Point* when it was released in 1945. Even thirty years later the work's theme wears well. As a film about war made in the midst of war it is atypical. The story focuses on the psychological strain of war on those who have to direct battles and face the prospect of more battles. Generals bent over their maps as they ponder the correctness of their decisions form the focal point of the film. The emotional anxieties and tensions of the command post dominate the usual battlefield scenes. The synthetic story makes no mention of Stalin or the city named after him. Unfortunately the film also marks the artistic turning point for Ermler.

Ermler's work after 1945 never measured up to the forcefulness or standards of his earlier films. After finishing the highly patriotic *Great Force,* he was to have started work in 1949 on a Cold War film *Guarding the Peace.* Illness seems to have prevented him from filming the project and he did not become active again until 1955. In the early 1960s he worked in Soviet television and then made a strong attempt to come back with *Before The Judgement of History.* His last film was a story about the events of the Russian Revolution seen in a fresh light, which failed to excite critics and did not reflect the Ermler of old. It is for his films of the 1920s that Ermler is best remembered and show that a film artist can attain a high standard of social criticism without descending into mere polemics.

Films: *Skarlatina* (1924), *Children of the Storm* (1926, with Eduard Ioganson), *Katka's Reinette Apples* (1926), *House on the Snow* (1928), *The Parisian Cobbler* (1928), *Fragment of an Empire* (1929), *Counterplan* (1933, with Sergei Yutkevich), *Peasants* (1935), *The Great Citizen* (1938, 1939), *She Defends Her Country* (1943), *The Great Turning Point* (1945), *Great Force* (1950), *Unfinished Story* (1955), *The First Day* (1958), *Before the Judgement of History* (1967).

GAIDAI, Leonid. b. 1923. Georgian.

A 1955 graduate of Moscow's State Institute of Cinematography, Gaidai has concentrated on comedy and social satire for which the Georgians are building a strong reputation. His films have been very popular and have been well received in the West.

Films: *The Long Way* (1956, with Nevzorov), *The Bridegroom From the Other World* (1958), *The Moonshiners* (1961), *The Businessmen* (1963), *Operation Laughter* (1965), *The Caucasian Prisoner* [also: *Kidnapping Caucasian Style*] (1967), *The Diamond Arm* (1968), *The Twelve Chairs* (1971), *Ivan Vasilievich* (1973).

GANIEV, Nabi. 1904-52. Uzbek. Actor and director.
A pioneer of the early Uzbek cinema, Ganiev started acting in
1927 as Umar in *The Second Wife* and later gave a memorable perform-
ance as the comical Baimat in *The Covered Wagon*.
Films (as director): *The Ascent* (1931), *Ramazan* (1932), *Yegit* (1936),
Tahir and Zuhra (1945).

GARDIN, Vladimir Rostislavovich. 1877-1965. Actor and director.
One of the grand old men of Russian and Soviet cinema whose
films have gone almost unstudied in the West. In the years prior to the
Revolution Gardin worked for the Thiemann and Reinhardt Studio and
became one of tsarist Russia's most popular film-makers along with
Yakov Protazanov and Yevgeni Bauer. In his early years as a director
Gardin endeavored to establish high artistic standards at at ime when
syrupy melodrama was much in vogue. He was one of the first directors
to declare that montage, or editing, was the key to film art, but his
work in this area became overshadowed by that of Eisenstein, Kuleshov,
and Pudovkin.

   After the October Revolution Gardin decided to remain in Russia
and early in 1918 volunteered his services to the newly organized
Moscow Cinema Committee for which he made a number of short
agitki. In the same year Gardin also proposed the establishment of a
state film school, an idea that was to insure the future development of
Soviet cinema by providing professional training for aspiring directors,
scriptwriters, actors, and cinematographers. He became the school's first
director as well as teaching in his own workshop. At that time many of
his colleagues looked upon him as a leftist progressive because of his
attempt to break away from the tradition of romaticist or drawing-
room melodrama.

   Gardin's workshop produced *Iron Heel*, a largely experimental
film based on Jack London's novel. The work enjoyed some popularity
when it was released for exhibition, but it was his next two films that
brought him more attention. *Hunger, Hunger, Hunger* and *Sickle and
Hammer* were filmed in a semi-documentary manner and dealt with recent Soviet experiences of the post-Civil War period. In both films
Gardin's chief assistant was Vsevolod Pudovkin who also had a featured
acting role in the latter film. The works were an important step in
moving away from the quick, simple *agitki* towards the first Soviet

theatrical feature films. Gardin's efforts in bringing the revolutionary experience to Soviet screens was later overshadowed by the more forceful manner of Eisenstein.

From 1922 through 1924 Gardin, along with Chardynin, helped to spark the Ukrainian cinema. For a brief time Pudovkin worked with him on his first film for VUFKU and then left to join the workshop of the more radical Lev Kuleshov. While in the Ukraine Gardin made a number of films that were popular and exhibit more realism in form if not in content. Three of the films, *The Locksmith and the Chancellor*, *Duel*, and *A Specter Is Haunting Europe*, all reflected the Russian revolutionary experience, but received less than warm receptions by critics. In these works Gardin reverted to allegorical symbolism and mythical backgrounds for which film commentators saw little need. Gardin apparently did not ignore the words of the critics because in his later films he made conscious attempts to use realistic Russian material for his stories.

Gardin returned to Moscow and joined the Mezhrabpom-Rus studio where he collaborated with Natan Zarkhi who later became a very prominent scenarist.

The House of the Golubins, for which Zarkhi wrote the script, is often cited as an example of the progress Gardin made in film editing. The story traces the destiny of two Russian families from the last years of the tsarist era to the end of the Civil War. Gardin maintained the parallel action through skillful cutting of the finished work. That Gardin's work proved excellent is seen in the fact that the film was quite popular with audiences and was actually commissioned as a simple culture film about tuberculosis and its treatment. Whatever skill Gardin showed in editing this film was all too quickly overshadowed by Eisenstein's *Potemkin* which came out in the same year.

Gardin's last five films, while popular, did not escape carping by critics and he left directing for acting. The choice may have been a fortunate one because he was never able to free himself entirely of traditional repertory drama or allegorical symbolism. After 1929 abstract symbolism and traditionalism came under increasingly heavy attack, making life for film-makers difficult.

Until 1950 Gardin remained in the Soviet cinema as an actor and is still remembered mainly for two performances, as the elderly worker Babchenko in *Counterplan* and the music teacher in *Song About Happiness*. Largely in recognition for his acting Gardin was awarded the title of People's Artist in 1935. In his later years he devoted his energies to writing his memoirs. His contributions to Soviet film as a progressive director in the early 1920s is usually recognized only by Soviet historians.

Films (as director): *The Keys of Happiness* (1912), *Anna Karenina* (1914), *Days of Our Life* (1914), *Ghosts* (1915), *A Nest of Gentlefolk* (1915), *Petersburg Slums* (1915, with Yakov Protazanov), *War and Peace* (1915, with Yakov Protazanov), *Thought* (1916), *Iron Heel* (1919), *Hunger, Hunger, Hunger* (1921, with Vsevolod Pudovkin), *Sickle and Hammer* (1921, with Vsevolod Pudovkin), *Great October* (1922), *Duel* (1923), *Khmel* (1923), *The Locksmith and the Chancellor* (1923), *A Specter Is Haunting Europe* (1923), *The Landowner* (1924), *Ostap Bandura* (1924), *Cross and Mauser* (1925), *The House of the Golubins* (1925), *In Memory of the Great Communards* (1925), *Marriage of the Bear* (1926, with Konstantin Eggert), *Poet and Tsar* (1927), *Kastus Kalinovski* (1928), *Spring Song* (1929), *400 Million* (1929).

[See also: Gardin, Vladimir R. *Vospominaniya* [Reminiscences]. Moscow: Goskinoizdat, 2 vols., 1949, 1952.
_____. *Zhizn i trud artista* [The Life and Work of an Artist]. Moscow: Iskusstvo, 1960.]

GERASIMOV, Sergei Apollinarievich. b. 1906, in the Urals. Actor and director.

At the age of 14 Gerasimov left school to go to work in order to help support his family. He then moved to Leningrad where he also studied painting and theater design in addition to full time work. The lure of the cinema won out and he joined the FEKS group to study acting. His first acting role was in *Mishka Against Yudenich* and for several years thereafter worked under Kozintsev and Trauberg as actor and assistant director. Gerasimov's association with FEKS exposed him a good deal to current American film styles, which were much admired by Kozintsev and Trauberg. Throughout the 1920s Gerasimov enjoyed popularity for his roles in *The Devil's Wheel*, *The Overcoat*, *S.V.D.*, and *Alone*.

When Gerasimov began directing after 1929 he broke away from the eccentrism of the FEKS group and moved into naturalism, at which he has been an acknowledged master. Throughout his film-making career Gerasimov often wrote his own film scripts, which was typical of many Soviet directors of his generation.

From his earliest films Gerasimov has extensively employed young actors and has focused his efforts on stories about young people. His first important film, *Do I Love You?* (1934), is still admired for its intelligent, natural approach in exploring the morals of Soviet youth, a theme that is much in vogue among Soviet directors in the 1960s and 1970s.

Not until 1936 was Gerasimov given the opportunity to make a sound film. His first two works with the new medium, *The Brave Seven* and *Komsomolsk* were highly popular and Kozintsev praised Gerasimov for *The Brave Seven*. With these two films Gerasimov became recognized as an important director whose work served as a model of heroic realism, a style that seems to have caught the spirit of the role of Soviet youth in the Second Five-Year Plan.

After *The Brave Seven* Gerasimov taught in the directors' seminar at Lenfilm Studios until the outbreak of war with Germany in 1941. After 1945 he again resumed teaching when he joined the faculty of Moscow's All-Union State Institute of Cinematography, where he was active right into the 1970s.

In 1938 Gerasimov began work on *The Teacher* which focused on the daily life and professional problems of Soviet educators. While he was at work on the script he consulted no less than 1,000 schoolteachers for their views. The revised script resulted in a film that was a commercial success, a critical triumph, and admired by the state which awarded Gerasimov a prize of 15,000 rubles.

After 1941 Gerasimov made a number of popular wartime films before he was appointed to supervise documentary films. In late 1944, in the same year that he joined the Communist Party, Gerasimov became the head of the Central Newsreel and Documentary Studios in Moscow. The appointment of a theatrical film director to supervise documentaries was to prove eminently successful. Gerasimov assigned top-notch dramatic directors (Yuli Raizman, Sergei Yutkevich, Iosif Heifitz, and Alexander Zarkhi) to make documentaries to cover the last stages of World War II. *Berlin, Liberated France,* and *The Defeat of Japan* were highly praised when they were released in 1945. By and large critics have continued to like them even today, proving the value of having dramatic film-makers in documentary work.

In 1946 Gerasimov began to work on *The Young Guard,* based on

Fadeev's popular, Stalin Prize novel about the role of the Komsomol in the defense of Krasnodon in 1941. Gerasimov used many of his students at the Moscow film school for the cast and crew, thus giving rise to a whole new generation of film-makers including Sergei Bondarchuk and Samson Samsonov. When the two-part film was released in 1947 it came under heavy attack for its negativism by having scenes of flight and panic that were not complimentary to the Soviet wartime efforts. Gerasimov thus became a target for Zhdanov's great cultural purge as were Pudovkin, Leonid Lukov, Eisenstein, and the team of Kozintsev and Trauberg. Gerasimov lost no time in revising the film, which received a Stalin Prize in 1948. *The Young Guard* is the least modest of Gerasimov's films because of the bombastic heroics that he put into the second version.

In 1949 Gerasimov was back in good graces and was a member of the Soviet delegation that attended the Cultural and Scientific Conference for World Peace in New York. There he publicly criticized American films for their overt concentration on social violence. Although Gerasimov's words at the time were dismissed as part of the then Cold War rhetoric they seem to have validity in view of the increasing level of violence in American films since that time.

Gerasimov did not receive any great attention until he made a strong artistic comeback with his two-part adaptation of Sholokhov's *The Quiet Don [Quiet Flows The Don]* which was one of the best Soviet films of the 1950s. In recent years he has enjoyed renewed popularity with Soviet audiences for *To Love A Man* and *Mothers and Daughters*.

Films (as director): *Twenty-two Misfortunes* (1930, with S. Bartenev), *The Forest* (1931), *The Heart of Solomon* (1932), *Do I Love You?* (1934), *The Brave Seven* (1936), *Komsomolsk* (1938), *Parade of Athletes* (1938, short documentary), *The Teacher* (1939), *Masquerade* (1941), *Meeting With Maxim* (1941), *The Old Guard* (1941), *Cine-Concert for the 25th Anniversary of the Red Army* (1943, with Mikhail Kalatozov and Yefim Dzigan), *The Invincible* (1943, with Mikhail Kalatozov), *Great Land* (1944), *The Young Guard* (1948), *Liberated China* (1950, documentary), *Country Doctor* (1952), *Nadezhda* (1954), *The Quiet Don* (1957, 1958), *The Sputnik Speaks* (1959), *Men and Beasts* (1962), *The Journalist* (1967), *By the Lake* (1969), *To Love A Man* (1973), *Mothers and Daughters* (1973).

[See also: Gerasimov, Sergei. "A Clash of Conscience," *Films and Filming*, 1961 (March), vol. 7, no. 6, p. 7.
_____. "Socialist Realism and the Soviet Cinema," *Films and Filming*, 1958 (December), vol. 5, no. 3, p. 11.]

HEIFITZ, Iosif. b. 1905.

Graduated the Leningrad Technicum of Cinema Art with Alexander Zarkhi in 1927 and the two men thereafter collaborated exclusively until 1950. They began work in films as scriptwriters for the Sovkino studio in Leningrad. As directors they did not come into prominence until their third film, *Baltic Deputy*, although their *Hectic Days* was appealing and featured the later prominent actor Nikolai Cherkasov.

Baltic Deputy is still regarded as one of the best Soviet films of the 1930s. The story dealt with the events of the October Revolution and an old Russian scientist, played with great sensitivity by Nikolai Cherkasov, who commits himself to the Bolshevik cause after being befriended by the Baltic sailors. Filmed naturalistically, the work was applauded for its nice blend of history, character development, and revolutionary ideals which muted what might have been overt propaganda.

Heifitz and Zarkhi repeated the triumph of *Baltic Deputy* with their next film, *Member of the Government* (shown abroad as *The Great Beginning*). Similar in treatment to their previous work, this film dealt with the improved status and role of women in Soviet society since 1917. Vera Maretskaya gained a good deal of attention as the simple peasant woman who attains high position. Through the life and eyes of this woman we see Soviet attainments in the struggle against illiteracy and social advancements in the years after the Revolution. Again the two directors produced a work that was to be long admired for its psychological insight into character revelation and while its aim was the idealization of Communist society it never descended into overt indoctrination.

Although little is known about their second war film, *Malakhov Kurgan*, it was shelved apparently for artistic rather than ideological shortcomings. Their feature-length war documentary, *The Defeat of Japan*, received a Stalin Prize and is one of the best of the Soviet wartime documentaries. The film is largely the result of edited newsreels and gives a good glimpse of the Soviet Far Eastern campaign against the Japanese in 1945.

After making three more films after the war, Heifitz and Zarkhi ended their long collaboration to go their separate ways. Their breakup was not politically motivated but apparently the result of individual desires after not enjoying great success in their postwar work.

Heifitz's second film as an independent director, *The Big Family* (1954), was a popular work that only in later years was recognized as one of the first forerunners of the post-Stalin rejuvenation of Soviet cinema. The story deals with one family against the background of the shipbuilding industry. The heroes of the film are ordinary people through whose eyes and lives the viewer sees the achievements of Soviet society. Heifitz's film was free of the overt, bombastic propaganda that had characterized so many films produced during the last years of Stalin's life and attempted to deal significantly with the problems of the individual rather than the masses.

Never a stylistic innovator Heifitz has consistently brought out good films. His artistic reputation received renewed international attention for his colorful and skillful film adaptations of Chekhov: *The Lady With The Little Dog* and *In The Town of "S"*. The former has enjoyed more acclaim by critics, but both are excellent in their depiction of 19th-century Russia as seen by one of its great writers.

Films: with Alexander Zarkhi — *Facing the Wind* (1929), *My Motherland* (1933), *Hectic Days* (1935), *Baltic Deputy* (1937), *Member of the Government* (1939), *His Name Is Sukhe-Bator* (1942), *Malakhov Kurgan* (1944, shelved), *Defeat of Japan* (1945, documentary), *In the Name of Life* (1947), *Precious Grain* (1948), *Fires of Baku* (1950); alone — *Spring in Moscow* (1953), *The Big Family* (1954), *The Rumyantsev Case* (1955), *My Dear Man* (1958), *The Lady With The Little Dog* (1959), *Horizon* (1961), *A Day of Happiness* (1964), *In the Town of "S"* (1966), *Salute Marya* (1970).

ILYENKO, Yuri. b. 1936. Ukrainian. Cinematographer and director.

Upon graduating Moscow's state film school Ilyenko's diploma film, *Goodbye to Pigeon Time*, was judged to have sufficient quality for general exhibition. Ilyenko had a few acting roles before gaining recognition and several international awards for his camera work on Paradzhanov's *Shadows of Our Forgotten Ancestors*.

Ilyenko made his debut as an independent director with an adaptation of a story by Gogol, *On the Eve of Ivan Kupala,* which was given good praise by Soviet film observers. It was his second film, *White Bird With a Black Mark,* that gave Ilyenko foreign attention. The film has been admired for its lyrical, poetic qualities and earned a gold medal at the 1971 Moscow Film Festival.

In the late 1960s Ilyenko joined the teaching staff of the Cinema Faculty of the Kiev Theatrical Institute. For some time he was reportedly working on a film script entitled *Kiev Rus,* a projected film about medieval Ukrainian history but which has not gone into production.

Films: *Good-bye to Pigeon Time* (1960), *On the Eve of Ivan Kupala* (1967), *White Bird With a Black Mark* (1971), *With Regards* ((1974).

[See also: Ilyenko, Yuri. "A Director's Credo," *Soviet Life,* 1972 (February).]

ISHMUHAMMEDOV, Elyer. b. 1942. Uzbek.

A director who has gained much popularity for his films about Soviet youth and love, which have a refreshing, easy and naturalistic style.

Films: *Rendezvous* (1963), *Tenderness* (1966), *In Love* (1968), *Meetings and Partings* (1973).

IVANOV-VANO, Ivan. b. 1900. Russian.

After graduating the Institute of Fine Arts in 1923 he went into film work and became a pioneer in cartoon films. His first picture employed dolls. Ivanov-Vano has based most of his work on Russian fables.

Films: *Soviet Toys* (1923), *Skating Rink* (1927, with Cherkes), *The Adventures of Baron Muchhausen* (1929), *Black and White* (1931), *Tale of Tsar Duranda* (1934, with the Brumberg sisters), *The Little Humpbacked Horse* (1948), *The Brave Hare* (1955), *The Left Hander* (1964), *The Mechanical Flea* (1964), *How One Peasant Kept Two Generals* (1965), *Go To Nowhere* (1966), *Legend of a Cruel Giant* (1968).

KALATOZOV, Mikhail Konstantinovich (real name: **Kalatozishvili**). 1903-73. Georgian.

When *The Cranes Are Flying* appeared in 1958 foreign commentators proclaimed it as the beginning of the rejuventation of Soviet cinema following the repressive Stalinist era. It is the film for which Kalatozov will always be remembered as a major film-maker.

As a young man Kalatozov first studied commerce before becoming excited by the cinema and taking up the study of cinematography. His training and early work as a cameraman became apparent in the films he directed. Exciting visual effects through bold and imaginative camera angles.

Kalatozov returned to his native Tiflis in 1925 and joined the young, budding Georgian film industry. Almost immediately he was exposed to the work of two major film-makers. He took a small acting role in Perestiani's *The Case of the Murder of Tariel Mklavadze* and then worked under Lev Kuleshove as a cameraman on *Locomotive No. 1000b*. For the next few years Kalatozov was employed on several short documentaries and popular science films. The greatest influence upon Kalatozov in these early years came from the work of two other documentarists, Esther Shub and Dziga Vertov. In 1927 he had an opportunity to meet Shub and greatly admired her editing style on *The Fall of the Romanov Dynasty*.

In 1928 he was given an opportunity to make a film as a director in collaboration with Nutsa Gogoberidze. *18-28* was a historical documentary on the role of the Mensheviks in Georgia in the Civil War. The film gave no hint of Kalatozov's future potential. Although the two men strove to pattern their work after that of Esther Shub they had not the resources or materials to make an equivalent work. Today *18-28* is recalled only by Soviet film historians as Kalatozov's first step in his desire to make artistically important films.

Kalatozov's first important film was *Salt for Svanetia* which stamped him as an important director although Soviet critics at the time of its release were divided as to its artistic importance. *Salt for Svanetia*, an outgrowth for an art film project, dealt with the life of a poverty-ridden people in a remote, undeveloped area of the Caucasus. Photographed in a semi-documentary style the film points up the beauty of isolation through grand sweeping camera shots. In total effect it is comparable to Luis Buñuel's great *Land Without Bread [Las Hurdes]*. The film now appears as a prelude to what Kalatozov was to accomplish photographically with *The Cranes Are Flying*. When the work was exhibited it was criticized for its formalism and naturalism and Kalatozov's talents were not to be appreciated for some time. After the poor reception of *Salt for Svanetia* Kalatozov left Tiflis in 1932 to make his second film and face a greater setback at the hands of the Red Army. *The Nail in the Boot* was made as an allegory on Soviet industry as symbolized by the poor quality of a nail in a soldier's boot which leads in the end to the defeat of a military unit on maneuvers. The film came at a time when other directors had already begun to feel the chill of criticism for abstract films. The symbolism of *The Nail in the Boot* was lost on the generals who viewed it as a negative image of the Army and the film was banned from exhibition. The bureaucratic meddling discouraged Kalatozov from doing any more directing for some time and he accepted an administrative post with the Tiflis Studio.

Two years after taking his new post Kalatozov seemed ready to try to make another film. He submitted a proposal for a biographical film on the great Caucasian hero, Shamil, who had resisted tsarist Russian colonialism in the 19th century. The subject may have been politically sensitive in view of its potential to inspire nationalism and the idea was quashed.

After seven years of artistic inactivity Kalatozov came back to Soviet screens in 1939 with *Manhood,* a drama about Soviet aviation that served as a prelude for his next film. *Valeri Chkalov* was a biographical film about the temperamental Soviet flyer who became a popular national hero for his flight from the USSR across the North Pole to Vancouver, Washington. The film's success seemed ready made in view of Chkalov's recent achievement and official interest in popularizing aviation. Kalatozov gave due regard to Chkalov's individualistic personality which became a highpoint of the film, not to mention the role of Stalin as Chkalov's benefactor. In the picture Kalatozov himself played the part of one of the Americans who greets Chkalov upon the latter's landing in the United States. The actors who portrayed the Americans made the film noteworthy according to the historian Jay Leyda because of the sympathetic and credible manner they portrayed their characters. The work was a triumph and comeback for Kalatozov.

During World War II Kalatozov served as Soviet Consul in Los Angeles, where he reportedly devoted his efforts to strengthening U.S.-Soviet film relations and exchanges. In 1943 he collaborated with

Sergei Gerasimov on *The Invincible*, a popular war drama about the defense of Leningrad. Although popular in its time *The Invincible* in no way compares to the films he made before or after. Kalatozov was not to make another film until 1949, when he made his bow to the Cold War with *Conspiracy of the Doomed*. This was to have been followed by a second anti-American film, *The Man From Wall Street*, which never got beyond the script stage. Kalatozov's next film, released a year after Stalin's death, in retrospect seems like an announcement that the cultural thaw in Soviet life was taking place.

Firm Friends was a subtle satire on Soviet political life. In the story three friends band together and struggle against the frustrations of dealing with bureaucrats. Humorous in a subtle, hesitant way, the film was the first of its genre to appear on Soviet screens since the 1920s.

With *The Cranes Are Flying*, a beautifully lyrical and tender love story set in World War II, Kalatozov firmly heralded the end of Stalinist repression in films. The sensitive, full-bodied characters in the story represented a welcome change. Not a few critics pointed out the near absence of political propaganda. Photographically the work is rich and dynamic in its heightening of the main narrative. Socially, too, the film made a breakthrough in the sympathetic way that it treated the problem of wartime adultery. For the first time in many years the issue of social morals was openly revealed and handled in an intelligent manner. Kalatozov did not surpass the triumph of *The Cranes Are Flying* in his last three films. *I Am Cuba*, which he co-scripted with the poet Yevgeni Yevtushenko and co-produced with Cuba, was a political tribute to the revolutionary spirit of the Cuban people after the abortive Bay of Pigs invasion.

Films: *18-28* (1928, with Nutsa Gogoberidze), *Salt for Svanetia* (1930), *The Nail in the Boot* (1932, banned), *Manhood* (1939), *Valeri Chkalov* (1941), *Cine-Concert for the 25th Anniversary of the Red Army* (1943, with Sergei Gerasimov and Yefim Dzigan), *Conspiracy of the Doomed* (1950), *Firm Friends* (1954), *The First Echelon* (1956), *The Cranes Are Flying* (1957), *The Letter That Was Not Sent* (1960), *I Am Cuba* (1962), *The Red Tent* (1969).

KALIK, Moisei. b. 1927.
Studied under Sergei Yutkevich at the State Institute of Cinematography which he graduated in 1958. Kalik's most admired work to

date is *A Man Follows the Sun* which is a tender story about a boy growing up.

Films: *The Youth of Our Fathers* (1958), *Ataman Kodr* (1958, with Ritsarev and Ulitskaya), *Cradle Song* (1959), *A Man Follows the Sun* (1962), *Goodbye Boys* (1965).

KARASIK, Yuli. b. 1923.

A rising film-maker whose early works had a charming and youthful style. Karasik gained international attention with *The Sixth of July*, a historical drama about the attempt to throw Lenin out of power in 1918. The film was remarkable in that Lenin was not idealized but was depicted as a harried political leader. Karasik's next film was a deeper study of Lenin in his early years in the Russian revolutionary movement, which has barely come to foreign notice. *The Seagull*, a colorful adaptation of Chekhov's work, is acknowledged to be his best.

Films: *Waiting for Letters* (1960), *Wild Dog Dingo* (1963), *The Man I Love* (1966), *The Sixth of July* (1968), *Lenin in 1903* (1970), *The Seagull* (1971), *The Hottest Month* (1974).

KARMEN, Roman. b. 1906, in Odessa.

After working as a photographer for the magazine *Ogonyok*, Karmen studied at the Moscow film school from which he graduated in 1932. He is one of the leading Soviet documentary film-makers and his works of the World War II period are especially admired.

Films: *Moscow* (1932), *On the Events in Spain* (1937), *China in Conflict* (1939), *A Day in the New World* (1940, with Mikhail Slutski), *In China* (1941), *Leningrad Fights* (1942), *Stalingrad* (1943, with L.V. Varlamov), *Berlin* (1945, with Yuli Raizman), *Albania* (1945), *Oil Workers of the Caspian Sea* (1953), *Vietnam* (1954), *How Broad Is Our Country* (1958), *Conquered Seas* (1959), *Indian Morning* (1959), *Cuba Today* (1960), *The Great Patriotic War* (1965), *Russian Adventure* (1966, with Leonid Kristi and Boris Dolin), *Granada, My Granada* (1967), *Comrade Berlin* (1968), *Continent Aflame* (1970), *Chile-Happenings* (1973).

KAUFMAN, Mikhail. b. 1897. Ukrainian. Director and cinematographer.
Brother of the irrepressible Dziga Vertov with whom he was associated on the *Kino-Eye* and *Kino-Pravda* series.
Today Kaufman is most remembered as the co-director and chief cameraman of the bedazzling documentary *Man With A Movie Camera*. As an independent director Kaufman's style veered away from that of his brother by its smoothness and soft lyricism, which was most evident in *Spring*. After receiving the title of Honored Art Worker in 1935 Kaufman became less publicized and his work little known.

Films: *Moscow* (1927, with Ilya Kopalin), *Man With A Movie Camera* (1929, with Dziga Vertov), *Spring* (1929), *These Won't Give Up* (1932), *The Great Victory* (1933), *March of the Air* (1936), *Poem on the Life of the People* (1958).

KAVALERIDZE, Ivan Petrovich. b. 1887. Ukrainian.
Film sculptor of the Ukraine is a fitting appelation for Kavaleridze who only in the past few years has received more attention by Soviet film historians, but is still largely overlooked in the West.
Kavaleridze first studied sculpture and art at the Kiev art institute and then went on to the St. Petersburg Academy of Arts and finally Paris. After returning to Russia in 1911 he joined the Thiemann and Reinhardt studio as a set designer and artist. After the October Revolution he left Moscow and returned to his native Ukraine, where he worked for a time in the theater. Kavaleridze's work in art during the 1920s was mainly in the cubist style and he produced a portrait sculpture of Lenin and was commissioned to do a monument of Taras Shevchenko.
In 1928, as the Golden Age of Soviet cinema ended, Kavaleridze decided to return to the cinema and submitted a film script to the Odessa Studio. The idea for a film about the revolutionary movement in the Ukraine that covered a two-hundred year span was quickly accepted by the studio head, Neches, who also assigned Kavaleridze to direct it. *The Cloudburst* was one of the most interesting Ukrainian films of the silent era and controversial. The film came out at a time when any sort of experimentation was singled out for criticism. Critics of the time either admired its monumental symbolism or disliked it. The sculptural composition of the film made it an experiment in form, but not in

theme. The characters in the film are photographed and posed as living sculptures which made the film so unique. Critics however tended to agree that Kavaleridze exhibited talent as a film-maker.

In his next important work, *Perekop*, Kavaleridze avoided the sculptured forms that had caused him grief in his first film. His second effort, again about the Revolution and Civil War in the Ukraine, received better treatment. After *The Koli Rebellion*, another story about revolution in the Ukraine, Kavaleridze received the Order of the Red Star in 1935. He now was at the zenith of his career. For his next, and biggest, film Kavaleridze again chose the theme of Russian and Ukrainian revolutionary movements based on two poems by Taras Shevchenko. *Prometheus* came under scathing attack for its distortion of history which indicated that Moscow did not like the apparent strain of nationalism in the film.

In his last two works, Kavaleridze chose safe subjects. *Cossack Beyond the Danube* and *Natalka Poltavka* were pretty but hollow romantic musical operettas that failed to bring much notice.

During World War II Kavaleridze remained in Kiev under Nazi occupation and survived the war, but nothing more has been heard of this talented, but luckless artist.

Films: *The Cloudburst* (1929), *Perekop* (1930), *Stormy Nights* (1931), *The Koli Rebellion* (1933), *Prometheus* (1936), *Cossack Beyond the Danube* (1937), *Natalka Poltavka* (1937).

KHITRUK, Fedor. b. 1917. Russian.

A leading director of cartoon films which have consistently been admired abroad. Khitruk joined the Soyuzmultfilm Studio in 1938 as an animator. After serving in the Soviet Army in World War II he rejoined Soyuzmultfilm in 1947. His 1969 film was a bright satire about film-makers and their problems.

Films: *Story of a Crime* (1962), *Teddy Bear* (1964), *Boniface's Holiday* (1965), *A Man In A Frame* (1966), *Othello-67* (1967), *Film, Film, Film!* (1969), *The Island* (1973).

KHRABOVITSKI, Daniil. b. 1923. Russian.

First worked as a journalist before going into films as a

scriptwriter. As a director Khrabovitski scored a much admired critical success with *The Taming of the Fire*, a work about contemporary Soviet life set against the background of missile engineering and space explorations.

Films: *Roll Call* (1965), *Relay* (1967), *The Taming of the Fire* (1972), *The Fourth Room* (1974).

KHUTSIEV, Marlen. b. 1925. Georgian.
Graduated the All-Union State Institute of Cinematography in 1950 as one of Igor Savchenko's students. Khutsiev has established himself as one of the noteworthy film-makers concerned with exploring contemporary Soviet social problems, especially that of youth. With Mironer he pointed up the growing trend of humanism in Soviet films with *Spring on Zarechnaya Street*, which is considered by some Soviet commentators to be one of the best films of the 1950s.
In 1963 Khutsiev caused such controversy with *Ilich Square* that it had to be revised and was retitled *I Am Twenty*. Despite the revisions the film is still important as a social document in pointing up the difference of outlook of Soviet youth as opposed to older generations.

Films: *Spring on Zarechnaya Street* (1956, with F. Mironer), *Two Fedors* (1958), *I Am Twenty* (1964), *July Rain* (1966).

KOBAKHIDZE, Mikhail. b. 1939. Georgian.
One of the "new wave" Soviet directors who has helped to rejuvenate the Georgian film industry with his fresh and sparkling comedies.

Films: *The Wedding* (1965), *The Umbrella* (1966).

[See also: "A Russian Six," *Films and Filming*, 1967 (September), vol. 13, no. 12, p. 27.]

KOLOSOV, Sergei. b. 1921. Scenarist and director.
Began studies at State Institute of Theater Art in 1939, but studies were interrupted by war. Served in the Soviet Army 1941-46 and thereafter resumed his studies, graduating in 1951. Kolosov has been active primarily in Soviet television. His two theatrical films

focused on stories set in World War II, a theme in which he has a strong interest because of his own wartime experiences. His last film was a joint Polish-Soviet co-production which has received good reviews by critics.

Films: *The Heart of a Soldier* (1957), *Remember Your Name* (1974).

KONCHALOVSKI (see MIKHALKOV-KONCHALOVSKI)

KOPALIN, Ilya. b. 1900.

A documentarist and newsreel specialist who began as a cameraman under Dziga Vertov on the *Kino-Eye* series and *Stride, Soviet!* After co-directing *Moscow,* Kopalin came to prominence for his so-called "Village" trilogy of 1929-30, which focused on the plight and poverty of old style peasant agriculture during the height of the collectivization campaign. *For the Harvest, Renewed Labor,* and *The Village,* despite their propaganda message, reflected a dynamic and dramatic style of editing.

During World War II Kopalin supervised the work of combat cameramen.

Films: *Moscow* (1927, with Mikhail Kaufman), *For the Harvest* (1929), *Renewed Labor* (1930), *The Village* (1930), *One of Many* (1931), *The Village Observed* (1935), *To the Danube* (1940, with Poselski), *Defeat of the German Armies Near Moscow* (1942, with L.V. Varlamov), *Czechoslovakia* (1946), *The Day of the Victorious Country* (1947), *The Unforgettable Years* (1957), *Inside the USSR* (1959), *City of Great Destiny* (1960), *First Trip to the Stars* (1961), *Pages of Immortality* (1965).

KORSH-SABLIN, Vladimir. 1900-74.

Began film work in the Belorussian cinema in the 1920s. Korsh-Sablin's *Born in Fire* and *The First Platoon* are regarded as among the best films about the revolutionary movement in Belorussia.

Films: *Born in Fire* (1930), *A Sunny Campaign* (1931), *The First Platoon* (1933), *Seekers of Happiness* (1934), *Golden Fires* (1935),

A Daughter of the Motherland (1937), *The Fiery Years* (1939), *My Love* (1940).

KOZINTSEV, Grigori Mikhailovich. 1905-73. As a young boy in Kiev Kozintsev was a friend of Sergei Yutkevich. During the Civil War he served with a theatrical group on an agit-train. In 1921 Kozintsev went to Petrograd where he met Leonid Trauberg, with whom he was to collaborate almost exclusively until their trouble with *Plain People* (1946). As a result of their common interest in American shorts and comedies, especially those of Charles Chaplin and Mack Sennet, they formed their own workshop, the Factory of the Eccentric Actor (FEKS), along with Sergei Yutkevich in December 1921.

Kozintsev and Trauberg issued a 15-page manifesto on "eccentrism', which was to be a theatrical style based on the circus and vaudeville, but using story material from real life. The curriculum for FEKS made wide use of pantomime and acrobatics, which was not too dissimilar from the training at Lev Kuleshov's workshop in Moscow. The group staged a number of plays, but were unable to do any actual filming until 1924 when Sevzapkino gave them an opportunity to make their first film.

Adventures of Oktyabrina was a short, comical fantasy which centered around a capitalist plot to rob the Soviets. Modest though it was, the film launched Kozintsev and Trauberg on their directing careers and they were assigned to make another short, thriller-comedy, *Mishka Against Yudenich.* Their second effort proved popular and they were assigned their first full length feature film.

With *The Devil's Wheel* they chose to focus on city street life and the corrupting influences of the NEP period. The film marked a turn away from their eccentric style and the two men did so consciously after having been affected by Eisenstein's *Strike.* The film was a critical success and in mood and tone not too dissimilar from Ermler's later *Katka's Reinette Apples.* They now made their first adaptation of classical literature, Gogol's *The Overcoat.*

The Overcoat was filmed in a subjective manner, using unusual camera angles to give greater, dramatic emphasis to the physical proportions of objects and city streets. In the film the overcoat itself almost takes on the aspect of a living character. Gestures and poses were struck in such a way as to heighten the melodramatic tones that were usually associated with 19th-century themes. The story was a natural vehicle and outlet for the eccentric style. The acclaim of this film continues today and critics consider Alexei Batalov's 1960 remake not as good, although Batalov was accorded high marks for the way he caught the style of the original.

Following the Civil War comedy *Little Brother,* Kozintsev and Trauberg scored another triumph with *S. V. D.* The film again dealt with 19th century Russia and dealt with an episode of the 1825 Decembrist Revolt. The acting style was more relaxed, but again the two men caught the melodramatic flavor of the 19th century. Sergei Gerasimov gave an extremely good performance as Medoks while the photography of Andrei Moskvin proved notable. With a good record of successes behind them they now embarked upon their biggest film to that time, *New Babylon.*

Their new work took a year and a half to make with filming taking place in Paris and Leningrad. *New Babylon* was the story of the events surrounding the Paris Commune of 1871, the first popular social revolt in modern times. The bourgeois world and social tensions within French society were depicted through various people connected with the New Babylon department store. The heroine, Louisa, comes to recognize her working class loyalties and joins the Communards while Jean, her young soldier lover, refuses to follow her and in the end watches her die as the Communards are executed. The emotional mood of the film was heightened by Dmitri Shostakovich's accompanying musical score. By any measure *New Babylon,* because of its revolutionary theme and working class bias, should have received critical acclaim. Unfortunately the film came out at a time when the whole atmosphere in the Soviet film industry was changing. Critics were not too happy with the film's expressionistic style which they saw as similar to Eisenstein's *October,* which had been criticized for being too intellectual. Only today is *New Babylon* considered by the Soviets to be the climax of Soviet silent film art.

If critics had not been happy with *New Babylon* they were with *Alone.* This was a quiet, heroic, and natural story about a young woman teacher living in the cold, isolated wilderness of the Altai. The photography vividly captured the bleakness of the region and was enhanced in its impact by the fine musical score of Dmitri Shostakovich. *Alone* was initially made as a silent film, but a limited sound track was added during editing and thus marks it as Kozintsev's and Trauberg's successful transition to sound films.

The two men next spent several years in making their masterpiece which time has not tarnished. The *Maxim Trilogy* reflected the best that Soviet cinema was capable of producing in the 1930s. The story traces the life, revolutionary activity, and political maturation of a Bolshevik. The main character, Maxim, is a composite synthetic based on extensive research that Kozintsev and Trauberg conducted on the period from 1910 to 1918. Maxim was carefully drawn and comes out a fully drawn character whose emotions range from anger and sadness to rough, folksy humor. After the release of *The Youth of Maxim* the two men were awarded the Order of Lenin, the highest decoration of the USSR. Critics and audiences were not disappointed by the remaining two parts, *The Return of Maxim* and *The Vyborg Side*. The character of Maxim proved so popular that he was to reappear in other Soviet films. The *Trilogy* was the finest and most enduring achievement of Kozintsev's and Trauberg's collaboration.

World War II interrupted their collaboration for a time but they teamed up again after a few years on a film that was to be a tribute to the Soviet people on the home front. *Plain People* was released and immediately banned in 1946 for containing negative references to lack of Party leadership during the war. Kozintsev and Trauberg were severely criticized for erroneous interpretation of the recent past, much like Eisenstein, Pudovkin, and Lukov. The furor of the criticism was such that the two men never again collaborated. Kozintsev was still able to continue directing, but not Trauberg who was barred for several years from making any films. *Plain People* was finally released in 1956, but in a highly edited version.

Kozintsev's career, despite his highly patriotic biographical film *Pirogov*, was under a cloud until after Stalin's death. In 1950, in an apparent effort to get back into good political graces, Kozintsev began writing a script with Ilya Ehrenburg for an anti-American film, *Great Heart*. The work never went into production for reasons still unknown.

In 1957 Kozintsev made a strong artistic comeback with *Don Quixote*. With his next two films, *Hamlet* and *King Lear*, Kozintsev added new luster to an already distinguished career. His last two works are regarded as excellent and faithful film adaptations of Shakespeare and *Hamlet* was awarded a special prize by the British Film Institute when it was released. Kozintsev was one of the few Soviet film-makers of his generation who were able to gain new, important stature in the film world after 1953.

Films: with Leonid Trauberg — *Adventures of Oktyabrina* (1924), *Mishka Against Yudenich* (1925), *The Devil's Wheel* (1926), *The Overcoat* (1926), *Little Brother* (1927), *S.V.D.* (1927), *New Babylon* (1929), *Alone* (1931), *The Maxim Trilogy — The Youth of Maxim* (1934), *The Return of Maxim* (1937), *The Vyborg Side* (1938), *Plain People* (1946 [1956]); alone — *Film Notes on Battles 1 and 2* (1941, with Lev Arnshtam), *Incident at the Telegraph Office* (1941), *Pirogov* (1947), *Bilinski* (1953), *Don Quixote* (1957), *Hamlet* (1964), *King Lear* (1970).

[See also: Kozintsev, Grigori. "Deep Screen," *Sight and Sound*, 1959 (Summer), vol. 28, no. 3/4, p. 156.

_____. "The Hamlet in Me," *Films and Filming*, 1962 (September), vol. 8, no. 12, p. 20.

_____. *Prostranstvo tragedii. Dnevnik regissera* [The Scope of Tragedy. Diary of a Director]. Leningrad: Iskusstvo, 1973.

_____. *Shakespeare: Time and Conscience*. New York: Hill and Wang, 1966.]

KRUMIN, Varis. b. 1931. Lithuanian.

Films: *The Heir of the Military Road* (1970).

KULESHOV, Lev Vladimirovich. 1899-1970. Director and film theoretician.

Along with Eisenstein, Pudovkin, and Dovzhenko, Kuleshov was one of the giants in the history of Soviet film. He was always held in high esteem as a teacher of Soviet film-makers and while he was alive liked to point out that among his students were Pudovkin, Eisenstein (for only a brief time), Barnet, Kalatozov, and Paradzhanov. Kuleshov's main contribution to the artistic development of Soviet cinema lay in his experiments in montage or editing and for his theoretical writings.

As a youngster Kuleshov had a strong interest in art and mechanics. At the age of 15 he enrolled in Moscow's school of fine arts to study painting. Two years later he went to work as a set designer for

Yevgeni Bauer, one of tsarist Russia's most respected film-makers. While working under Bauer Kuleshov began to study American techniques of editing and began to see film as a selective, plastic art in which the director had great potential for restructuring his material. This later became known as the "Kuleshov effect" through which different emotions can be evoked by varying the juxtaposition of different scenes. In one experiment Kuleshov photographed the eminent actor Ivan Mozhukhin followed by a shot of a different object. Throughout each sequence Mozhukhin's face remained immobile and impassive, yet viewers maintained he had gone through a whole series of different emotions based only on the objects. It was from such experiments that Kuleshov maintained that film had to be edited and structured frame by frame. His ultimate aim was emotional montage while Eisenstein strove for intellectual montage.

In 1918 the first of Kuleshov's articles, "The Tasks of the Artist in Cinema," was published. Kuleshov believed that an actor's body movements were most important in doing a scene and in his early teaching stressed bio-mechanics as part of the acting curriculum. He long maintained that actors for the cinema had to be trained differently than those for the stage.

Kuleshov's first film, *The Project of Engineer Prite*, was made in 1917 but not released until the following year. In theme the film was not unusual, a romantic adventure against an industrial background, but was significant in its painstaking structure.

During the Civil War Kuleshov made a number of short *agitki* and then formed his own workshop as part of the newly established state film school in Moscow. His older colleagues looked upon him as a radical and he was thus not strictly a part of the regular teaching faculty. It was at this time that Kuleshov began working out his theoretical principles about directing based on the relationships between an actor's movements, scene composition, and film editing. Like so many others at that time, Kuleshov was unable to do filming because of the shortage of film stock, but did stage film plays and short skits which he called *etudes*.

In 1920 Kuleshov, along with his students, made an *agitka* about the 1920 Russo-Polish War. *On the Red Front* was an experimental film in which Kuleshov blended in documentary sequences with enacted sequences. Lenin is reported as having liked the film, but some officials disliked it because of its atypical pattern of editing. Kuleshov was to wait another four years before Soviet officials were to give him another chance.

The Extraordinary Adventures of Mr. West in the Land of the Bolsheviks was an amusing satire on Western misconceptions about communism and the Soviet state as seen through the eyes of an American senator, Mr. West. Although the acting style was exaggerated at times, the overall result was a popular, wild parody on American yellow journalism and the mistaken notions it publicized. The film was all the more remarkable because it was made in a studio that had no heat, no props, and no technicians. Everything was done or made by Kuleshov's students.

Kuleshov's next film, *The Death Ray*, proved commercially successful but did not please all the critics. The film came out only a short time after Eisenstein's *Strike* and bore some structural resemblance to the latter's mass scenes. Pudovkin, who wrote the script, was later to turn to Kuleshov for help on the mass scenes in *Mother*. *The Death Ray*, involving foreign intrigue and conspiracy to steal the invention of a Soviet engineer, was criticized because the structure of the plot was presented in an episodic, almost confusing manner. Kuleshov's editing technique stood in the way of presenting the whole story in an easily comprehensible manner. Kuleshov's next film was to be his best.

Dura Lex (or *By the Law*), like practically all Kuleshov films, was made on one of the lowest budgets in Soviet cinema. The film, based on a novel by Jack London, was unusual for its time because it had no hero, no parallel action, very few sets, and only three actors. The film, however, became an international success for the breadth and depth of its emotional range. The acting typified Kuleshov's efforts at having actors work in a carefully orchestrated ensemble that resulted in well sustained harmony. Despite the film's success, Kuleshov's career declined from this point on.

The Journalist Girl (or *Your Acquaintance*), *The Gay Canary*, and *Two-Buldi-Two*, all received criticism on political grounds and the experimental style. His imitation of American techniques drew increasing negative attention. *Horizon*, his first sound film, was a critical failure because the acting style was too melodramatic coupled with a poor sound technique. Yet Soviet officials were willing to give him another chance, although again a limited budget.

The Great Consoler, based on the life and stories by and about O. Henry during the time of his imprisonment for embezzlement. While regarded as impressive by those who were able to see it, the film was complex in its structure and told at different levels. Although officials disliked its abstract elements, it was a production masterpiece. Filmed in less than fifty days, *The Great Consoler* never exceeded its budget or allocation of film. Sets were sparse and had no major crowd scenes. Each scene was carefully staged and rehearsed prior to filming so that time, effort and film were not wasted. Unfortunately the timing for the film was all wrong. The abstract, intellectual elements did not meet the need for "socialist realism." Stalin is known to have berated Kuleshov after a preview of the film and it was quickly withdrawn. Kuleshov was not to make another film for several years afterwards. How low his prestige had sunk was seen in 1935 when he and another outcast, Eisenstein, received the low ranking title of Honored Art Worker.

Until his death Kuleshov remained active in teaching and writing. In 1944, largely at Eisenstein's suggestion, Kuleshov was appointed as director of Moscow's State Institute of Cinematography. His contributions to the development of Soviet cinema were belatedly recognized in 1967 when he received the Order of Lenin. After his death a memorial scholarship in his name was established at the Moscow film school. Although his last films were not outstanding Kuleshov left behind two books that are still admired today by film students, *The Art of Cinema* (1929) and *Fundamentals of Film Direction* (1941).

Films: *The Project of Engineer Prite* (1918), *On the Red Front* (1920), *The Extraordinary Adventures of Mr. West in the Land of the Bolsheviks* (1924), *The Death Ray* (1925), *Dura Lex* (1926), *Locomotive No. 1000b* (1926), *The Journalist Girl* (1927), *The Gay Canary* (1929), *Two-Buldi-Two* (1929), *Horizon* (1932), *The Great Consoler* (1933), *The Siberians* (1940), *Happening On the Volcano* (1943), *Timur's Oath* (1943), *We Are From the Urals* (1944).

[See also: Hill, S.P. "Prophet Without Honor?" *Film Culture*, 1967 (Spring, no. 44, p. 1.

Levaco, Ronald. "Kuleshov," *Sight and Sound*, 1971 (Spring), vol. 40, no. 2, p. 86.

——————, trans. and ed. *Kuleshov On Film*. Berkeley and Los Angeles: University of California Press, 1974.

"Selections From Lev Kuleshov's 'Art of the Cinema,' " *Screen*, 1971/72 (Winter), vol. 12, no. 4, p. 103.]

KULIDZHANOV, Lev. b. 1924.
Graduated the State Institute of Cinematography in 1954 as a student of Sergei Gerasimov. Kulidzhanov early established a reputation for colorful realism. Soviet critics have much admired his *When The Trees Grew Tall*, a romantic, yet probing look at contemporary society.

Films: *Ladies* (1954, with Oganissian), *It Started Like This* (1956, with Yakov Segel), *The House I Live In* (1957, with Segel), *The Lost Photograph* (1959), *Our Father's House* (1959), *When The Trees Grew Tall* (1961), *The Blue Notebook* (1963), *Crime and Punishment* (1970).

MEDVEDKIN, Alexander Ivanovich. b. 1900. Director and scenarist.
Began working in films in 1927 as a scriptwriter for Gosvoyenkino Studio and later assisted Okhlopkov on *The Way of Enthusiasts*, which seems to have set Medvedkin on his course to comedy and satire.

In 1932-34 Medvedkin was made head of a travelling film train which made and exhibited films in rural areas. His first two short comedies were preludes for his later eccentric, near outrageous satires. *Happiness* is his best film, a bizarre satire on Soviet farm life and search for individuality. In view of the struggle for agricultural collectivization in the mid-1930s it is a wonder the film was allowed to be made. *Happiness* continues to enjoy revivals among film societies and is an example of Soviet film humor at its best.

During World War II Medvedkin served as a combat cameraman and after the war concentrated on documentary filming.

Films: *Extraordinary Adventures of an Artillery Observer* (1932), *Tale of a Big Spoon* (1932), *Happiness* (1935), *Marvellous Girl* (1937), *Liberated Earth* (1946).

[See also: Roud, Richard. "SLON: Marker and Medvedkin," *Sight and Sound*, 1973 (Spring), vol. 42, no. 2, p. 82.]

METALNIKOV, Budimir. b. 1925. Scenarist and director.
After war service with the Soviet Army Metalnikov studied at the State Institute of Cinematography. His early work in films was primarily as a scenarist before he turned to direction.

Films: *House and Master* (1967), *The Silence of Doctor Ivens* (1973).

MIKHALKOV-KONCHALOVSKI, Andrei. b. 1937. Scenarist and director.

The son of Sergei Mikhalkov, a poet, and grandson of Pyotr Konchalovski, an artist, he is often called simply Konchalovski. He first studied piano before deciding on a career in film-making. While a student at the State Institute of Cinematography, from which he graduated in 1961, he became associated with Andrei Tarkovski. Both are now among the leading, and controversial, directors of contemporary Soviet films.

The film that first brought him to critical attention was *The First Teacher*, which was a cool, probing reappraisal of the early years of Soviet power. His next film, *The Story of Asya Kliachina, Who Loved But Did Not Marry*, caused a good deal of controversy because of its depiction of Soviet youth and morals. The film was held up for three years before it was released in an edited version. Konchalovski's experience pointed up once more that contemporary Soviet themes were sensitive political topics for film-makers.

As a scriptwriter Konchalovski has been active in television and films. He teamed up with his friend Tarkovski on the script for *Andrei Rublev*, another controversial film that was criticized mostly on historical grounds. His next two films, *A Nest of Gentlefolk* and *Uncle Vanya*, were well received and enjoyed extensive foreign exhibition. He also received much acclaim for writing the script of Tolomush Okeyev's very successful *The Ferocious One*.

Films: *The Boy and the Pigeon* (1958), *The Skating Rink and the Violin* (1959, with Andrei Tarkovski), *The First Teacher* (1965), *The Story of Asya Kliachina, Who Loved But Did Not Marry* (1966 [1969]), *A Nest of Gentlefolk* (1969), *Uncle Vanya* (1971), *Romance of Lovers* (1974).

[See also: "A Russian Six," *Films and Filming*, 1967 (September), vol. 13, no. 12, p. 27.]

MITTA, Alexander. b. 1933.

After studying at the Institute of Construction Engineering, Mitta worked for the satirical magazine *Krokodil* as a political cartoonist. He then studied at the State Institute of Cinematography, graduating in 1961. His films have been well received and enjoy popularity with audiences. He is known for a light, satirical style.

Films: *My Friend Kolka* (1963, with Alexei Saltykov), *Without Fear and Reproach* (1964), *The Bell Rings, Open the Door* (1966), *Period, Period, Comma* (1973), *Moscow — My Love* (1974, with Kenji Ishida).

MOSKALENKO, Nikolai. 1926-74. Actor and director.

First went into theatrical work in 1943 as a student as Moscow's State Theatrical Institute. After graduation Moskalenko joined the Minsk Drama Theater and later returned to Moscow where he joined the Mossoviet Theater. Until 1957 Moskalenko acted on stage and in films before he decided to become a film director. At Ivan Pyriev's urging Moskalenko joined Mosfilm Studios as an assistant director rather than enrolling at the State Institute of Cinematography. After working under various directors he made his debut as an independent film-maker in 1969. Moskalenko died suddenly while in the midst of production of *Opening of The Abyss*, which was temporarily suspended.

Films (as director): *Little Crane* (1969), *The Newlyweds* (1971).

NARLIEV, Khodzhakuli. b. 1937. Turkmenian.

Films: *The Daughter-in-Law* (1971).

NAUMOV, Vladimir. b. 1927. Russian.

Graduated the State Institute of Cinematography in 1951 and has collaborated exclusively with Alexander Alov. For films see ALOV.

OKEYEV, Tolomush. b. 1935. Turkmenian.

Graduate of the Leningrad Institute of Cinema Engineering. Okeyev has established a reputation as a bright and noteworthy film-maker at the Kirghizfilm Studios. He received a good deal of attention for his controversial *Bow to the Fire*, which had to be revised because of its almost unvarnished portrayal of the social consequences of the agricultural collectivization campaign of the 1930s. *The Ferocious One*, an allegory on the struggle between good and evil, gave a warm portrayal of rural life.

Films: *These Are Horses* (1965), *Bakai's Pasture* (1966), *The Sky of Our Childhood* (1967), *Bow to the Fire* (1970 [1973]), *The Ferocious One* (1974).

OKHLOPKOV, Nikolai. 1900-67. Russian. Actor and director.
Okhlopkov first studied acting under Vsevolod Meyerhold before going into film work. He joined the Odessa Studio in 1927 when he directed his first film *Mitya* in which he also acted. This satire about Soviet rural life proved popular and Okhlopkov proved himself a skillful director of comedy.

His second film was a burlesque comedy about the capitalistic West, *The Sold Appetite*. The film was released at a time when the direction of Soviet cinema was undergoing a basic change and away from satire. Moreover, Okhlopkov began his third film at a time when Stalin was energetically pushing collectivization.

The Way of Enthusiasts was a satire about the mutual suspicions between Soviet urban workers and peasants. Although the film was reportedly quite humorous, Party critics saw little that was amusing at a time when the peasants were bitterly resisting collectivization. Okhlopkov was severely criticized and the film was banned. This was Okhlopkov's last film as a director although he remained in the cinema as an actor. His decision not to make any more films was later regretted by Soviet film historians who felt his decision was a blow to the future development of Soviet film comedy.

Films (as director): *Mitya* (1927), *The Sold Appetite* (1928), *The Way of Enthusiasts* (1930, banned).

OZEP, Fedor. 1895-1949.
While a student at Moscow University in 1916 Ozep wrote the script for Yakov Protazanov's *The Queen of Spades*, which critics later thought was a very successful film adaptation of Pushkin's story. Ozep thereafter remained active in the film industry and remained in Russia for several years after the 1917 October Revolution.

He served as Alexander Sanin's assistant director on *Polikushka* (1919), which some critics feel is the first true theatrical feature film that was produced under the Soviets. Ozep next received prominence as the co-director of the highly popular *Miss Mend*.

His first independent film, *Earth in Chains*, was viewed as an auspicious beginning, but it proved to be Ozep's last, true Soviet film. He was next assigned to work on the German-Soviet co-production of *The Living Corpse*, which was begun under the more stringent political climate following Stalin's rise to dominance within the Party. After finishing the Soviet sequence, Ozep went with the cast and crew to Germany. Trained in a more traditional style of film drama, Ozep appears not to have been in the mainstream of Soviet cinema and might well have fallen under criticism as his other pre-1917 colleagues. Ozep chose not to return to the USSR and made films in Europe and Hollywood, including a wartime American version of *The Girl From Leningrad*.

Films: *Miss Mend* (1926, with Boris Barnet), *Earth in Chains* (1928), *The Living Corpse* (1928).

OZEROV, Yuri. b. 1921. Russian.

Ozerov has been highly acclaimed in the Soviet and foreign press for his epic war film *Liberation* which dealt with the last days of World War II. The film commemorated the 25th anniversary of the Soviet victory over Nazi Germany. The film was several years in the making and included an international cast of players. Marshal Zhukov served as Ozerov's consultant on the film.

Films: *Liberation* (1970).

[See also: "The Coming of the Russians," *Action*, 1971 (March/April), vol. 6, no. 2, p. 4.

"The Russians Are Here," *Making Films*, 1971 (June), vol. 5, no. 3, p. 10.]

PARADZHANOV, Sergei. b. 1924. Georgian.

First studied at the Tiflis Conservatory before deciding on a career in film-making. In 1951 he graduated Moscow's State Institute of Cinematography, where he had been a student of Igor Savchenko and Lev Kuleshov.

Paradzhanov began his directing career at the Kiev Studios, where he became known as a director with a deep interest in films dealing with rural legends and folk traditions. His *Shadows of Our Forgotten*

Ancestors was highly acclaimed abroad for its lyricism and colorful style. In 1968 Paradzhanov joined the Armenfilm Studios.

Films: *Andriesh* (1954, with Bazelian), *The First Lad* (1958), *Ukrainian Rhapsody* (1961), *Shadows of Our Forgotten Ancestors* (1964), *Sayat Novar* (1969).

[See also: Paradzhanov, Sergei. "Shadows of Our Forgotten Ancestors," *Film Comment*, 1968 (Fall), vol. 5, no. 1, p. 39.]

PERESTIANI, Ivan Nikolaevich. 1870-1959. Russian. Actor and director.

A pioneer of Soviet Georgian cinema. Perestiani began working in films as a scriptwriter and wrote the scenario for Yevgeni Bauer's *The Revolutionary* (1917). He then made three films as an independent director prior to the October Revolution.

During the Civil War he made a short propaganda drama, *Father and Son*, which was popular for a number of years. At the time of the Russo-Polish War of 1920 Perestiani made the three-reel agit-prop film *In the Days of Struggle*, which Soviet historians still admire.

In 1921 Perestiani accepted an appointment to head the Cinema Section of the Georgian Commissariat of Education. Despite worn out equipment, little money, and almost no studio facilities, Perestiani energetically proceeded to make films about Georgian life and history. He often wrote his own film scripts because of the lack of qualified scenarists. In his first year in Georgia Perestiani made the first Georgian feature film, *Arsen Georgiashvili*, under adverse physical conditions. The film proved popular because of its Civil War theme and featured Mikhail Chiaureli, who later became a director and made a remake of the film.

Georgian film officials next requested Perestiani to make a feature film based on socially important national literature. *Fortress of Suram* was a story of unrequited love which proved very successful in its time and even found bookings in Germany, France, Turkey, and Iran. Yet this film's success was nothing compared to Perestiani's next work and one for which he is best remembered.

Little Red Devils was an unusual Soviet film for it featured a young Negro, Kader Ben-Salim in the role of Jackson. The story was about three young Komsomols during the Civil War who fight against the bandit leader Makhno. A skillful blend of humor, mystery, and adventure made *Little Red Devils* an all-time popular hit with Soviet audiences. The Soviet press praised Perestiani for the way in which he caught the spirit of the Civil War as reflected in the actions of the three young circus artists whom Perestiani employed in the feature roles. This Soviet version of a cowboy adventure was the first Soviet film to be reviewed in the New York *Times* which considered it a success by any standard. The film was so popular and long run that it was refurbished with a limited sound track in 1943. The triumph of the film was all the more noteworthy because Perestiani improvised the script as he went along, although he would fall down badly when he tried this again a few years later.

Perestiani's next two films, *Three Lives* and *The Case of the Murder of Tariel Mklavadze,* enjoyed good critical notices but not the same degree of popularity as *Little Red Devils.* Both films centered on the complex social relationships that resulted from class consciousness with the establishment of capitalism in Georgia in the 19th century. Perestiani now exhibited a growing sophistication in his handling of complex story lines and control over parallel action, which had been one of the weaknesses of *Fortress of Suram. Three Lives* brought to prominence the young actress Nato Vachnadze and Mikhail Gelovani, who in a few years would gain so much attention for his frequent portrayals of Stalin.

Perestiani then decided to try to repeat his tremendous success of *Little Red Devils* with three sequels: *Savur's Grave, Illan-Dilli,* and *The Crime of Princess Shirvanskaya.* He made all three in the same manner as the original, without formal scripts. All three proved to be critical flops because they lacked the freshness of the original. Perestiani's work on these sequels seemed tired and strained, and what was worse offered nothing new.

For his last three films Perestiani concentrated on Georgian life and revolutionary backgrounds. His last films were well received and he showed a fine ability for handling highly emotional moods, especially in *Zamallu.* Later Perestiani retired from directing, but remained active as an actor.

Films: *Eva* (1917), *Goat, Kid, Ass* (1917), *Love, Hate, Death* (1917), *Father and Son* (1919), *In the Days of Struggle* (1920), *Arsen Georgiashvili* (1921), *Fortress of Suram* (1923), *Little Red Devils*

(1923), *The Case of the Murder of Tariel Mklavadze* (1925), *Three Lives* (1925), *The Crime of Princess Shirvanskaya* (1926), *Illan-Dilli* (1926), *Savur's Grave* (1926), *Zamallu* (1930), *Anush* (1931), *Two Friends* (1937).

PETROV, Vladimir. 1896-1965. Russian.

After having studied theater in St. Petersburg and London, Petrov joined the film workshop of Vyacheslav Viskovski. In 1925 Petrov began his film career as an assistant director to Kozintsev and Trauberg on *The Overcoat.* As an independent film-maker Petrov initially specialized in children's films at which he proved successful. With *Fritz Bauer* and *The Fugitive* Petrov began moving into adult themes and showed a strong liking for the German expressionistic style, but this may have been determined largely by the stories which were set in the Germany of the 1920s.

Although Petrov was accorded the title of Honored Artist of the Republic in 1935 he was not considered an exciting director. Pudovkin thought *The Thunderstorm* was theatrical and photographically without distinction. His early training in the theater and study under the traditionalist Viskovski may have been very strong influences upon his style.

Petrov's first big film was the two-part *Peter the Great,* which was a good, patriotic film that did little to advance film art. The film was made with a lavish budget but failed to excite critics. Measured against some of the other great films of the 1930s *Peter the Great* seems dated.

In the midst of World War II Petrov was again assigned a big, historical film, *Kutuzov in 1812,* sometimes called merely *Kutuzov.* The film explained how Kutuzov's strategic withdrawal toward Moscow ultimately defeated Napoleon and was something of a justification for the large scale Soviet retreats in 1941. The workmanlike production proved popular, but again Petrov failed to do anything that was exciting.

After the war Petrov made his third big film, the lavish *Battle of Stalingrad,* which became highly controversial and thereby assured that Petrov would not be forgotten as a film-maker. Coming out at an intense period of the Cold War, the film engendered, and still does, much discussion about the god-like portrayal of Stalin. The victory at this crucial stage of the Soviet-German war is attributed almost wholly to Stalin. Petrov used sharp contrasts in depicting the calm, confident mood at Stalin's Stavka with the near frenzy at Hitler's headquarters.

Critics have sometimes been fond of swiping at Petrov for the rigid, almost liturgical tone and rhythm of the dialog in the scenes with Stalin. Yet the film even today is worthy of a second look. From all the post-Stalin Soviet military memoirs it would seem that Petrov caught the true spirit of the atmosphere that surrounded Stalin at the time. To be sure the work of the Soviet generals takes second place in the film to Stalin, but the mood was essentially correct. Petrov's later films went by largely unnoticed.

Films: *Golden Honey* (1928, with N. Beresnev), *The Address of Lenin* (1929), *Fritz Bauer* (1930), *The Dam* (1932), *The Fugitive* (1933), *The Thunderstorm* (1934), *Peter the Great* (1937, 1939), *Kutuzov in 1812* (1943), *Jubilee* (1944), *Guilty Without Guilt* (1945), *Battle of Stalingrad* (1949), *Revizor* (1953), *300 Years Ago* (1956), *The Duel* (1957).

PROTAZANOV, Yakov Alexandrovich. 1881-1945. Russian.

Energetic and widely respected for his professional attainments as a film-maker prior to the October Revolution, Protazanov has increasingly been admired by Soviet writers. Protazanov entered films as an actor in 1905 and four years later made his debut as a director. In the years prior to 1917 he directed the Golden series of films for Thiemann and Reinhardt. His early work showed a steady, progressive development of sophistication in dramatic style. When film was hardly more than an entertaining novelty he strove constantly to bring it up to the same level as other art forms. During his work in the Soviet cinema Protazanov stood between the innovators and traditionalists, and was more of an eclectic in matters of style. He was, however, revolutionary in content and his Soviet films were strongly satirical. His films were almost always popular with audiences, but not always pleasing to or understood by Party critics while he was alive.

When *Father Sergius*, a frank denunciation of the church, was released in 1918 it was admired not only for its drama but for its social importance as well. Although the film was made in 1917 it was not until after the October Revolution that the controversial film could be exhibited. Over the years *Father Sergius* has been acknowledged as representing a sharp break in content as opposed to the works of Protazanov's contemporaries.

After the October Revolution Protazanov first went to Odessa and then emigrated to Paris in 1920. For the next two years he made films in France and Germany working largely with other Russian emigres. Then, in 1922, Protazanov decided to return to Russia, where he joined the Mezhrabpom-Rus Studio in Moscow.

Protazanov's first Soviet film, *Aelita*, enjoyed great success abroad and was one of the most talked about films until *Battleship Potemkin*. While not revolutionary in style, *Aelita*, as a science-fiction fantasy, did much to keep social satire alive on Soviet screens as it was a parody on the contemporary world.

For a few years after returning to the USSR Protazanov worked on a projected remake of *War and Peace*, which he was never able to realize. His 1915 film had enjoyed popularity for a period of time. Although he was not to realize his hope for a remake of *War and Peace*, Protazanov was to enjoy success and popularity.

His most important films were those of the 1920s, perhaps because of their politically controversial themes. Soviet writers today feel that Protazanov's films of the NEP period were often misunderstood by critics. The acting in a Protazanov film was always good, though individual performances varied. Unlike Kuleshov who strove to create a harmonic, unified acting ensemble, Protazanov tended to focus on individual performances, but his films were almost always profitable.

Like other directors of the pre-1917 generation Protazanov suffered from official Party criticism as the NEP period ended in 1928. In *The Forty-First* Protazanov probed deeply into the emotions of a tragic love affair between a Red girl guerilla commander and a White Guards officer who was her captive. In the end, true to her duty, she kills him to prevent his rescue. Critics, however, could not accept a White officer in the lyrical and moving way that Protazanov presented him. The story has since become a classic about the Russian Civil War. Years later official critics could accept the 1956 remake with more equanimity, but Protazanov's film is considered the better of the two.

With *The White Eagle*, which featured Anna Sten in a role specially written for her, Protazanov again received rough handling for the compassionate way he revealed the inner torment of a tsarist governor who is responsible for shooting workers and their children during a protest demonstration. Again critics could not endure sympathy being shown for a former class enemy. Today Soviet film historians have acknowledged *The White Eagle* as one of the outstanding films of its time.

Protazanov came under attack once more for *The Man From the Restaurant,* in which the last years of tsarist Russia serve as a backdrop to this story. Skorokhodov, the lowly waiter, undergoes a strengthening of character as a result of suffering humiliation at the hands of the upper classes. Rather than looking at the content of the film, critics chose to focus on surface aspects of the story which they felt appealed to bourgeois tastes.

Despite his troubles with narrow, myopic critics, Protazanov continued to make socially satirical films. Even Pudovkin admired the way Protazanov subtly wove in propaganda into a melodrama as in *His Call. The Holiday of St. Jorgen* was the best and most admired of Protazanov's later films. This story was an anti-religious and anti-Western satire on the commercialism of religion and marked a highpoint of humor and satire on Soviet screens.

Despite lingering ill health during the war Protazanov kept on working. He was collaborating with Boris Barnet on a projected film adaptation of N.A. Ostrovski's *Wolves and Sheep* when he died.

Films: *The Fountains of Bakhisarai* (1909), *The Prisoner's Song* (1911), *Anfisa* (1912), *Departure of a Grand Old Man* (1913), *How Fine, How Fresh the Roses Were* (1913), *The Shattered Vase* (1913), *Nikolai Stavrogin* (1915), *Plebeian* (1915), *Petersburg Slums* (1915, with Vladimir Gardin), *War and Peace* (1915, with Vladimir Gardin), *The Queen of Spades* (1916), *Sin* (1916, with Georgi Azagarov), *Woman With A Dagger* (1916), *Andrei Kozhukhov* (1917), *Blood Need Not Be Spilled* (1917), *Cursed Millions* (1917), *The Public Prosecutor* (1917), *Satan Triumphant* (1917), *Father Sergius* (1918), *Secret of the Queen* (1919), *Aelita* (1924), *His Call* (1925), *Tailor From Torzhok* (1925), *A Lawsuit for Three Million* (1926), *Don Diego and Pelagea* (1928), *The Forty-First* (1928), *The White Eagle* (1928), *The Man From the Restaurant* (1929), *Ranks and People: A Chekhov Almanac* (1929), *The Holiday of St. Jorgen* (1930), *Tommy* (1931), *Marionettes* (1934), *The Dowerless* (1936), *Pupils of the Seventh Grade* (1938), *Salavat Yulaev* (1941), *Nasreddin in Bokhara* (1943).

[See also: *Yakov Protazanov.* Moscow: Iskusstvo, 1957.]

PTUSHKO, Alexander. b. 1900. Ukrainian.

A leading director of animated films. Ptushko followed the work of Wladyslaw Starewicz in using three-dimensional figures and wax dolls, a true Russian form of animated film. His first big film was *The New Gulliver* which took three years to make and employed live actors along with wax dolls. Parts of the film were shown at the Venice Film Exhibition of 1934 and were much admired. Largely for his work on this film he received the title Honored Artist of the Republic in 1935.

In 1945 Ptushko was put in charge of Soyuzmultfilm Studio and worked on *The Stone Flower,* which was filmed partly in Prague and made use of the newly acquired Agfacolor process. Ptushko's postwar films are adaptations of Russian folk stories.

Films: *Occurrence in the Stadium* (1928), *Master of Existence* (1932), *The New Gulliver* (1935), *The Little Gold Key* (1939), *The Stone Flower* (1946), *Sadko* (1951), *Ilya Muromets* (1956), *The Tale of Tsar Sultan* (1967).

[See also: Ptushko, A. "Stepping Out of the Soviet," *Films and Filming,* 1960 (January), vol. 6, no. 4, p. 29.]

PUDOVKIN, Vsevolod Illarionovich. 1893-1953. Russian. Actor, director, and film theoretician.

As one of the giants of Soviet, if not world, cinema Pudovkin continues to have strong interest for film scholars. His theoretical writings on techniques of film direction and editing are still considered important. In his works he more closely approached Kuleshov and Dovzhenko rather than Eisenstein. As the French film historian Leon Moussinac wrote "Pudovkin's films resemble a song, Eisenstein's a shout." Pudovkin appealed to emotions, Eisenstein to intellect.

Pudovkin grew up in Moscow and as a student at the gymnasium studied painting and music, but his interests shifted to physics and chemistry when he entered the university. At the outbreak of World War I he was drafted into the Army and later became a prisoner of war for three years. After returning to Moscow in 1918 Pudovkin worked in the chemical laboratory of a military plant. He soon decided to embark upon a career in films and enrolled in the state film school at the then old age of 27. He studied and worked first under Vladimir Gardin.

While a member of Gardin's workshop Pudovkin was assistant director and actor on *Sickle and Hammer,* which was considered a transitional film between the simple *agitka* and the true theatrical film.

Vsevolod Pudovkin (The Museum of Modern Art/Film Stills Archive)

Pudovkin played the role of the heroic Andrei Krasnov and was to be an actor in many films throughout his life. His screen credits as a player included *The Extraordinary Adventures of Mr. West in the Land of the Bolsheviks, The Death Ray, The Living Corpse, New Babylon,* and *Ivan the Terrible.* Although Gardin was one of the more progressive of the older generation of film-makers, Pudovkin opted to join Lev Kuleshov's workshop in 1922 after doing some work on the scenario for *The Locksmith and the Chancellor.*

Pudovkin always acknowledged Kuleshov as his mentor and intellectual benefactor. It was under Kuleshov's tutelage that Pudovkin formulated his own ideas about the art of editing for emotional content. Everything on film, according to Pudovkin, had to say something about a character's personality and emotions — movement, background, and expression. The wide use Pudovkin made of close-up and brief shots, which stemmed from Kuleshov's work, helped to heighten emotional impact in his three great films, *Mother, The End of St. Petersburg,* and *Descendant of Genghis Khan.*

In 1925 Pudovkin left Kuleshov although the two men were to remain close friends throughout the years. Pudovkin's background in science made him a natural choice for *Mechanics of the Brain,* a study of Pavlov's experiments in the physiological functioning of living organisms. The film was scientifically and logically structured, and it was done so well that it set the pace for other directors of popular science films. During pauses in production Pudovkin made a short comedy, *Chess Fever,* which was set against the 1925 International Chess Tournament. *Chess Fever* was released first and was noteworthy because of the clever editing by which the actual tournament players came off as comics although they never knew they were being photographed for a film.

After completing *Mechanics of the Brain* Pudovkin began work on the first of his three great revolutionary films, *Mother,* based on Maxim Gorki's novel. He collaborated on the scenario with Natan Zarkhi, with whom he worked closely for many years and who had also had his start in films under Gardin. The project was threatened early when Soviet bank officials refused the relatively unknown director the loan of 85,000 rubles until after Pudovkin showed them a few filmed scenes. The officials liked what they saw and Pudovkin was given the money to proceed. When the film came out it proved to be a great triumph and confirmed Pudovkin's ideas about montage. Unlike

Eisenstein, he chose an individual to characterize and represent the revolutionary masses. In the same year that *Mother* was released Pudovkin had two monographs published, *The Film Scenario* and *The Film Director and Film Material.*

Pudovkin's next great film, *The End of St. Petersburg,* was made to commemorate the tenth anniversary of the October Revolution and came out a little before Eisenstein's *October.* Although it was popular enough, critics began to dislike it for its symbolic, abstract composition and charging Pudovkin with formalism, though most of their abuse was heaped on Eisenstein's *October.* A grander film than *Mother, The End of St. Petersburg* still focused on one individual, Paren, as representative of the Russian masses from 1912 through 1917. The film was another product of the collaboration of Pudovkin with the scenarist Zarkhi. Briefly the two men parted company when Pudovkin made *Descendant of Genghis Khan,* the last of three great epic revolutionary films. The work was more naturalistic than its two predecessors and attracted audiences for its elements of the exotic Orient. Pudovkin again had a great triumph with the film. Moods and emotions were expressed so well that a whole sequence was made without the use of titles in this last silent film by Pudovkin. *Descendant of Genghis Khan* represented a zenith in the development of Soviet silent film art, and Pudovkin never again attained the same level of success.

After playing the part of Fedor Protasov in Ozep's *The Living Corpse* Pudovkin returned to the USSR from Germany and enthusiastically began work on his next project, *Life Is Beautiful.* Work began on this Civil War and love story in 1929, but was not finished until 1932 and came out briefly under the title *A Simple Case.* Almost from the start Pudovkin encountered difficulties. The story line underwent changes which Pudovkin made to please Party critics as he was joining the Communist Party at the time. The sound equipment was poor and the film thus suffered from a technical deficiency. To compound these problems Pudovkin experimented with so-called "time loops" in the story narrative and left himself open to criticism for a confusing structure. *A Simple Case* became Pudovkin's first failure and was quickly followed by a second.

The Deserter proved so bad that it was removed from exhibition after only eight days. The story dealt with the revolutionary movement in Germany. After location shooting in Hamburg Pudovkin had to revise much of the footage because of Hitler's rise to power. *The*

Deserter, dealing with current events, had become outdated because of the quickly changing political scene in Germany. To add to this Pudovkin once more was charged with formalism.

Despite two poor films Pudovkin remained in such good graces that he received the Order of Lenin in January 1935. The same year however brought a great shock to Pudovkin six months later. Pudovkin, a motor enthusiast, suffered an auto accident which resulted in Natan Zarkhi's death. The incident deeply depressed Pudovkin and work on his new film, *Victory,* lagged badly. The film and Pudovkin were both saved when Mikhail Doller stepped in as co-director. With the film's release Pudovkin recovered his old drive and enthusiasm, and in short order completed three more films.

Minin and Pozharski and *Suvorov* were big, lavish historical films that are admired even today. The first was anti-Polish in theme and came out just as Stalin signed his pact with Hitler that sealed Poland's fate, while *Suvorov* commemorated the great military deeds of one of the most famous tsarist Russian military leaders. Both films reflected Pudovkin's developing ability to control grand, sweeping films and also showed that his days of exciting innovation were over. His last pre-war film was *Twenty Years of Cinema,* a documentary that commemorated the twentieth anniversary of the Soviet film industry which he made with Esther Shub.

After the outbreak of war with Germany Pudovkin served as a member of the editorial board of the *Fighting Film Albums* series in 1941-42, during which time he made one of the series' featurettes *Feast at Zhirmunka.* His first feature wartime film, *Murderers Are On Their Way,* was never released. The film was based on a pre-war anti-Nazi film and its portrayal of a now much hated enemy was so tame that Pudovkin decided to shelve it. He enjoyed a new triumph with *In the Name of the Fatherland* which was a stirring film about the Soviet partisan movement. Pudovkin then selected a theme which proved troublesome.

Admiral Nakhimov was begun in 1945 and dealt with the diplomatic aspects of the Russo-Turkish conflicts of the 19th century and the Crimean War. Had the film been released sooner it might have fared well. As it was the first version was released in 1946 when Soviet foreign policy was stiffening towards the West. Pudovkin received a chilling reception at the hands of critics who accused him of inaccurate historical interpretation and worse, "cosmopolitanism." This new heresy was worse than "formalism" as it meant that Pudovkin had not given sufficient attention to his Russian cultural heritage. Pudovkin was able to revise the film accordingly. The second variant came out in 1947 and had more battle scenes and ended on an anti-Western note as the Russian frigates dissolve into modern day Soviet destroyers. The new version earned Pudovkin the Stalin Prize which meant he was in good political standing.

Pudovkin's last two films came out during the most intense period of the Cold War and last years of Stalin's life. *Zhukovski* was one of several, pro-Russian biographical films and paid tribute to the Russian pioneer of aeronautics. *The Return of Vasili Bortnikov* held promise of a new beginning. The film touched on the problem of postwar social readjustment of returning war veterans. Unfortunately the film had an almost formula-like plot. Bortnikov suddenly returns after having been reported killed and finds his wife married to another. Personal emotions are tamed down thanks to the wisdom of a Party official who in the end helps to put things right again. There was probably little that Pudovkin could have done with this film given the very tight censorship restrictions at the time.

When Pudovkin died in July 1953 the Soviet cinema lost one of its true virtuosos. His theoretical writings and films of the 1920s continue to be admired by film-makers and scholars.

Films: *Hunger, Hunger, Hunger* (1921, with Vladimir Gardin), *Chess Fever* (1925), *Mechanics of the Brain* (1926, semi-documentary), *Mother* (1926), *The End of St. Petersburg* (1927, with Mikhail Doller), *Descendant of Genghis Khan* (1928), *A Simple Case* (1932, with Doller), *The Deserter* (1933), *Victory* (1938, with Doller), *Minin and Pozharski* (1939, with Doller), *Suvorov* (1940, with Doller), *Twenty Years of Cinema* (1940, documentary, with Esther Shub), *Feast at Zhirmunka* (1941), *Murderers Are On Their Way* (1942, shelved), *In the Name of the Fatherland* (1943), *Admiral Nakhimov* (1946 [1947]), *Zhukovski* (1950), *The Return of Vasili Bortnikov* (1952).

[See also: Iezutov, N. *Pudovkin*. Moscow: Iskusstvo, 1937.

Pudovkin, Vsevolod. *Film Acting: A Course of Lectures Delivered at the State Institute of Cinematography, Moscow*. London: George Newnes, 1935.

—————. *Film Techniques and Film Acting*. New York: Lear, 1954.

_____. *Sobranie sochineni* [Collected Works]. 3 vols.
Moscow: Iskusstvo, 1974-.
_____. "Stanislavski's System in the Cinema," *Sight and
Sound,* 1953 (January/March), vol. 22, no. 3, p. 115.
Weinberg, H. G. "Vsevolod Pudovkin," *Films in Review,* 1953
(August/September), vol. 4, no. 7, p. 325.
Wright, B. "Homage to Pudovkin," *Sight and Sound,* 1953
(October/December), vol. 23, no. 2, p. 105.]

PYRIEV, Ivan Alexandrovich. 1901-68. Russian.
Began working as a boy by selling newspapers and then was
drafted into the Russian Army in World War I. After the Civil War
Pyriev studied directing at the dramatic arts institute in Moscow and
from there worked in *avant-garde* theater. He began his film career as
assistant director to Yuri Tarich on *Wings Of a Serf.*
Pyriev never reached the same high stature of an Eisenstein or
Dovzhenko, but enjoyed a rather long series of popular films. Naturalistic in style, Pyriev always chose themes that consistently fit within
Party policies of the time. Only once in his career did Pyriev suffer official displeasure and that only mildly.
His first film, *The Other Woman,* was a witty social satire which
came out while that genre was still being tolerated. After two political
films Pyriev gained a strong reputation for musical romantic, and innocuous, comedies. At a time when comedy was at its nadir in Soviet
cinema Pyriev was at least able to enjoy popularity.
Immediately after World War II, during which he made two
notable films, he was dismissed as editor-in-chief of *Iskusstvo kino,* the
leading journal of the Soviet film industry. The reason for his dismissal
lay in his publishing an article by Sergei Eisenstein, though he himself
had occasionally joined in the criticism of Eisenstein. The incident in
no way harmed Pyriev who continued on at Mosfilm Studios. Prior to
his death Pyriev enjoyed a good measure of critical acclaim for *The
Idiot, White Nights,* and *The Brothers Karamazov.*

Films: *The Other Woman* (1929), *Assembly Line of Death* (1933), *The
Party Card* (1936), *The Rich Bride* (1938), *Tractor Drivers* (1939), *The
Swineherd Girl and the Shepherd* (1941), *The Raikom Secretary*
(1942), *At 6 P.M. After the War* (1944, Stalin Prize), *Tale of the*

Siberian Land (1948), *Cossacks of the Kuban* (1950), *We Are For Peace* (1951, with Joris Ivens), *Test of Fidelity* (1954), *The Idiot* (1957), *A Summer to Remember* (1959), *White Nights* (1959), *Our Mutual Friend* (1961), *Light of A Distant Star* (1965), *The Brothers Karamazov* (1969).

[See also: Donskoi, Mark. "While His Heart Beat: A Tribute to Ivan Pyriev," *Film Comment*, 1968 (Fall), vol. 5, no. 1, p. 34.]

RAIZMAN, Yuli. b. 1903.

First studied literature at the University of Moscow before going into film work as an assistant director to Yakov Protazanov and then under Konstantin Eggert. After leaving Eggert through dissatisfaction he joined the little known State Military Film Studio, Gosvoyenkino, in 1927. His first film was a modest comedy, *The Circle*, which was almost unnoticed and gave no hint as to the extent of his talents. Raizman had critics paying attention with his next work.

Forced Labor (or *Katorga*) was a powerful and grim look at penal servitude and political imprisonment under the tsars. The film proved very controversial and critics disliked it because of its dark, pessimistic tone and theme. The criticism was not blunted until the Russian Society of Political Exiles came to the film's defense with its endorsement of Raizman's work. From then on the film was a critical success.

Raizman's films of the 1930s all proved popular with audiences and were well received by critics. During the popularization of Soviet aviation in the mid and late 1930s, Raizman's *Aviators* became a model for other film-makers who unfortunately imitated the plot pattern too frequently.

During World War II Raizman continued his triumphs with *Mashenka*, a lyrical and moving romance about a Red Army woman and her soldier fiance, *Moscow Sky* paid tribute to the fighter pilots that defended the Soviet capital in the early stages of the war, while *Berlin* proved an excellent feature documentary that he did jointly with Karmen.

After 1945 Raizman had mixed success, but his best efforts were *The Communist*, a tough and searing Civil War drama, while *What If It Is Love?* was considered by Soviet critics an uncompromising look at social hypocrisy in contemporary times. He has not received as much attention as his contemporaries.

Films: *The Circle* (1927), *Forced Labor* (1928), *The Earth Thirsts* (1930), *Aviators* (1935), *The Last Night* (1937), *Virgin Soil Upturned* (1939), *Mashenka* (1942), *Moscow Sky* (1944), *Towards An Armistice With Finland* (1944, documentary), *Berlin* (1945, documentary with Roman Karmen), *The Train Goes East* (1948), *Rainis* (1949), *Cavalier of the Golden Star* (1950), *The Lesson of Life* (1955), *The Communist* (1958), *What If It Is Love?* (1961), *Your Contemporary* (1967).

[See also: Raizman, Yuli. *Vchera i segodnia. Rasskaz o tvorcheskom puti narodnogo artista* [Yesterday and Today. The Story of The Creative Path of a People's Artist]. Moscow: Iskusstvo, 1969.]

ROMM, Mikhail Ilyich. 1901-71. Born in eastern Siberia of Jewish parents.

Throughout his life Romm was well liked for his charm and wit, and among his close friends was Vsevolod Pudovkin.

During the Civil War Romm served in the Red Army, 1918-21, and then attended an art school in Moscow where he specialized in sculpture. After graduating in 1925 Romm found sculpture unexciting and went into film work in 1928 as a scriptwriter. Largely because of his close observation of the introduction and use of sound during the late 1920s and early 1930s Romm easily adapted to the new medium. He never experienced difficulty with dialog as some of the first generation of film-makers, notably Pudovkin.

After assisting Alexander Macheret on *Jobs and Men* Romm went into independent directing and almost always made films that were commercially and critically successful. *Boule de Suif*, his first work, won a good deal of praise at the 1934 Venice Film Exhibition, although some critics felt Romm strained the work by interjecting Marxist ideology. Romm's next effort came directly from the cinema tsar Boris Shumyatski.

After seeing John Ford's *Lost Patrol* Shumyatski wanted a socialist equivalent and the result was Romm's triumph *The Thirteen*. The film was made largely on location in Central Asia, but Romm almost did not finish it. In the midst of filming members of the cast and crew were suddenly taken away for other projects. Then budgetary problems began to plague Romm. Yet he managed to stick it out with the devoted help from the remaining players and crew. After returning to Moscow Romm had to reshoot many of the close ups in order to intensify the feeling of heat and thirst which did not come through well enough in the original exterior shots. The film was well received and Stalin personally requested Romm to undertake a film to commemorate the twentieth anniversary of the October Revolution.

Work on *Lenin in October* started late in 1937, but Romm finished it in just three months, a miraculous achievement for any Soviet film-maker in those days. Despite the rush work, *Lenin in October* became one of Romm's best and a near classic of the Soviet cinema. The excellent reception that this film received encouraged Romm further and he went into production almost immediately on *Lenin in 1918*. Both films were done in a dignified manner and Romm's direction proved to be far more subtle in the portrayal of Stalin than that of Chiaureli in his Stalin films. Many of the obvious pro-Stalin distortions in the original versions were cut out during the refurbishing of the two films prior to their rerelease in the 1960s.

Romm, with an unbroken series of successful films behind him, began work in 1941 on his first unlucky film, *The Dream*. The story dealt with the moral decay of bourgeois society in pre-1939 Poland and might have done well if it had been made a few years earlier. As it was Romm began filming on the day that German armies crossed the Soviet frontier. When it was released *The Dream* seemed dry, tame, and rather pointless during a war. The film was a failure at the time, but Soviet film historians, in a retrospective look, feel the work was skillfully done and had an interesting plot.

In contrast to the failure of *The Dream*, Romm scored a victory with *Girl No. 217* (or *Person No. 217*). A harsh, realistic and tragic story about the fate of a Russian girl who is deported to Germany as a household servant made the film in its emotional impact equivalent to *Zoya* and *The Rainbow*.

After the war Romm was the first to come out with an anti-American Cold War film, *The Russian Question*. Though the film was skillfully executed in a technical sense, the film marked Romm's decline in Western eyes. However the film was quickly answered by a series of virulent anti-Soviet films that emanated from Hollywood.

Romm did not receive favorable international attention until the release of *Nine Days of One Year*. A second triumph, though not without controversy, came as a result of his feature documentary *Ordinary Pascism*. In this retrospective look at the rise of Hitler and the Nazis, Romm blended bestial cruelty with scenes of near childlishness that characterized Hitler's entourage. The film was a chilling lesson about recent history, but came close to verging on political propaganda at the end where Nazi Germany is compared with the political system of the Federal Republic of Germany. Romm, nevertheless, was one of the more important directors of the Soviet film industry.

Films: *Boule de Suif* (1934), *The Thirteen* (1937), *Lenin in October* (1937), *Lenin in 1918* (1939), *The Dream* (1943), *Girl No. 217* (1944), *Lenin* (1948, documentary with Vasili Belayev), *The Russian Question* (1948), *Secret Mission* (1950), *Admiral Ushakov* (1953), *Ships Storm the Bastion* (1953), *Murder on Dante Street* (1956), *Nine Days of One Year* (1961), *Ordinary Fascism* (1964), *A Night of Thought* (1966).

ROOM, Abram. b. 1894 in Vilnius, Lithuania, of Polish descent.
After studying psychiatry and neurology Room entered the Red Army and served as a doctor during the Civil War. After demobilization Room went to Moscow where he joined the Theater of the Revolution and also worked as a journalist.

Room's films of the 1920s are regarded as his best as they exhibited his strong interest in the psychology and motivation of people.

After the wild and eccentric short comedy, *The Vodka Chase*, Room in quick succession pleased audiences and critics alike with *Death Bay, Bed and Sofa*, and *Ruts*. However he received such rough treatment for *The Traitor*, mainly because of its traditional style, that even its scriptwriters disavowed it.

After the successful *The Ghost That Never Returns* Room tried his hand at sound. *Plan for Great Works* was an experimental sound documentary on the First Five-Year Plan and used documentary episodes from other films. Room's next film largely resulted in his decline.

In 1936 *A Strict Youth* caused a furor and Room was barred from making films for a few years. The story dealt with the role of the intelligentsia in modern society and neither the critics nor the Party liked the intimation that an intellectual elite might well provide leadership for the future. Room's efforts after *A Strict Youth* were workmanlike but failed to recapture his successes of the 1920s. His *Bed and Sofa* is considered his best and a classic of the silent era of Soviet cinema.

Films: *The Vodka Chase* (1924), *Death Bay* (1926), *The Traitor* (1926), *Bed and Sofa* (1927), *The Jew on the Land* (1927), *Ruts*

(1928), *The Ghost That Never Returns* (1929), *Plan for Great Works* (1930), *A Strict Youth* (1936), *Squadron No. 5* (1939), *Wind From the East* (1940), *Invasion* (1944), *In the Mountains of Yugoslavia* (1946), *Court of Honor* (1948), *School for Scandal* (1952), *Silver Dust* (1953), *The Heart Beats Again* (1956), *The Untimely Man* (1973).

ROSHAL, Grigori. b. 1899.

Began working in films in the Ukraine in 1919 and made his first independent film in 1926, *The Skotinins*, an eccentric satire. Roshal specialized mostly in film adaptations of literature and biographic films which were usually sober in manner. In the 1930s he married his co-director Vera Stroyeva. Roshal's first important film was *The Oppenheim Family*, an anti-Nazi film that is still highly regarded. He was applauded for the manner in which he caught the atmosphere of Hitler's Germany and anti-Semitism. Roshal also had a good deal of success in his next film, *The Artamanov Affair*, which might have been guided strongly by Eisenstein who supervised Mosfilm Studios while Roshal made the film.

In the post-Stalin era Roshal gained a notable success for his *The Way of Sorrows* Trilogy, a realistic family sage of the revolutionary and Civil War era.

Films: *The Skotinins* (1926), *His Excellency* (1927), *Salamander* (1928), *Two Women* (1929), *Petersburg Night* (1934, with Vera Stroyeva), *People of the Eleventh Legion* (1937), *The Oppenheim Family* (1939), *The Artamanov Affair* (1941), *Song of Abai* (1946), *Academician Ivan Pavlov* (1949), *Mussorgski* (1950), *Rimski-Korsakov* (1953), *Aleko* (1954), *The Way of Sorrows Trilogy — The Sisters* (1957), *The Eighteenth Year* (1958), *Gloomy Morning* (1959); *They Are Neighbors* (1968).

ROSTOTSKI, Stanislav. b. 1922. Russian.

During World War II Rostotski served with Soviet Army cavalry and was badly wounded. After demobilization he enrolled at the State Institute of Cinematography where he initially studied under Eisenstein. He left his studies at the Institute in 1946 to join the directors' workshop at Mosfilm Studios, and in 1950 returned to the Institute and graduated in 1952 as one of Kozintsev's students.

Rostotski used some of his own wartime experiences as a basis for *May Stars,* a film dealing with the final period of World War II. He has gained wide acclaim for his last film, a tender and tragic story about a women's anti-aircraft unit in World War II.

Films: *Land and People* (1955), *It Happened In Penkovo* (1957), *May Stars* (1959), *In the Seven Winds* (1962), *Pechorin's Notes* (1967), *Let's Live Until Monday* (1968), *And the Dawns Are Quiet Here* (1972).

RYAZANOV, Eldar Alexandrovich. b. 1927. Russian.

Studied under Grigori Kozintsev at the State Institute of Cinematography from which he graduated 1950. Joined Mosfilm Studios in 1955 and quickly established himself as a master of comedy and contemporary social satire. Hi s work reflects the fresh, light spirit in film comedies that all but disappeared during Stalin's time. A favorite target in Ryazanov's films is bumbling bureaucracy. Admired by Soviet critics and actors for his affable manner and high standard of professionalism.

Films: *Voices Of Spring* (1955), *Carnival Night* (1957), *The Girl Without An Address* (1957), *How Robinson Was Created* (1961), *Man From Nowhere* (1961), *The Hussar's Ballad* (1962), *Complaints Book, Please* (1964), *Beware, Automobile!* (1966), *Zigzag Of Fortune* (1969), *The Old Brigands* (1971), *The Incredible Adventures Of Italians In Russia* (1974).

SALTYKOV, Alexei. b. 1934. Russian.

Graduated the State Institute of Cinematography 1961 as one of Mikhail Romm's students. His realistic *The Chairman* created a stir among Soviet and foreign critics who regard it as one of the best Soviet films of the 1960s. Saltykov has a preference for themes in which the destiny of the individual is related to the destiny of the nation.

Films: *Boys From Our Courtyard* (1959, with Yastrebov), *Beat The Drum* (1962), *My Friend Kolka* (1963, with Alexander Mitta), *The Chairman* (1965), *The Kingdom Of Women* (1967), *The Director* (1970), *Breakup* (1971), *No Return* (1974), *Ivan and Marya* (1975).

SAMSONOV, Samson (real name: **Samson Iosifovich Edelstein**).
b. 1921.

First studied acting in Moscow and joined the Central Theater of Transport with which he was associated until 1943. After 1945 he enrolled at the State Institute of Cinematography and studied under Sergei Gerasimov along with Sergei Bondarchuk. Samsonov, while still a student, was Gerasimov's assistant director on *The Young Guard*. Gained acclaim for his tender handling of *The Grasshopper* and *An Optimistic Tragedy*, the former receiving the Silver Lion at Venice and the latter a special prize at Cannes.

Films: *Shop Window* (1955), *The Grasshopper* (1955), *The Fiery Miles* (1957), *As Old As The Century* (1960), *An Optimistic Tragedy* (1963), *The Arena* (1968), *The Three Sisters* (1969).

SAVCHENKO, Igor Andreevich. 1906-51. Ukrainian, born in Vinnitsa.

Son of a soldier and music teacher. At the age of 13 Savchenko joined Orda Svetlova's theater in Vinnitsa. In 1925 he organized the agit-theater 'Krasnyi Galstuk' [Red Necktie] with Viktor Eisimont and a year later enrolled in the directors' course at the Leningrad Technicum of Screen Arts. Prior to graduation Savchenko went to Baku in 1929 where he worked as an actor and art director for the Theater of the Young Worker. While in Baku Savchenko took a role in Shengelaya's *Twenty-six Commissars* and made his first, educational, film *People Without Hands*.

Savchenko went to Moscow in 1932 and was there commissioned to direct what has since been acknowledged as a Soviet landmark film, *Accordion*, the first Soviet musical. Although critics were not overjoyed with it the film proved quite popular. Savchenko then worked on historical and war films. *Bogdan Khmelnitski* was his first big film and was lauded for its direction despite its anti-Polish bias that seemed to justify the Soviet annexation of the western Ukraine.

During World War II Savchenko made two popular feature war dramas, *Partisans in the Steppes of the Ukraine* and *Ivan Nikulin, Russian Sailor*. The latter film briefly marked a return of color films to Soviet screens. In 1944 Savchenko was appointed to the Artistic Council of the Committee on Cinema Affairs which served as an advisory body for film production planning. In the same year he took over as head of Soyuzdetfilm Studios when Sergei Yutkevich left. During his tenure, as well as that of Yutkevich's, Soviet children's films improved qualitatively and assumed more importance in the film industry.

After leaving Soyuzdetfilm in 1947 Savchenko made one of the big films about World War II, *The Third Blow*. The film concentrated on portraying Stalin as a military genius, but it was quickly overshadowed by the more grandiose works of Petrov *(Battle of Stalingrad)* and Chiaureli *(The Fall of Berlin)*.

Savchenko reached a peak in his career posthumously with *Taras Shevchenko* which was completed after his sudden death by his students Alov and Naumov. The work proved to be a powerful film about the life of the Ukrainian poet who was played notably by Sergei Bondarchuk.

Films: *People Without Hands* (1931), *Accordion* (1934), *A Thought About Cossack Golotu* (1937), *Riders* (1939, with A. Golovanov), *Bogdan Khmelnitski* (1941), *Block 14* (1942), *Partisans in the Steppes of the Ukraine* (1942), *Ivan Nikulin, Russian Sailor* (1944), *The Third Blow* (1948), *Taras Shevchenko* (1951).

SEGEL, Yakov. b. 1923.
Studied under Sergei Gerasimov at State Institute of Cinematography; graduated 1954.

Films: *Secret of Beauty* (1955, with Vasili Ordinski), *It Started Like This* (1957, with Lev Kulidzhanov), *The House I Live In* (1957, with Kulidzhanov), *The Day The War Ended* (1960), *Goodbye Doves* (1961), *The Volga is Flowing* (1964), *Wake Mukhin Up* (1965).

SHENGELAYA, Eldar. b. 1933. Georgian.
Has concentrated on fantasies and adaptations of folk legends.

Films: *Legend of the Ice Heart* (1957, with Alexei Sakharov), *A Snow Fairy Tale* (1959, with Alexei Sakharov), *White Caravan* (1964), *He Did Not Want to Kill* (1967).

SHENGELAYA, Nikolai. 1903-43. Georgian.
One of the pioneer film-makers of Soviet Georgian cinema.

Shengelaya's first three films were popular and critical successes in which he exhibited progressive sophistication as a director. *Twenty-six Commissars* still stands as a classic of the Soviet cinema of the 1930s. Shengelaya, following the triumph of this work, began to collaborate with Mikhail Sholokhov on a film adaptation of the latter's novel, *Virgin Soil Upturned.* Filming started in January 1934, but the work was suddenly halted and the project was shelved. Although the reasons for the stoppage were never explained, even Soviet film historians agree that the incident had a traumatic effect upon Shengelaya whose later works never recaptured his earlier success. *Virgin Soil Upturned* was later made by Raizman.

Films: *Giulli* (1972), *Eliso* (1928), *Twenty-six Commissars* (1932), *The Golden Valley* (1937), *Motherland* (1939), *He'll Come Back Again* (1942).

SHEPITKO, Larissa. b. 1939. Ukrainian.

A beautiful woman director whose films have caught the attention of Soviet and foreign critics for their sharp, probing manner. While a student at the State Institute of Cinematography Shepitko made two short films prior to her graduation in 1963. Her first feature film, *The Heat*, caused a stir among Soviet critics for its sharp photography and the depth of passion between the protagonists. *Wings*, which proved controversial because of its theme of social adjustment, marked her as one of the important film-makers of the Soviet new wave. In *You and I* Shepitko strove to depict people reaching a psychological watershed in their lives and was partly a look at her own generation.

Films: *The Blind Cook* (1961), *Living Water* (1962), *The Heat* (1963), *Wings* (1969), *You and I* (1972).

SHNEIDEROV, Vladimir. b. 1900.

Specialist in adventure, documentary, and popular science films.

Films: *Great Flight* (1925), *Great Tokyo* (1925), *Pamir* (1928), *El-Yemen* (1930), *The Golden Lake* (1935), *Julbars* (1937), *Gaichi* (1938), *The Beginning of Life* (1950), *Among the Reeds in the Volga Delta* (1950), *A Journey With A Movie Camera* (1952), *Charles Darwin* (1960), *Under Ancient Desert Skies* (1961), *Otto Yulevich Shmidt* (1963), *Across Zangezur* (1967).

Larissa Shepitko on the set of *You and I*. (British Film Institute)

SHUB, Esther. 1894-1959. Ukrainian.

One of the few Soviet women directors to have achieved international recognition for her creative and dramatic style of editing historical documentaries. Because of her early and laborious work in gathering historical film footage Shub provided great stimulus toward the establishment of Soviet film archives.

During the Civil War Shub began her work in films as an editor and continued along this line in the early 1920s for Goskino and Sovkino. She worked on editing foreign films before working on Soviet theatrical films, most notably on Yuri Tarich's *Wings of a Serf.*

Her debut as an independent film-maker was marked by her famous historical trilogy of the Russian Empire and Soviet Union. Her first film, *The Fall of the Romanov Dynasty* (1927), was produced by Sovkino in cooperation with the Museum of the Revolution. Her work required patient collection of old and forgotten news film which she wove into a dramatic work that included the little 'home movies' of the tsar's entourage. The film covered the years 1912-17 and was very well received. Her next effort, *The Great Road*, was a film chronicle of the first ten years of the Soviet state. A year later Shub again gained remarkable acclaim for *The Russia of Nikolai II and Lev Tolstoi*, which commemorated Tolstoi's centenary and focused on the era of 1897 to 1912. The film was noteworthy for the skillful way that Shub blended in the little amount of film on Tolstoi that was available. Despite these triumphs Shub was denied author rights to her trilogy by Sovkino, which according to Jay Leyda was a shabby episode.

Shub's later career suffered from charges of "formalism", but in recent Soviet studies she is now highly acclaimed. In a ceremony that honored the Soviet film industry in January 1935, Shub's contributions to documentary film were acknowledged when she was awarded the title Honored Artist of the Republic. After making the well received *Twenty Years of Cinema* with Vsevolod Pudovkin, Shub concentrated on editing and her talents ignored.

Films: *The Fall of the Romanov Dynasty* (1927), *The Great Road* (1927), *The Russia of Nikolai II and Lev Tolstoi* (1928), *Today* (1930), *Komsomol — The Guide to Electrification* (1932), *The Metro By Night* (1934), *Spain* (1937), *Land of the Soviets* (1938), *Twenty Years of Cinema* (1940, with Vsevolod Pudovkin).

SHUKSHIN, Vasili. 1929-74. Russian. Director, actor, scriptwriter.
Shukshin's last film marked him as one of the bright, important
directors of Soviet cinema. *The Red Snowball Tree* reflects the deep
interest Shukshin had in contemporary problems of Soviet society. The
film's release was delayed because of its unvarnished depiction of the
problems facing ex-convicts as they return to society and its sharp satire
on bureaucrats. Shukshin had barely completed his feature role and
script collaboration on Bondarchuk's *They Fought for Their Motherland* when he died.

Films (as director): *There Was A Lad* (1964), *Your Son and Brother*
(1966), *Strange People* (1970), *The Red Snowball Tree* (1974).

SKUIBIN, Vladimir. 1929-62.
Soviet critics admired Shuibin's second film and he was considered to have great talent. Skuibin was suffering from an incurable illness
and was partially disabled when he died in the midst of his last film.

Films: *On the Ruins of the Estate* (1956), *Cruelty* (1959), *The Miracle
Worker* (1960), *The Trial* (1963).

SOLNTSEVA, Yulia. b. 1901.
Studied at the University of Moscow before making her debut as
the statuesque queen in Protazanov's *Aelita*. Solntseva also is still
remembered for her leading performance in *Cigarette Girl From
Mosselprom*. After starring in *Earth* she married Alexander Dovzhenko
and from that time on became his devoted assistant and co-director.
After Dovzhenko died she worked tirelessly to complete his un-
realized film projects. Her work as a director has been admired internationally, but critics have usually agreed that while she has skillfully
portrayed Dovzhenko's focus and intent she has not succeeded in main-
taining his poetic flavor. Solntseva's *Poem of the Sea, Story of the
Flaming Years,* and *The Enchanted Desna* have been much acclaimed.

Films (as director): *Shchors* (1939, with Dovzhenko), *Battle for the
Ukraine* (1943), *Victory in the Ukraine* (1945), *Igor Bulichov* (1953),
The Unwilling Inspectors (1954), *Poem of the Sea* (1957), *Story of the
Flaming Years* (1961), *The Enchanted Desna* (1965), *Unforgettable*
(1969), *Golden Gates* (1970).

STABOVOI, Georgi. 1894-1968. Scenarist and director.

After serving with the Red Army during the Civil War Stabovoi was demobilized in 1923 and joined VUFKU, the Ukrainian film industry as a scriptwriter. His first film as a director, *Fresh Wind*, had a good deal of attention for its well rounded character portrayals in a story about socialized economy. Stabovoi's second effort, *P.K.P.*, intended to commemorate Polish aggression against the Ukraine in 1920, was judged by Soviet critics to be so historically inaccurate that it was hastily withdrawn, reedited and reissued in abbreviated form. Today Stabovoi is little remembered except by Soviet film historians largely for his successful and very dramatic portrayal of divided loyalties and inner conflict during the Civil War in *Two Days*. The film is an example of the best that VUFKU produced in the 1920s. After the critical failure of his last film Stabovoi ceased directing.

Films: *Fresh Wind* (1926), *P.K.P.* (1926, with A. Lundin), *Two Days* (1927), *The Break* (1929), *They Interfere With Our Stride* (1932).

STOLPER, Alexander. b. 1907. Director and scenarist.

First worked as a journalist and stage director before going into film work. Stolper began his film career as a scenarist and received complimentary attention for his work on the script of *The Road to Life* along with Ekk and Yanushkevich. Stolper's debut as a director was met with severe criticism because of the uncomplimentary portrayal of Komsomol behavior.

Since World War II Stolper concentrated on war films and has been accorded much acclaim for his realistic and intelligent handling of story material. His last two films brought him renewed attention because of their fresh reexamination of the Soviet military in the first two years of war with Nazi Germany.

Films: *Law of Life* (1940, with Boris Ivanov), *A Lad From Our Town* (1942), *Wait For Me* (1944, with Boris Ivanov), *Days and Nights* (1945), *Our Heart* (1946), *Story of A Real Man* (1948), *Far From Moscow* (1951), *The Road* (1955), *Unrepeatable Spring* (1957), *The Difficult Happiness* (1958), *The Living and the Dead* (1964), *None Are Born Soldiers* (1967).

TALANKIN, Igor. b. 1927. Russian.
Studied at the Glasunov Theater and Music School, and in the directors' course at Mosfilm Studios. His third film gained him international attention when it won a special prize at the Venice Film Festival. Talankin is one of the promising directors of the Soviet cinema.

Films: *Seryozha* (1960, with Georgi Daneliya), *There Are Also People* (1960, with Daneliya), *Starting Out* (1962), *Day Stars* (1968), *Tchaikovski* (1969), *A Choice of Goal* (1974).

TARICH, Yuri. 1885-1967.
First worked in films as a scriptwriter and then became one of the pioneering film-makers in Belorussian cinema. Traditionalist in style and sober in mood his films have largely been overlooked. Tarich's one great success, and internationally most memorable film, was *Wings of a Serf* which was edited by Esther Shub. The film, entitled *Ivan the Terrible* abroad, was a historical drama that attempted to reveal the historical processes of the Russian people as viewed from the aspect of class struggle. Although Tarich never again had such a critically admired film he continued to focus his efforts on historical and revolutionary themes.

Films: *A Forest Tale* (1926), *Wings of a Serf* (1926), *Bulat Batyr* (1928), *The Captain's Daughter* (1928), *Until Tomorrow* (1929), *Hatred* (1930), *Path of a Ship* (1937), *The Eleventh of July* (1938), *The Sky* (1940).

TARKOVSKI, Andrei. b. 1932. Russian.
Son of Arseni Tarkovski the poet. Tarkovski studied under Mikhail Romm at the State Institute of Cinematography and graduated in 1960. While a student Tarkovski made two films, his diploma project was in collaboration with Mikhalkov-Konchalovski and brought them international recognition when *The Skating Rink and the Violin* received first prize at the New York Students' Film Competition. From then on Tarkovski established an enviable record as a film-maker.

Ivan's Childhood reflected an artful blend of reality and surrealism in a tender story about a young boy in the midst of war, and took prizes at the Venice, Acapulco, and San Francisco Film Festivals.

With *Andrei Rublev,* which took a prize at the 1969 Cannes

Festival, Tarkovski received even more prominence because of controversy that delayed the release of this work. The film was officially criticized because it reflected a negative view of medieval Russia. There is some belief that the criticism was motivated primarily on the grounds of history rather than politics. Rublev still remains an obscure historical character with more being known about his paintings than his personality. What Tarkovski depicted was a man's rise to greatness and his search for beauty despite the darkness that may surround him. The film reflects, as does *Ivan's Childhood*, Tarkovski's interest in historical subjects as they have relevance for our understanding of the present.

With *Solaris* Tarkovski received a special jury prize at the 1972 Cannes Festival and aroused the interest of critics, some of whom have been fond of comparing it to Stanley Kubrick's *2001: A Space Odyssey*. Where Kubrick intended a non-subjective theme Tarkovski portrays man's psychological readiness to face the challenges of space and space technology.

Tarkovski's works have engendered much discussion which has made him one of the foremost Soviet film-makers.

Films: *There Will Be No Leave Today* (1959), *The Skating Rink and the Violin* (1959, with Andrei Mikhalkov-Konchalovski), *Ivan's Childhood* (1962), *Andrei Rublev* (1967 [1969]), *Solaris* (1972), *A White, White Day* (1974).

[See also: Montagu, Ivor. "Man and Experience: Tarkovski's World," *Sight and Sound*, 1973 (Spring), vol. 42, no. 2, p. 89.]

TASIN, Georgi. 1895-1956. Director and scenarist.

After completing studies at the Psycho-Neurological Institute in Petrograd Tasin joined the Red Army during the Civil War and served as a political worker, primarily as a scriptwriter for *agitki*. In 1920 Tasin joined the young Ukrainian film industry as a scriptwriter and worked most notably on the scenario of *A Specter Is Haunting Europe*.

As a director Tasin scored only one big success, *Night Coachman*, which in theme was similar to Stabovoi's *Two Days*. The film featured Amvrosi Buchma as Gerdei Yaroshchuk who becomes a Bolshevik after seeing his daughter, a revolutionary, die. *Night Coachman* became one of the important films of Ukrainian cinema. From then on Tasin's work declined.

Jimmie Higgins was based on the novel by Upton Sinclair and featured the performances of Amvrosi Buchma and Yulia Solntseva. The film also had the services of Isaac Babel as scenarist. The story dealt with an American soldier who comes to realize the nature of moral decay under capitalism while stationed in Arkhangelsk during the Allied intervention in the Russian Civil War. Tasin, despite all the good material he had to work with, was severely criticized for the weak and inaccurate portrayal of Americans and the American way of life that had been based only on weak second hand sources. His later career was undistinguished.

Films: *Night Coachman* (1928), *Jimmie Higgins* (1929), *Salty Fellows* (1930), *Great Gamble* (1935), *Nazar Stodolia* (1936).

TRAUBERG, Ilya. 1905-48. Director and scenarist.

Younger brother of Leonid Trauberg. Entered film work in 1927 as one of Eisenstein's assistants on *October*. He scored notable triumphs with *The Blue Express,* an effective drama about anti-colonialism in Asia, and *Son of Mongolia,* one of the most exotic Soviet films.

Films (as director): *Leningrad Today* (1927, documentary), *The Blue Express* (1929), *There Will Be Work For You* (1932), *A Singular Affair* (1934), *Son of Mongolia* (1936), *Concert Valse* (1940), *Waiting for Victory* (1941), *Spider* (1942, with I. Zemgano), *The Actress* (1943).

TRAUBERG, Leonid. b. 1902.

Long associated with Grigori Kozintsev dating back to the early 1920s when they jointly established the Factory of the Eccentric Actor (FEKS). Trauberg's collaboration with Kozintsev ended as a result of the heavy official criticism of *Plain People.* Although both men admitted their so-called "errors", Trauberg bore the brunt of the criticism by being barred from film-making until after Stalin's death. In his comeback as a director Trauberg never again enjoyed the acclaim that he received during his collaboration with Kozintsev.

Films: for films with Kozintsev see KOZINTSEV; alone — *The Year 1919* (1939), *Soldiers on the March* (1958), *Dead Souls* (1961), *Wind of Freedom* (1961).

TURIN, Viktor. 1895-1945.

Born in a well-to-do family Turin went to the United States and studied at the Massachusetts Institute of Technology. For a time he worked for the Vitagraph Studios and then decided to return to Russia in the early 1920s.

Turin's *Turksib* still stands as a classic documentary which surprised everyone when it was first released for its clean, natural style. Following the success of this film Turin was appointed to an administrative post in the Ukrainian film industry, but never again attained the triumph of his *Turksib*.

Films: *Order of the Day of October 8th* (1925), *Struggle of the Giants* (1926), *When the Dead Awake* (1928), *Turksib* (1929, documentary), *The White Sea Canal* (1933), *Baku People* (1938).

URUSEVSKI, Sergei. b. 1908. Russian. Cinematographer and director.

Joined the film industry in 1935 after studying fine arts and photography. During World War II Urusevski served as a combat photographer. After 1945 he became a leading cinematographer and worked mostly with Donskoi and Kalatozov. Began directing in 1969.

Films: *The Ambler's Race* (or *The Trotter's Gait,* 1970), *Sergei Yesenin* (1970, with Shpalikov), *Sing Your Song, Poet* (1973).

VASILIEV, Georgi (1899-1946) and **Sergei** (1900-59).

Though unrelated they took the pseudonym Vasiliev Brothers during their professional collaboration. They met while students of Sergei Eisenstein's seminar at the State Institute of Cinematography. Eisenstein encouraged and helped them in their early work.

After almost two years of work they scored a huge triumph with *Chapayev,* a pleasing and naturalistic film about the renowned Red Army commander of the Civil War. Stalin was so pleased by the film that many directors apparently tried to imitate its style. Try as they might, the Vasilievs never again had such a critical victory. Their very next film, *Volochaevka Days,* seemed a mechanical self-imitation and offered nothing new. Their later work was always in the shadow of *Chapayev,* which critics were never able to forget.

In 1944 Sergei relieved Ermler as head of Lenfilm Studios when the latter became heavily engaged in *The Great Turning Point.*

Films: jointly — *Exploit on the Ice* (1928, documentary), *The Sleeping Beauty* (1930), *A Personal Matter* (1932), *Chapayev* (1934), *Volochaevka Days* (1937), *Defense of Tsaritsyn* (1942), *The Front* (1944); Georgi alone — *Unlikely But True* (1928); Sergei alone — *The Heroes of Shipka* (1955), *October Days* (1958).

VENGEROV, Vladimir. b. 1920. Russian.
Studied under Sergei Eisenstein at the State Institute of Cinematography.

Films: *The Living Corpse* (1953, filmed theater play), *The Forest* (1954), *Dirk* (1954), *Two Captains* (1956), *The Lights Go On in the City* (1958), *Baltic Sky* (1961), *Home Trip* (1963), *A Factory Town* (1965), *The Living Corpse* (1969, free film adaptation).

VERTOV, Dziga (real name: **Denis Arkadievich Kaufman**). 1896-1954. Ukrainian.
Brother of Mikhail Kaufman. Acknowledged as the father of Soviet newsreel and documentary film.

Prior to 1917 Vertov studied at Moscow's Psycho-Neurological Institute and while a student experimented with sound. After the October Revolution he volunteered his services to the Bolsheviks and served as a film editor with an agit train. By the early 1920s Vertov was recognized as an inspired, energetic, and occasionally eccentric documentarist.

Vertov organized a group of documentarists which came to be known as Kino-oki, or Kino-Eyes. The movement, which was characterized by a revolutionary militancy in believing that true film art had to be unacted, that is true *cinema-verite* or only showing life as it was. During Soviet cinema's Golden Age Vertov's view that the newsreel and documentary was the only true form of revolutionary film art gained a sizeable following. Vertov also became engaged in hot theoretical debates with other film directors for his extreme views, even going so far as to suggest that theatrical films should not exceed twenty-five per cent of total annual film production.

In the 1930s Vertov lost his official favor and even his works took on a more poetic, mellower style that was noticeable as early as *October Without Ilyich* and then in *The Eleventh[Year]*, the film poem *Three Songs of Lenin*, and *Lullaby*. His other important films include *Leninist Film Truth, A Sixth Part of the Earth, Stride, Soviet!, Man With A Movie Camera*, and *Enthusiasm*.

Vertov's personal manner was at times very eccentric. He once almost drove the audience out of a London theater during the showing of *Enthusiasm* when he raised the sound to near ear shattering intensity.

Despite reported troubles with film officials in his later years Vertov continued to supervise newsreels and documentaries right up to the time of his death. His work has a sizeable following of *cinema-verite* enthusiasts.

Films: *Kino Week* (1918-21, newsreel series), *Anniversary of the Revolution* (1919), *The Mironov Trial* (1919), *Opening of the Reliquary of Sergei Radonerski* (1919), *The Battle of Tsaritsyn* (1920), *Agit-Train 'Vtsik'* (1921), *History of the Civil War* (1921), *Trial of the Social Revolutionaries* (1922), *Kino Pravda* (1922-24, film magazine), *Yesterday, Today, Tomorrow* (1923), *Give Us Air!* (1924), *Kino Eye* (1924), *Leninist Film Truth* (1925), *October Without Ilyich* (1925), *A Sixth Part of the Earth* (1926), *Stride, Soviet!* (1926), *The Eleventh [Year]* (1928), *Man With A Movie Camera* (1929, with Mikhail Kaufman), *Enthusiasm* (or *Donbas Symphony*, 1931), *Three Songs of Lenin* (1934), *Lullaby* (1937), *Memories of Sergo Ordzhonikidze* (1937), *Glory to Soviet Heroines* (1938), *Three Heroines* (1938), *Blood for Blood, Death for Death* (1941), *In the Line of Fire* (1941), *In the Region of Height 'A'* (1941), *For You, Front!* (1942), *In the Mountains of Ala-Tau* (1944), *The Oath of the Young* (1944), *News of the Day* (1944-54, newsreel series).

[See also: Abramov, N.P. *Dziga Vertov*. Lyon: SERDOC, 1965.

Bordwell, D. "Dziga Vertov," *Film Comment*, 1972 (Spring), vol. 8, no. 1, p. 38.

Sadoul, Georges. *Dziga Vertov*. Paris: Editions Champ Libre, 1971.

Vertov, Dziga. *Stati. Dnevniki. Zamysli* [Articles. Diaries. Thoughts]. Moscow: Iskusstvo, 1966.

"The Writings of Dziga Vertov," *Film Culture*, 1962 (Summer), no. 25, p. 50.]

VISKOVSKI, Vyacheslav. 1881-1933. Director and actor.
Was an established film director and producer prior to 1918.
After the October Revolution he established his own teaching film workshop in Leningrad. Viskovski's films exhibited a high degree of organization and discipline. Viskovski directed Ermler in *Red Partisans* and then later was directed by Ermler in *Fragment of an Empire.* His *The Ninth of January* was one of the biggest revolutionary films and employed thousands. Viskovski's last film was *The Minaret of Death,* which in its time was one of the most popular.

Films (as director): *Red Partisans* (1924), *The Minaret of Death* (1925), *The Ninth of January* (1925).

YARMATOV, Kamil. b. 1903. Uzbek. Director and actor.
One of the early pioneer actor-directors in Uzbek and Tadzhik films. Began film acting in 1924 and worked under Russian and Ukrainian directors who were making films in Central Asia. Studied at the Workers' Faculty (Rabfak) in Moscow in 1926 and then returned to acting in 1926-27. Graduated the State Institute of Cinematography in 1931 and made his directorial debut in the Tadzhik cinema.

Yarmatov has concentrated on social and revolutionary themes, and gained much notice for *Alisher Navoi, Storm Over Asia,* and *Horsemen of the Revolution.*

Films (as director): *The Emigrant* (1935), *Friends Meet Again* (1939), *Road Without Sleep* (1946), *Alisher Navoi* (1947), *Pakhta-Oi* (1952), *Rakhmanov's Sisters* (1954), *When Roses Bloom* (1959), *Storm Over Asia* (1965), *Poem of Two Hearts* (1967), *Horsemen of the Revolution* (1968).

YOSELIANI, Otar. b. 1934. Georgian.
His films have proved very popular for their light, satirical view of the contemporary Soviet social scene.

Films: *Watercolor* (1958), *Song About Flowers* (1959), *April* (1961), *Cast Iron* (1964), *Falling Leaves* (1968), *The Singing Thrush* (1970), *Day After Day* (1971).

[See also: "A Russian Six," *Films and Filming,* 1967 (September), vol. 13, no. 12, p. 27.]

YUTKEVICH, Sergei Iosipovich. b. 1904 in Kiev.

With his boyhood friend Grigori Kozintsev he put on puppet shows in the streets of Kiev. In 1920, already characterized by a humorous and engaging personality, Yutkevich went to Moscow to study theater and became friendly with fellow student Sergei Eisenstein. With Kozintsev and Trauberg he helped to establish the Factory of the Eccentric Actor (FEKS) in Leningrad in 1922. A year later he returned to Moscow and joined Meyerhold's workshop while earning a living as a set designer.

After making a short comedy, *Give Us Radio!*, which was a parody on American adventure thrillers and while Yutkevich was without any formal training in film work, he was taken on by Abram Room as set designer and assistant director for *The Traitor* and *Bed and Sofa*. In later years Yutkevich credited Room as being his teacher in film work while acknowledging Mayakovski and Meyerhold as his mentors in dramatic art.

Throughout his directing career Yutkevich gained much popularity for his lively and visually pleasing films. He became an excellent artist of the spectacle and of the closely intimate drama. Thanks to his efforts the Soviet cinema was spared the loss of Donskoi and Ermler.

In 1938 Yutkevich joined the teaching staff of Moscow's State Institute of Cinematography and had a critical triumph in the same year with *The Man With The Gun*. From this time on Yutkevich made several films that featured Maxim Shtraukh in the role of Lenin. Over the years their work together was to show a steady polish in the way Lenin was portrayed and reached a triumphant climax in *Lenin in Poland*.

During much of World War II Yutkevich headed Soyuzdetfilm Studio and is credited for giving children's films more attention and qualitative improvement. After the war his career was threatened when *Dawn Over Russia* was suddenly and inexplicably banned. His comeback was slow but remarkable when the colorful historical spectacle *Skanderbeg* was released.

Yutkevich received acclaim for *Othello*, which featured Sergei Bondarchuk in the lead role. The film gave a more humanistic interpretation of Shakespeare's character. Since then Yutkevich has enjoyed renewed critical attention. During the 1967 film exhibition in Moscow audiences were pleasantly surprised by the static film of Eisenstein's *Bezhin Meadow*, which Yutkevich supervised.

Films: *Give Us Radio!* (1925), *Lace* (1928), *The Black Sail* (1929), *The Golden Mountains* (1931), *Counterplan* (1933, with Friedrich Ermler), *Ankara, Heart of Turkey* (1934, documentary with Lev Arnshtam), *How the Elector Will Vote* (1937), *Miners* (1937), *The Man With The Gun* (1938), *Yakov Sverdlov* (1940), *The Elixir of Courage* (1941), *Schweik in the Concentration Camp* (1941), *The White Raven* (1941), *The New Adventures of Schweik* (1942), *Liberated France* (1945, documentary), *Moscow Calling* (1945), *Our Country's Youth* (1946), *Dawn Over Russia* (1948, banned), *Three Meetings* (1948), *Przhevalski* (1953), *Skanderbeg* (1954), *Othello* (1955), *Yves Montand Sings* (1957), *Stories About Lenin* (1958), *Meeting With France* (1960, documentary), *The Bath House* (1962, partly animated), *Peace To Your House* (1963), *Lenin in Poland* (1966), *Subject for A Short Story* (1969).

[See also: Yutkevich, Sergei. *Chelovek na ekrane* [Man on the Screen]. Moscow: Goskinoizdat, 1947.

_____. "Cutting It To Style," *Films and Filming*, 1962 (March), vol. 8, no. 6, p. 10.

_____. "My Way With Shakespeare," *Films and Filming*, 1957 (October), vol. 4, no. 1, p. 8.]

ZALAKEVICIUS, Vitautas. b. 1930. Lithuanian. Director and scenarist.

Graduated the State Institute of Cinematography 1956.

Zalakevicius is one of the "new wave" of Soviet film-makers whose films have made a strong impact on domestic and foreign critics. His films have focused on contemporary life and have exhibited a high degree of boldness. His last film continues to be widely exhibited abroad.

Films (as director): *It is Not Too Late* (1958, with Fogelman), *Adam Wants To Be A Man* (1959), *Living Heroes* (1960, fourth episode or novella), *Chronicle of One Day* (1963), *No One Wanted To Die* (1966), *Feelings* (1971), *That Sweet Word — Liberty* (1973).

ZARKHI, Alexander Grigorievich. b. 1908.

Graduated the Leningrad Technicum of Screen Arts in 1927 along with Iosif Heifitz. The two men were in constant collaboration until 1947. They began their careers as scriptwriters for Sovkino-Leningrad Studio and later to enjoy much success for their films.

The reason for their breakup as a directing team has never been explained, but they apparently did not fall into the same difficulties as Kozintsev and Trauberg. As an independent film-maker Zarkhi scored an admirable triumph with *The Heights*, which reflected a turn towards greater humanism in Soviet films after Stalin's death. His *Anna Karenina* was a well done and visually pleasing film although it failed to excite critics.

Films: for films with Heifitz see HEIFITZ; alone — *Pavlinka* (1952), *Nesterka* (1955), *The Heights* (1957), *Men on the Bridge* (1960), *My Younger Brother* (1962), *Anna Karenina* (1967), *Cities and Years* (1973).

ZHELIABUSHSKI, Yuri Andreevich. 1888-1965. Director and cinematographer.

The son of a prominent Russian actress, Zheliabushski entered film work before 1917 as an assistant cameraman as a result of being a good amateur photographer. After the October Revolution Zheliabushski joined the Cinema Committee of the Commissariat of Education and made a number of *agitki*, thereby teaching himself how to direct films. Of his Civil War efforts *The Domestic Agitator* was his best and is regarded as a transitional step between the *agitka* and the theatrical feature film.

Zheliabushski was one of the first film-makers to pioneer in educational and popular science films with *Gidrotorf*, released in 1920. His most memorable film is *The Cigarette Girl From Mosselprom* which was a satire about the remnants of bourgeois society in the USSR during the period of the New Economic Policy. Following this film Zheliabushski worked as a photographer under Dziga Vertov in filming Lenin's funeral for the *Kino Pravda* series. He was then assigned to make a new version of *Mother* after the unsuccessful 1920 film of Alexander Razumni. Although Zheliabushski took on the project seriously he was unable to satisfy himself in choosing a player for the lead role. He allowed the project to fall through and be made in a short time into a worldwide success by Vsevolod Pudovkin.

In 1928 he came under heavy criticism for *No Entrance to the*

City similar to what Protazanov experienced for *The White Eagle* and *The Forty-First*. Zheliabushski then concentrated entirely on documentaries and joined the faculty of the State Institute of Cinematography, where he taught until the late 1940s.

Films: *Children Are The Flowers of Life* (1919), *The Dream of Taras* (1919), *The Emperor's New Clothes* (1919), *Peter and Alexis* (1919), *What Were You?* (1919), *The Domestic Agitator* (1920), *Gidrotorf* (1920), *The Cigarette Girl From Mosselprom* (1924), *Father Frost* (1924), *The Stationmaster* (or *The Collegiate Registrar*, 1925), *Dina Dza-Dzu* (1926), *Svanetia* (1927), *A Woman's Victory* (1927), *Abkhazia* (1928), *Along the Mountains and Glaciers of the Caucasus* (1928), *A Man Is Born* (1928), *No Entrance to the City* (1928).

SOVIET CINEMA

SELECTED SOVIET FILMS
1918-1975

[**Note.** Readers who wish to know about Russian films produced and released prior to 1918 should consult the work by Jay Leyda cited in the General Bibliography.]

ABKHAZIYA — 1928 - Yuri Zheliabushski (Mezhrabpomfilm)
Geographical and social documentary film.

ABORTION — 1924 — N. Baklin (Kultkino)
Popular science film on the effects of abortion on women.

ABU RAYHAN BIRUNI — 1974 - Shurat Abasov (Uzbekfilm)
Biographical film about the great Oriental scholar Biruni (973-1048), whose interests ranged over all the sciences and philosophy. The film focuses on Biruni's quest for truth at a time of ignorance and darkness. The work traces Biruni's life from childhood through his adulthood under the Sultan Mahmud of Ghazni.

ACADEMICIAN IVAN PAVLOV — 1949 - Girgori Roshal (Lenfilm)
Dramatized account of the life of the famous Russian physiologist. While patriotic in theme the film depicts the nonconformist nature of Pavlov.

ACCORDION — 1934 - Igor Savchenko (Mezhrabpomfilm)
First Soviet musical. Savchenko made this film in the then record time of eight months. The story is about a young collective farm worker who routs a band of rowdy kulaks (rich peasants) by his music and wins the heart of his girl. Critics did not particularly like the film and Savchenko viewed it as a simple, light musical comedy. Proved very popular with audiences. The film came out at a time when Stalin was relentlessly pushing collectivization which had peaked out a few years earlier.

ACROSS ZANGEZUR — 1967 - Vladimir Shneiderov
Expeditionary adventure film.

THE ACTRESS — 1943 - Ilya Trauberg
One of the first feature comedies made during the war. The story focused on a young musical comedienne evacuated from Moscow.

ADAM WANTS TO BE A MAN — 1959 - Vitautas Zalakevicius
(Lithuanian Film Studio)

THE ADDRESS OF LENIN — 1929 - Vladimir Petrov
(Mezhrabpomfilm)
 A children's film which dealt with a group of young Pioneers who
establish a club and park at a home once occupied by Lenin.

ADMIRAL NAKHIMOV — 1946 [1947] - Vsevolod Pudovkin
(Mosfilm)
 The first version came out when relations between the USSR and
the West were already cooling. The film stressed the diplomacy re-
volving around 19th-century Russo-Turkish conflicts. Pudovkin was
criticized for not giving sufficient scope to Russian naval victories,
especially at the Battle of Sinope. The film was revised accordingly and
won a Stalin Prize when it was rereleased in 1947. An indication of
Soviet foreign policy was given in the end scene when tsarist frigates
dissolve into modern Soviet warships, intimating Soviet preparedness
for defense of Black Sea interests.

ADMIRAL USHAKOV — 1953 - Mikhail Romm (Mosfilm)
 A colorful biographical film of an outstanding Russian naval com-
mander of the 18th century who has only lately been given his due by
Western historians. The film had extravagant ship and battle scenes.

ADVENTURES OF A MANUFACTURER — 1926 - P. Sazonov
(VUFKU) — Also entitled *In the Clutches of Soviet Power.*
 A social satire on Russian bourgeois emigrants during the Civil
War period. A rich businessman, Volfer, finds himself impoverished by
the Revolution and joins the Whites. His fortunes decline steadily to the
point where he ekes out a living as a clown in Parisian night clubs.

ADVENTURES OF A YELLOW SUITCASE — 1970 - Ilya Frez
(Maxim Gorki Studios)
 Story about a little boy who helps an absent-minded doctor
search for a misplaced suitcase, which contains many magical items such
as pills for bravery. The boy discovers he needs no pills for personal
courage.

THE ADVENTURES OF BARON MUNCHHAUSEN — 1929 -
Ivan Ivanov-Vano (Mezhrabpom-Rus)
Animated film.

ADVENTURES OF OKTYABRINA — 1924 - Grigori Kozintsev and
Leonid Trauberg (Sevzapkino)
An eccentric, burlesque comedy that was made under appalling
physical conditions. The story was about a bizarre attempt by Coolidge,
Poincare, and Lord Curzon to rob the Soviet State Bank. The machina-
tions of the capitalist leaders are foiled by a daring youngster.

ADVENTURES OF PETRUSHKA — 1937 - K. Isayev (Ukrainfilm)
Children's film.

AELITA — 1924 - Yakov Protazanov (Mezhrabpom-Rus)
Based on a novel by Alexei Tolstoi. The cast included Konstantin
Eggert, Yulia Solntseva, and Nikolai Batalov. The story dealt with three
Soviets who fly to Mars. A love affair develops between the Martian
queen, Aelita, and one of the Soviet men while a revolution takes place
on the planet. The film received much attention and acclaim when it
was released. The film's posters were accorded a prize at the 1925 International Exhibition of Decorative Arts in Paris. The costumes and sets
were designed in the constructivist style which was then gaining popularity in the USSR, but Protazanov found the original designs too
extreme and toned them down for more conventional taste.

AEROGRAD — 1935 - Alexander Dovzhenko (Mosfilm and Ukrainfilm)
Also entitled *Frontier.*
Set in a mythical Far Eastern Soviet city and air base, the film reflects Soviet anxieties about Japanese aggression. In the story Glushak,
a Siberian hunter, kills his long-time friend who is exposed as a traitor
to the USSR. Eduard Tisse's camera work was excellent and gave a
poetic quality to the Siberian countryside. The film in its scenario stage
was threatened by bureaucrats until Dovzhenko had a personal meeting
with Stalin, who insured the film's completion. Considered one of
Dovzhenko's best.

AGAINST THE WIND — 1930 - Iosif Heifitz and Alexander Zarkhi (Sovkino-Leningrad) — Also entitled *Facing the Wind*.

The story is set in the late NEP period and focuses on the efforts of a group of Komsomols to stamp out the vestiges of the bourgeois past. In one sequence, which caused the film to be criticized, the Young Communists stage a violent raid on a tavern in order to end alcoholism.

AGIT-TRAIN 'VTSIK' — 1921 - Dziga Vertov
Documentary.

AGONY — 1974 - Elem Klimov (Mosfilm)
Drama about the monk Rasputin.

AIR CHAUFFEUR — 1943 - Herbert Rappoport
World War II drama.

ALBANIA — 1945 - Roman Karmen (Central Documentary and Newsreel Studio)
Documentary on post-war life in Albania.

ALCOHOL — 1928 - Yu. Genik (Sovkino)
Popular science film on the negative effects of alcohol on animals and humans.

ALEKO — 1954 - Grigori Roshal

ALENKA — 1961 - Boris Barnet (Mosfilm)

ALEXANDER NEVSKI — 1938 - Sergei Eisenstein (Mosfilm)
Originally was to have been entitled *Rus*. The film was released after Hitler's takeover of Austria and the Sudetenland. The film was patriotic in theme. The story focused on the Russian resistance to the Teutonic Knights in the 13th century. Although very costly this historical film recouped all its expenditures from foreign earnings. The most memorable scene is the Battle on the Ice, which was filmed in the sultry heat of mid-July. This film, which pleased Stalin very much, marked Eisenstein's return to creative work and to Party favor, and earned Eisenstein the Order of Lenin. In addition to its outstanding photography the film had an excellent music score by Sergei Prokofiev, who worked closely with Eisenstein during the scoring.

ALEXANDER PARKHOMENKO — 1942 - Leonid Lukov, under supervision of Alexander Dovzhenko (Kiev and Tashkent Studios)
Drama about the Civil War which focused on a Ukrainian worker who led in driving German forces out of the Ukraine in 1919. Filming had barely begun when it was interrupted by the German capture of Kiev in 1941.

ALEXANDER POPOV — 1950 - Viktor Eisimont and Herbert Rappoport
A film biography of the Russian inventor of radio.

ALIEN RELATIVES — 1955 - M. Shveitser (Lenfilm)
A drama about kolhoz workers in which personal desires are in conflict with communal goals. One of the first post-Stalin films that probed deeply into the fabric of Soviet society by asking if society owed anything to the individual.

ALIEN SHORE — 1930 - Mark Donskoi

ALISHER NAVOI — 1947 - Kamil Yarmatov (Tashkent Studio)

ALITET GOES TO THE HILLS — 1950 - Mark Donskoi (Maxim Gorki Studios)
Banned after a very brief period of exhibition. The film in part was a satire on Soviet bureaucrats which failed to please the Party. Reportedly Stalin had parts of it destroyed.

ALMAS — 1936 - A. Kuliev and G. Braginski (Baku Studio)
Story of a young woman who takes up a struggle against opponents of socialist development in a rural area. The film continued the theme of political and social liberation of Caucasian women from the old ways of life.

ALONE — 1931 - Grigori Kozintsev and Leonid Trauberg (Soyuzkino-Leningrad)
Good photography and interesting ethnographical background highlighted this drama about a young woman teacher who is assigned a post in the Altai wilderness. At first she yearns for the familiar, warm surroundings of Leningrad (much, reportedly like Kozintsev and

Trauberg felt when they began location shooting), but slowly accepts her surroundings and the people around her. One of the first satisfactory Soviet sound films, which was recorded by Lev Arnshtam.

ALONG AZERBAIDZHAN — 1924 - Abas-Mirza Sharif-zade (AFKU)
Documentary on the life of the young Azerbaidzhan Soviet republic.

ALONG RUSSIAN PATHS — 1969 - Fedor Filipov
Drama about Russia near the turn of the century; based on stories by Maxim Gorki.

ALONG THE MOUNTAINS AND GLACIERS OF THE CAUCASUS — 1928 - Yuri Zheliabushski (Mezhrabpom-Rus)
Popular science film.

AMANGELDI — 1939 - Moisei Levin (Lenfilm)
Commissioned specifically by Kazakh cinema officials and intended as a Kazakh counterpart of *Chapayev* and *Shchors*. This is a drama about Amangeldi Imanov, a Kazakh revolutionary and how he matures from a simple anti-tsarist rebel to a devoted Bolshevik.

THE AMBLER'S RACE — 1970 - Sergei Urusevski — Also entitled *The Trotter's Gait.*
Based on the story "Farewell Gulsary" by Chinghiz Aitmanov, who also wrote the script.

THE AMERICAN WOMAN — 1930 - L. Esakiya (Goskinprom-Gruziya)
Historical drama about the underground Bolshevik press at the time of the 1905 Revolution.

AMOK — 1927 - Kote Mardzhanishvili [Konstantin Mardzhanov] (Goskinprom-Gruziya)

AMONG PEOPLE — (See *Out In The World*)

AMONG THE REEDS IN THE VOLGA DELTA — 1950 - Vladimir Shneiderov
Popular science film.

AND THE DAWNS ARE QUIET HERE — 1972 - Stanislav Rostotski
(Maxim Gorki Studios)
   World War II drama that has been extremely well received by
critics. A lyrical, moving story about a Soviet women's anti-aircraft
unit. The women talk about their lives and hopes when they are suddenly attacked by German paratroops. No mock heroics in this struggle
for life.

ANDREI RUBLEV — 1967 [1969] - Andrei Tarkovski (Mosfilm)
   Release was delayed while Party critics discussed Tarkovski's
negative and gloomy image of medieval Russia in this dramatized biography of the famous icon painter. Man's struggle to rise above ignorance
and injustice was the theme behind this study of a man who is still
wrapped in historical obscurity.

ANDRIESH — 1954 - Sergei Paradzhanov with Bazelian
(Kiev Film Studios)

ANKARA, HEART OF TURKEY — 1934 - Lev Arnshtam and
Sergei Yutkevich, with Esther Shub
   Documentary.

ANNA KARENINA — 1967 - Alexander Zarkhi (Mosfilm)
   Based on the novel by Tolstoi. A 1953 film was a filmed stage
play by the Moscow Art Theater.

ANNENKOVSHCHINA — 1933 - N. Bersenev
   A Civil War drama about the Bolshevik struggle against the White
ataman Annenkov.

ANNIVERSARY OF THE REVOLUTION — 1919 - Dziga Vertov
   Documentary chronicle.

ANNUSHKA — 1959 - Boris Barnet

ANTHRACITE — 1972 - Alexander Surin (Mosfilm)
   Considered by some foreign observers to be an intelligent, well
handled drama about a Russian coal miner as he attempts to cope with
personal problems. The film reflects the strong tendency in Soviet films
to focus on the individual since 1953.

ANTICHRIST — (See *Peter and Alexis*)

ANTON IVANOVICH GETS MAD — 1941 - Alexander Ivanovski,
supervised by Friedrich Ermler (Lenfilm) — Also entitled *Spring Song.*
Musical comedy.

ANTOSHA RYBKIN — 1941 - Konstantin Yudin
Short featurette as part of *Fighting Film Album No. 3.*

ANTOSHA RYBKIN — 1942 - Konstantin Yudin
Full length feature and expansion of the featurette above. Light
war comedy.

ANUSH — 1931 - Ivan Perestiani (Armenkino)
Adapted from the poem by O. Tumanian. Nonprofessional actors
were used in this love story set against the background of social struggles during agricultural collectivization. The film, which had the quality
of a film poem, suffered from uneven acting and sketchy revelation of
innercharacter.

APARTMENT IN MOSCOW — 1961 - Viktor Eisimont
(Maxim Gorki Studios)
Love story about contemporary Soviet youth.

APRIL — 1961 - Otar Yoseliani

THE ARENA — 1968 - Samson Samsonov (Mosfilm)

ARSEN — 1937 - Mikhail Chiaureli (Goskinprom-Gruziya)
Based on a play by A. Shanshiashvili. Story about a legendary
Georgian folk hero and a remake of Perestiani's *Arsen Georgiashvili* of
1921. Perestiani was part of the cast.

ARSEN GEORGIASHVILI — 1921 - Ivan Perestiani (Cinema Section,
Georgian Commissariat of Education)
Mikhail Chiaureli had the lead role in this story about the legendary Georgian national hero. The film was made with wornout equipment and under poor physical conditions because of the lack of studio
facilities.

ARSENAL — 1929 - Alexander Dovzhenko (VUFKU) — Also entitled *The January Uprising in Kiev in 1918.* Filming was completed in six months. The story was about the workers' uprising at the Arsenal plant and was less complex and symbolic in structure than Dovzhenko's *Zvenigora.* Nationalism was viewed in the film as detrimental to the interests of the Ukrainian people while Communism was seen as the solution to the nationality problem.

THE ARSENALISTS — 1925 - Les Kurbas (VUFKU)
Although Kurbas dealt with the same events as Dovzhenko (see above) the style is more of the ingrigue-suspense type of thriller. Kurbas made interesting use of the split-screen in the climactic battle scene to heighten tension as the opposing forces converged.

ARSHIN MAL-ALAN — 1945 - Rza Takhmasib and Nikolai Leshchenko (Baku Studio)
An Azerbaidzhanian musical comedy based on the work by Uzeir Gadzhibekov. Stalin Prize.

THE ARTAMANOV AFFAIR — 1941 - Grigori Roshal (Mosfilm)
Based on the novel by Maxim Gorki. The story centered on life and personal conflicts of an industrial family in the years before the 1917 Revolution. Considered to be one of Roshal's better films and may have been influenced by Sergei Eisenstein.

ARUT — 1933 - P. Armanda (Armenfilm)
The Armenian equivalent of Dovzhenko's *Earth.* The story was about Armenian farm laborers and their struggles for a better life at the time of agricultural collectivization. When the film was first released critics were not too happy with it, but in retrospect Soviet film historians take a kindlier view of it.

AS OLD AS THE CENTURY — 1960 - Samson Samsonov (Mosfilm)

ASAL — 1940 - M. Yegorov and B. Kozachkov (Uzbekfilm)
A light romantic story about a young Uzbek girl who is an optimistic archetype in the textile industry.

THE ASCENT — 1931 - Nabi Ganiev (Uzbekgoskino)
 A story about the lives and hopes of Young Communists (Komsomols) in a cotton mill. The original scenario was heavily propagandistic, but Ganiev changed it and infused more human drama.

ASSEMBLY LINE OF DEATH — 1933 - Ivan Pyriev — Also entitled *The Death Conveyor.*
 This film is in marked contrast to many of the satirical political films of the 1920s. The story is set in Germany at the time of Hitler's rise to power and follows the destinies of three young German girls. Suicide, hunger, and depression abound in the film and gives the viewer a harsh look at life in the capitalist West. One girl falls into prostitution, another goes after dissolute luxury while the heroine joins the Communist Party, which offers the true course to salvation.

ASYA — 1928 - Alexander Ivanovski
 An adaptation of a story by Turgenev. The film proved unpopular as too much social comment and moralizing were injected into what should have been a costume drama of 19th-century Russia.

AT A DISTANT OUTPOST — 1952 - Konstantin Yudin
 A Cold War film. Two American spies, passing themselves off as scientists are at work in the border region of Central Asia. They are finally caught by the vigilant Soviet border troops, a plot similar to many Soviet films of the 1930s in which the spies were usually German or Japanese.

AT A HIGH COST — 1957 - Mark Donskoi (Alexander Dovzhenko Studios)
 Based on the works of Kotsubinski. An emotional drama about a group of Ukrainians and Gypsies who band together for common defense in 1830.

AT 6 P.M. AFTER THE WAR — 1944 - Ivan Pyriev (Mosfilm)
 One of the best known Soviet films of World War II and Stalin Prize winner. A light, romantic musical comedy about two Soviet soldiers and their girl friends who are reunited in Moscow on the day of victory. The film told Soviet audiences that ultimate victory was a certainty.

AT THE OLD NURSE's — 1941 - Yevgeni Chervyakov
Featurette, *Fighting Film Album No. 2.*

ATAMAN KODR — 1958 - Moisei Kalik

AUTUMN OF HOPE — 1962 - Viktor Lisakovich
Documentary.

AUTOMOBILE, VIOLIN, AND THE DOG BLOB — 1975 -
Rolan Bykov (Mosfilm)
A musical comedy for children set in a mythical country with a
carnival-like background. Lavish, colorful sets.

AVE VITA — 1971 - Almantis Gricaevicius (Lithuanian Film Studio)

AVIATORS — 1935 - Yuli Raizman (Mosfilm) — Also entitled *Flyers*
and *Men On Wings*.
This may well be the grandad of all Soviet aviation films and was
surpassed only by Kalatozov's *Manhood* and *Valeri Chkalov*. A serious
story which is set against the background of a Soviet pilot training
school. The theme of devotion to duty is the framework for a triangle
of love involving an aviatrix, a young pilot, and an older flying instruc-
tor. The film was very popular and came out at a time when the Soviet
government was pushing for the expansion and modernization of the air
forces. Raizman's film stimulated a whole series of aviation movies, but
few matched the quality of this one.

AZAMAT — 1939 - A. Kordium (Uzbekfilm)
Story about life on an Uzbek collective farm that Soviet critics
felt was unrealistic.

AZIADE — 1918 - Iosif Soifer

A BAD JOKE — 1969 - Alexander Alov and Vladimir Naumov
(Mosfilm)
Adaptation from a work by Dostoevski.

BAD TROUBLE — 1930 - Alexei Popov (Sovkino) — Also entitled
An Extremely Unpleasant Incident.
    An antireligious satire told in a light amusing fashion. The story
involves a priest and an atheistic lecturer who bear a strong physical
resemblance. From this arises a series of comical errors.

BAKAI'S PASTURE — 1966 - Tolomush Okeyev (Kirghizfilm)
    Lyrical story about rural life in Central Asia.

BAKU IS READY — 1940 - Ye. Yeremeyev and M. Mustafeyev
(Azerfilm)
    Documentary on civil defense preparedness.

BAKU PEOPLE — 1938 - Viktor Turin (Azerfilm)
    Story about the revolutionary underground in Baku in 1905.
Filming began in 1935. Turin reportedly strove to imitate *The Maxim
Trilogy* with this film but failed.

BALLAD OF A SOLDIER — 1959 - Grigori Chukhrai (Mosfilm)
    One of several films that marked the post-Stalin renascence of
Soviet cinema. Chukhrai himself looked upon this film as a statement
about and tribute to his own generation, which had barely finished
school and was thrown into the cauldron of war. The story is about a
young soldier who is rewarded with six days home leave for combat
heroism. His journey home to see his mother is complicated by a series
of people, including a girl that he falls in love with. The final scene is
poignant, for he has only ten minutes to be with his mother before
going back to the front and death. Excellent, interesting photography.
The English-language dubbed version is poor when compared to the
original version. Won a prize at the 1960 Cannes Film Festival.

A BALLAD OF LOVE — 1966 - Mikhail Bogin (Riga Film Studio)
    Contemporary love story.

BALTIC DEPUTY — 1937 - Iosif Heifitz and Alexander Zarkhi
(Lenfilm)
    Considered one of the best Soviet films of its time. The film
brought much acclaim to its directors and to Nikolai Cherkasov who
played in the lead role. Based in part on the life of the scientist

K.A. Timiriazev. In the film the Russian scientist Polezhaev is forsaken by many of his friends during the 1917 Revolution because of his beliefs. He joins the Bolsheviks and the Baltic Fleet sailors at Kronstadt elect him as their deputy to the Petrograd Soviet. The film was lauded because of the strength of its revelation of character change and inner conflict.

BALTIC SAILORS — 1938 - Alexander Faintsimmer (Sovetskaya Belarus)
A popular film about the Bolshevik defense of Petrograd in 1919. Critics however thought it was nothing new and a facile attempt to capitalize on the success of Dzigan's *We Are From Kronstadt.*

BALTIC SKY — 1961 - Vladimir Vengerov

THE BATH HOUSE — 1962 - Sergei Yutkevich (Mosfilm)
A partly animated and updated adaptation of the 1928 play by Vladimir Mayakovski. The film is a satire on bureaucracy and the Stalinist cult of personality. Special effects and settings gave the film a 1920s style.

BATTLE FOR THE UKRAINE — 1943 - Alexander Dovzhenko, supervisor; Yulia Solntseva and Yakov Avdeyenko co-directors (Central Newsreel and Kiev Newsreel Studios)
War documentary which was given a poetic flavor by Dovzhenko. One of the best Soviet documentaries of World War II.

THE BATTLE OF OREL — 1943 - G. Gikov and L. Stepanova (Central Newsreel Studio)
Documentary on the Soviet counteroffensive following the Battle of Kursk.

BATTLE OF STALINGRAD — 1949, two parts - Vladimir Petrov (Mosfilm)
This film glorified Stalin's role in planning and conducting the famous battle, and supported Stalin's campaign to lower the autonomy and prestige of the military officer corps. A majestic film that was made with a lavish budget, much like Chiaureli's *The Fall of Berlin.* The film offers a view of war that is almost operatic in scenes of battle. Critics

have unfairly criticized Petrov for the way he contrasted the scenes of Hitler's and Stalin's headquarters. In Hitler we see hysteria, in Stalin cool, almost icy, calm. Postwar memoirs of generals indicate Petrov's handling accurately portrayed the atmosphere in the two headquarters.

THE BATTLE OF TSARITSYN — 1920 - Dziga Vertov
   Documentary.

BATTLE PAGES — 1939 - D. Babichenko
   Cartoon film on Soviet military history.

BATTLESHIP POTEMKIN — 1925 - Sergei Eisenstein
(First Factory Goskino)
   Made to commemorate the 1905 Revolution and originally was to have been only one of eight episodes for a larger film originally entitled *The Year 1905*. Eisenstein then decided that the Potemkin mutiny reflected the essence of the Revolution of 1905 and concentrated on it. Filming was done in three months and Eisenstein was still doing final editing right up to the hour of its special jubilee showing at the Bolshoi Opera Theater in Moscow, December 21, 1925. Since then the work has been judged as one of the most influential in the history of world cinema. When it was shown in Pennsylvania in 1926 it was banned for fear it would incite American sailors to mutiny. Censors in England and France worried over it, while in Germany the film received its greatest acclaim. Surprisingly Soviet critics at the time treated it initially with indifference. An epic tribute to revolutionary masses, the film's most memorable sequences are the close-up of the maggots on the meat and the Odessa Steps sequence. Sound tracks were added to the Soviet version in 1930 and again in 1950.

BEACON — 1942 - Mark Donskoi
   Featurette, *Fighting Film Album No. 9.*

THE BEAR — 1938 - Isidor Annenski (Sovetskaya Belarus)
   This comedy based on a work by Anton Chekhov was Annenski's diploma project at the State Film Institute.

BEAST OF THE FOREST — 1924 - Axel Lundin (Odessa Studio)
   A Civil War story which focused on Soviet defeat of the bandit

Battleship Potemkin, Odessa Steps sequence, Sergei Eisenstein (Museum of Modern Art/Film Stills Archive)

gang of Ataman Zabolotnyi who operated near Odessa in 1921. The main character is Yukhin, who goes over to the Bolsheviks and fights against his former bandit leader. The action thriller was long popular with Soviet audiences and Lundin's work was on the screens throughout the 1920s.

BEAT THE DRUM — 1962 - Alexei Saltykov (Mosfilm)

BEAUTY — 1971 - Arunas Zebriunas (Lithuanian Film Studio)
    A tender story about a 10-year old girl and her attitude towards and definition of 'beauty.'

THE BEAUTY AND THE BOLSHEVIK — (See *Brigade Commander Ivanov*)

BED AND SOFA — 1927 - Abram Room (Sovkino-Moscow) — Also entitled *The Third Philistine, Triangle Love,* and *In The Cellars of Moscow.*
    One of Room's best works and one of the best satires during and about the NEP period. The film points up the social consequences of the Soviet housing shortage. A husband and wife invite a friend to live with them and sleep on the sofa. Soon the husband winds up on the sofa and in the end the wife leaves both men.

BEETHOVEN CONCERT — 1936 - V. Shmidtgof and M. Gavronski (Sovetskaya Belarus)
    A musical film made primarily for children.

BEFORE THE DAWN — 1933 - Suleiman Khodzhayev (Uzbekgoskino)
    Story about the Uzbek revolutionary movement prior to the October Revolution with focus on the Uzbek uprising of 1916. When the film was first released Khodzhayev was severely criticized for his politically inaccurate portrayal of the events, but film historians in the 1960s have "rehabilitated" him.

BEFORE THE JUDGEMENT OF HISTORY — 1967 - Friedrich Ermler (Mosfilm)
    A drama that portrayed the Russian revolutionary era in a new examination, but failed to arouse much foreign interest. Ermler's last film.

THE BEGINNING OF LIFE — 1950 - Vladimir Shneiderov
Popular science film on biology.

BEHIND CONVENT WALLS — 1928 - Pyotr Chardynin (VUFKU)
A virulent antireligious film that portrayed nuns as depraved. Not considered one of the best films of Ukrainian cinema.

BELA — 1927 - Vladimir Barski (Goskinprom-Gruziya)
An adaptation of Lermontov's *Hero of Our Time*. The film was praised for its inclusion of the ethnography of Cherkass life and customs.

THE BELL RINGS, OPEN THE DOOR — 1966 - Alexander Mitta (Mosfilm)
Story about two youngsters and their view of the adult world. Through their actions and thoughts the viewer is told that one should always seek and retain enthusiasm for life.

BELORUSSIAN STATION — 1971 - Andrei Smirnov (Mosfilm)
Despite mixed reviews by foreign critics, Smirnov's film is one of the important works of the 1970s for the theme rather than the story or plot. Four Soviet war veterans meet twenty-five years after the war and they look at their lives since 1945. The film is at times quite somber as the human values of Soviet society since 1945 are examined.

THE BENCH — 1968 - Lev Atamanov (Soyuzmultfilm)
Cartoon.

BENYA KRIK — 1928 - Vladimir Vilner (VUFKU - Odessa Studio)
The scenario for this film was written by Isaak Babel. The final scene is what caused Soviet critics to dislike the film. Benya Krik, leader of the Odessa underworld, decides to cast his lot with the Bolsheviks during the Civil War. After a short time the Bolsheviks believe Krik is a detriment to them and decide that he must be executed. An army officer invites Krik to have dinner with him and shoots him in the back of the head.

[Note. Reportedly this form of execution was much in favor with the secret police because it was so humane.]

BERLIN — 1945 - Roman Karmen and Yuli Raizman
(Central Documentary and Newsreel Studio)
An excellent documentary about the last days of war against
Germany and the fall of Berlin in 1945. Final editing of the film was
completed in 16 days.

BEWARE, AUTOMOBILE! — 1966 - Eldar Ryazanov (Mosfilm)
A satire on the contemporary Soviet social scene.

BEZHIN MEADOW — 1936-37 [1967] - Sergei Eisenstein (Mosfilm)
Banned because of displeasure over Eisenstein's portrayal of rural
life. Over two million rubles were spent on this film which was made in
two variants because of changes in state policies and interruptions resulting from Eisenstein's illnesses. The peasants were portrayed sympathetically and collectivization almost as coercion. Much of the original
film was destroyed when Mosfilm Studios were struck by a German air
attack in 1941. Naum Kleiman, working under Sergei Yutkevich's supervision, was able to make a static film from remaining frames and
showed it at the 1967 Moscow Film Festival where it was considered a
technical success.

[See also: Leyda, Jay. "Eisenstein's Bezhin Meadow," *Sight and Sound,*
1959 (Spring), vol. 28, no. 2, p. 74; and Robinson, David. "The Two
Bezhin Meadows," *Sight and Sound,* 1967/68 (Winter), vol. 37, no. 1,
p. 33.]

THE BIG FAMILY — 1954 - Iosif Heifitz (Lenfilm)
Based on the novel *Zhurbiny* by V. Kochetov. Released a year
after Stalin's death this film signalled something new in Soviet cinema,
the interests, needs, and problems of everyday common people.
Through the eyes of the chief character, Matvei Zhurbin, and the destinies of his families we see the social and industrial development of the
USSR. The film is remarkably free of Party meetings, speeches, and
sermonizing. The film featured a strong performance by Alexei Batalov.

BILINSKI — 1953 - Grigori Kozintsev
Patriotic biographical film.

BIRDS OVER THE CITY — 1975 - Sergei Nikonenko
(Maxim Gorki Studios)
World War II drama.

BLACK AND WHITE — 1931 - Ivan Ivanov-Vano (Mezhrabpomfilm)
Feature cartoon.

BLACK MOUNTAIN — 1971 - Alexander Zguridi
Indian-Soviet coproduction. Documentary on nature study made
primarily for youth.

BLACK RUSKS — 1972 - Herbert Rappoport (Lenfilm/DEFA, Potsdam)
East German-Soviet coproduction.

THE BLACK SAIL — 1929 - Sergei Yutkevich (Sovkino-Leningrad)
Story about Young Communists who triumph over individualistic-
minded fisherman during the collectivization and nationalization of the
economy.

BLACK SUN — 1972 - Alexei Speshnev (Belarusfilm)
Story about politics and revolutionary struggle in contemporary
Africa.

BLACK SUNDAY — (See *The Ninth of January*)

THE BLIND COOK — 1961 - Larissa Shepitko
Short film satire.

BLOCK 14 — 1942 - Igor Savchenko
Featurette, *Fighting Film Album No. 9.*

BLOCKADE — 1975 - Mikhail Yershov (Lenfilm)
Released in two parts: Part I — *The Luga Defense Line* and
Part II — *The Pulkovo Meridian.* A color 70mm film about the epic
siege of Leningrad in 1941. Two further parts were in production in
1975.

BLOOD FOR BLOOD, DEATH FOR DEATH — 1941 - Dziga Vertov
War documentary.

BLUE CRAGS — 1942 - Vladimir Braun
Featurette, *Fighting Film Album No. 9.*

THE BLUE EXPRESS — 1929 - Ilya Trauberg (Sovkino-Leningrad)
Also entitled *China Express.*
The story takes place aboard a train and entails a wholesale revolt by Orientals against Westerners. The various tensions among the passengers reflects the struggle against colonialism in China. The film was originally made as a silent, but a sound track and extra scenes were added after its completion.

BLUE ICE — 1970 - Viktor Sokolov
A love story about two Soviet ice figure skaters.

THE BLUE NOTEBOOK — 1963 - Lev Kulidzhanov

BOGDAN KHMELNITSKI — 1941 - Igor Savchenko (Kiev Studios)
A dramatized historical and biographical film about the Ukrainian hetman who led a revolt against Polish rule in 1648 and established an independent Ukraine. In this rich costume drama, with an anti-Polish bias, Khmelnitski appears as a precursor of the Bolsheviks in cementing the policy of friendship between Russians and Ukrainians.

BOLSHOI BALLET '67 — 1967 - Leonid Lavrovski and Alexander Shelenkov (Mosfilm)
Filmed ballet.

BONIFACE'S HOLIDAY — 1965 - Fedor Khitruk (Soyuzmultfilm)
Feature cartoon adapted from the story "Boniface and His Relatives" by Milan Mazourek. The story deals with a circus lion, Boniface, and his adventures when he takes a vacation.

THE BORDER — 1935 - Mikhail Dubson
Story about the Communist underground and class struggle in a small Polish town only four kilometers from the Soviet border.

BORDER TROOPS — 1939 - A. Makovski (Turkmenfilm)
Soviet border troops were often depicted in a large number of films of the 1930s and 1940s in what might well be called the "border"

genre of Soviet film. Today even Soviet film historians wonder about this work in which Soviet troops, while often and loudly singing, manage to catch foreign saboteurs. The film, like many of its kind, pointed up the need to maintain vigilance against foreign intrusions in border or frontier areas.

BORDERLAND — (See *Okraina*)

BORIS GODUNOV — 1955 - Vera Stroyeva (Mosfilm)
Filmed opera in color and based on the work by Mussorgski.

BORN IN FIRE — 1930 - Vladimir Korsh-Sablin (Belgoskino)
Also entitled *Giant*.
Considered one of the better films of early Belorussian cinema. The story is about the revolutionary struggle in Belorussia and is structured in three parts. Korsh used tempo and rhythm of action in an interesting manner. In the first part the poverty and agony of the Belorussian people prior to 1917 is presented slowly. As the story moves through the Revolution and establishment of the Soviet government the tempo picks up in speed and intensity. In its manner, time span, and camera work the film seems to have been influenced by Dovzhenko's *Zvenigora*, though freer of symbolism. The film was specifically made to commemorate the tenth anniversary of the Soviet Belorussian republic.

BOULE DE SUIF — 1934 - Mikhail Romm (Mosfilm)
An adaptation of Maupassant's story with a generous sprinkling of Marxist ideology. The film was praised when it was exhibited at the 1934 Venice Film Exhibition. Originally made as a silent, but a sound track was added prior to its rerelease in 1958.

BOUNTIFUL SUMMER — 1951 - Boris Barnet (Mosfilm)

BOW TO THE FIRE — 1970 [1973] - Tolomush Okeyev
Official release of this film was delayed because of the controversial theme. Okeyev gave the agricultural collectivization campaign of the 1930s a probing second look in a way that would have been unthinkable during Stalin's era.

THE BOY AND THE PIGEON — 1958 -
Andrei Mikhalkov-Konchalovski

BOYS FROM OUR COURTYARD — 1959 - Alexei Saltykov with
Yastrebov (Mosfilm)

THE BRAVE HARE — 1955 - Ivan Ivanov-Vano (Soyuzmultfilm)
Feature cartoon.

THE BRAVE LITTLE TAILOR — 1964 - Ventina and Zenaeda
Brumberg (Soyuzmultfilm)
Feature cartoon.

THE BRAVE NAZAR — 1940 - A. Martirosian (Armenfilm)
Amernian folk comedy and social satire.

THE BRAVE SEVEN — 1936 - Sergei Gerasimov (Lenfilm)
Long praised as a model of heroic realism. This is the story of
seven Komsomols and their hardships in the development of the Soviet
Arctic during the 1930s. Remarkably free of melodrama.

BRAVERY — 1966 - Leonid Makhnach
Documentary.

BREAD — 1918 - Boris Shushkevich and Richard Boleslawski
(Moscow Cinema Committee)
Agitka or agit-prop film.

THE BREAK — 1929 - Georgi Stabovoi and L. Zamkovoi
Story about the revolutionary movement among sailors in the
Russian Navy in 1917.

BREAKUP — 1971 - Alexei Saltykov (Mosfilm)
Based on a play by Boris Lavreniev. Story about the crew of the
cruiser *Aurora* on the eve of the October Revolution.

THE BREATH OF NEW LIFE — 1923 - N. Saltykov (VUFKU -
Odessa Studio)
A theatrical film that was made to show the unity between the
interests of peasants and workers.

THE BREMEN MUSICIANS — 1969 - I. Kovalevskaya (Soyuzmultfilm)
Cartoon fantasy based on a theme by the Brothers Grimm.

THE BRIDEGROOM FROM THE OTHER WORLD — 1958 -
Leonid Gaidai (Gruziyafilm)
Satirical comedy.

BRIEF ENCOUNTERS IN A LONG WAR — 1975 - Abdusalom
Rakhimov and Stanislav Chaplin (Tadzhikfilm)
A love story involving three Tadzhik youths, whose romantic involvement is complicated by World War II. The girl, Gulshot, joins the air force while her beloved Rustam becomes a war correspondent. The second boy, Umar, observes their lives and nobly bears his unfulfilled love for Gulshot.

BRIGADE COMMANDER IVANOV — 1923 - Alexander Razumni
(Proletkino) — Also entitled *The Beauty and The Bolshevik*.
Lenin is reported to have walked out before the finish of this film because he thought its propaganda value was nil. This is an antireligious story in theme in which a Red Army commander persuades a priest's daughter to marry him without a religious ceremony. First seen in the United States in 1928.

BRIGHT ROAD — 1940 - Grigori Alexandrov (Mosfilm)
Occasionally entitled or cited as *Tanya*.
A musical comedy about a young Soviet girl who attains happiness as a leading Stakhanovite worker. The film gave a true representation of life in a Soviet provincial city of the late 1930s. In a severely edited version the film had modest success in the United States.

BROTHER OF A HERO — 1940 - Mark Donskoi (Soyuzdetfilm)

THE BROTHERS KARAMAZOV — 1969 - Ivan Pyriev (Mosfilm)
Pyriev's last film. Based on Dostoevski's novel. Widely exhibited abroad, but undistinguished because of a slow, plodding style.

BRUISED BY THE STORMS OF LIFE — 1918 - Iosif Soifer
(Merkazor)

BRUSSELS 1958 – 1958 - Roman Grigoriev (Central Documentary Studios)
   Documentary on world's fair.

BUDAPEST – 1945 - Vasili Belayev (Central Newsreel Studios)
   Documentary on the Soviet capture of Budapest and contained some good segments on Soviet air operations.

BUILDING BLOCKS – 1925 - L. Obolenski and Mikhail Doller

BUKOVINA – *UKRAINIAN EARTH* – 1940 - Alexander Dovzhenko, supervisor; Yulia Solntseva and Lazar Bodik co-directors (Kiev Film Studios)
   Documentary on the annexation of Bukovina to the USSR 1940.

BULAT-BATYR – 1928 - Yuri Tarich (Belgoskino)
   A historical drama about the Tatars who fought along side Emelyan Pugachev during his revolt against Catherine II.

BULGANIN – 1946 - Roman Grigoriev (Central Documentary Studios)
   Script by Ilya Ehrenburg. A biographical film tribute to Stalin's then Minister of Defense.

THE BUSINESSMEN – 1963 - Leonid Gaidai (Gruziyafilm)
   Comedy and social satire.

BUYING A DADDY – 1963 - Ilya Frez (Maxim Gorki Studios)
Also entitled *Dimka*.
   Story about a five-year old boy who sets out to buy himself a father with only twenty kopecks in his pocket.

BY THE BLUEST OF SEAS – 1936 - Boris Barnet and S. Mardanov (Azerkino and Mezhrabpomfilm)
   A light-hearted, lyrical story about a triangular romance within a fishing collective on the Caspian Sea.

BY THE LAKE – 1969 - Sergei Gerasimov (Maxim Gorki Studios)
   Winner of the jury prize at the 1970 Karlovy Vary Film Festival. A contemporary story about a conflict between Soviet biologists and

engineers who want to construct a factory on the shores of Lake Baikal. Based in part on actual events, the film depicts the concern over environmental safeguards and pollution in the USSR.

BY THE LAW — (See *Dura Lex*)

BY THE PIKE'S DECREE — 1938 - Alexander Rou (Mosfilm)
A comedy based on motifs from Russian folk tales and proved very popular. Rou was the only film-maker to venture into this particular genre of comedy.

CANDIDATE FOR PRESIDENT — 1924 - Pyotr Chardynin (VUFKU)
Also entitled *Not Caught-No Thief.*
Satire on the capitalist West. The story focuses on the relationship of money to politics as seen in a partnership between a scheming banker and smooth political adventurist.

THE CAPRICIOUS PRINCESS — 1969 - Valentina and Zenaeda Brumgerg (Soyuzmultfilm)
Animated fantasy based on a theme by the Brothers Grimm.

THE CAPTAIN'S DAUGHTER — 1928 - Yuri Tarich (Belgoskino)
1959 - V. Kaplunovski (Mosfilm)
Based on the story by Alexander Pushkin. The drama is about Emelyan Pugachev and his revolt against Catherine II.

THE CAREER OF LIEUTENANT GOPP — 1942 - N. Sadkovich
Featurette, *Fighting Film Album No. 11.*

CARNIVAL NIGHT — 1957 - Eldar Ryazanov (Mosfilm)
Light musical comedy about Soviet youth.

CAROUSEL — 1971 - Mikhail Shveitser (Mosfilm)

CARROT HEAD — 1961 - Ilya Frez (Maxim Gorki Studios)
Children's comedy.

THE CASE OF THE MURDER OF TARIEL MKLAVADZE — 1925 - Ivan Perestiani (Goskinprom-Gruziya)

Based on the story "A Knight of Our Time" by E. Ninoshvili. Dealt with the difficulties of Georgian peasants in the late 19th century and social injustices arising out of class differences. The film enjoyed a good deal of popularity with Russian and Georgian audiences.

CAST IRON — 1964 - Otar Yoseliani (Gruziyafilm)

THE CAUCASIAN PRISONER — 1967 - Leonid Gaidai (Gruziyafilm)

Georgian comedy and social satire. Also entitled *Kidnapping Caucasian Style*.

CAVALIER OF THE GOLDEN STAR — 1950 - Yuli Raizman (Mosfilm)

Story about the conflict between individual happiness and social duty to the collective community. À decorated war hero joins a collective farm and soon puts aside notions of personal interest for the sake of collective improvement and the construction of a power station. An excellent performance by Sergei Bondarchuk.

THE CAVALRY LEAPS — 1929 - N. Beresnev

Adventure and action thriller about a Red Army cavalry unit that battles a White force for control of a strategic bridge.

CEMENT — 1927 - Vladimir Vilner (VUFKU - Odessa Studio)

Based on the novel by F. Gladkov. A drama about the struggle of workers to rehabilitate the national economy in the years immediately after the Civil War.

CHADRA — 1927 - Mikhail Averbakh (Uzbekgoskino)

Filmed during the so-called "offensive" period of the campaign to emancipate and enfranchise Uzbek women. The film was intended also to commemorate the tenth anniversary of the October Revolution in Uzbekistan. In the story the heroine, Lola, leaves her husband to whom she had been sold as a young bride. Lola is caught and beaten by her husband, but she is later rescued by the police who jail her husband.

THE CHAIRMAN — 1964 - Alexei Saltykov (Mosfilm)
A huge box-office success and one of the more controversial Soviet films of the 1960s. The story depicted life on a Russian kolkhoz in the years immediately after World War II and centered on the efforts of the farm chairman, Mikhail Ulianov, who wrestles against obstructionists and problems of daily life. The film depicted the problems of the late Stalinist era and the need to return to Leninist principles. Despite the controversy over this film Ulianov received a Lenin Prize for his acting.

CHALIAPIN — 1972 - Mark Donskoi
Biographical film of the Russian singer who gained international renown in the 1930s when he emigrated from the USSR. Donskoi explores the problems Chaliapin encountered as an emigre.

CHAPAYEV — 1934 - Georgi and Sergei Vasiliev (Lenfilm)
The Vasilievs spent two years in making this film about the legendary, gruff Civil War commander which proved a tremendous success. Stalin was enthusiastic about it and directors rushed to imitate it. The National Association of Critics applauded the film when it was shown in New York in 1935. The film portrayed Chapayev, played by Boris Babochkin, as a warm and human character who becomes more dedicated to Bolshevism as a result of his association with his political commissar, Furmanov. The film was in fact inspired by Furmanov's reminiscences about Chapayev. The highlight of the film was the "psychological attack" by cigar puffing Whites. Neither the Vasilievs nor Babochkin ever again enjoyed as much success. Widely rereleased during World War II and still considered a Soviet classic film.

CHARLES DARWIN — 1960 - Vladimir Shneiderov
Biographical film, mostly about Darwin's work and theories.

CHEREVICHKI — 1927 - Pyotr Chardynin (VUFKU)
1944 - Shapiro and Koshevarova
An adaptation of Gogol's *Christmas Eve*.

CHESS FEVER — 1925 - Vsevolod Pudovkin (Mezhrabpom-Rus)
A satire, with clever editing, on the 1925 World Chess Tournament in Moscow. Many of the tournament players appeared comically, unaware they were being filmed for feature comedy.

The Childhood of Maxim Gorki, Mark Donskoi (British Film Institute)

A CHILD OF THE SUN — 1932 - P. Barkhudarian (Armenkino)
Drama about an Armenian cotton worker, Aram, who emigrates prior to 1917. After working under near feudal conditions in Egypt Aram returns to Soviet Armenia, where he discovers that peasants can find security and happiness only through collective effort.

THE CHILDHOOD OF MAXIM GORKI — 1938 - Mark Donskoi (Soyuzdetfilm)
First part of the Maxim Gorki trilogy. Based on Gorki's autobiographical stories. The story is set in late 19th-century Russia and depicts the hardships of life when Gorki was a child. The film ends when the boy decides to leave home to make his own way in the world.

[See also *Out In The World* and *My Universities.*]

CHILDREN — 1928 - A. Soloviev (VUFKU)

CHILDREN ARE THE FLOWERS OF LIFE — 1919 - Yuri Zheliabushski (VFKO)
Early attempt at popular science film. The work focused on life's beginning and the need for better care of children.

THE CHILDREN OF CAPTAIN GRANT — 1936 - V. Vainshtok
Based on the novel by Jules Verne. Adventure story about an expedition in Patagonia and made primarily for children.

CHILDREN OF THE SOVIET ARCTIC — 1941 - Mark Donskoi
Adapted from the novel by Tikhon Semushkin.

CHILDREN OF THE STORM — 1926 - Friedrich Ermler and Eduard Ioganson (Leningradkino)
Story about the role of Communist youth in the defense of Petrograd during the Civil War.

THE CHILDREN OF VANYUSHIN — 1974 - Yevgeni Tashkov (Mosfilm)

CHILE — HAPPENINGS — 1973 - Roman Karmen (Central Documentary Studios)
Feature documentary on the political events in Chile during the time of its elected Marxist president, Salvador Allende.

CHINA AFLAME — 1925 - Animation Workshop
Political and social cartoon on events in China. Made to show how animation techniques could be used for serious films.

CHINA EXPRESS — (See *The Blue Express*)

CHINA IN CONFLICT — 1939 - Roman Karmen (Central Newsreel Studios)
War documentary.

A CHOICE OF GOAL — 1974 - Igor Talankin (Mosfilm)
Drama about Soviet nuclear physicists who reluctantly decide to create a nuclear deterrent after the Americans drop the atomic bomb on Hiroshima. The story stresses the ethical struggles among Soviet and foreign scientists in their attempts to determine the correct choice of making a nuclear weapon or not.

CHRONICLE OF ONE DAY — 1963 - Vitautas Zalakevicius (Lithuanian Film Studio)

CHRONICLE WITHOUT SENSATION — 1966 - Viktor Lisakovich
Documentary.

THE CIGARETTE GIRL FROM MOSSELPROM — 1924 - Yuri Zheliabushski (Meshrabpom-Rus)
Satire about Moscow life and remnants of bourgeois society during the NEP period. The story focuses on several class enemies who fall in love with a cigarette girl, played by Yulia Solntseva, and find misfortune waiting for them. One of the better films of its time.

CINDERELLA — 1959 - Rostislav Zakharov and Alexander Rou (Mosfilm)
A filmed performance by the Bolshoi Ballet.

CINE-CONCERT FOR THE 25TH ANNIVERSARY OF THE RED ARMY — 1943 - Yefim Dzigan, Sergei Gerasimov, and Mikhail Kalatozov

THE CIRCASSIANS OF SUNNY TADZHIKISTAN — 1935 -
A. Stepanov (Tadzhik-kino)
Documentary about Tadzhik horsemen.

THE CIRCASSIANS OF SUNNY TURKMENISTAN — 1936 -
A. Makovski (Turkmenfilm)
Documentary.

THE CIRCLE — 1927 - Yuli Raizman (Gosvoyenkino)
Short comedy.

CIRCUS — 1936 - Grigori Alexandrov (Mosfilm)
A musical comedy, though laced with propaganda. The story features an American woman who flees to the USSR to escape racial bigotry in the United States.

CITIES AND YEARS — 1930 - Yevgeni Chervyakov (Soyuzkino-Leningrad) — 1973 - Alexander Zarkhi (Mosfilm)
Drama about the Russian Civil War and the Bolshevik struggle against occupying German forces. Chervyakov's film contains a scene of advancing German troops that is occasionally viewed as a precursor of the "psychological attack" sequence in *Chapayev.*

THE CITIES CHANGE THEIR FACE — 1958 - Leonid Makhnach
Documentary on Soviet urban development.

THE CITY OF CRAFTSMEN — 1966 - V. Bychkov (Belarusfilm)
A tale about medieval times based on the play by T. Gabbe.

CITY OF GREAT DESTINY — 1960 - Ilya Kopalin
(Central Documentary Studios)

CLEAR PONDS — 1966 - Alexei Sakharov (Mosfilm)

CLEAR SKY — 1961 - Grigori Chukhrai (Mosfilm)
Received grand prize at the 1961 Moscow Film Festival despite its controversial theme. The film made open reference to the negative aspects during the Stalin era. The story is about a Soviet pilot who is shot down during World War II and becomes a prisoner of war. After

his return to the USSR the hero is thrown out of the Party and suffers social disgrace. Later, after Stalin's death, he is rehabilitated and readmitted to the Party but not before suffering internal turmoil.

CLEVERNESS — 1973 - A. Haidarov (Kazakhfilm)
Animated. Based on a Central Asian folk tale about man's search for truth.

THE CLOUDBURST — 1929 - Ivan Kavaleridze (VUFKU-Odessa Studio)
A controversial film about the life of Ukrainian serfs from the 18th to the 20th century. The work was a remarkable piece of art, using film as a plastic sculpture. This and the use of symbolism caused Kavaleridze a good bit of trouble from critics. Kavaleridze was acknowledged as talented but was not given the same high regard as he is today.

THE COLLEGIATE REGISTRAR — (See *The Stationmaster*)

THE COLT — 1959 - V. Fetin (Mosfilm)
Based on the story by Mikhail Sholokhov.

COMEDIENNE — 1923 - Alexander Ivanovski

COMING OF AGE — 1935 - B. Shreiber (Sovetskaya Belarus)
A Civil War drama about the Bolshevik struggle for power in a provincial Belorussian town.

COMMANDER OF THE RESERVE — (See *Sixty Days*)

COMMOTION — 1971 - Yuri Erzinkian (Armenfilm)
A comedy of errors adapted from a classical Armenian play.

THE COMMUNIST — 1958 - Yuli Raizman (Mosfilm)
Story about the first years of the new Soviet state and the strong spirit of a young Communist who overcomes the severe hardships of economic dislocation.

COMPETITION — 1963 - B. Mansurov (Turkmenfilm)
Drama about the legendary Turkmenian hero, Shukur-bakhshi, at

the turn of the century. The story focused on the divisive social conflicts among Turkmenians and the revolutionary movement. Received first prize at the Exhibition of Films of the Central Asian Republics.

COMPLAINTS BOOK, PLEASE — 1964 - Eldar Ryazanov (Mosfilm)
Satire about contemporary Soviet society.

THE COMPOSER GLINKA — 1952 - Girgori Alexandrov (Mosfilm)
Biographical and patriotic film.

[See also *Glinka*.]

COMRADE ABRAM — 1919 - Alexander Razumni (Moscow Cinema Committee)
An agitka about a Jew who joins the Bolsheviks during the Civil War after surviving tsarist pogroms.

COMRADE BERLIN — 1968 - Roman Karmen (Central Documentary Studios)
Feature documentary about life and contemporary development in East Berlin.

CONCERT — 1940 - A. Andreevski under supervision of Semyon Ivanov (Stereo Studio)
One of the first truly successful stereoscopic films for which special viewing glasses were not needed.

CONCERT VALSE — 1940 - Ilya Trauberg (Lenfilm)
Concert musical.

CONGRESTION — 1918 - Alexander Panteleev, D. Pashkovski and A. Dolinov (Petrokino)
Propaganda comedy made in only eight days.

CONQUERED SEAS — 1959 - Roman Karmen (Central Documentary Studios)
Documentary.

THE CONQUEST OF THE LAND — 1930 - V. Vainshtok
(Sovetskaya Belarus)
   Documentary on the economic benefits to be derived from the swamp drainage program in Belorussia.

CONSCIENCE — 1966 - Sergei Alexeiev (Mosfilm)

CONSPIRACY OF THE DEAD — 1930 - Semyon Timoshenko
   Story about the Bolshevik defense of Petrograd in 1919.

CONSPIRACY OF THE DOOMED — 1950 - Mikhail Kalatozov
(Mosfilm)
   Espionage and intrigue abound in this Cold War drama about a conspiracy between the Vatican and American intelligence to undermine communism in an East European country. The focus is on an American ambassador who plans to murder a Communist Party leader, but the plot is exposed and the supporters of the Marshall Plan are defeated.

CONTINENT AFLAME — 1970 - Roman Karmen
(Central Documentary Studios)
   Documentary on political unrest in Latin America; in two parts.

CONVICTS — 1936 - Yevgeni Chervyakov
   Drama about the rehabilitation of former class enemies against the background of the construction of the White Sea Canal. The system of retraining is seen as beneficial as former enemies are turned into useful Soviet citizens.

COSMIC VOYAGE — 1936 - V. Zhuravlev
   The Russian rocket scientist K.E. Tsiolkovski was technical consultant for this film. The story is about a young boy and his dreams about man's flight to the moon.

COSSACK BEYOND THE DANUBE — 1937 - Ivan Kavaleridze
(VUFKU)
   A film opera based on the work by Gulak-Artemovski.

COSSACKS OF THE KUBAN — 1950 - Ivan Pyriev (Mosfilm)
A musical comedy that portrays life on a kolkhoz in light-hearted fashion.

COUNTERPLAN — 1933 - Friedrich Ermler and Sergei Yutkevich (Rosfilm-Leningrad) — Also entitled *Shame*.
Made during the first enthusiastic and optimistic five-year plan for the industrialization of the USSR. The story dealt with industrial workers and the need to increase production while at the same time showing generational differences among workers. The new Soviet man in this film is not portrayed in heroic terms but in appealing human terms. Ermler directed the actors representing the older generation while Yutkevich worked with the younger actors. One of the better Soviet films of the 1930s.

THE COUNTRY CALLS — 1936 - Alexander Macheret
A story about Soviet pilots and the need to build a strong air force. Largely overshadowed by Raizman's *Aviators*.

COUNTRY DOCTOR — 1952 - Sergei Gerasimov (Mosfilm)
Drama about the life and work of a woman doctor in a provincial town in Siberia. Initially she is distrusted by her patients because of her ideas but manages in the end to gain their confidence.

A COUNTRY OF HAPPINESS — 1939 - G. Balasanian and L. Isaakian (Armenfilm)
Documentary on Armenian life and customs.

THE COUNTRY TEACHER — 1948 - Mark Donskoi (Soyuzdetfilm)
Also entitled *The Village Teacher*.
One of Donskoi's best and much admired by critics. Vera Maretskaya gave a warm and appealing performance as a woman who selflessly devotes forty years of her life to teaching rural children after her revolutionary fiance is killed by tsarist police in 1914.

THE COUPLE — (See *There Was An Old Man and An Old Woman*)

COURT OF HONOR — 1948 - Abram Room (Mosfilm)
Patriotism during the Cold War was the framework for this drama

about two Soviet scientists who relay scientific information to American counterparts. They are exposed by their Soviet colleagues and considered traitors.

THE COVERED WAGON — 1927 - Oleg Frelikh (Uzbekgoskino)
Story about the Civil War in Uzbekistan done with a mixture of satire and humor.

CRADLE SONG — 1959 - Moisei Kalik (Mosfilm)

THE CRANES ARE FLYING — 1957 - Mikhail Kalatozov (Mosfilm)
Considered as one of the highpoints in the post-Stalin renascence of Soviet cinema as well as an artistic triumph for Kalatozov. Received grand prize for acting at 1958 Cannes Film Festival. The photography was considered outstanding. This wartime love story was presented with an emotional honesty that was lacking in many films of the Stalin era. In the story the young heroine loses her fiance who dies in battle and through adultery marries his cousin. The work was notably free of any moralizing or political harangues.

CREATION CANNOT BE BOUGHT — 1918 - Nikandr Turkin (Antik)
An adaptation of Jack London's *Martin Eden.*

CRIME AND PUNISHMENT — 1970 - Lev Kulidzhanov (Mosfilm)
Considered a good adaptation of Dostoevski's novel.

THE CIME OF PRINCESS SHIRVANSKAYA — 1926 -
Ivan Perestiani (Goskinprom-Gruziya)
Adventure thriller that was an unsuccessful sequel to *Little Red Devils.*

CROSS AND MAUSER — 1925 - Vladimir Gardin (VUFKU)
One of the more ambitious antireligious dramas. The story is about Catholic priests who oppose the Bolsheviks and cast as instigators of pogroms.

CROSSROAD — 1963 - Shaken Aimanov (Kazakhfilm)

THE CROWN OF THE RUSSIAN EMPIRE — 1971 - Edmond Keosaian
A popular drama about four youngsters and their daring adventures during the Russian Civil War. An updated spin-off from Perestiani's memorable *Little Red Devils.*

CRUELTY — 1959 - Vladimir Skuibin (Mosfilm)
Based on the novel by P. Nilin who also wrote the script. The story is about a vestigial group of Whites in Siberia in 1923 and the campaign against it by a Bolshevik force. The film was not entirely free of controversy, yet Soviet commentators admired the work for its honest portrayal of the problem of rehabilitating former White Guards in the years immediately following the Civil War.

THE CRUISER 'VARANGIAN' — 1946 - Viktor Eisimont (Mosfilm)
Stalin Prize film. Drama about the heroism of the crew of the Russian cruiser *Varangian* during the Russo-Japanese War of 1904-05. The film emphasized naval traditions and patriotism while also reviving a Russian naval song of 1905.

CRUSADE — 1930 - B. Antonovski
Antireligious cartoon film.

CUBA TODAY — 1960 - Roman Karmen (Central Documentary Studios)
A Cuban-Soviet coproduction. Documentary on Cuban life following Fidel Castro's ascension to power.

CZECHOSLOVAKIA — 1946 - Ilya Kopalin (Central Newsreel Studio)
Documentary on postwar reconstruction.

THE DAM — 1932 - Vladimir Petrov
Based on a factual episode, the film dealt with a Rumanian attempt to divert the flow of the Danube River and seize Soviet territory.

DANGEROUS GAMES — 1974 - Veljie Kiasper (Tallinfilm)
Drama about the resistance movement in Nazi-occupied Estonia.

DAREDEVIL — 1919 - M. Narokov and Nikandr Turkin
(Moscow Cinema Committee)
Civil War *agitka* written by V. Lunacharski.

DARIKO — 1937 - Siko Dolidze (Goskinprom-Gruziya)
Based on motifs from the stories of the 19th-century Georgian writer Egnate Ninoshvili. Drama about the rising revolutionary spirit of the Georgian people as reflected in the tragic life of a young woman, Dariko. The cast included Sergo Zakariadze as Simon.

THE DAUGHTER-IN-LAW — 1971 - Khodzhakuli Narliev
(Turkmenfilm)
A drama about World War II and the ties between soldiers and their homes. The story focuses on a young war widow who finds inner strength to go on with life despite her great loss. Good direction prevented the film from being too maudlin.

DAUGHTER OF A PARTISAN — 1935 - Mayevskaya and Masliukov
(Ukrainfilm)
A film made primarily for children. The story is about young Communists who succeed in exposing saboteurs.

DAUGHTER OF A SAINT — 1931 - Oleg Frelikh (Uzbekgoskino)
A melodrama which exposed the social and religious hypocrisy of the old way of life in Uzbekistan. As if in answer to their prayers a childless couple give birth to a daughter. Unknown to the father, the child is the result of the mother's assignation with a holy man. Later the mother, Khakima, is abused when the truth is discovered and this leads to her protest against the old, hypocritical way of life. Reportedly Frelikh was heavily influenced by the work of Pudovkin when he made this film.

A DAUGHTER OF GILIAN — 1928 - Leo Mur (Azerkino)
Story about social struggle and love in the Persian province of Gilian.

A DAUGHTER OF THE MOTHERLAND — 1937 -
Vladimir Korsh-Sablin (Sovetskaya Belarus)
The leading character is Pasha, a young chairwoman of a

collective farm who succeeds in discovering and defeating enemies of the Soviet state. One of a large number of films that dealt with the need to maintain vigilance against domestic enemies.

DAUGHTER OF THE STEPPES — 1955 - Shaken Aimanov (Kazakhfilm)
A lyrical romance.

DAVID BEK — 1943 - Amo Bek-Nazarov (Erevan Studio)
Biographical film about the dedicated Armenian national hero who led his people in the struggle against Persian rule in the 18th century.

DAWN OVER RUSSIA — 1948, banned - Sergei Yutkevich (Mosfilm)
Also entitled *Light Over Russia*.
Based on the play *Kremlin Chimes* by Nikolai Pogodin and dealt with Lenin's plan for wide scale electrification of Soviet Russia. Officials never gave a full explanation for the banning and Yutkevich reportedly experienced difficulties in his career for a time.

DAWN OVER THE NEMAN — 1952 - Alexander Faintsimmer
Cold War intrigue. The Vatican plots to ruin the harvests of Polish collective farms by distributing poisoned seeds and aiding anti-Communist groups.

DAY AFTER DAY — 1971 - Otar Yoseliani (Gruziyafilm)
A light comedy about Georgian life which proved very popular.

A DAY IN A NEW WORLD — 1940 - Roman Karmen and Mikhail Slutski (Central Newsreel Studio)
Inspired by an idea by Maxim Gorki this documentary shows ordinary occurrences in the daily life of the Soviet people. Filmed by one hundred cameramen throughout the USSR on August 24, 1940.

A DAY OF HAPPINESS — 1964 - Iosif Heifitz (Mosfilm)

THE DAY OF THE VICTORIOUS COUNTRY — 1947 - Ilya Kopalin
(Central Newsreel Studio)
  Documentary.

A DAY OF WAR — 1942 - Mikhail Slutski (Central Newsreel Studio)
  A well edited war documentary incoporating film footage from
one hundred cameramen recording a single day's combat along the
entire Soviet-German front.

THE DAY THE WAR ENDED — 1960 - Yakov Segel
(Maxim Gorki Studios) — Also entitled *First Day of Peace*.
  Drama about the end of World War II.

DAYS AND NIGHTS — 1945 - Alexander Stolper (Mosfilm)
  A faithful and popular adaptation of Konstantin Simonov's novel
of the same name. The story is about Red Army soldiers and officers,
their thoughts and anxieties, during the Battle of Stalingrad.

DAYS OF WORK — 1940 - B. Shreiber (Mosfilm/Sovetskaya Belarus)
  Story about Soviet Air Force pilots and their activities on the eve
of German invastion. Not as successful as Raizman's earlier *Aviators*.
The film stressed the need for defense preparedness.

DEAD SEASON — 1968 - Savva Kulish
  Espionage and suspense thriller. Story about preparations for
bacteriological warfare in an unnamed country.

DEAD SOULS — 1961 - Leonid Trauberg (Mosfilm)
  Based on Gogol's novel and not very successful.

THE DEADLY ENEMY — 1971 - Yevgeni Matveyev (Mosfilm)
  War drama based on two stories by Mikhail Sholokhov.

DEATH BAY — 1926 - Abram Room (Goskino)
  A melodrama about the Russian Civil War based on a story by
Alexei Novikov-Priboi. The story was about a ship's machinist who
scuttles his ship to prevent its capture by the Whites. The film was very
popular and critics liked Room's direction of the actors in portraying
fully developed characters.

THE DEATH CONVEYOR — (See *Assembly Line of Death*)

THE DEATH RAY — 1925 - Lev Kuleshov (Goskino)
An espionage drama about a capitalist attempt to steal the plans for a new secret weapon invented by a Soviet scientist. Proved to be profitable, but Soviet critics at the time found it deficient in ideology. The cast featured Vsevolod Pudovkin as the sinister abbot Revo. The film is sometimes regarded as a reflection of Kuleshov's imitation of American film technique.

THE DEBUT — 1971 - Gleb Panfilov (Mosfilm)
Story about a young actress who is more fortunate in her career than in love.

THE DECEMBRISTS — 1926 - Alexander Ivanovski (Leningradkino)
A costume and psychological drama about the 1825 Decembrist Revolt in Russia. A critical and commercial failure. The film was produced at a reported cost of 340,000 rubles and did not recover expenditures after two years of exhibition.

DEEP RAID — 1937 - A. Malakhov
Story about Soviet preparedness against possible aggressors.

DEFEAT OF JAPAN — 1945 - Iosif Heifitz and Alexander Zarkhi (Central Newsreel Studio)
Stalin Prize film. Edited largely from newsreel footage, the film emphasized the Soviet role in the war against Japan in 1945.

DEFEAT OF THE GERMAN ARMIES NEAR MOSCOW — 1942 - Ilya Kopalin and L. Varlamov (Central Newsreel Studio) — Also entitled *Moscow Strikes Back*.
The film depicts the Soviet Army's winter counteroffensive of 1941/42 at Moscow. One of the best Soviet wartime documentary films and was widely exhibited in the United States. Reissued in 1975 during the commemoration activities of the thirtieth anniversary of the Allied victory over Nazi Germany.

DEFENSE OF TSARITSYN — 1942 - Georgi and Sergei Vasiliev (Lenfilm) — Also entitled *Fortress On the Volga.*

The film was actually completed just before the German invasion in 1941, but not released until 1942. This Civil War drama about the crucial battle for Tsaritsyn (Stalingrad) depicted Stalin as the genius behind the Bolshevik defense.

A DEGREE OF RISK — 1968 - Ilya Averbakh (Lenfilm) — Also entitled *The Risk.*

Based on a novel by Nikolai Amosov this drama deals with a heart surgeon and the life-and-death decisions that confront him. His professional skills are put to a severe test when a close friend becomes a patient. The film had a high degree of realism in portraying a hospital atmosphere, possibly because Averbakh himself was a former surgeon.

DEPOT FOR CATASTROPHES — 1941 - R. Perelstein and L. Altsev
Featurette, *Fighting Film Album No. 7.*

DESCENDANT OF GENGHIS KHAN — 1928 - Vsevolod Pudovkin (Mezhrabpomfilm) — Also entitled *Heir of Genghis Khan* and *Storm Over Asia.*

One of Pudovkin's finest and most exotic films. This revolutionary drama centers on a young Mongol who is thought to be descended from the great Genghis Khan. Imperialists, obviously British, seek to use the young man to further their expansionist schemes in the Far East. However, the young man soon turns against the foreigners and the final scene shows a mounted Mongolian force that symbolizes a growing storm to sweep away the imperialists. Filmed on location in the Buriat-Mongolian Republic. The work includes some good scenes of the Festival of the Lamas. Because of foreign protests the word 'British' was deleted from the titles of this silent film. Pudovkin enjoyed a good deal of critical acclaim for this work. A limited sound track was added when the film was technically refurbished in 1949.

THE DESERTER — 1933 - Vsevolod Pudovkin (Mezhrabpomfilm)

Pudovkin blended a documentary style into this story about a German dockworker who leaves Nazi Germany and emigrates to the USSR. Later he decides to return to his native country in order to participate in the political struggle against the Nazis. The film was

Pudovkin's least successful and was removed from exhibition after eight days. Filming had begun on location in Hamburg in 1932 prior to Hitler's rise to power. By the time filming resumed in Odessa and Leningrad Pudovkin had to revise the work to account for changing conditions. Despite revisions the film was criticized for its intellectualism and bore a poor resemblance to actual events.

DESTINY OF A MAN — 1959 - Sergei Bondarchuk (Mosfilm)
This film marked Bondarchuk's directorial debut and in the lead role as Andrei Sokolov. This may well be Bondarchuk's best work as a director and actor. Bondarchuk received a Lenin Prize for his performance in this adaptation of a story by Mikhail Sholokhov. Sokolov is the hero of the story, a prisoner of war. After escaping from a prison camp and humiliation he learns of the death of his wife and children during the war. He must start life anew and adopts a homeless orphan. Bondarchuk brought great poignancy to his role and later indicated he wanted to plumb the depths of the Russian soul. The theme in this film would have been unthinkable during the time of Stalin, who looked upon prisoners of war as traitors. Received a grand prize at the 1959 Moscow Film Festival. The film is noteworthy for its strong emphasis on humanism.

THE DEVIL'S WHEEL — 1926 - Grigori Kozintsev and Leonid Trauberg (Leningradkino)
Sometimes cited as *Sailor From The 'Aurora'*. Unusual photography gave this work a near bizarre style and at times approached expressionism. The story dealt with underworld figures who victimized the people of Petrograd during the Civil War.

THE DIAMOND ARM — 1968 - Leonid Gaidai (Gruziyafilm)

THE DIFFICULT HAPPINESS — 1958 - Alexander Stolper (Mosfilm)

DIMKA — (See *Buying A Daddy*)

DINA DZA-DZU — 1926 - Yuri Zheliabushski (Azerkino)
Ethnographical film about the province of Svanetia.
[See also *Svanetia* and *Salt For Svanetia*.]

Destiny Of A Man, Sergei Bondarchuk (Artkino Pictures)

DIPLOMATIC POUCH — 1927 - Alexander Dovzhenko (VUFKU)
One of the so-called "Red detective" mystery thrillers that were much liked by Soviet audiences. The story is about a Soviet diplomatic courier and the theft of Soviet state papers which are recovered. Dovzhenko himself played a small role in the film.

DIPLOMATIC SECRET — 1923 - Boris Chaikovski
A "Red detective" mystery thriller.

THE DIPLOMATS — 1968 - Viktor Lisakovich (Central Documentary Studios)
Documentary on recent diplomatic history.

THE DIRECTOR — 1970 - Alexei Saltykov (Mosfilm)
Filming started in 1965 but production was halted for a few years after the original lead actor, Yevgeni Urbanski, died in a car accident in 1966. The story deals with a Baltic Fleet sailor who eventually becomes the manager of the first automobile plant in Soviet Central Asia.

DIRK — 1954 - Vladimir Vengerov

THE DISTANT BRIDE — 1948 - Yevgeni Ivanov-Barkov (Ashkhabad Studio)
Light, fanciful romance.

DO I LOVE YOU? — 1934 - Sergei Gerasimov
An intelligent probing into moral and ethical aspects of love, marriage and family life in Soviet society. After the rather free-wheeling approach to life styles in the 1920s this film signalled a call for greater morality and traditional values in social life.

DR. AI BOLIT — 1967 - Rolan Bykov (Mosfilm)
An allegory on the eternal struggle between good and evil.

A DOG AND A CAT — 1938 - Lev Atamanov (Armenfilm)
Feature cartoon based on a classical story from Armenian literature by O. Tumanian.

THE DOMESTIC AGITATOR — 1920 - Yuri Zheliabushski (VFKO)

An *agitka* about the poverty of rural life. The photography of this film was almost unusual and innovative for its time. Zheliabushski strove to give the work a Gogolesque visual flavor. Now considered one of the transitional works between the simple crude *agitka* and true theatrical film of Soviet cinema.

DONBAS SYMPHONY — (See *Enthusiasm*)

DON DIEGO AND PELAGEA — 1928 - Yakov Protazanov (Mezhrabpom-Rus)

An example of Soviet political satire at which Protazanov was so skillful, though often misunderstood by Soviet critics. The story is about a petty bureaucrat who causes the arrest of an old woman for a minor breach of the law. In the end the incident is happily resolved when a group of Komsomols come to the aid of Pelagea. This theme about pricking the balloon of overblown bureaucrats was revived after 1953.

DON QUIXOTE — 1957 - Grigori Kozintsev (Lenfilm)

An artistic comeback for Kozintsev. This was a well made and successful adaptation of the novel by Cervantes. The main role was played by the venerable film actor Nikolai Cherkasov of *Alexander Nevski* and *Ivan the Terrible* fame.

DONETS MINERS — 1951 - Leonid Lukov

This film brought the director back into good graces following the banning and severe criticism of his earlier *Great Life*. The story centers around coal miners and their endeavors to increase production. Stalin is their benefactor.

DON'T GRIEVE! — 1970 - Georgi Daneliya (Gruziyafilm)
Also entitled *Cheer Up!*

A light comedy adapted from the novel *My Uncle Benjamin* by Claude Tiller.

THE DOOM OF THE SQUADRON — 1966 - Vladimir Dovgan (Alexander Dovzhenko Studios)

THE DOWERLESS — 1936 - Yakov Protazanov (Mezhrabpomfilm)
Also entitled *Without Dowry*.
    Based on the play by N.A. Ostrovski. A satire depicting the improved status of women in the Soviet era as opposed to tsarist times.

THE DREAM — 1943 - Mikhail Romm (Mosfilm)
    Commercially unsuccessful and critically unnoticed when it was released two years after its completion. The story takes place in eastern Poland at about the time of its annexation to the USSR in 1939. This was a condemnation of the shallowness of beourgeois life and morals, and unrealized hopes. The characters were fully developed and Romm attempted to reveal their psychological depths and motivations. Unfortunately the Soviet people were engaged in a life or death war and a classical plot on the evils of capitalist life held little immediate relevance for them. Today Sovet film historians give the work high marks but acknowledge that its timing was all wrong.

DREAM IN THE HAND — 1941 - Ya. Nekrasov
    Featurette, *Fighting Film Album No. 1.*

THE DREAM KNIGHT — 1964 - Vadim Derbenev (Moldovafilm)

THE DREAM OF TARAS — 1919 - Yuri Zheliabushski
    An *agitka* about a Red Army soldier during the Civil War who goes AWOL after he dreams he is in the tsarist army. The film was intended to show the need for military discipline.

THE DREAMERS — 1934 - D. Maryan
    This drama came out as Stalin was making his final preparations to eliminate all opposition to him. The destinies of two brothers, Andrei and Sergei, are traced from the Civil War to the Five Year Plan. Andrei becomes more devoted to the Party while Sergei becomes a member of the Party opposition. Maryan posed the question Is Man to serve the Revolution or is the Revolution to serve Man? Andrei was the true hero.

DREAMS OF LOVE — 1971 - Marton Keleti
    A Hungarian-Soviet coproduction that was a dramatized biography of the composer Franz Liszt.

DREAMS WITHOUT END — 1965 - Viktor Lisakovich
(Central Documentary Studios)

A DROP OF POISON — 1965 - Leonid Makhnach
Feature documentary.

DUBROVSKI — 1936 - Alexander Ivanovski
Based on a work by Alexander Pushkin. The writer of the first
script, Adrian Piotrovski, was arrested and exiled as his work was
politically suspect.

THE DUEL — 1923 - Vladimir Gardin (VUFKU) — Also entitled *The
Last Stake of Mr. Enniok.*
Based on the novel *The Life of Gnorr* by A. Grin. An allegory on
the world struggle between the proletariat and the bourgeoisie. The
protagonists are Enniok, the capitalist, and Gnorr, the worker, who
have a final confrontation in a game of cards in which the stake is the
life of the loser. Later Enniok's deceit is discovered by workers who rise
in revolt and kill him. The film was liked by critics at the time for the
quality of the acting performances but on the whole found the style
too reminiscent of bourgeois melodrama.

THE DUEL — 1944 - Vladimir Legoshin (Soyuzdetfilm)
Wartime drama about the selfless struggle of Soviet intelligence
agents against the Nazi Gestapo.

THE DUEL — 1957 - Vladimir Petrov — 1961 - T. Bereżantseva and
L. Rudnik (Mosfilm)
Film adaptations of the story by Anton Chekhov.

DURA LEX — 1926 - Lev Kuleshov (Goskino) — Also entitled
By The Law.
Based on Jack London's *The Unexpected.* Soviet and Western
critics generally agree that this is Kuleshov's best film. The story is
about a husband and wife and their manservant who undergo inner
turmoil as a result of their complicity in a murder. Then the husband
and wife decide, strictly "by the law", that the manservant must be
hung for his crime. This allegory on the hypocrisy of capitalistic and
bourgeois life was made on one of the smallest of Soviet film budgets.

Despite its avant-garde style it was one of the most well received of all
Soviet films abroad, though it was not shown in English-speaking
countries until the late 1930s.

DURSUN — 1940 - Yevgeni Ivanov-Barkov (Turkmenfilm)
A popular film and one of the few from Turkmenian cinema that
enjoyed critical success. The heroine of the story is Dursun, who faces a
problem in her marriage when she becomes an outstanding agricultural
worker. Her husband Nuri becomes jealous and then is unable to accept
the fact that he is her subordinate in a work unit. In a fit of pique Nuri
leaves, but after a while they are reunited. The story pointed up the
need for men to readjust their thinking in view of women's economic
equality in Soviet life.

DZHAMBUL — 1952 - Yefim Dzigan (Alma-Ata Studio)
A dramatized biography of Dzhambul Dzhabaev the Kazakh poet
who glorified Stalin in his writings.

DZHAMBUL-ATA — 1935 - I. Kolsanov (Kazakhfilm)
Documentary about the Kazakh poet.

DZHUT — 1932 - M. Karostin (Vostokfilm)
Story about the awakening of class consciousness and revolutionary movement in Kazakhstan.

EACH DAY OF DR. KALINNIKOVA — 1974 - Viktor Titov (Mosfilm)
A woman doctor attempts to maintain her creative, scientific
drive to find new methods in science while at the same time searching
for meaning in human relationships.

EARLY MORNING — 1966 - Tatiana Lioznova (Maxim Gorki Studios)

EARTH — 1930 - Alexander Dovzhenko (VUFKU-Kiev)
Often considered to be Dovzhenko's best film. This was a poetic
and lyrical story of peasant toil in the Ukrainian countryside at the time
of agricultural collectivization. The class struggle between kulaks and
poor peasants was amply treated, but the film left some in the Party in
doubt as to Dovzhenko's intent. The old, simple way of rural life was
not all that bad. Although several sequences were cut prior to release

the film still shows Dovzhenko's love for his native Ukraine, a theme often repeated in his films.

EARTH IN CHAINS — 1928 - Fedor Ozep — Also entitled *The Yellow Passport.*
Tragic drama about a woman who succumbs to commercial prostitution.

THE EARTH THIRSTS — 1930 - Yuli Raizman (Vostok-kino)
Originally made as a silent film but was rereleased with a synchronized sound track in 1931. Sharp, vivid photography of sun-baked soil heightened the dramatic flavor of this story about class struggle and agricultural collectivization in Turkmenia. The focus is on a group of Komsomols who come to help a peasant collective in irrigating the land while struggling against proponents of the old way of life.

18-28 — 1928 - Mikhail Kalatozov and Nutsa Gogoberidze (Goskinprom-Gruziya)
Documentary historical chronicle about the development of Georgia from 1918 to 1928. A highlight of the film was the Menshevik counterrevolt against the Bolsheviks.

THE EIGHTEENTH YEAR — 1958 - Grigori Roshal (Mosfilm)
Part II of *The Way of Sorrows* Trilogy.

EL-YEMEN — 1930 - Vladimir Shneiderov
Expeditionary adventure and popular science film.

THE ELDER VASILI GRIAZNOV — 1924 - Cheslav Sabinski (Goskino)
An antireligious story about deceit and commercialization involved in the manufacture of so-called holy items.

THE ELEPHANT AND THE SKIPPING ROPE — 1946 - Ilya Frez (Maxim Gorki Studios)
Light comedy for children.

THE ELEVENTH [YEAR] — 1928 - Dziga Vertov (VUFKU)
Vertov's last silent documentary on the achievements of Soviet society eleven years after the October Revolution.

THE ELEVENTH OF JULY — 1938 - Yuri Tarich (Sovetskaya Belarus)
Civil War drama centering on the Bolshevik struggle for control of
Minsk.

ELISO — 1928 - Nikolai Shengelaya (Goskinprom-Gruziya)
Very popular in its time, the film had a synchronized sound track
added in the 1930s when it was reissued. The story is about tsarist
colonialism in Georgia in the 1860s and focuses on a tsarist takeover of
valuable land from a Georgian village. Rich in Georgian folklore.

THE ELIXIR OF COURAGE — 1941/42 - Sergei Yutkevich
Featurette, *Fighting Film Album No. 7.*

ELIZAVETA UVAROVA — 1974 - Gleb Panfilov (Lenfilm)

ELUSIVE JAN — 1944 - Isidor Annenski and Vladimir Petrov
A drama about World War II and the Czech resistance to Nazi
occupation.

THE EMIGRANT — 1935 - Kamil Yarmatov (Tadzhik-kino)
This was a drama about the fate of a Tadzhik peasant, Kamil
(played by Yarmatov), who is deceived by enemy propaganda and
emigrates from the Soviet Union to an Islamic country. In his new land
Kamil slowly becomes aware that he is little more than a feudal slave
and goes back to the USSR. The film depicted the hardships of workers
in Middle Eastern countries and the social struggle in the USSR.
Yarmatov succeeded in avoiding reliance on exotic elements in this film
and used a large number of nonprofessional actors. Today this film is
regarded as one of the most significant, artistically and socially, of the
early years of Tadzhik cinema.

THE EMPEROR'S NEW CLOTHES — 1919 - Yuri Zheliabushski
(Rus and VFKO)
Based on the story by Hans Christian Andersen.

THE ENCHANTED DESNA — 1965 - Yulia Solntseva
(Alexander Dovzhenko Studios)
The script was initially written by Dovzhenko which was made
after his death. A beautifully idyllic picture of the life of a small boy in

the Ukraine in the years before the 1917 Revolution. The story is partly based on Dovzhenko's own life.

THE ENCHANTED ISLAND — 1973 - Moisei Levin (Mosfilm)
A romantic fantasy which took the Silver Dragon award at the 1973 Cracow Film Festival.

THE END OF ST. PETERSBURG — 1927 - Vsevolod Pudovkin with Mikhail Doller (Mezhrabpom-Rus)
Commissioned, like Eisenstein's *October,* to commemorate the tenth anniversary of the October Revolution. This was the second of Pudovkin's three great films on man's revolutionary spirit. The story is about a young worker, Paren, and his growing dedication to the revolutionary movement in Russia in the years 1914-1917. The photography was impressive, though Soviet critics at the time found it too abstract to their liking. Now one of the classics of silent Soviet cinema.

THE END OF THE ATAMAN — 1970 - Shaken Aimanov (Kazakhfilm)
A Civil War drama about the White Guards General Dutov in Kazakhstan and his defeat at the hands of the Bolsheviks.

ENEMIES — 1938 - Alexander Ivanovski
Based on the play by Maxim Gorki about the workers' movement in Russia.

THE ENEMY'S PATH — 1940 - Olga Preobrazhenskaya and Ivan Pravov
A story about a villainous kulak who conceals his past and joins a collective farm. His intention to disrupt the collective's work is discovered in time. This was one more in a series of films that emphasized the need to maintain vigilance against internal class enemies.

ENGINEER KOCHIN'S ERROR — 1940 - Alexander Macheret (Mosfilm)
Counterespionage thriller. An average Soviet man willingly volunteers his services to the secret police in order to expose an industrial saboteur.

ENTHUSIASM — 1931 - Dziga Vertov (Ukrainfilm) — Also entitled *Donbas Symphony.*
This was Vertov's lyrical sound and musical documentary about

the coal miners of the Donets Basin during the First Five-Year Plan. While well received abroad, some Soviet critics found fault with its near 'formalistic' structure. The film reflected a mellowing of Vertov's usual *cinema-verite* technique. The film historian Jay Leyda in his book relates how Vertov almost drove a British audience right out of a London theater when he turned the sound volume up to an unbearable crescendo so that the full beauty of the film could be better appreciated.

ESTONIAN EARTH — 1941 - Vasili Belayev (Central Newsreel Studio)
Documentary on Estonian life.

EVERLASTING SORROW — 1922 - A. Panteleev (Sevzapkino)
One of the earliest feature theatrical films which was a transition from the simpler wartime propaganda to a more sophisticated dramatic structure. The story dealt with the famine in the Volga region at the end of the Civil War.

EVIL SPIRIT — 1928 - P. Barkhudarian (Armenfilm)
A drama about poverty and class structure in Armenian society as seen through the life of a deaf man.

EXACTLY AT SEVEN — 1941 - A. Bendelstein and Alexander Rou
Featurette, *Fighting Film Album No. 7.*

EXPLOIT ON THE ICE — 1928 - Georgi and Sergei Vasiliev (Lenfilm)
Documentary about Soviet efforts to rescue the survivors of Nobile's dirigible crash in the Arctic.
[See also *The Red Tent.*]

EXTRAORDINARY ADVENTURES OF AN ARTILLERY OBSERVER — 1932 - Alexander Medvedkin (Soyuzkino)
Short, eccentric military comedy.

THE EXTRAORDINARY ADVENTURES OF MR. WEST IN THE LAND OF THE BOLSHEVIKS — 1924 - Lev Kuleshov (Goskino)
A satire on Western misconcpetions about the new Soviet state which are the result of yellow journalism. In the film, the American Senator West decides to see the Soviet Union firsthand, though really expecting to find wild-eyed bomb-throwing revolutionaries. On his

arrival he is victimized by hooligans, but is then helped out of his difficulties by Red militiamen and alter his preconceived notions. Made on a tiny budget, as were many of Kuleshov's films, and under severe physical conditions, the film still stands as a classic of Soviet silent cinema. The wild, eccentric style of the film is sometimes seen as a reflection of Kuleshov's interest in American technique.

THE EXTRAORDINARY COMMISSAR — 1971 - Ali Khamraev (Uzbekfilm)
A drama about the Russian Civil War in Central Asia and the Bolshevik struggle for power as seen through the actions of one man.

THE EXTRAORDINARY TRAVELS OF MISHKA STREKACHEV — 1959 - Ilya Frez (Maxim Gorki Studios)
A children's comedy about the adventures of an irrepressible youngster.

AN EXTREMELY UNPLEASANT INCIDENT — (See *Bad Trouble*)

AN EYE FOR AN EYE — 1924 - A. Litvinov (AFKU)
An Azerbaidzhanian thriller about American spies who attempt to steal the secrets of a new war gas developed by the Soviets.

THE EYES WERE OPENED — 1919 - Cheslav Sabinski
Civil War *agitka*.

FACING THE WIND — (See *Against The Wind*)

A FACTORY TOWN — 1965 - Vladimir Vengerov

THE FALL OF BERLIN — 1950, in two parts - Mikhail Chiaureli (Mosfilm)
A lavishly budgeted war film that monumentalized the role of Stalin as war leader. Chiaureli offered sharp contrasts between the calm Stalin and hysterical Hitler and grumbling Churchill. The film was luxurious in its epic, sweeping battle scenes that were complemented by the musical score of Dmitri Shostakovich. The film also featured a scene of Hitler's suicide as Soviet forces entered the German capital. Chiaureli, like Petrov for *Battle of Stalingrad*, was perhaps unfairly criticized for

The Fall of Berlin, Mikhail Chiaureli (Artkino Pictures)

what was believed to be an exaggeration in portraying the calm atmosphere in Stalin's headquarters. If postwar memoirs are to be believed
Chiaureli was more accurate than critics have admitted. The film was
cited by Khrushchev during the 1956 Party Congress as an example of
the worst of Stalinism as it portrayed Soviet generals as mere messen-
gers. Technically the film is of a high standard.

THE FALL OF THE ROMANOV DYNASTY — 1927 - Esther Shub
(Sovkino)
 A historical documentary that included rare footage of film of the
tsar and his family taken by the imperial court photographer. Considered one of Shub's best works. The film reconstructs the events leading
up to the 1917 February Revolution and the abdication of Nicholas II.

THE FALLING LEAVES — 1968 - Otar Yoseliani (Gruziyafilm)
 Wry satire about a young engineer who struggles to overcome
industrial laxness and abuse of work regulations in a Georgian wine
plant. The film points up Georgian national feelings when a group of
Great Russians are given poor wine to drink.

FAR FROM MOSCOW — 1951 - Alexander Stolper (Mosfilm)
 Drama about the Soviet labor front during World War II. The
theme of the story is the struggle between individual and group interests. A selfish, egotistic engineer who cares little about others is slowly
made to see the error of his ways by a patient, benevolent Party worker.

FATHER AND SON — 1919 - Ivan Perestiani (Moscow Cinema
Committee)
 Popular for many years after the Civil War this was a simple
drama about an elderly White soldier who joins the Bolshevik after
seeing the suffering of his son, a Red, in a prisoner of war camp.

FATHER FROST — 1924 - Yuri Zheliabushski (Mezhrabpom-Rus)
 Based on a Russian folk tale and widely exported to European
countries in the 1920s.

FATHER SERGIUS — 1917 [1918] - Yakov Protazanov
 Based on the story by Lev Tolstoi and filmed prior to the October
Revolution. The work was so controversial that release was delayed

until May 1918 when the Bolsheviks were in power. Protazanov's work was considered to be one of the most socially significant theatrical films of its time. The story is about an officer during the time of Nicholas I who decides to give up his fortune and become a monk. As Father Sergius the hero sees the human weaknesses of the Russian priesthood, which came as a surprise to those who saw it.

FATHERS AND SONS — 1957 - A. Bergunker and N. Rashevskaya (Lenfilm)
   An adaptation of Turgenev's novel.

FEAST AT ZHIRMUNKA — 1941 - Vsevolod Pudovkin

FEAT OF A SCOUT — 1948 - Boris Barnet (Kiev Film Studios —
Also entitled *Secret Agent*.
   Drama about the courageous exploits of a Soviet intelligence officer working behind German lines during World War II. The Soviet film historian Pisarevski considers this one of the better films of Soviet cinema because Barnet transcended the usual tale of adventure and intrigue. The story depicts the agent in direct collision with a social and political psychology which is alien to his own.

THE FEAT OF LENINGRAD — 1973 - Mikhail Yershov (Lenfilm)
   Drama about the blockade and siege of Leningrad in 1941-43.

[See also *Blockade*.]

FEDKA — 1937 - N. Lebedev
   A children's film which tells the story about a young boy who joins the Red Army after seeing his father, the chairman of a village soviet, murdered by class enemies.

FEELINGS — 1971 - Vitautas Zalakevicius (Lithuanian Film Studio)
   World War II drama. Story about conflicting personal and political loyalties in Nazi-occupied Lithuania.

THE FEROCIOUS ONE — 1974 - Tolomush Okeyev (Kazakhfilm)
   Script by Andrei Mikhalkov-Konchalovski. A warm story about a young Kazakh orphan boy who is in search of love and warmth. He tries

to domesticate a wolf, but in time the animal becomes the most ferocious in the pack and reflects the problem of good vs. evil. Excellent photography gives a lyrical view of peasant life and nature.

THE FIERY MILES — 1957 - Samson Samsonov (Mosfilm)
War drama.

FIERY VOYAGE — 1930 - Ya. Urinov
Civil War melodrama about a Siberian Red partisan who is ordered to blow up a train carrying the White troops of Admiral Kolchak. At the last minute the hero sees his wife and child aboard the train. Mission uncompleted.

THE FIERY YEARS — 1939 - Vladimir Korsh-Sablin
(Sovetskaya Belarus)
Civil War action story about the battles along the Berezina River and struggle for control of Belorussia.

THE FIGHTERS — 1936 - G. Vangenheim
Anti-Nazi film.

FILM, FILM, FILM! — 1969 - Fedor Khitruk (Soyuzmultfilm)
A feature cartoon satire on the problems of film-making.

FILM NOTES ON BATTLES 1 AND 2 — 1941 - Lev Arnshtam and Grigori Kozintsev
War film, semi-documentary.

FIND ME — 1970 - Algirdas Araminas (Lithuanian Film Studio)
An autobiographical story about childhood.

FIRE — 1930 - Mark Donskoi (Belgoskino)

FIRES OF BAKU — 1950 - Iosif Heifitz and Alexander Zarkhi

FIRM FRIENDS — 1954 - Mikhail Kalatozov (Mosfilm)
Grand prize winner at 1955 Karlovy Vary Film Festival. The scenario was studied by officials for two years before approval for production was given. The story is about three friends who band

together to overcome the frustrations encountered in dealing with petty bureaucrats. The film marked the return of genuine humorous satire to Soviet screens after many years' absence of this genre.

THE FIRST DAY — 1958 - Friedrich Ermler (Lenfilm)

FIRST DAY OF PEACE — (See *The Day The War Ended*)

THE FIRST ECHELON — 1956 - Mikhail Kalatozov (Mosfilm)

THE FIRST GRADER — 1948 - Ilya Frez (Maxim Gorki Studios)
Story about a young boy and his thoughts during his first days of school.

FIRST IN THE DESERT — 1932 - M. Bystritski (Turkmenfilm)
A semi-theatrical, semi-documentary story about the beginnings of industrialization in Turkmenia.

THE FIRST KOMSOMOL [BRIGADE] — 1930 - B. Medvedev and I. Frolov (Azerkino)
Story about a group of Young Communist shock workers and their efforts to increase production in the Azerbaidzhanian oil industry.

THE FIRST LAD — 1958 - Sergei Paradzhanov (Alexander Dovzhenko Studios)

FIRST LIEUTENANT STRESHNEV — 1928 - Mikhail Chiaureli and Yefim Dzigan (Goskinprom-Gruziya)
Civil War drama about a tsarist soldier who, as a result of increased class consciousness and love for his revolutionary son, joins the Bolshevik cause. The film was quite popular but the theme was often repeated with mixed success.

FIRST LOVE — 1934 - B. Shreiber (Sovetskaya Belarus)
Bozhena, the heroine of this story, is a young Communist from a Western country who comes to Belorussia. She soon falls in love with Semyon, a young worker. Despite their love for each other, Bozhena decides to return to her own country in order to carry on the struggle for peace. In the end she is accused by Fascists as being responsible for the death of a policeman.

THE FIRST PLATOON — 1933 - Vladimir Korsh-Sablin
(Sovetskaya Belarus)
     This was the first sound film in which Boris Babochkin of later
Chapayev fame acted. Babochkin played the role Makar Bobrik who
personified the revolutionary masses. The story was about the destiny
of a platoon of soldiers as they fight their way through World War I and
then join the cause of the Bolsheviks in the Civil War. This was one of
the better films of the time, but it was too quickly overshadowed by
Chapayev which certainly was given more publicity. Quite popular with
audiences.

FIRST RUSSIANS — 1967 - Alexander Ivanov (Lenfilm)

THE FIRST TEACHER — 1965 - Andrei Mikhalkov-Konchalovski
(Mosfilm)
     Drama and love set against the first few years of Soviet rule.

FIRST TRIP TO THE STARS — 1961 - Ilya Kopalin
(Central Documentary Studios)
     Soviet space program and exploration.

THE FIRST VISITOR — 1966 - Leonid Kvinikidze (Lenfilm)

FIVE IN A LITTLE APPLE — 1928 - P. Barkhudarian (Armenfilm)
     An agit-prop drama about an illiterate villager who joins the Red
Army, becomes educated, returns home, and earns the respect of his
fellow citizens.

FLAG OF THE NATION — 1928 - V. Shmidtgof (Belgoskino)
     A somber story about class struggle in the United States. A
proletarian newspaperman investigates the activities of a corrupt oil
millionaire. In the end the journalist is a victim of the capitalist's
treachery.

FLAMES — 1975, in two parts — Vitali Chetverikov (Belarusfilm)
     A wide-screen drama about the Belorussian partisan movement
and its harassment of German forces from 1941 to July 1944. The
growing power of the partisans is contrasted with the increased anxiety
of German General Reinhardt. The film also shows daily life in a

partisan camp such as a wedding and a young man making a toy for a war orphan.

THE FLIGHT — 1971 - Alexander Alov and Vladimir Naumov (Mosfilm)
A surprising film because of its compassionate treatment of the fate of Russian exiles after the October Revolution.

FLYERS — (See *Aviators*)

THE FLYING CARPET — 1958 - G. Kazanski (Lenfilm)
Whimsical story based on the novel by L. Lagin.

FOLLOWING THE SUN — (See *A Man Follows The Sun*)

FOMA GORDEEV — 1959 - Mark Donskoi (Soyuzdetfilm)
Story about prerevolutionary Russia based on the novel by Maxim Gorki.

THE FOP — 1929 - Mark Donskoi (Belgoskino)

FOR THE HARVEST — 1929 - Ilya Kopalin (Sovkino)
The first of the so-called Village Trilogy about contemporary agriculture. Intended as educational propaganda about the benefits to be derived from collectivized agriculture. The old style agriculture is portrayed in terms of grim poverty.

FOR THE RED BANNER — 1919 - Vladimir Kasianov (Moscow Cinema Committee)
Civil War *agitka*.

FOR THOSE WHO ARE AT SEA — 1948 - Alexander Faintsimmer (Mosfilm)
Drama about a Soviet sailor who puts his own personal interests ahead of those of the group. In time he is won over to the needs of the Party and country as a result of the benevolence of Party workers.

FOR YOU, FRONT — 1942 - Dziga Vertov (Central Newsreel Studio)
War documentary.

FORCED LABOR — 1928 - Yuli Raizman (Gosvoyenkino) —
Also entitled *Katorga*.

A stirring and grim story about a tsarist Siberian prison camp in the early 1900s and an unsuccessful revolt by political prisoners. Controversial for a time the film in time won over many critics after the Russian Society of Political Exiles endorsed it.

THE FOREST — 1931 - Sergei Gerasimov — 1954 - Vladimir Vengerov

FOREST SYMPHONY — 1967 - Alexander Zguridi
Nature study film.

A FOREST TALE — 1926 - Yuri Tarich (Belgoskino)

Based on the play *The Swineherd* by Mikhas Charota. A Civil War drama and romance set in Belorussia and focuses on the Bolshevik struggle against the Poles.

FORTRESS OF SURAM — 1923 - Ivan Perestiani
(Goskinprom-Gruziya)

Based on the story by Daniil Chonkadze who adapted it from folk legends. Melodrama of unrequited love in feudal Georgia. The hero, Durmishkhan, after being freed from feudal obligations by Vardo, a peasant girl who loves him, goes off and marries another.

FORTRESS ON THE VOLGA — (See *Defense of Tsaritsyn*)

THE FORTY-FIRST — 1928 - Yakov Protazanov (Mezhrabpom-Rus)
1956 - Grigori Chukhrai (Mosfilm)

A classic story of love and duty during the Russian Civil War. The heroine is a Red partisan commander with forty kills to her credit. After capturing a White officer she falls in love with him. In the end she must make a decision whether to let him be rescued or follow the obligation of duty. Despite her love he becomes the forty-first. Both films were international successes. Protazanov shot his in a record two months and was severely criticized for his humane treatment of a White. Chukhrai's version signalled a new turn for Soviet cinema following Stalin's death.

THE FOUNDLING — 1940 - T. Lukashevich
A comedy about erroneous notions. Mulia, a little girl, leaves her house one day and is unable to find her way back home. A couple comes upon her and makes plans to adopt the homeless orphan. At a time when comedy was at a low ebb this was one of the best.

400 MILLION — 1929 - Vladimir Gardin (Mezhrabpomfilm)
Drama about a Chinese workers' uprising in Canton.

THE FOURTH ROOM — 1974 - Daniil Khrabovitski (Mosfilm)

THE FOX AND THE HARE — 1973 - J. Norstein (Soyuzmultfilm)
Cartoon feature.

FRAGMENT OF AN EMPIRE — 1929 - Friedrich Ermler
(Sovkino-Leningrad)
One of Ermler's best films. A satire about Soviet life at the beginning of the First Five-Year Plan with a good deal of humor. The story centers on a Russian soldier who suffers amnesia at the time of the October Revolution. Twelve years later he begins to recover his memory and, in a series of flashbacks, grasps the quality of social changes that have occurred. Fedor Nikitin gave one of his best performances as the soldier.

FREEDOM FOR YOU AND FOR US — 1968 - Leonid Makhnach
Political and social documentary.

FRIENDS — 1938 - Lev Arnshtam (Mosfilm)
Story about friendship among different nationalities in the Soviet Union.

FRIENDS MEET AGAIN — 1939 - Kamil Yarmatov (Tadzhikfilm)
In the prologue a group of military engineers are mapping a little known desert region for a future irrigation project and city. Within the unit is a bandit and foreign spy, Daniar. Years later the group is reunited and Daniar is exposed. Originally made only as a Russian-language film, but later dubbed in Tadzhik.

FRITZ BAUER — 1930 - Vladimir Petrov (Mezhrabpomfilm)
Based on the story by N. Satz and V. Selikhova. Filmed on location in Germany. This was a drama about workers' children and their role in the German revolutionary movement. Photographically the film was quite interesting because Petrov made a conscious attempt to use an expressionistic style that was much in vogue in German cinema and thus gave the film a German flavor.

FROM MAN TO MAN — 1958 - Grigori Alexandrov (Mosfilm)

FROM SPARKS — FLAMES — 1924 - Dmitri Bassaligo (Proletkino)
One of the first big films of early Soviet cinema. The story dealt with the revolutionary activities of Russian textile workers.

THE FRONT — 1944 - Georgi and Sergei Vasiliev (Mosfilm)
War drama about the early period of the 1941-45 conflict. The early Soviet defeats were attributed to the older generals while acknowledging the contributions of young commanders to Soviet victories.

FRONT WITHOUT FLANKS — 1974 - Igor Gostev (Mosfilm)
World War II drama based on the novel *We Shall Return* by Semyon Tsvigan. A small Red Army unit suddenly finds itself encircled by a German force. Surrender initially seems like an easy option, but the commander persuades his men to keep on fighting.

FRONTIER — (See *Aerograd*)

FRONTLINE COMPANIONS — (See *The Girl From Leningrad*)

THE FUGITIVE — 1933 - Vladimir Petrov (Mezhrabpomfilm)
Petrov's first sound film in which he again used the German expressionistic style. Based on the story by K. Wittfogel. A German revolutionary who is in hiding decides to surrender to the authorities. He concludes that he can best serve his cause by turning his trial into a public forum for airing his political and social views.

THE GADFLY — 1928 - Kote Mardzhanishvili (Goskinprom-Gruziya)
Drama about the revolutionary movement in Italy.

GADZHI-KARA — 1929 - Abas-mirza Sharif-zade (Baku Studio) —
Also entitled *Sona*.
Adapted from a 19th-century comedy by Mirza Akhundov. The
story depicted Azerbaidzhanian life in the 1850s and emphasized the
lowly social status of women. While not a critical triumph, the film
proved popular and was important for its emphasis on the need to increase human rights for women.

GAICHI — 1938 - Vladimir Shneiderov
A children's adventure film about life in the taiga.

THE GANG OF FATHER KNYSH — 1924 - Alexander Razumni
Civil War espionage thriller about a group of Whites who pass
themselves off as Red Army men until their capture.

THE GARDEN — 1938 - N. Dostal (Tadzhikfilm)
First dramatic sound film of Tadzhik cinema. A simple story that
seems topical for the 1970s. Mamed-Ali is an old gardener who decides
to leave the collective farm when oil is discovered under the garden he
has been tending so lovingly. A year later he returns and is surprised to
find his garden beautifully restored side by side with oil wells. Originally made only in Russian with Tadzhik dubbed in later.

GAVROCH — 1937 - T. Lukashevich
A children's drama about a young French boy who joins in the
struggles of the Paris Commune of 1871.

THE GAY CANARY — 1929 - Lev Kuleshov
Set against the Civil War in Odessa, this was a drama about a
Bolshevik agent who disguises himself as a prince to spy on the Whites.
Withdrawn from exhibition after a short time as critics found the film
politically naive, but is better treated by film historians today.

THE GENERAL FROM THE OTHER WORLD — 1925 -
Pyotr Chardynin (VUFKU-Kiev)
A comedy that in form and theme was a forerunner of Ermler's
later *Fragment Of An Empire*. In this story a tsarist general falls into a
deep ten-year sleep and awakens in the midst of the Soviet era. While
popular the film was not too well liked by critics because Chardynin

emphasized the funny aspects of tsarist times rather than stressing the achievements of Soviet society.

GENERATION OF VICTORS — 1936 - Vera Stroyeva (Mosfilm)
    Drama about the revolutionary struggle against tsarist autocracy in the years 1896-1905 with attention to the work of Lenin and Bukharin. An initial version was remade after some Party criticism. The main hero is Sasha Mikhailov and his life from the time he is expelled from a university to his actions as a fighter on the street barricades in Moscow.

THE GENTLEMAN AND THE ROOSTER — 1929 - Vladimir Ballyuzek (Belgoskino)
    A satire (and political protest) about the territorial division of Belorussia. The comedy was about a landlord whose holdings were split evenly between the USSR and Poland. He is constantly bedevilled by his roosters who insist on crossing the border into the USSR. At the time this eccentric comedy lost favor with the critics who were becoming more militant in their taste. The film was a subtle message that the Belorussian people would not allow themselves to be divided forever.

GEORGI SAAKADZE — 1943, in two parts - Mikhail Chiaureli (Tbilisi Studio)
    Stalin Prize winner. Dramatized biography of the 17th-century Georgian national hero.

GERASIM AND MUMU — 1918 - Cheslav Sabinski
    Based on a story by Turgenev.

THE GHOST THAT NEVER RETURNS — 1929 - Abram Room (Sovkino-Moscow)
    Based on a novel by Henri Barbusse. The setting of the story is Mexico and concerns the struggle of a Mexican prisoner to lead his people against the government. Photography is done in an interesting manner. Sound track added after 1930.

GIANT — (See *Born In Fire*)

GIDROTORF — 1920 - Yuri Zheliabushski
An early popular science-educational film about new methods of peat mining. Lenin used this film as an example for expanding the production of educational films.

GIKOR — 1934 - A. Martirosian (Armenfilm)
Last silent film of Armenian cinema. This is the story of Gikor, who as a young boy is sold into personal service by his poor father. The harshness of Gikor's life is used to illustrate the plight of the Armenian lower classes before the October Revolution.

GIRL FRIENDS — 1936 - Lev Arnshtam (Lenfilm)
This warm, naturalistic story about three young Red Army nurses during the Civil War made this one of the better films of Soviet cinema. The film depicts the solidarity of the younger and older generations in the struggles of the Bolsheviks.

THE GIRL FROM A DISTANT RIVER — 1928 - Yevgeni Chervyakov (Sovkino-Leningrad)
A fanciful story about a young girl in a remote area who dreams of going to Moscow and living a revolutionary life.

THE GIRL FROM KHIDOBANI — 1940 - D. Antadze (Goskinprom-Gruziya)
Love, music, and comedy form the basis for this film about life on a Georgian collective farm.

THE GIRL FROM LENINGRAD — 1941 - Viktor Eisimont (Lenfilm)
Also entitled *Frontline Companions* and *Natasha*.
A warm and tender love story against the backdrop of the Russo-Finnish War of 1939-40. The film was highly popular because it avoided sensationalism without hiding the hardships of war. American distributors decided the original version, because of its anti-Finnish bias, would not do well and it was largely remade under Fedor Ozep's direction as *Russian Girl*. Zoya Fyodorova, who starred in the cast, was later imprisoned for her wartime love affair with an American naval officer. Fyodorova's daughter emigrated to the United States in 1975 to be with her natural father.

THE GIRL FROM THE UPPER DECK — 1928 - A. Pereguda and G. Kravchenko

Based on Alexei Novikov-Priboi's story "The Woman On The Sea." This film reflected the social and economic emancipation of women under the Soviet system. In the story a young woman wins the right to become a sailor just like men.

THE GIRL HASTENS TO A MEETING — 1936 - M. Verner

Comedy about people and their tribulations as a result of misplaced passports.

GIRL NO. 217 — 1944 - Mikhail Romm (Mosfilm at Tashkent Studio) Also entitled *Person No. 217*.

A grim film about human tragedy and humiliation in war. This is a story about a young Russian girl who is deported to Germany to serve as a household slave. Visually a harsh film and one of the best Soviet wartime films. Stalin Prize winner.

GIRL OF THE ARARAT VALLEY — 1950 - Amo Bek-Nazarov

GIRL WITH A GUITAR — 1957 - A. Reintsimmer (Mosfilm)

Fanciful romance.

GIRL WITH A HAT BOX — 1927 - Boris Barnet (Mezhrabpom-Rus)

Considered one of the finest examples about social satire of the NEP period. The young heroine, Natasha, is a seamstress who works in a hat factory run by Madame Iren and her husband. Natasha refuses to surrender her feelings or ethics for the temptations of money.

THE GIRL WITH CHARACTER — 1939 - Konstantin Yudin

A young, hard-working girl, Katya Ivanova, comes to Moscow from the Soviet Far East. At a time when Soviet managers are looking for conscientious workers, Katya creates more problems when she decides to return home and takes several hard-working girls with her.

THE GIRL WITHOUT AN ADDRESS — 1957 - Eldar Ryazanov (Mosfilm)

Satire on Soviet social scene and bureaucracy.

GIVE US AIR! — 1924 - Dziga Vertov (Sovkino)
Documentary.

GIVE US RADIO! — 1925 - Sergei Yutkevich
Short eccentric comedy and parody on American comedies.

GLINKA — 1946 - Lev Arnshtam (Mosfilm)
Stalin Prize winner. Patriotic and dramatized biography of the
Russian composer.
[See also *The Composer Glinka.*]

GLOOMY MORNING — 1959 - Grigori Roshal (Mosfilm)
Part III of *The Way of Sorrows* Trilogy.

GLORY OF PEACE — 1932 - V. Vainshtok (Sovetskaya Belarus)
Drama about the Communist underground in a Western country.
The hero, Bill Parker, with the help of his fiance, Martha, blows up an
arms shipment that is to be used in a war against the USSR. During the
explosion Martha goes blind.

GLORY TO SOVIET HEROINES — 1938 - Dziga Vertov
A film poem and tribute to Soviet women.

GLUMOV'S DIARY — 1924 - Sergei Eisenstein
Eisenstein's first attempt at film-making. A short, surrealistic
interlude to a stage play.

GO TO NOWHERE — 1966 - Ivan Ivanov-Vano (Soyuzmultfilm)
Feature cartoon.

THE GOALKEEPER — 1937 - Semyon Timoshenko
Light comedy about Soviet soccer players.

GOBSECK — 1935 - Konstantin Eggert (Mezhrabpomfilm)
Based on a story by Balzac. Shortly after completing this film
Eggert was arrested by the NKVD and disappeared. Following severe
criticism for his *Harbor of Storms,* Eggert tried to revise Balzac's story
to fit Marxist ideology but failed. The film was later banned.

GOD OF WAR — 1929 - Yefim Dzigan (Goskinprom-Gruziya) —
Also entitled *White Horseman*.
    An antireligious film that used a highly innovative style. A simple
soldier and his wife symbolize injustice and hardship as the result of the
symbolic union of the cross and the machine gun. Priests, pastors,
mullahs, and rabbis are pictured as instigators of war.

GOGI RATIANI — 1927 - Kote Mardzhanishvili (Goskinprom-Gruziya)

THE GOLDEN ANTELOPE — 1954 - Lev Atamanov (Soyuzmultfilm)
    Feature cartoon based on folk stories.

THE GOLDEN BEAK — 1929 - Yevgeni Chervyakov
    Story about Russian serfs who dream of a life in which they work
for themselves in the 18th century.

THE GOLDEN CALF — 1969 - Mikhail Shveitser
Based on Ilf and Petrov's novel.

GOLDEN FIRES — 1935 - Vladimir Korsh-Sablin (Sovetskaya Belarus)
    An intrepid group of Komsomols endeavor to unmask industrial
saboteurs.

THE GOLDEN GATES — 1970 - Yulia Solntseva
(Alexander Dovshenko Studios)

GOLDEN HONEY — 1928 - Vladimir Petrov and N. Beresnev
(Mezhrabpom-Rus)
    Film for children.

THE GOLDEN LAKE — 1935 - Vladimir Shneiderov
    Adventure and popular science film about the Altai taiga.

THE GOLDEN MOUNTAINS — 1931 - Sergei Yutkevich
(Soyuzkino-Leningrad)
    Story about a peasant working in a factory in the 1914-17 period.
He slowly becomes aware of the hardships of his life because he is being
exploited by the upper classes. He decides to lead other workers in revolt against the factory owners. This was Yutkevich's first sound film

and is considered interesting for the way he used sound as a counterpoint to visual image. Good musical score by Dmitri Shostakovich.

THE GOLDEN RING — 1975 - Fedor Tiapkin
(Central Popular Science Studio)
Color documentary on the art and architecture of the old Russian cities of Vladimir and Suzdal. Focuses on recent restoration of these historic cities.

GOLDEN STEPMOTHER — 1966 - Valentina and Zenaeda Brumberg
(Soyuzmultfilm)
Feature cartoon based on a Russian fairy tale.

GOLDEN TAIGA — 1937 - G. Kazanski with Ruf
Melodrama about the daily life of young Komsomol workers in a Siberian gold mine.

THE GOLDEN VALLEY — 1937 - Nikolai Shengelaya
(Goskinprom-Gruziya)
Story about the life and work of Georgian peasants.

THE GOOD SOLDIER SCHWEIK — 1935 - B. Antonovski
Animated adaptation of the novel.

GOODBYE BOYS — 1965 - Moisei Kalik (Moldovafilm)

GOODBYE DOVES — 1961 - Yakov Segel (Maxim Gorki Studios)

GOODBYE TO PIGEON TIME — 1960 - Yuri Ilyenko
(Maxim Gorki Studios)
Ilyenko's student diploma film.

GOYA — 1970 - Konrad Wolf (DEFA/Mosfilm)
An East German-Soviet coproduction. Dramatized biography of the Spanish artist based on the biography by Lion Feuchtwanger.

GRANADA, MY GRANADA — 1967 - Roman Karmen
(Central Documentary Studios)
Retrospective political documentary about the Spanish Civil War.

GRAND MASTER — 1974 - Sergei Mikaelian (Lenfilm)
Drama about the life of Soviet chess players.

GRANDMA, ILIKO, ILLARION AND ME — 1963 - Tengiz Abuladze
(Gruziyafilm)
A tender story about a young Georgian boy, Zuriko, his life and
that of his family. Much admired for its warmth mixed with humor and
tragedy. Throughout the film ran the theme that man's strength lay in
his love and compassion for others. One of the best films of the 1960s.

THE GRASSHOPPER — 1955 - Samson Samsonov (Mosfilm)
Based on the story by Anton Chekhov. Received a Silver Lion
award at 1955 Venice Film Festival and featured a fine performance by
Sergei Bondarchuk.

THE GREAT CITIZEN — 1938, 1939, two parts — Friedrich Ermler
(Lenfilm)
A dramatized and Stalinized version of the life and death of
Sergei Kirov as seen through the film's central character Shakhov.
Despite its official bias, the film gave a good depiction of the intra-
Party debates and struggles of the late 1920s and early 1930s. The main
focus is on debates and discussions, or political life. Even Soviet critics
feel this is an unusual film because it is so remarkably free of expres-
sions of human love. Production of the film was delayed for several
months because of disputes over the scenario which were resolved by
arrests of so-called 'obstructionists.' Critics, Western and Soviet, see it
as one of the important films of Soviet cinema. The film was largely intended as a justification for the Moscow show trials of the 1930s.

THE GREAT CONSOLER — 1933 - Lev Kuleshov (Mezhrabpomfilm)
One of the more controversial films made by Kuleshov. Shortly
after its initial release Kuleshov was called to a personal meeting with
Stalin which resulted in its banning. This was Kuleshov's last important
film. Soviet cirtics have admitted it was a significant film of Soviet
cinema, but the work was never reissued after Stalin's death and few
people have seen it. The story is about an American convict, Jimmy
Valentine, and is based on the life, the stories by, and the stories about
O. Henry. Fact is blended into fantasy and results in work that is often
confusing. Drama is followed by eccentric, exaggerated humor. If the

The Great Citizen, Friedrich Ermler (Museum of Modern Art/Film Stills Archive)

film was meant to be a condemnation of capitalist life it was executed in an abstract manner. Like all Kuleshov films this one was made on a small budget and produced in two months after careful, painstaking rehearsals. The cast included William Rudd as the Negro convict.

GREAT FLIGHT — 1925 - Vladimir Shneiderov
Sponsored by the Soviet Society for Air and Chemical Warfare Defense. Documentary on a Soviet flight from Moscow to Tokyo and made to popularize aviation.

GREAT FORCE — 1950 - Friedrich Ermler (Lenfilm) — Also entitled *Great Power*.
Drama about a campaign by Soviet scientists to end the slavish following of foreign science. Soviet patriotism is emphasized in this film which was intended to show that the Soviets too had a record of scientific achievement. A related film is *Court of Honor*.

GREAT GAMBLE — 1935 - Georgi Tasin
This story is about a German engineer who is sent to the USSR to conduct industrial sabotage. As a result of observing the Soviet people he undergoes a change of heart and devotes himself to the Soviet cause.

THE GREAT GLOW — 1938 - Mikhail Chiaureli
Drama about the early days of the 1917 October Revolution. Lenin and Stalin are portrayed as equals and as the great benefactors of Soviet society.

GREAT HEIGHT — (See *The Heights*)

GREAT LAND — 1944 - Sergei Gerasimov (Mosfilm)
Wartime drama about the efforts of devoted Leningrad workers to restore a factory that had earlier been evacuated to Siberia.

GREAT LIFE — 1939, 1946 [1958], in two parts - Leonid Lukov (Kiev Studios)
The first part of this film dealt with young coal miners in the Donets Basin, their efforts to increase production and the unmasking of class enemies. The second part was severely criticized and banned after its initial release. Lukov's career was threatened because the Party

deemed the film as a ridicule of the realities of Soviet life. In its original version the second part was about the grim and harsh conditions of life as coal miners struggled to reconstruct the war damaged mines. After Stalin's death the film was released but in a greatly edited version.

GREAT OCTOBER — 1922 - Vladimir Gardin (VUFKU)
Historical documentary compiled from other film sources to commemorate the fifth anniversary of the October Revolution.

THE GREAT PATRIOTIC WAR — 1965 - Roman Karmen (Central Documentary Studios)
Historical documentary that commemorated the twentieth anniversary of the Soviet victory over Nazi Germany in 1945.

GREAT POWER — (See *Great Force*)

THE GREAT ROAD — 1927 - Esther Shub (Sovkino-Moscow)
A historical documentary that showed Soviet achievements in the ten years since the October Revolution. The film was compiled from many newsreel and documentary film sources, including footage purchased in the United States. One of Shub's best films.

THE GREAT TEST — 1975 - Leonid Avtonomov (Ukrainian Documentary Studios)
Historical documentary on the industrial and labor fronts of the Soviet Union during World War II. One of a large number of films made to commemorate the thirtieth anniversary of Soviet victory in the war against Nazi Germany.

GREAT TOKYO — 1925 - Vladimir Shneiderov
Social and travel documentary.

GREAT TROUBLES — 1961 - Valentina and Zenaeda Brumberg (Soyuzmultfilm)
Animated feature film.

THE GREAT TURNING POINT — 1945 - Friedrich Ermler (Lenfilm)
One of Ermler's best. Originally was to have been entitled *General of the Army*. This war drama was inspired by the Battle of Stalingrad

and by the generals who fought in it. Filmed among the ruins of Leningrad, the story focuses on generals, their decisions, and the psychological strain under which they must act. This was an atypical war film in that most of the action takes place at the command level at a crucial point of the war. Neither Stalin nor Stalingrad are mentioned. Stalin Prize.

THE GREAT VICTORY — 1933 - Mikhail Kaufman
     Documentary on Soviet economic advances and the First Five-Year Plan.

GRISHKA THE SWINEHERD — 1927 (Belgoskino)
     First Belorussian children's film that was made largely from unused footage of Yuri Tarich's *A Forest Tale.*

GROWN-UP CHILDREN — 1961 - Villen Azarov (Mosfilm)
     Social satire.

GRUNYA KORNAKOVA — (See *Nightingale, Little Nightingale*)

GUERRILLA BRIGADE — (See *Riders*)

GUILTY WITHOUT GUILT — 1945 - Vladimir Petrov (Mosfilm)
     Stalin Prize winner based on the play by N.A. Ostrovski.

GYULLI — 1927 - L. Push and Nikolai Shengelaya (Goskinprom-Gruziya)
     Based on the story by Shio Aragvispireli. Dealt with a young Moslem girl, Gyulli, who, while in love with a young worker, Mitro, is sold for 100 sheep to the shepherd Ali. Mitro attempts to rescue Gyulli from her bondage, but Ali kills her rather than see her in the arms of another. A very popular film in its time and Shengelaya looked upon it as instructional for himself.

HAMBURG — 1926 - Vladimir Ballyuzek (VUFKU)
     A drama about the German Communist Party and revolutionary movement that centered on events leading to the Hamburg uprising of 1923. Ballyuzek employed an interesting semi-documentary style, but the Soviet press at the time found the approach too traditional when compared to *Battleship Potemkin* which was gaining more favor.

HAMLET — 1964 - Girgori Kozintsev (Lenfilm)
   Based on Boris Pasternak's translation of Shakespeare's work and still considered one of the finest film adaptations of Shakespeare. The film was a realization of a dream that Kozintsev had since 1938. The work has been well received abroad and won an award from the British Film Institute. The film has been admired for the realism in the performance of the actors, satisfying photography, and good set design. The preparations for the film took several years and Kozintsev strove to transform Shakespeare's words into visual poetry.

HAPPENING ON THE VOLCANO — 1941 - Lev Kuleshov

HAPPINESS — 1935 - Alexander Medvedkin (Mosfilm) — Also entitled *Snatchers*.
   A surrealistic and bizarre comedy about farm life in the tsarist and Soviet eras. The antihero, Khmir, is something like Don Quixote, bent on pursuing individuality while his wife Anna, the heroine, happily adapts to collectivization. One of the more notable Soviet films of the 1930s and example of better Soviet film satire. Revived in the late 1960s and the early 1970s.

HARBOR OF STORMS — 1933 - Konstantin Eggert (Mezhrabpomfilm)
   Based on a novel by Balzac. Eggert is reported to have exceeded the film's budget by one million rubles because he insisted on using real ships for extravagant naval battle sequences. Despite the inordinate expenditures, the film was banned for political reasons and Eggert's career declined.

HATRED — 1930 - Yuri Tarich (Belgoskino)
   A political melodrama about the revolutionary workers' movement in Poland. Critics were displeased with the work because of its inaccurate portrayal of Polish realities.

HE DID NOT WANT TO KILL — 1967 - Eldar Shengelaya (Gruziyafilm)

HE MUST BE ACCUSED — 1963 - Viktor Lisakovich

THE HEART BEATS AGAIN — 1956 - Abram Room (Mosfilm)

HEART OF A MOTHER — 1966 - Mark Donskoi (Maxim Gorki Studios) — Also entitled *A Mother's Heart* and *Sons and Mothers.*
 A poetic portrait of life in Russia before the Revolution. Lenin in this story is portrayed humanistically and not in hagiographic terms. The mother in the story is that of Lenin. Well received abroad.

THE HEART OF A SOLDIER — 1957 - Sergei Kolosov (Mosfilm)
 Devotion to duty marks this story about the peacetime Soviet Army and the training of officer cadets.

THE HEART OF A SOLDIER — 1974 - Anatoli Slesarenko (Ukrainian Documentary Studios)
 A true life documentary about Viktor Zeliony, who in the closing days of World War II saved the life of a young German boy and later adopted him.

THE HEART OF SOLOMON — 1932 - Sergei Gerasimov

THE HEAT — 1963 - Larissa Shepitko (Kirghizfilm)
 This was Shepitko's diploma film and received excellent reviews, including a special jury prize at the Karlovy Vary Film Festival. The theme of this well photographed film was the conflict of different generations on a collective farm as reflected in the protagonists Abakir, an old, experienced tractor driver, and Kemel, a young Komsomol. The story depicts a growing antagonism between different generations and their views about life and society. The photography evokes a feeling of intense heat and sun baked earth.

THE HEAVENS CALL — 1960 - Alexander Kosir (Mosfilm)
 A low budget science-fiction space adventure set in the 21st century.

HECTIC DAYS — 1935 - Iosif Heifitz and Alexander Zarkhi (Mosfilm)
 Story about a young Red Army tank officer and his gril friend set against the background of military modernization and rearmament during the Second Five-Year Plan.

THE HEIGHTS — 1957 - Alexander Zarkhi (Mosfilm) — Also entitled *Great Height.*
 Based on the novel by E. Vorobiev. The story dealt with the

construction of a metallurgical plant and the romance between a young worker and young woman. In plot the film was reminiscent of the many "industrial" films of the 1930s, but character development was deeper and it focused on average rather than heroic people. Grand prize winner at Karlovy Vary Film Festival.

HEIR OF GENGHIS KHAN — (See *Descendant of Genghis Khan*)

THE HEIR OF THE MILITARY ROAD — 1970 - Varis Krumin (Lithuanian Film Studio)

HE'LL COME BACK AGAIN — 1942 - Nikolai Shengelaya (Tbilisi Studio)
War drama about love of country and devotion to duty.

HELLO CHILDREN — 1962 - Mark Donskoi (Maxim Gorki Studios)

HELLO, IT'S ME — 1965 - Frunze Dovlatian (Armenfilm)
Story about contemporary Armenian society, people, and youth. Focused on a group of young physicists and their lives during the war and afterwards, including a wartorn romance.

THE HEROES OF SHIPKA — 1955 - Sergei Vasiliev
Drama about the Balkan Wars.

HEROES OF THE BLAST FURNACE — 1928 - Yevgeni Ivanov-Barkov
Based on the novel *Blast Furnace* by Nikolai Liashko.

HEROIC STALINGRAD: THE CITY THAT STOPPED HITLER — (See *Stalingrad*)

HIGH RANK — 1973 - Yevgeni Karelov (Mosfilm) — Also entitled *A Lofty Calling.*
A biographic and war drama about the life and career of a synthetic Soviet general. Popular and well received by Soviet audiences and critics.

HIS CALL — 1925 - Yakov Protazanov (Mezhrabpom-Rus)
Drama about a White emigrant who returns to the USSR after the Civil War to search for jewels that his father had hidden. The story also

dealt with the attempted murder of the heroine, Katya. The film ends at the time of Lenin's death and his call to support communism. Protazanov is usually accorded compliments for this film for acting direction and the successful way he subtly wove in propaganda into a melodrama.

HIS EXCELLENCY — 1927 - Grigori Roshal (Belgoskino)
Story about Jewish life in the tsarist era and focuses on the attempt of a Jewish revolutionary to kill the tsarist governor of Minsk.

HIS NAME IS SUKHE-BATOR — 1942 - Iosif Heifitz and Alexander Zarkhi (Tashkent Studio)
War drama made in Mongolia.

HIS NAME WAS FEDOR — 1963 - Viktor Lisakovich
Documentary.

HISTORY OF THE CIVIL WAR — 1921 - Dziga Vertov
Documentary.

THE HOLIDAY OF SAINT JORGEN — 1930 - Yakov Protazanov (Mezhrabpomfilm)
A very popular and much admired satire on religion. The story dealt with the financial and political aspects of religion and their relationship to big business and petty thievery. Made as a silent, but a sound track was added later.

HOME TRIP — 1963 - Vladimir Vengerov

HONOR — 1932 - Mikhail Averbakh (Sovetskaya Belarus)
Story about a tractor plant in which Party officials exhort the workers to produce better machines for their agricultural comrades.

HORIZON — 1932 - Lev Kuleshov
Kuleshov's first sound film which was unsuccessful.

HORIZON — 1961 - Iosif Heifitz (Mosfilm)

HORSEMEN OF THE REVOLUTION — 1968 - Kamil Yarmatov
(Uzbekfilm)
An action drama about the establishment of Soviet rule in
Uzbekistan during the Civil War.

HOT SNOW — 1973 - G. Egiazarov (Mosfilm)
World War II drama.

HOTEL SAVOY — 1930 - Alexander Feintsimmer (Belgoskino)
Civil War drama about the struggle of Belorussian Bolsheviks for
control of Gomel in 1919.

THE HOTTEST MONTH — 1974 - Yuli Karasik (Mosfilm)
Based on the play *The Steel Makers* by Gennadi Bokarev. The
story touches on a problem that has often plagued Soviet plant managers. In this drama personalities conflict sharply when the management
and workers of a plant try to reach ambitious production targets without sacrificing qualitative standards.

AN HOUR UNTIL THE MEETING — 1965 - Valentina and
Zenaeda Brumberg (Soyuzmultfilm)
Feature cartoon film.

HOUSE AND MASTER — 1967 - Budimir Metalnikov (Mosfilm)

THE HOUSE I LIVE IN — 1957 - Lev Kulidzhanov and Yakov Segel
(Mosfilm)
World War II setting for a warm and tender story about average
people. Has proven very popular.

HOUSE OF ICE — 1928 - Konstantin Eggert (Mezhrabpom-Rus)
Drama about tsarist court intrigue. Based on the novel by Ivan
Lazhechnikov.

THE HOUSE OF THE DEAD — 1932 - V. Fedorov (Mezhrabpomfilm)
Drama about the life and work of the Russian novelist Dostoevski.

THE HOUSE OF THE GOLUBINS — 1925 - Vladimir Gardin
(Mezhrabpom-Rus)

Screenplay by Natan Zarkhi who later became one of the leading scenarists in the Soviet cinema. The story dealt with the lives and destinies of two families, the aloof bourgeois Golubins, and the poor Skvortsovs who live in the basement. Parallel action was strong in this film which pointed up Soviet concern for the health and welfare of its citizens as opposed to the tsarist era. The work is now highly regarded by Soviet film historians.

HOUSE ON A VOLCANO — 1928 - Amo Bek-Nazarov
(Azerkino and Armenkino)

The revolutionary movement in Baku is the background for this story about a group of oilworkers who become discontented and angry when they learn their living quarters stands over a treacherous pocket of natural gas.

HOUSE ON THE SNOW — 1928 - Friedrich Ermler (Sovkino-Leningrad)

A trilogy of stories about the people who live in one house during the Civil War.

HOW AND HOW NOT TO DO IT — 1929 - Nikolai Ekk
(Mezhrabpom-Rus)

A culture film on the leather trade which brought Ekk much attention as a rpomising director.

HOW BROAD IS OUR COUNTRY — 1958 - Roman Karmen
(Central Documentary Studios)

On Soviet life and potential.

HOW ONE PEASANT KEPT TWO GENERALS — 1965 -
Ivan Ivanov-Vano (Soyuzmultfilm)

Animated feature film based on Russian folk tales.

HOW PETYUNKA TRAVELLED TO SEE ILYICH — 1924 -
M. Doronin

One of the first Soviet films made for children. The story was inspired largely by Lenin's death and is about a boy who leaves his orphanage in order to attend Lenin's funeral. Photographically interesting because it portrayed the social tone of the times.

HOW ROBINSON WAS CREATED — 1961 - Eldar Ryazanov (Mosfilm)
Contemporary satire.

HOW THE ELECTOR WILL VOTE — 1937 - Sergei Yutkevich

HOW THE STEEL WAS TEMPERED — 1942 - Mark Donskoi
(Kiev and Ashkabad Studios)
Adapted from the novel by N.A. Ostrovski and dealt with the
Civil War. Donskoi adapted only those portions of the novel that had
relevance for the then current war against Nazi Germany. The story was
about Ukrainian resistance to the German forces that were occupying
the Ukraine in 1918.

[See also *Pavel Korchagin.*]

HOW WOMEN SOLD THEIR HUSBANDS — 1972 - I. Gurvich
(Kievnauchfilm)
Animated film based on a Ukrainian folk tale.

A HUNDRED FOR ONE — 1941 - Herbert Rappoport
Featurette, *Fighting Film Album No. 2.* A tragic story about
Yugoslav hostages under Nazi terror.

HUNGER AND THE STRUGGLE AGAINST IT — 1922 - N. Saltykov
(VUFKU-Kiev)
A semi-documentary account of the reasons for the famine in the
Ukraine in 1921 and the steps being taken to combat it.

HUNGER, HUNGER, HUNGER — 1921 - Vladimir Gardin with
Vsevolod Pudovkin
Made primarily to obtain funds for the victims of famine in the
Volga area in 1921.

THE HUSSAR'S BALLAD — 1962 - Eldar Ryazanov (Mosfilm)

I AM CUBA — 1962 - Mikhail Kalatozov (Mosfilm) — Cuban title:
Soy Cuba.
A Cuban-Soviet coproduction. Script by Yevgeni Yevtushenko. A
documentary and poetic tribute to the ideals of the Cuban revolution.

I AM TWENTY — 1964 - Marlen Khutsiev (Maxim Gorki Studios)
Release of the original version was refused and Khutsiev had to revise this film about Soviet youth. The story is about young Soviet people, their life, their work, and most importantly their view about their world. Khutsiev wanted to show the social outlook of young people and how it was related to older revolutionary ideals. The film includes interesting shots of Moscow locales. The Soviet film historian Pisarevski regards it as one of the 100 important films of Soviet cinema.

I, FRANCIS SKORINA — 1970 - Boris Stepanov (Belarusfilm)
A dramatized film biography of a 16th-century Belorussian philosopher and doctor.

I LOVE — 1940 - Leonid Lukov (Ukrainfilm)
Based on the novel by Alexander Avdeenko. This story about a coal miner in tsarist times was well liked because of the naturalism of unrestrained folk humor. The hero endures exploitation until he becomes class conscious.

I LOVED YOU — 1968 - Ilya Frez (Maxim Gorki Studios)
A tender story about Kolya, a 15-year old boy, who falls in love for the first time in his life. When his romantic illusions are shattered he realizes he must search within himself for the meaning of life.

I WILL RETURN — 1935 - A. Ledashchev (Turkmenfilm)
Based on the poem "The Farm Laborer" by Oraz Tashnazarov. During the great purges Tashnazarov was arrested and the film was banned until after 1956 when it was briefly revived. The story was about the growth of class consciousness and revolution among Turkmenian peasants. Ledashchev was one of Pudovkin's students and his work enjoyed a good deal of popularity when it was first released.

THE ICEBREAKER — 1963 - K. Kiisk (Tallinfilm)
A drama about the resistance movement in Nazi-occupied Estonia. The story centers on a group of fishermen on a small Estonian island and their efforts to stand up to the Germans.

THE IDIOT — 1957 - Ivan Pyriev (Mosfilm) — Also entitled *Natasha Filipovna.*
Pyriev wrote the script for this adaptation of Dostoevski's novel.

Reportedly Pyriev planned two parts for this film but the second was never begun. A colorful film which more closely approaches theater by having a series of acts in single, fixed sets.

IF YOU WANT TO BE HAPPY — 1974 - Nikolai Gubienko (Mosfilm)
Social satire.

IGOR BULICHOV — 1953 - Yulia Solntseva (Kiev Studios)

IGOR BULICHOV AND OTHERS — 1972 - S. Soloviev

ILLAN-DILLI — 1926 - Ivan Perestiani (Goskinprom-Gruziya)
Sequel to *Little Red Devils.*

ILYA MUROMETS — 1956 - Alexander Ptushko (Mosfilm)
Partly animated film about a folk hero of Russian legends in the dragon-slayer tradition. Has occasionally been exhibited on American television.

IMMORTAL GARRISON — 1956 - Zakhar Agranenko and Eduard Tisse (Mosfilm)
Based on the novel by Konstantin Simonov. Although overlooked by many foreign film observers, this is one work that heralded the post-Stalin renascence of Soviet cinema. The drama is about the heroism and fall of the Soviet garrison at Brest-Litovsk in the face of overwhelming German forces in June 1941. The story indicated that the Soviet Army was not fully prepared for war. During Stalin's years Brest-Litovsk was hardly mentioned in official histories of the war.

IN CHINA — 1941 - Roman Karmen (Central Newsreel Studio)
War documentary.

IN LOVE — 1968 - Elyer Ishmuhammedov

IN PEACETIME — 1951 - Vladimir Braun
Cold War drama. An American submarine lays mines along Soviet shipping lanes and is sunk by a Soviet warship while on its way to rescue a Soviet submarine that had been damaged by the American mines.

IN THE BIG CITY — 1929 - Mark Donskoi (Belgoskino)
   Story about a young, dream-filled poet who comes to Moscow from the countryside. In his encounter with city life the poet's talents are slowly eroded in his pursuit of cheap, easy success.

IN THE CELLARS OF MOSCOW — (See *Bed and Sofa*)

IN THE CLUTCHES OF SOVIET POWER — (See *Adventures of A Manufacturer*)

IN THE DAYS OF STRUGGLE — 1920 - Ivan Perestiani
   Civil War *agitka*.

IN THE DEPTHS OF THE SEA — 1933 - Alexander Zguridi
   Documentary on marine life and oceanography.

IN THE FAR EAST — 1937 - D. Maryan
   Foreign espionage and intrigue against the Soviet Union.

IN THE HOUSE OF A RICH LADY — 1970 - Leonid Leimanis
(Riga Film Studio)

IN THE ICY OCEAN — 1952 - Alexander Zguridi
   Popular science film on Arctic oceanography.

IN THE LAND OF AVALANCHES — 1931 - Siko Dolidze
(Goskinprom-Gruziya)
   A semi-feudal, isolated region of Georgia is the setting for a contest between old and new ways of life in the early Soviet era.

IN THE LAST HOUR — 1928 - Mikhail Chiaureli
(Goskinprom-Gruziya)
   Chiaureli's first independent film and one that marked his liking for political themes. A Civil War melodrama about a train carrying Red Army men to rescue some beleaguered workers and is stopped by a railway repair team headed by a treacherous foreman. After a quarrel the track is hastily repaired and the train speeds off to its destination. The film gave no hint of Chiaureli's later, brighter talent.

IN THE LINE OF FIRE — 1941 - Dziga Vertov
Frontline documentary during early period of Soviet-German war.

IN THE MOUNTAINS OF ALA-TAU — 1944 - Dziga Vertov
Documentary.

IN THE MOUNTAINS OF YUGOSLAVIA — 1946 - Abram Room
(Mosfilm)
A war drama about the struggle of Tito and his partisans against
German forces in Yugoslavia. The film was removed from exhibition be-
cause of Stalin's feud with Tito.

IN THE NAME OF GOD — 1925 - Abas-mirza Sharif-zade (AFKU)
An antireligious story about repugnant and feudal aspects of the
Moslem religion in Azerbaidzhan.

IN THE NAME OF LENIN — 1932 - Mikhail Slutski
Documentary on the building of the Dneprostroi Dam.

IN THE NAME OF LIFE — 1947 - Iosif Heifitz and Alexander Zarkhi
(Lenfilm)

IN THE NAME OF THE FATHERLAND — 1943 - Vsevolod Pudovkin
(Consolidated Studios, Alma-Ata)
Adapted from the play *Russian People* by Konstantin Simonov. A
popular war film about the heroism of Russian partisans behind German
lines.

IN THE PACIFIC — 1957 - Alexander Zguridi
Popular science film.

IN THE PILLORY — 1924 - Amo Bek-Nazarov (Goskinprom-Gruziya)
A drama about depotism and lack of human rights in tsarist
Georgia.

IN THE REAR OF THE ENEMY — 1941 - Yevgeni Shneider under
supervision of Sergei Yutkevich (Soyuzdetfilm)
A drama about the Russo-Finnish War of 1939-40.

IN THE REAR OF THE WHITES — 1925 - Boris Chaikovski and O. Rakhmanova
Civil War espionage thriller.

IN THE REGION OF HEIGHT A — 1941 - Dziga Vertov
Frontline documentary.

IN THE SANDS OF CENTRAL ASIA — 1943 - Alexander Zguridi (Kievtekhfilm)
Nature documentary which won the Stalin Prize.

IN THE SEVEN WINDS — 1962 - Stanislav Rostotski (Mosfilm)

IN THE SHADOW OF DEATH — 1972 - Gunar Piyesis (Riga Film Studio)
Drama about exploration and life in the Arctic. Based on the novel by Rudolf Blauman.

IN THE SMOKE OF NEP — 1924 - B. Svetozarov
Adventuristic melodrama about social moral decay in the NEP period. The story was about a man who surrenders his virtues to the temptations of a vamp.

IN THE STEPS OF OUR ANCESTORS — 1961 - Alexander Zguridi
Popular science film on evolution.

IN THE TOWN OF "S" — 1966 - Iosif Heifitz (Lenfilm)
A colorful costume drama based on the work by Chekhov about a young physician who falls into a hopeless love for a carefree, wealthy girl.

IN THE WHIRLWIND OF REVOLUTION — 1922 - Alexander Chargonin
Romantic and class-conscious melodrama about a coal miner who falls in love with the daughter of the mine's director.

INCIDENT AT THE TELEGRAPH OFFICE — 1941 - Grigori Kozintsev
Featurette, *Fighting Film Album No. 2*. One of the best remembered of the Soviet wartime shorts in which Napoleon sends a telegram to Hitler warning him of the dangers of invading Russia.

THE INCREDIBLE ADVENTURES OF ITALIANS IN RUSSIA —
1974 - Eldar Ryazanov (Mosfilm/Dino di Laurentis)
   Social satire; Italian-Soviet coproduction.

INDIAN MORNING — 1959 - Roman Karmen
(Central Documentary Studios)
   Indian-Soviet coproduction; documentary.

INSIDE THE USSR — 1959 - Ilya Kopalin
(Central Documentary Studios)
   On daily life of the Soviet people.

INTERNATIONALE — 1933 - Girgori Alexandrov
   Experimental short documentary.

INTERPLANETARY REVOLUTION — 1924 - Animation Workshop
   A Cartoon parody on *Aelita.*

INTO THE STORM — 1966 - Sergei Mikaelion (Lenfilm)

THE INTRACTABLE — (See *Nadya's Charges*)

INVASION — 1944 - Abram Room (Consolidated Studios, Alma-Ata)
   The hero of this story returns home from prison prior to the Nazi
invasion. Alienated from friends and family because of his prison experiences he is on the verge of leaving home when the Germans attack.
After much inner turmoil he decides to fight against the invaders. In the
end he is captured and tortured by the Gestapo. An unusual theme that
points up the intensity of the Soviet campaign to foster patriotism by
using a former political prisoner as a hero.

THE INVINCIBLE — 1943 - Sergei Gerasimov and Mikhail Kalatozov
(Tashkent Studio)
   A popular war drama about the defense of Leningrad, 1941-43.
Filmed in Central Asia.

IRON HEEL — 1919 - Vladimir Gardin
   Based on the novel by Jack London.

THE ISLAND — 1972 - Fedor Khitruk (Soyuzmultfilm)
    Animated story about a man stranded on an uninhabited island.

ISMET — 1934 - M. Mikaelov (Azerkino)
    This film was inspired by Mikaelov's meeting with Leila Mamedbekova, the first Azerbaidzhanian aviatrix. Generational differences, internal conflicts, and the struggle of old and new forces dominate this story about Ismet, a young Azerbaidzhanian woman, who battles to gain her rightful place as an equal to men in Soviet society in the 1930s.

IT HAPPENED IN PENKOVO — 1957 - Stanislav Rostotski (Mosfilm)

IT IS NOT TOO LATE — 1958 - Vitautas Zalakevicius with Fogelman (Lithuanian Film Studio)

IT STARTED LIKE THIS — 1956 - Lev Kulidzhanov and Yakov Segel (Mosfilm)

IUDUSHKA GOLOVLEV — 1934 - Alexander Ivanovski (Mezhrabpomfilm)
    Based on the novel *The Golovlev Family* by Mikhail Saltykov-Shchedrin about life in tsarist Russia. Heavily theatrical and sentimental. Only Vladimir Gardin's acting saved the film from failure in the eyes of Soviet critics.

IVAN — 1932 - Alexander Dovzhenko (Ukrainfilm)
    Dovzhenko's first sound film which did not quite enjoy the success of his earlier or later films. The theme of the story is the conflict between the new, productive Soviet man and the social idler as seen in the lives of three men named Ivan. The background for the story is the building of the Dneprostroi Dam. While critics liked the lyrical photography the structure of the drama was too unorthodox.

IVAN AND MARYA — 1975 - Alexei Saltykov (Mosfilm)

IVAN NIKULIN, RUSSIAN SAILOR — 1944 - Igor Savchenko (Mosfilm)
    Dramatic exploits of a Russian war hero. One of the few Soviet wartime films made in color.

IVAN THE TERRIBLE — 1945, 1946 [1958], in two parts — Sergei Eisenstein (Consolidated Studios, Alma-Ata)

Originally planned as a trilogy, but the third part was never filmed. One of the most celebrated and controversial films of Soviet cinema. The scenario was begun in 1940 at Stalin's request to glorify the first tsar of Russia. Filming was delayed by the German invasion of Russia until 1943. Part I had its premiere in January 1945 and pleased all who saw it with the result that Eisenstein received a Stalin Prize. Part II was quickly banned because it showed a less admirable aspect of Ivan's character. The second part is best summarized by the critic Bosley Crowther who wrote "He [Eisenstein] shows in this panorama of the pitfalls of absolute power the ageless axiom that the man who must be tyrant must inevitably lose his own soul." The last part of the film was not released until five years after Stalin's death. The work exacted a heavy physical and psychological toll of its director. In contrast to the first part Eisenstein used color in the second, but for dramatic enhancement rather than visual appeal. The photography by Andrei Moskvin and Eduard Tisse, coupled with excellent art and set design give a brooding, apprehensive atmosphere that marked Ivan and his time. A grand historical film about the man who undertook to unify Russia and thereby established autocracy.

IVAN VASILIEVICH — 1973 - Leonid Gaidai (Gruziyafilm)

A light fantasy about tsarist and Soviet Russia.

IVAN'S CHILDHOOD — 1962 - Andrei Tarkovski (Mosfilm)

Shared a grand prize at the 1962 Venice Film Festival, although it met a mixed reception by Soviet critics. A poignant and occasionally surrealistic story about a young boy who must all too swiftly grow up in the midst of a cruel war. There never was a childhood for Ivan.

JACK FROST — 1966 - Alexander Rou (Maxim Gorki Studios)

A children's film based on a Russian fairy tale.

JAMILYA — 1972 - Irina Poplavskaya

Based on a story by Chingiz Aitmatov.

THE JANUARY UPRISING IN KIEV IN 1918 — (See *Arsenal*)

JAZZ COMEDY — 1934 - Grigori Alexandrov (Mosfilm) — Also entitled *Jolly Fellows.*

A musical comedy which was very popular with Soviet audiences and set the pace for other films of this genre. After Eisenstein refused to do it Alexandrov accepted the assignment for it and patterned it after American comedy and musicals.

THE JEW ON THE LAND — 1927 - Abram Room

A semi-documentary about a Jewish experimental agricultural settlement.

JEWISH LUCK — 1926 - Alexander Granovski (Goskino)

Script written by Isaak Babel and was an adaptation of a story by Sholem Aleichem. The hero is a luckless but amusing Jewish matchmaker who is confounded by poor luck at every turn. The climax occurs when he inadvertently arranges to marry one girl to another. A highpoint of the film was the matchmaker's hope and dream of importing girls from America by the shipload.

JIMMIE HIGGINS — 1931 - Georgi Tasin (VUFKU)

Isaak Babel wrote the scenario which was based on the novel by Upton Sinclair. A young American soldier, already a victim of capitalism, comes to Arkhangelsk with the American intervention forces during the Russian Civil War. While in Russia he realizes that Communism is the best way of life for himself. Tasin was badly criticized for the poor and thin portrayal of American realities. The saving grace of the work was Amvrosi Buchma's acting.

JOBS AND MEN — 1932 - Alexander Macheret (Soyuzkino-Moscow)

Early sound film that centered on the conflict of views between an American technician and a Russian worker during the construction of the Dnieper Dam. The main theme is the Soviet urge to surpass the United States.

JOLA — 1920 - Wladyslaw Starewicz (Rus Studio)

JOLANTHE — 1963 - Vladimir Gorikker (Riga Film Studio)

A colorful film opera based on the work by Tchaikovski. Performed by the orchestra and chorus of the Bolshoi Opera.

JOLLY FELLOWS — (See *Jazz Comedy*)

THE JOURNALIST — 1967 - Sergei Gerasimov (Mosfilm)
Story about contemporary Soviet society.

THE JOURNALIST GIRL — 1927 - Lev Kuleshov (Sovkino-Moscow)
Also entitled *Your Acquaintance.*
A witty satire about Soviet journalists and influential persons
which did not endear Kuleshov to Soviet critics.

JOURNEY INTO APRIL — 1963 - Vadim Derbenev (Moldovafilm)

JOURNEY TO ERZURUM — 1937 - Moisei Levin
Dealt with an episode in the life of the Russian poet Alexander
Pushkin and his travels to the Caucasus.

A JOURNEY WITH A MOVIE CAMERA — 1952 - Vladimir Shneiderov
Popular science film.

JUBILEE — 1944 - Vladimir Petrov (Mosfilm)
Comedy based on a work by Chekhov.

JUDAS — 1930 - Yevgeni Ivanov-Barkov
An antireligious drama about a priest who undergoes inner
turmoil as he questions his faith and later renounces religion.

JUDGE REITANESCU — 1929 - F. Lopatinski (VUFKU)
Story about the revolutionary struggle and workers' movement in
Rumania. The plot revolved around the fact that the stern judge and
arrested revolutionary bore a striking physical resemblance to one another. The hero manages to escape and put the judge into his cell to
await the sentence of death.

JULBARS — 1937 - Vladimir Shneiderov
Adventure drama about a Soviet police dog who was the counterpart of the American Rin Tin Tin.

JULY RAIN — 1966 - Marlen Khutsiev (Maxim Gorki Studios)
A film about Soviet youth and young love that was not controversial like Khutsiev's earlier *I Am Twenty.*

JUNGLE TRACK — 1959 - Alexander Zguridi
(Central Popular Science Studios)
    Nature film.

KADZHETI — 1940 - I. Mikaberidze (Gruziyafilm)
    Based on Shota Rustaveli's classic Georgian poem "The Man In
The Panther Skin."

KAIN AND ARTEM — 1929 - P. Petrov-Bytov
    Based on a work by Maxim Gorki which is about a Volga porter,
Artem, and a Jewish cobbler, Khaim. Under Khaim's influence and
tutelage Artem stirs with a revolutionary spirit and awakens to class
consciousness. The film was liked by critics for the way it caught the
spirit of Gorki's work. A sound track was added to the film in Paris and
rereleased.

THE KARABEKAUL CANAL — 1931 - Ye. Terpilin (Turkmenfilm)
    A drama about efforts to irrigate the Turkmenian steppes.

KARL BRUNNER — 1936 - A. Masliukov
    Anti-Nazi drama and story about the revolutionary struggle in
Hitler's Germany.

KARO — 1937 - A. Ai-Artian and S. Taits (Armenfilm)
    An Armenian children's film adapted from A. Gaidar's story "The
School." Dealt with the fate and plight of children during the Civil War.

KASHTANKA — 1925 - Olga Preobrazhenskaya
    Based on a story by Chekhov and filmed for children.

KASTUS KALINOVSKI — 1928 - Vladimir Gardin (Belgoskino)
    Initially a controversial film because it was thought too national-
istic in content. The film was an action and romantic drama about a
Belorussian revolutionary folk hero which was well liked by audiences.
Gardin's work is now credited with raising the artistic and production
standards of the Belorussian cinema, and introducing the historical-
revolutionary genre.

KATERINA IZMAILOVA — 1926 - Cheslav Sabinski —
1969 - Mikhail Shapiro (Mosfilm)
    Based on Nikolai Leskov's novel *Lady Macbeth of Mtsensk
District.* Both versions were popular with Soviet audiences. In 1962 the
Polish director Andrzej Wajda also made an adaptation of Leskov's
classic entitled *Siberian Lady Macbeth.*

KATKA'S REINETTE APPLES — 1926 - Friedrich Ermler
(Sovkino-Leningrad)
    One of Ermler's best and a work that is still regarded as a good
portrayal of the NEP period of Soviet history. This is a warm, tender
story about Katka, a young woman who comes to Petrograd in the early
1920s and has to sell apples to earn a livelihood. After being seduced
and cheated she is rescued by Fedka, a gentle man of the streets. Fedor
Nikitin's performance was a highlight of the film.

KATORGA — (See *Forced Labor*)

KAZAKHSTAN IN THE GREAT PATRIOTIC WAR — 1975 -
Asylbek Mugmanov (Kazakhfilm)
    A feature historical documentary made to commemorate the role
of the Kazakh SSR in the war against Nazi Germany.

KEEP YOUR HANDS OFF CHINA — 1925 - N. Saltykov (VUFKU)
    A semi-documentary drama about the aggressive policies of
Western imperialism in China.

KENDLILIAR — 1939 - S. Mardanov (Azerfilm)
    Mardanov died after the filming had been finished and final
editing was done by Amo Bek-Nazarov. Drama about the uprising of
Azerbaidzhanian peasants against the bourgeoisie in 1919-20.

THE KEY — 1961 - Lev Atamanov (Soyuzmultfilm)
    Feature cartoon film.

KHABARDA — (See *Out Of The Way!*)

KHANUMA — 1926 - A. Tsutsunova (Goskinprom-Gruziya)
    Comedy based on the play by A. Tsagareli.

THE KHARKOV TRIAL — 1945 - Alexander Dovzhenko
Documentary on Nazi atrocities in the Ukraine.

KHAS-PUSH — 1927 - Amo Bek-Nazarov (Armenkino)
This film represented a noticeable change in Bek-Nazarov's style toward more revolutionary, innovative structuring. Based on stories by Raffi and Vrtanes Papzian the work was about the poverty and exploitation of the Khas-push minority in Iran in 1891. The poor peasants become aware of their feudal conditions and rise in revolt against foreign imperialists.

KHMEL — 1923 - Vladimir Gardin (VUFKU)
A revolutionary and Civil War drama set in the Ukraine. The story is about the Red Army's campaign against the ataman Khmel.

KHOVANSHINA — 1958 - Vera Stroyeva (Mosfilm)
Filmed opera based on the work by Mussorgski and performed by the Moscow Opera.

KIDNAPPING CAUCASIAN STYLE — (See *The Caucasian Prisoner*)

A KIEV COMEDY — 1962 - Viktor Ivanov
(Alexander Dovzhenko Studios)
Social satire.

KIKOS — 1931 - M. Darbinian (Armenfilm)
Satire about the changing political conditions in Armenia during the Civil War. The story focuses on a simple peasant who is often bedevilled by the necessity to readjust himself to changing political fortunes.

KING LEAR — 1970 - Grigori Kozintsev (Mosfilm)
Winner of the grand prize at the 1972 Tehran Film Festival and of the Silver Hugo award at the 1972 Chicago Film Festival. This film has proved to be the crowning achievement in Kozintsev's film-making career. This adaptation of Shakespeare has been applauded for Kozintsev's handling of the dramatic and psychological aspects of the play. One of the most prestigious Soviet films of the 1970s.

[See also: Yutkevich, Sergei. "The Conscience of the King: Kozintsev's King Lear," *Sight and Sound*, 1971 (Autumn), vol. 40, no. 4, p. 192.]

THE KINGDOM OF WOMEN — 1967 - Alexei Saltykov (Mosfilm)

KINO EYE — 1924 - Dziga Vertov
Documentary series.

KINO PRAVDA — 1922-24 - Dziga Vertov
Film news magazine.

KINO WEEK — 1918-21 - Dziga Vertov
Newsreel series.

KIRA KIRALINA — 1927 - Boris Glagolin (VUFKU)
Based on the novel by Panait Istrati.

KLYCH — 1936 - Yuldash Agzamov (Uzbekgoskino)
First Uzbek children's film. Klych is a young boy who finally realizes his dream of seeing a train and takes a trip to the big city of Tashkent.

THE KOLI REBELLION — 1933 - Ivan Kavaleridze (VUFKU)
A drama about the revolt of Ukrainian serfs against their Polish masters in the 18th century. Critics chided Kavaleridze for depicting the event in national rather than class terms.

KOLKHOZ SPRING — 1930 - A. Martirosian (Armenfilm)
Drama about the sharp and bitter struggles between rich and poor peasants in Armenia during the campaign to collectivize agriculture.

KOMSOMOL — GUIDE TO ELECTRIFICATION — 1932 - Esther Shub
Documentary on the work of Young Communists in the drive to electrify the country.

KOMSOMOL CELEBRATION — 1958 - Leonid Makhnach
Documentary.

KOMSOMOLSK — 1938 - Sergei Gerasimov (Lenfilm)

The film was made at Stalin's suggestion and dramatized the work of Komsomol laborers in building the new city named after them in the Soviet Far East. In addition to portraying the hardships faced by the young workers the story also included the theme of vigilance against domestic class enemies. Considered less melodramatic than Gerasimov's earlier *The Brave Seven* and an example of heroic realism at its best.

THE KREMLIN CHIMES — 1970 - V. Georgiev (Mosfilm)

Based on the play of the same name. The film centers on Lenin's work in planning the electrification of the USSR.

[See also *Dawn Over Russia.*]

KURDY-EZIDY — 1933 - P. Barkhudarian (Armenfilm)

One of the few films to deal with the life of the Kurdish minority in the USSR. The story deals with the struggle of the poor Kurds against rich peasants at the time of agricultural collectivization.

KUTUZOV IN 1812 — 1943 - Vladimir Petrov (Mosfilm)

Historical drama about General Kutuzov's strategic withdrawals in the face of Napoleon's invasion of Russia in 1812. The film indirectly explained the reasons for the Soviet Army's retreats of 1941 and 1942 as being strategically justified.

LACE — 1928 - Sergei Yutkevich (Sovkino)

An idealistic story about the Komsomol in its endeavors to end the rowdy behavior of young workers.

A LAD FROM OUR TOWN — 1942 - Alexander Stolper

Konstantin Simonov wrote the screenplay which was based on his novel of the same name. A war drama about the heroism of a young Soviet soldier.

LADIES — 1954 - Lev Kulidzhanov and Oganissian (Mosfilm)

THE LADY WITH THE LITTLE DOG — 1959 - Iosif Heifitz (Lenfilm)

An adaptation of Anton Chekhov's story about a hopeless love affair between two lonely people, both married, while on vacation in

Yalta. One of Heifitz's best films and an excellent adaptation of Chekhov. The spirit of life in pre-1917 Russia is excellently evoked by the manner of Andrei Moskvin's photography and art design.

THE LAME NOBLEMAN — 1928 - Konstantin Eggert
(Mezhrabpom-Rus)
Based on a story by Alexei Tolstoi which dealt with a dissolute nobleman before the 1917 Revolution. The aristocrat deserts the woman he loves but later returns to her after enduring hardship and poverty. Prior to the film's release Eggert made several changes in response to Party criticism. Despite the revisions the film was removed from exhibition after a short time.

LAND AND PEOPLE — 1955 - Stanislav Rostotski (Mosfilm)

LAND OF OUR FATHERS — 1967 - Shaken Aimanov (Kazakhfilm)

LAND OF THE SOVIETS — 1938 - Esther Shub
Documentary.

THE LANDOWNER — 1924 - Vladimir Gardin (VUFKU)
Based on the poem by N. Ogarev. The film is now lost. When it was first released the work received little critical notice and what little it did was negative. Gardin was panned for catering to bourgeois tastes in this melodrama about the Russian gentry prior to the Revolution.

THE LANFIERE COLONY — 1970 - Jan Schmidt (Barrandov/Mosfilm)
A Czechoslovak-Soviet coproduction. The pressures and false values of civilization drive a man to seek solitude on a desert island.

THE LAST ATTRACTION — 1929 - Ivan Pravov
Adventure drama about a Russian circus troupe in southern Russia caught in the turmoil of the Civil War.

THE LAST CROSS BEARERS — 1934 - Siko Dolidze
(Goskinprom-Gruziya)
This film marked the screen debut of actor Sergo Zakariadze in the role of Torgvai. The story dealt with the ending of a centuries-old feud between various Georgian mountain tribes.

THE LAST GAME — 1961 - Yevgeni Karelov (Mosfilm)

THE LAST MASQUERADE — 1937 - Mikhail Chiaureli
(Goskinprom-Gruziya)
A social drama about class differences in Georgia from the pre-1914 era to the first years of the Soviet republic as seen through the lives of a nobleman and a young worker.

THE LAST MONTH OF AUTUMN — 1965 - Vadim Derbenev
(Moldovafilm)
E. Lebedev received the Southern Cross prize for best male actor at the 1966 Mar del Plata Film Festival for his lead performance in this film. The film was awarded a grand prix at the 1967 Cannes International Youth Film Festival. The story explores the relationship between an old man and his four sons. He finds himself in the autumnal years of his life and decides to visit his sons, perhaps for the last time, in order to see what kinds of people they have turned out to be. A warm, poignant story.

THE LAST NIGHT — 1937 - Yuli Raizman (Mosfilm)
The destinies of two families, one wealthy and one poor, are explored during the last night of the old order and the first night of the Revolution against the background of Bolshevik takeover of power in Moscow. One of Raizman's best.

THE LAST PAGES OF LENIN — 1963 - Fedor Tyapkin
Documentary.

THE LAST PORT — 1932 - A. Kordium
Drama about the revolutionary movement in the Russian Navy on the eve of the October Revolution.

THE LAST RELIC — 1971 - Grigori Kromanov (Tallinfilm)
A historical drama about the struggle of the Estonian peasantry against the Germans and Swedes in the 16th century.

THE LAST STAKE OF MR. ENNIOK — (See *The Duel (1923)*)

LATIF — 1930 - M. Mikaelov (Azerkino)
Set against the collectivization struggles in Azerbaidzhan. Two poor peasants decide to revolt against their master, a rich peasant, and organize a kolkhoz.

LAUTARI — 1973 - Emil Lotyani (Moldovafilm)

LAW AND DUTY — 1927 - Kote Mardzhanishvili (Goskinprom-Gruziya)
Drama about attempted British colonial expansion into the Caucasus.

LAW OF GREAT LOVE — 1945 - Boris Dolin
Nature documentary. Stalin Prize.

LAW OF LIFE — 1940 - Alexander Stolper and Boris Ivanov (Mosfilm)
Reportedly made at the suggestion of Lavrenti Beria, then chief of the secret police. The film was exhibited in Leningrad for only two days before it was banned because of its unvarnished portrayal of the low morals of Komsomol members.

A LAWSUIT FOR THREE MILLION — 1926 - Yakov Protazanov (Mezhrabpom-Rus)
A witty social satire and comedy about three kindly, clever thieves based on the novel *The Three Thieves* by Umberto Notari. Despite a negative reaction by Soviet critics the film was a financial success.

THE LEFT HANDER — 1964 - Ivan Ivanov-Vano (Soyuzmultfilm)
Feature cartoon.

LEGEND OF A CRUEL GIANT — 1968 - Ivan Ivanov-Vano (Soyuzmultfilm)
Feature cartoon.

LEGEND OF THE ICE HEART — 1957 - Eldar Shengelaya and Alexei Sakharov (Gruziyafilm)

THE LEGEND OF THE MAIDEN'S TOWER — 1924 —
Vladimir Ballyuzek (AFKU)
     First Azerbaidzhanian theatrical film to be made with an all-Azerbaidzhanian cast. While the exotic elements appealed to audiences the critics were displeased by the overdramatization of this story. A legendary drama about a Prince who harbors a secret lust for his own daughter. When she falls in love the Prince imprisons her in a tower built out on the Caspian Sea. In despair she throws herself into the sea.

LENIN — 1948 - Vasili Belayev and Mikhail Romm (Mosfilm)
     Documentary.

LENIN IN 1918 — 1939 - Mikhail Romm (Mosfilm)
     Made largely under the control and supervision of Lavrenti Beria which insured that Stalin's historical role in the film was emphasized. Boris Shchukin played the title role in this dramatization of the problems that confronted Lenin and the Bolsheviks in their first and most critical year of political power. Still considered one of Romm's best works and one of the better films of the 1930s. The film was renovated in 1965 at which time many historically inaccurate sequences were cut out prior to the film's rerelease.

LENIN IN 1903 — 1970 - Yuli Karasik (Mosfilm)
     Drama about Lenin's early struggle for leadership in the Russian revolutionary movement.

LENIN IN OCTOBER — 1937 - Mikhail Romm (Mosfilm)
     Made in a very few months to commemorate the twentieth anniversary of the October Revolution. The part of Lenin was played by Boris Shchukin in this drama about the Bolshevik preparations for revolution. Stalin was depicted as an equal to Lenin.

LENIN IN POLAND — 1966 - Sergei Yutkevich (Mosfilm/Polska Studio)
     A Soviet-Polish corporduction which gained for Yutkevich the prize for best direction at the 1966 Cannes Film Festival. A warm and rather charming film about Lenin's hopes and dreams in the years prior to the 1917 Revolution. Maxim Shtraukh played the lead role and showed Lenin as a man rather than as a demi-god.

LENIN IN SWITZERLAND — 1966 - Grigori Alexandrov (Mosfilm)
Dramatization about Lenin and his life among other Russian
exiles in the years before the 1917 Revolution.

LENINGRAD FIGHTS — 1942 - Roman Karmen
(Central Newsreel Studios)
Documentary on the defense and siege of Leningrad.

LENINGRAD SYMPHONY — 1957 - Zakhar Agranenko (Lenfilm)
A dramatized story about Dmitri Shostakovich's composition of
the Seventh or Leningrad Symphony which was written at the height of
the siege of Leningrad in 1941.

LENINGRAD TODAY — 1927 - Ilya Trauberg
Documentary.

LENINIST FILM TRUTH — 1925 - Dziga Vertov
Documentary chronicle and tribute to Lenin.

LEON COUTURIER — 1927 - Vladimir Kasianov
Civil War espionage drama about a Bolshevik agent operating behind enemy lines disguised as a Frenchman. After being exposed he dies
a hero.

THE LEPROUS WOMAN — 1928 - Oleg Frelikh (Uzbekgoskino)

LERMONTOV — 1943 - A. Gendelstein (Soyuzdetfilm)
A dramatized biography of the famous Russian poet.

THE LESSON OF LIFE — 1955 - Yuli Raizman (Mosfilm)

THE LESSON OF HISTORY — 1957 - Lev Arnshtam (Mosfilm)

LET'S LIVE UNTIL MONDAY — 1968 - Stanislav Rostotski
(Maxim Gorki Studios) — Also entitled *Until Monday*.
A drama about the problems and lives of Soviet teachers.

THE LETTER THAT WAS NOT SENT — 1960 - Mikhail Kalatozov
(Mosfilm)

LIBERATED CHINA — 1950 - Sergei Gerasimov
(Central Documentary Studios)
    Documentary on the Communist victory and the defeat of
Chiang Kai-shek.

LIBERATED EARTH — 1946 - Alexander Medvedkin
(Sverdlovsk Studio)
    Documentary on the Kuban area.

LIBERATED FRANCE — 1945 - Sergei Yutkevich
(Central Documentary Studios)
    Documentary on Allied victory in France 1944-45 which was
made primarily from reedited newsreels.

LIBERATION — 1940 - Alexander Dovzhenko and Yulia Solntseva
(Kiev Studios)
    Documentary on the annexation of western Ukraine to the USSR
after Hitler's victory in Poland.

LIBERATION — 1970 - Yuri Ozerov (Mosfilm)
    A multi-part epic drama of World War II for which Marshal
Zhukov served as technical consultant. The film had an international
cast and has been widely admired since its release.

LIEUTENANT BASIL — 1970 - Yuri Lysenko
(Alexander Dovzhenko Studios)
    Story about a Ukrainian World War II hero who joined the French
partisans after escaping from a Nazi concentration camp.

LIEUTENANT KIJE — 1934 - Alexander Faintsimmer (Sovetskaya
Belarus) — Also entitled *The Tsar Wants To Sleep.*
    A fanciful and at times exaggerated comedy about the era of Tsar
Paul I. Based on the story by Yu. Tynianov. Contained a good musical
score by Prokofiev. Proved very popular despite eccentric acting.

LIFE — 1927 - Mark Donskoi (Belgoskino)

LIFE IN A CITADEL — 1947 - Herbert Rappoport (Lenfilm)
    Stalin Prize film based on the Estonian play by Avgust Yakobson.

LIFE IN BLOOM — (See *Michurin*)

THE LIGHT OF A DISTANT STAR — 1965 - Ivan Pyriev (Mosfilm)

LIGHT OVER RUSSIA — (See *Dawn Over Russia*)

THE LIGHTS GO ON IN THE CITY — 1958 - Vladimir Vengerov

LILEYA — 1958 - Vasili Lapoknysh and Vakhtang Vronski
(Kiev Studios)
Film ballet performed by the Shevchenko Theater.

THE LING — 1938 - S. Sploshnov (Sovetskaya Belarus)
Adaptation of a story by Anton Chekhov.

LITTLE BROTHER — 1927 - Grigori Kozintsev and Leonid Trauberg
(Sovkino-Leningrad)
A lyrical comedy set in the time of the October Revolution about
a driver and his problems in repairing a truck. The film has been reported lost.

LITTLE CRANE — 1969 - Nikolai Moskalenko (Mosfilm)
A lyrical romance based on Mikhail Alexeiev's story "Bread Is A
Noun."

LITTLE EAGLE — 1967 - V. Bordzilovski (Soyuzmultfilm)
Animated film about a young boy who visits the Museum of the
Revolution and there relives the events of the Russian Civil War in his
fantasies.

THE LITTLE FRUITS OF LOVE — 1926 - Alexander Dovzhenko
(VUFKU)
This short, frenzied comedy about the results of love marked
Dovzhenko's directorial debut.

THE LITTLE GOLD KEY — 1939 - Alexander Ptushko
(Soyuzmultfilm)
Feature animated film.

THE LITTLE HUMPBACKED HORSE — 1941 - Alexander Rou
(Mosfilm) — 1948 - Ivan Ivanov-Vano (Soyuzmultfilm) —
1961 - Alexander Radunski (Mosfilm)
Adaptations of the Russian fairy tale of the same name. Rou's
film was a delightful, enchanting comedy. Ivanov-Vano's version was a
feature cartoon. The last was a filmed ballet adaptation performed by
the Bolshoi Ballet.

LITTLE RED DEVILS — 1923 - Ivan Perestiani (Goskinprom-Gruziya)
Also called *Red Imps* occasionally.
One of the earliest Georgian theatrical films. The work was so
popular that the film was repaired and refurbished with a limited sound
track in 1943. A wild, impish adventure thriller in the American cowboy tradition about three youngsters, including one Negro, and their
struggles against the bandit leader Makhno during the Civil War.
Perestiani tried to recapture his success with this film by making three
sequels, none of which proved successful.

THE LITTLE STRIPED ELEPHANT — 1971 - I. Gurvich
(Kievnauchfilm)
Feature cartoon about the explorations of an adventurous baby,
striped elephant.

LITTLE TARAS — 1926 - Pyotr Chardynin (VUFKU)
Dramatization of the boyhood of the great Ukrainian poet Taras
Shevchenko.

THE LITTLE TIME MACHINE — 1967 - Valentina
and Zenaeda Brumberg (Soyuzmultfilm)
Animated science-fiction for children.

THE LIVING AND THE DEAD — 1964 - Alexander Stolper (Mosfilm)
Won first prize at the 1964 Leningrad All-Union Film Festival and
grand prize at the Karlovy Vary Film Festival. Based on the novel by
Konstantin Simonov. A war drama about the Soviet Army's defeats in
1941 told with compassion and insight. Central to the story is the heroism of the Soviet soldier despite disastrous defeats. The characters are
well rounded and the most interesting is that of General Serpilin, a victim of the great purges who is suddenly recalled to active duty.

Stolper's work has been well received and given high marks for the bold probing into the reasons for the Army's disasters in the first summer of war.

THE LIVING CORPSE — 1918 - Cheslav Sabinski — 1928 - Fedor Ozep (Mezhrabpomfilm/Prometheus) — 1953 - Vladimir Vengerov (Mosfilm) — 1969 - Vladimir Vengerov (Mosfilm)
     Adaptations of the play by Lev Tolstoi. Ozep's film was a German-Soviet coproduction which was only moderately successful. Vengerov's first version was a filmed play while his second was a free-form film.

THE LIVING GOD — 1935 - M. Verner and D. Vasiliev (Tadzhik-kino)
     Story about the Ismail sect and Aga Khan, both depicted as agents of Western imperialism. Filmed on location in the Pamirs. Soviet critics were displeased by the film's weak portrayal of national life.

LIVING HEROES — 1960 (Lithuanian Film Studio)
     Made as four film novellas: "We Do Not Need It", M. Gedris; "Solovushka", B. Bratkauskas; "The Last Round", A. Zebriunas; and "Living Heroes", Vitautas Zalakevicius. The novellas trace contemporary and wartime episodes in the lives of a group of Lithuanian children.

LIVING WATER — 1962 - Larissa Shepitko
     Short film.

THE LOCKSMITH AND THE CHANCELLOR — 1923 - Vladimir Gardin (VUFKU)
     An adaptation of the play by Anatoli Lunacharski. The script was prepared by Vsevolod Pudovkin. This was another of Gardin's abstract allegories about the recent Russian revolutionary experience which did not altogether please critics. The drama begins with a war between two mythical countries, Nordlandia and Galikania. As the war drags on the workers of Nordlandia become discontented and rebel. The bourgeoisie flees the country and the proletariat seizes political power.

LOCOMOTIVE NO. 1000b — 1926 - Lev Kuleshov
     Experimental short film.

A LOFTY CALLING — (See *High Rank*)

LONE WHITE SAIL — 1937 - Vladimir Legoshin (Soyuzdetfilm)
Adapted from the novel by Valentin Katayev. The story deals with two young boys who witness the revolutionary events of 1905 in Odessa.

A LONG HAPPY LIFE — 1966 - Gennadi Shpalikov (Mosfilm)

THE LONG WAY — 1956- Leonid Gaidai with Nevzorov (Gruziyafilm)

LOOK AT THE ROOT — 1932 - B. Antonovski
Animated film.

LOST PARADISE — 1937 - David Rondeli (Goskinprom-Gruziya)
Comedy and social satire based on the highly successful Georgian play *Autumn Noblemen.*

THE LOST PHOTOGRAPH — 1959 - Lev Kulidzhanov (Mosfilm)

THE LOST SUMMER — 1963 - Rolan Bykov (Mosfilm)

LOST TREASURES — 1924 - Amo Bek-Nazarov (Goskinprom-Gruziya)
Based on a story by P. Morskoi. Mystery and intrigue thriller with a secondary antireligious theme. During the Civil War a group of priests take valuable relics from a monastery and attempt to hand them over to anti-Soviet counterrevolutionaries.

LOVE FOR THREE ORANGES — 1970 - Viktor Titov
A Bulgarian-Soviet coproduction. Film version of Prokofiev's opera.

THE LUGA DEFENSE LINE — (See *Blockade*)

LULLABY — 1937 - Dziga Vertov
A lyrical film poem on Soviet motherhood and one of Vertov's best.

MABUL — 1926 - Yevgeni Ivanov-Barkov

Based on a novel by Sholem Aleichem. Drama about tsarist pogroms and anti-Semitic terrorism.

MACDONALD — 1925 - Les Kurbas (VUFKU-Odessa Studio)

Bizarre satire about the leader of the British Labor Party and his espousal of an anti-Soviet policy. The highlight of the film is the sequence showing MacDonald, well dressed, run into a workers' club to avoid journalists and emerges dirty, torn, and abused.

MACHEKHA SAMANISHVILI — 1927 - Kote Mardzhanishvili (Goskinprom-Gruziya)

A satire on the parasitic elements of Georgian society at the end of the 19th century. An aging Georgian widower-landowner suddenly decides to remarry which throws his son and daughter-in-law into despair over the prospects of sharing the old man's wealth with another possible heir.

THE MADONNA OF ROMNY — 1974 - Anatoli Slesarenko (Ukrainian Documentary Studios)

A true life documentary about Alexandra Derevskaya, who took in and cared for forty-five children during World War II. The film features a reunion of her charges, now adults, as they reminisce about Derevskaya.

MAGDANA'S DONKEY — 1956 - Tengiz Abuladze and Revas Chkeidze (Gruziyafilm)

The story is set in a small Georgian village in the 1890s and is about Magdana, who is a poor widow and ekes out a livelihood by selling milk. The future brightens when she and her children find a sick, abandoned donkey. Love and hope are focused on the animal even when the owner returns and reclaims it. This film heralded the arrival of a new generation of film-makers in Soviet cinema and its warm humanism marked a new trend in Soviet films.

THE MAGIC CARPET — 1947 - Lev Atamanov (Armenfilm)

Cartoon feature.

MAGNETIC ANOMALY — 1924 - Pyotr Chardynin (VUFKU)
Satire on the contemporary Soviet scene. A petty bureaucrat takes no action on the requests of a metallurgical plant for more supplies of ore except to note that the requests are improperly filled out. In desperation a plant engineer searches for local sources of iron ore and stumbles across a large stockpile of ore. In the end the plant reopens with an abundant supply of ore.

MAGNIFICENT ISLANDS — 1965 - Alexander Zguridi
Popular science documentary.

MAIDS OF THE MOUNTAIN — 1918 - Alexander Sanin (Rus Studio)
Melodrama on the struggle between good and evil and was the culmination of the romanticist "satanic" style. Filmed in 1917.

MAINLAND — (See *Great Land*)

MAKSIM MAKSIMICH — 1927 - Vladimir Barski
(Goskinprom-Gruziya)
Popular and commercially successful partial adaptation of Mikhail Lermontov's *Hero Of Our Time*.

MALAKHOV KURGAN — 1944 - Iosif Heifitz and Alexander Zarkhi
A war drama which was shelved because of artistic shortcomings.

MAN AND WORDS — 1973 - E. Sivokon (Kievnauchfilm)
An animated satire on the use and misuse of words.

A MAN FOLLOWS THE SUN — 1962 - Moisei Kalik (Moldovafilm)
Also entitled *Following The Sun*.
This is a story about one day in the life of a six-year old boy, Sandu, and his feelings and experiences.

MAN FROM NOWHERE — 1961 - Eldar Ryazanov (Mosfilm)

THE MAN FROM THE RESTAURANT — 1929 - Yakov Protazanov
(Mezhrabpomfilm)
A social drama about prerevolutionary Russian society. Skorokhodov is a waiter who endures humiliation from the wealthy

classes until one day he finds an inner strength and pride that he never realized he had. In the story the waiter symbolized the Russian masses, but the subtle point was apparently lost on Soviet critics at the time who unfairly dismissed it as appealling to bourgeois tastes. Now considered one of Protazanov's better films and one of the more important ones of Soviet cinema.

THE MAN I LOVE — 1966 - Yuli Karasik (Mosfilm)

MAN IN A CASE — 1939 - Isidor Annenski (Sovetskaya Belarus)
Based on the story by Chekhov.

A MAN IN A FRAME — 1966 - Fedor Khitruk (Soyuzmultfilm)
Feature cartoon.

A MAN IS BORN — 1928 - Yuri Zheliabushski
Adultery and human compassion are the themes of this social drama about a husband who forgives his wife's transgression and acknowledges her child by another man as his own.

MAN WITH A MOVIE CAMERA — 1929 - Dziga Vertov and Mikhail Kaufman (VUFKU)
A dazzling documentary on Soviet life executed with intricate and novel camera work.

THE MAN WITH THE GUN — 1938 - Sergei Yutkevich (Lenfilm)
Historical drama about the roles of Lenin and Stalin in the October Revolution as seen through the hero, a simple peasant, who at the beginning is apolitical and then becomes dedicated to the Bolshevik cause. Yutkevich received the Order of the Red Banner for Labor for this film, which featured a fine score by Dmitri Shostakovich.

MANHOOD — 1939 - Mikhail Kalatozov
Drama about Soviet aviation which included foreign espionage.

MANHOOD — 1941 - Boris Barnet
Featurette, *Fighting Film Album No. 3.*

THE MANNERHEIM LINE — 1940 - Vasili Belayev
　　Documentary on the Russo-Finnish War of 1939-40.

MARCH-APRIL — 1943 - V. Pronin
　　War film.

MARCH OF THE AIR — 1936 - Mikhail Kaufman
　　Documentary.

MARIONETTES — 1934 - Yakov Protazanov (Mezhrabpomfilm)
　　One of Protazanov's least successful films. A satire on political
intrigue that takes place in the mythical European country of Bufferia,
where a barber becomes a king over the rightful heir to the throne.

MARITE — 1947 - Vera Stroyeva (Mosfilm)
　　War drama about the personal heroism and Party loyalty of a
young Lithuanian girl who is tortured and killed by the Germans.

MARRIAGE — 1936 - E. Gardin and Lokshina
　　An adaptation of the story by Gogol.

THE MARRIAGE OF JAN KNUKKE — 1935 - Alexander Ivanov
　　Silent comedy.

MARRIAGE OF THE BEAR — 1926 - Vladimir Gardin and
Konstantin Eggert (Mezhrabpom-Rus)
　　A commercially successful film which dealt with an insane and
dissolute nobleman who kills his young bride.

MARVELLOUS GARDEN — 1935 - L. Frenkel (Kiev Studios)
　　A children's film about a youth musical group.

MARVELLOUS GIRL — 1937 - Alexander Medvedkin
　　Bizarre satire and fantasy about Soviet rural life and the miracles
performed by a peasant girl.

MASHENKA — 1942 - Yuli Raizman (Mosfilm and Alma-Ata Studios)
　　V. Karayeva in the lead role of Mashenka Stepanova, Red Army
woman, captured the hearts of Soviet wartime audiences when this film

was released. The story examines the warmth and strength of the love between Mashenka and her soldier boy friend, Alyosha. Originally begun as a drama about the Russo-Finnish War it was revised when Germany invaded the USSR. The film, poignant and heart warming, was filled with optimism for the future and is still regarded as one of the finest films of wartime Soviet cinema.

THE MASK — 1938 - S. Sploshnov (Sovetskaya Belarus)
    Based on a story by Chekhov.

MASQUERADE — 1941 - Sergei Gerasimov (Lenfilm)
    Based on a play by Mikhail Lermontov.

MASTER OF EXISTENCE — 1932 - Alexander Ptushko
    Animated sound film.

MASTER OF THE BLACK CLIFFS — 1923 - Pyotr Chardynin (VUFKU)
    Antireligious satire about a young man who becomes disillusioned with religion after seeing its falseness.

MATZI HVITIA — 1967 - Georgi Shengelaya (Gruziyafilm)

MAY NIGHT — 1941 - Nikolai Ekk (Kiev Studios)
    Based on a story by Gogol.

MAY STARS — 1959 - Stanislav Rostotski (Mosfilm)
    Inspired by Rostotski's wartime experiences. The story was about the Soviet Army's offensive to liberate Czechoslovakia in 1944-45.

THE MECHANICAL FLEA — 1964 - Ivan Ivanov-Vano (Soyuzmultfilm)
    Feature cartoon.

THE MECHANICAL TRAITOR — 1932 - Alexander Andreevski
    A satire about the First Five-Year Plan which proved unpopular with audiences and critics. Comedies about food shortages were no laughing matter.

MECHANICS OF THE BRAIN — 1926 - Vsevolod Pudovkin (Mezhrabpom-Rus)
 A semi-documentary on the work and experiments of the Russian physiologist Ivan Pavlov. The filming took a year to complete, partly because Pudovkin approached the matter with much care and planning. Became a model popular science film and established Pudovkin as a major director.

MEET LEONID ENGIBAROV — 1966 - Viktor Lisakovich
 Documentary.

MEETING — 1941 - V. Feinberg
 Featurette, *Fighting Film Album No. 2.*

MEETING ON THE ELBE — 1949 - Grigori Alexandrov (Mosfilm)
 A Cold War drama about anti-Soviet policies of American forces in postwar, occupied Germany. Technically a fine film. Stalin Prize.

MEETING WITH FRANCE — 1960 - Sergei Yutkevich (Mosfilm)
 Documentary.

MEETING WITH MAXIM — 1941 - Sergei Gerasimov
 Featurette, *Fighting Film Album No. 1.* Reintroduction of the character created in Kozintsev and Trauberg's *Maxim* trilogy.

MEETING WITH THE PAMIR MOUNTAINS — 1960 - Leonid Makhnach
 Science-adventure film.

MEETINGS AND PARTINGS — 1973 - Elyer Ishmuhammedov (Uzbekfilm)
 A tender drama about the lives and destinies of Uzbek emigrants.

MELODIES OF THE VERY NEIGHBORHOOD — 1974 - Georgi Shengelaya (Gruziyafilm)
 Received an honorary diploma at the 1974 San Sebastian Film Festival. Story on the theme of human optimism and the triumph of good over evil.

MEMBER OF THE GOVERNMENT — 1939 - Iosif Heifitz and Alexander Zarkhi (Lenfilm)
Widely acclaimed as one of the better Soviet films of the 1930s.
Alexandra Sokolova, excellently played by Vera Maretskaya, is a simple and mistreated peasant woman who slowly struggles out of her bleak and bitter life to become, first, the director of her collective farm and later a member of the Supreme Soviet. No other film on the theme of emancipation of women reflected as much depth of character development as this one. Political propaganda is subtly underplayed throughout the work.

MEMORIES AT CHKALOV — 1967 - Viktor Lisakovich
Documentary.

MEMORIES OF SERGO ORDZHONIKIDZE — 1937 - Dziga Vertov
Biographical documentary.

MEMORY — 1970 - Grigori Chukhrai (Mosfilm) — Also entitled *Stalingrad.*
A historical and retrospective documentary on the Battle of Stalingrad in which Chukhrai fought.

MEMORY OF THE PEOPLE — 1964 - Viktor Lisakovich
Documentary.

IN MEMORY OF THE GREAT COMMUNARDS — 1925 - Vl adimir Gardin (VUFKU)
A propaganda and commemorative film on the Paris Commune of 1871.

MEN AND BEASTS — 1962 - Sergei Gerasimov

MEN AND WOMEN — 1973 - Vladimir Khmelnitski (Kievnauchfilm)
Sports documentary.

MEN OF THE BLACK SEA — 1943 (Central Newsreel Studio)
War documentary on the actions of Soviet marines.

MEN ON THE BRIDGE — 1960 - Alexander Zarkhi (Mosfilm)

MEN ON WINGS — (See *Aviators*)

THE METRO BY NIGHT — 1934 - Esther Shub
Documentary.

THE MEXICAN DIPLOMATS — 1931 - L. Kalantar and A. Martirosian
(Armenfilm)
One of the most popular comedy-satires of its time. The story takes place during the Civil War and concerns the efforts of a minor official to pass off two barbers, Aram and Khechan, as Mexican diplomats as Bolshevik forces draw nearer. The official's attempt to train the two men in diplomatic etiquette turns into a disaster and he flees as the Red units enter the city. Aram and Khechan are in their barber shop, amused by the frenzy of fleeing Dashnaks.

MICHURIN — 1949 - Alexander Dovzhenko and Yulia Solntseva
(Mosfilm) — Also entitled *Life In Bloom.*
Filming was started on this biographical film in 1946 and was plagued by changes in official policy toward the life and work of the Russian scientist. Despite Dovzhenko's frustrations in working on the film it was a lyrical, almost poetic, work that is highlighted by the scene of Michurin sitting in his garden and reminiscing with his wife.

MIGHTY STREAM — 1939 - D. Varlamov and B. Nebylitski
(Central Documentary and Tashkent Studios)
Documentary on the building of the Ferghana Canal.

THE MINARET OF DEATH — 1925 - Vyacheslav Viskovski
(Sevzapkino)
Filmed on location in Bokhara, this exotic suspense thriller was based on an Oriental legend of the 16th century. Proved very popular.

MINERS — 1937 - Sergei Yutkevich (Lenfilm)
The film was in production for three years because of changing political requirements. The drama centered about a conflict of views between two Party officials regarding living conditions for miners in the Donets Basin. The proponent for better standards in living finally wins out. While the film lauded the Stakhanovite movement the propaganda elements were underplayed. Gave an accurate portrayal of life and conditions in inudstrial areas.

MININ AND POZHARSKI — 1939 - Vsevolod Pudovkin and
Mikhail Doller (Mosfilm)
   A critically admired historical drama about the alliance between
the commoner Kuzma Minin and Prince Mikhail Pozharski in the 17th
century to oppose Polish and Swedish invaders. The story emphasized
the theme that even the ruling classes contained elements that were
progressive in thought and defended the cause of the masses. The film
did not enjoy popularity among American audiences at the time because of its anti-Polish bias and appearance after the Nazi-Soviet Pact.

MIRABEAU — 1930 - A. Kordium (VUFKU-Odessa Studio)
   Drama about the Allied Intervention in southern Russia during
the Civil War. The action takes place aboard the French cruiser
Mirabeau and focuses on the refusal of its sailors to take up arms against
Ukrainian workers and peasants.

MIRACLE MAKER — 1922 - Alexander Panteleev (Sevzapkino)
   Antireligious drama that reportedly was well liked by Lenin.

THE MIRACLE WORKER — 1960 - Vladimir Skuibin (Mosfilm)

MIRACLES — 1967 - Vl adimir Monakhov (Mosfilm)

THE MIRONOV TRIAL — 1919 - Dziga Vertov
   Documentary.

MISHKA AGAINST YUDENICH — 1925 - Grigori Kozintsev and
Leonid Trauberg (Sevzapkino)
   Espionage comedy about youngsters involved in fighting against
the Whites.

MISS MEND — 1926 - Boris Barnet and Fedor Ozep (Mezhrabpom-Rus)
   A "Red detective" thriller which is set in the United States and
similar to American mystery films of the time. The action revolves
around three left-wing journalists and their girl friend who set out to
expose the crimes of a villainous capitalist. Highly successful with
audiences.

MITKA LELIUK — 1938 - A. Masliukov and M. Mayevskaya
(Odessa Studio)
A Ukrainian children's film.

MITYA — 1927 - Nikolai Okhlopkov (VUFKU-Odessa Studio)
An eccentric comedy and social satire about a young man who causes a great deal of commotion when he reveals some questionable morals in a small village.

MOLBA — 1973 - Tengiz Abuladze (Gruziyafilm)

THE MOONSHINERS — 1961 - Leonid Gaidai (Gruziyafilm)
Satire on social folkways.

THE MOONSTONE — 1935 - Adolf Minkin and I. Sirokhtin
Popular science adventure about a geological team exploring the mountains of Central Asia.

MORNING STAR — 1961 - R. Tikhomirov (Lenfilm and Frunze Studios)
Musical based on the libretto by L. Kramarovski and O. Sarbagishev with songs by the Kirghiz State Opera.

MOSCOW — 1927 - Mikhail Kaufman and Ilya Kopalin (Sovkino) — 1932 - Roman Karmen
Documentaries on Moscow life and achievements since the October Revolution.

MOSCOW AND MUSCOVITES — 1956 - Roman Grigoriev
(Central Documentary Studios)
Documentary on the Soviet capital and its people.

MOSCOW CALLING — 1945 - Sergei Yutkevich (Mosfilm)
World War II story and romance.

MOSCOW IN OCTOBER — 1927 - Boris Barnet (Mezhrabpom-Rus)
One of a series of feature films made to commemorate the tenth anniversary of the Revolution. The film depicted the revolutionary events in Moscow. Barnet undertook this work reluctantly and was not too happy with it.

MOSCOW—MY LOVE — 1974 - Alexander Mitta and Kenji Ishida (Mosfilm)
    A Japanese-Soviet coproduction.

MOSCOW SKY — 1944 - Yuli Raizman (Mosfilm)
    World War II drama based on the life of Soviet fighter pilot Viktor Tomalikhin.

MOSCOW STRIKES BACK — (See *Defeat of The German Armies Near Moscow*)

THE MOSLEM WOMAN — 1925 - Dmitri Bassaligo (Turkgoskino)
    Dealt with one of the most socially sensitive and contested issues in the Moslem regions of the USSR, the enfranchisement and social emancipation of women. The film's release coincided with resolutions passed by the I Congress of the Uzbek Communist Party which called for increasing the number of women members in the Party. Although the film was officially supported religious leaders were still influential enough to delay its exhibition in Bokhara for some time. The Russian cast gave an uneven performance, but the social impact of the film was significant. The story is about a young woman, Saodat, who is sold as a wife to a wealthy old man. She then runs away and is eventually sent to Moscow for an education.

THE MOST IMPORTANT — 1970 - V. Bordzilovski (Soyuzmultfilm)
    Animated fantasy based on the story by B. Tikhomolov.

THE MOST VALIANT — 1941 - Klimenti Mints
    Featurette, *Fighting Film Album No. 7.*

MOTHER — 1920 - Alexander Razumni (Moscow Cinema Committee) — 1926 - Vsevolod Pudovkin (Mezhrabpom-Ru s) — 1956 - Mark Donskoi (Kiev Studios)
    A classic film of Soviet cinema based on Maxim Gorki's novel of the same name which dealt with the era of the 1905 Revolution. The story dealt with a poor, peasant woman who slowly becomes class conscious through the activities and imprisonment of her revolutionary son. In structure the films varied. Razumni's version was episodic, largely because of shortage of film. Pudovkin's, considered the best, eliminated

some of the maternal motivations that were in the novel. Nikolai Batalov played the son in Pudovkin's film while his nephew Alexei had the same role in Donskoi's version. Pudovkin's version, which was banned in New York when first exhibited in the United States, was voted by critics in 1958 in Brussels as one of the 12 best films of world cinema.

MOTHERLAND — 1939 - Nikolai Shengelaya (Goskinprom-Gruziya)
    Patriotic drama about Georgian collective farm workers who discover class enemies in their midst.

THE MOTHERLAND'S SOLDIER — 1975 - Yuri Chulukin (Mosfilm)
    Filmed partly at the former concentration camp at Mauthausen. A dramatization of the 1,320 days of captivity that was endured by Soviet General Dmitri Karbyshev while a prisoner of war of the Nazis. Although subjected to psychological and physical pressures Karbyshev refused to join the Nazi-sponsored anti-Soviet Russian Liberation Army. After the war Karbyshev remained forgotten until after Stalin's death when he was finally and posthumously awarded the title of Hero of the Soviet Union.

A MOTHER'S DEVOTION — 1966 - Mark Donskoi
(Maxim Gorki Studios)
    A tender and charming story about the life of Lenin's mother.

[See also *Heart of A Mother.*]

A MOTHER'S HEART — (See *Heart of A Mother*)

MOTHERS AND DAUGHTERS — 1973 - Sergei Gerasimov (Mosfilm)
    One of the most popular of all films with Soviet audiences in 1973-74. This is a story about a young woman, Olga Vasilieva, who was abandoned as a young child by her mother for whom she is searching. Olga comes upon another Vasiliev family which is not related to her. The Vasilievs however invite Olga to stay with them and it is through their lives that Olga finds more meaningfulness to her own life. The story ends on an optimistic note as Olga is informed as to the possible whereabouts of her real mother.

THE MOUNTAIN MARCH — 1939 - S. Kevorkov (Armenfilm)
Drama about the Civil War in Armenia. Kevorkov's work is applauded for a skillful blending of folk humor and tragedy which upgraded what might have been a simple adventure-action thriller.

A MOUNTAIN STREAM — 1940 - P. Barkhudarian (Armenfilm)
Light, fanciful musical about life on a collective farm.

MOUNTAIN WOMAN — 1975 - Irina Poplavskaya (Mosfilm)
Social shock from technological change is the theme of this story about an old mountain village which is suddenly confronted by the prospect of having a dam built nearby.

MURDER ON DANTE STREET — 1956 - Mikhail Romm (Mosfilm)

MURDERERS ARE ON THEIR WAY — 1942 - Vsevolod Pudovkin (Consolidated Studios, Alma-Ata)
Adapted from plays by Berthold Brecht. An anti-Nazi war film which was shelved after completion because it was felt that the enemy characters were too weak.

MUSHFIKI GOES AFTER THE BIRDS — 1975 - Ali Khamraev (Uzbekfilm)

A MUSICAL STORY — 1940 - Alexander Ivanovski and Herbert Rappoport (Lenfilm)
A musical concert comedy about a chauffeur who becomes a renowned singer. The film featured the popular opera singer Sergei Lemeshev and Zoya Fyodorova who a year later scored great success for her role in *The Girl From Leningrad.*

MUSSORGSKI — 1950 - Grigori Roshal (Lenfilm)
Dramatized and patriotic biography of the Russian composer.

MY DAUGHTER — 1958 - Viktor Zhilin (Odessa Studio)

MY DEAR MAN — 1958 - Iosif Heifitz — 1974 - Ravil Batyrov
Based on the novel *Impudence* by U. Nazarov.

MY FRIEND KOLKA — 1963 - Alexei Saltykov and Alexander Mitta (Mosfilm)

The world of adults as seen through the eyes of youngsters.

MY LOVE — 1940 - Vladimir Korsh-Sablin (Sovetskaya Belarus)

A lyrical comedy about Soviet youth which is similar to the Hungarian film *Little Mama.*

MY MOTHERLAND — 1933 - Iosif Heifitz and Alexander Zarkhi

Story of life and social aspirations on both sides of the Soviet-Chinese border. The common aims are represented by Vaska, a Red Army soldier, and Vana, a Chinese laborer.

MY SON — 1928 - Yevgeni Chervyakov (Sovkino-Leningrad)

Drama about marriage and infidelity in which the husband accepts his wife's child by another man as his own.

[See also *A Man Is Born.*]

MY UNIVERSITIES — 1940 - Mark Donskoi (Soyuzdetfilm)

Third part of the *Maxim Gorki Trilogy.* Based on Maxim Gorki's autobiographical writings this part deals with the writer's life in the slums of Kazan and his rebellion against the hard, sweaty labor under squalid conditions. The oppressiveness of life among the common people on the eve of revolutionary outbursts in Russia is excellently evoked by the photography. One of Donskoi's best works.

MY YOUNGER BROTHER — 1962 - Alexander Zarkhi (Mosfilm)

NADEZHDA — 1954 - Sergei Gerasimov (Mosfilm)

NADYA'S CHARGES — 1959 - Yuri Chulukin (Mosfilm) — Also entitled *The Intractable.*

A light, refreshing comedy about two happy-go-lucky and un-disciplined young factory workers. Their behavior is so outlandish that the local Party officials assign a young Komsomol girl activist to straighten them out, a task well nigh impossible. This was the first, and much admired, film to be made by Chulukin who was a student of Yuli Raizman.

THE NAIL — 1973 - H. Pars (Tallinfilm)
    Animated feature.

THE NAIL IN THE BOOT — 1932 - Mikhail Kalatozov
    Banned at the request of the Red Army in the belief that this
satire about a bad nail in a soldier's boot would give a negative impression about military preparedness.

NAMUS — 1926 - Amo Bek-Nazarov (Goskinprom-Gruziya and
Armenkino)
    This film was a popular hit with audiences in the USSR and
abroad. The story is based on a novel by A. Shirvanadze and dealt with
the hard life of Armenian women. Regarded as the first Armenian film
to portray accurately the realities of national life without reliance on
Oriental exotica.

NASREDDIN IN BOKHARA — 1943 - Yakov Protazanov
(Tashkent Studio)
    A social satire based on Leonid Soloviev's novel *Disturber Of The
Peace*. Nasreddin is a Central Asian Robin Hood who not only protects
the peasantry from the vagaries of the wealthy classes, but makes life
uncomfortable for noblemen and petty bureaucrats. Very popular and a
fitting climax to Protazanov's career.

NATALKA POLTAVKA — 1937 - Ivan Kavaleridze (Ukrainfilm)
    Ukrainian operetta.

NATASHA — (See *The Girl From Leningrad*)

NATASHA FILIPOVNA — (See *The Idiot*)

NATELLA — 1928 - Amo Bek-Nazarov (Goskinprom-Gruziya)
    Bek-Nazarov's last Georgian film and heavily criticized for its
exotic appeal and romanticist style.

NATIVE FIELDS — 1944 - Boris Babochkin and A. Bosulaev
    War story about the labors of kolkhoz workers to keep the front
supplied with food.

NAZAR STODOLIA — 1936 - Georgi Tasin (Ukrainfilm)
Drama about Cossacks in the 18th century based on the drama by Taras Shevchenko.

A NEST OF GENTLEFOLK — 1969 - Andrei Mikhalkov-Konchalovski (Mosfilm)
A well received and visually attractive adaptation of Ivan Turgenev's novel.

NESTERKA — 1955 - Alexander Zarkhi (Belarusfilm)
Filmed play.

THE NEW ADVENTURES OF SCHWEIK — 1942 - Sergei Yutkevich (Soyuzdetfilm and Stalinabad Studios)
An amusing and popular satire adapted from the novel by Hasek. The work reflected the current war and Schweik, a man unsuited to discipline, is recast as a Fascist soldier.

THE NEW BABYLON — 1929 - Grigori Kozintsev and Leonid Trauberg (Sovkino-Leningrad)
An expressionistic and symbolic drama about class tensions in French society that led to the Paris Commune of 1871. The department store "New Babylon" serves as a focal point in this story about love and class loyalties that eventually lead to what some historians consider to be the first popular social revolt of modern times. The musical accompaniment was written by Dmitri Shostakovich, his first for a film. Although the film was, and is, lauded for its aesthetic composition, it was received only lukewarmly by audiences who found it too abstract. Today Soviet film historians look upon it as a culmination of Soviet silent film art.

THE NEW GULLIVER — 1935 - Alexander Ptushko (Mosfilm)
The film was three years in the making and well received when parts of it were shown at the 1934 Venice Film Festival. Ptushko used real actors in combination with doll figures to produce an interesting adaptation of Jonathan Swift's classic. The theme stressed class struggle.

NEW HOMELAND — 1935 - Eduard Arshanski (Mezhrabpomfilm)
A German engineer comes to the USSR and helps to develop a

mine during which time he helps to uncover a spy, another German. Later the engineer comes to appreciate the Soviet way of life so much that he decides to become a Soviet citizen. The story stressed the idea that the USSR was the true motherland for the world's workers.

NEW HORIZON — 1941 - A. Kuliev and G. Braginski (Azerfilm)
Drama about generational conflict as represented by differences between a professor and his student regarding the location of new oil reserves. With Party support the student proves that his views are correct. The original version of the film had the professor committing suicide at the end but this was deleted as it was felt to be too harsh.

THE NEW TEACHER — (See *The Teacher*)

THE NEWLYWEDS — 1971 - Nikolai Moskalenko (Mosfilm)
Social satire.

NEWS OF THE DAY — 1944-54 - Dziga Vertov
Filmed news series.

NIGHT COACHMAN — 1928 - Georgi Tasin (VUFKU)
Regarded as one of the better films of early Ukrainian cinema and one of the more emotionally compelling dramas about the Civil War. Tasin made the film as a silent but a sound track was added to it after 1930. The hero of the story is Gordei Yaroshchuk, a simple train coachman and antirevolutionary. He is estranged from his daughter Katya, who unknown to him is a Bolshevik. Unwittingly Yaroshchuk exposes his own daughter to the police who execute her. Katya's death is a great traumatic experience and through it Yaroshchuk undergoes significant change in his social outlook. In the end he too becomes aligned with the Bolsheviks. Amvrosi Buchma gave one of his better performances as Yaroshchuk. In theme and quality of drama it is often compared to Stabovoi's *Two Days*.

A NIGHT IN SEPTEMBER — 1939 - Boris Barnet (Mosfilm)
Industrial sabotage thriller which touched on Sergo Ordzhonikidze's work in heavy industry.

A NIGHT OF THOUGHT — 1966 - Mikhail Romm (Mosfilm)

NIGHT OVER BELGRADE — 1942 - Leonid Lukov
Featurette, *Fighting Film Album No. 8.*

THE NIGHTINGALE — 1937 - Eduard Arshanski (Sovetskaya Belarus)
  Drama about revolutionary class struggle in feudal Belorussia based on the story by Z. Biadula.

NIGHTINGALE, LITTLE NIGHTINGALE — 1936 - Nikolai Ekk
(Mezhrabpomfilm) — Also entitled *Grunya Kornakova.*
  First Soviet color film. Class struggle is the theme of this story about women factory workers who revolt when the owner-capitalist refuses to compensate a woman for the death of her husband in a factory fire, which he started.

NIKITA THE TANNER — 1965 - N. Vasilenko (Kievnauchfilm)
  An animated folk tale about medieval Kiev and the struggle against invading Mongols.

NINE DAYS OF ONE YEAR — 1961 - Mikhail Romm (Mosfilm)
  Grand prize winner at the 1962 Karlovy Vary Film Festival. Story about Soviet atomic scientists and their personal and social problems. The hero is played by Alexei Batalov, a physicist who feels honor bound to sacrifice his life and love for his work. Romm focused on the theme of man's responsibility for his fellow man and future generations.

THE NINTH OF JANUARY — 1925 - Vyacheslav Viskovski
(Sevzapkino) — Also entitled *Black Sunday.*
  A drama about the Russian revolutionary movement filmed in Leningrad. The biggest film of its time, employing 367 actors, 2,500 extras, and 340 soldiers.

NO ENTRANCE TO THE CITY — 1928 - Yuri Zheliabushski
(Mezhrabpomfilm)
  Loosely based on the life of the Socialist Revolutionary Boris Savinkov. The main character is Boris, a White Guardist who returns to Russia to engage in sabotage against the Bolsheviks. He is forced to flee again and dies when his father renounces him. The film was banned because Boris continued his struggle against the Bolsheviks despite his disillusionment with the Whites. Today historians give the film high marks for its deep sense of human tragedy.

NO FORD THROUGH THE FIRE — 1969 - Gleb Panfilov (Mosfilm)
Revolutionary drama which won the Bronze Leopard award at
the 1969 Locarno Film Festival.

NO GREATER LOVE — (See *She Defends Her Country*)

NO HAPPINESS ON EARTH — 1923 - A. Panteleev
A melodrama which attempted to point up the social evils of the
tsarist era through the eyes of a woman who is married to a lowly government servant and is seduced by a nobleman.

NO ONE WANTED TO DIE — 1966 - Vitautas Zalakevicius
(Lithuanian Film Studio)
A surprising and bold drama about the postwar anti-Soviet resistance in Lithuania. The story centers around a small collective farm
which is attacked by nationalists. The farm manager is killed and his
four sons take up the struggle against the bandits. The call for Soviet
patriotism was low key and the struggle was seen primarily on the personal, ethical level. The heroes are average citizens, not MVD border
troops as was usual with such films of the 1930s and 1940s.

NO RETURN — 1974 - Alexei Saltykov (Mosfilm)
As in his earlier *The Chairman*, Saltykov shows that there is a relationship between the destiny of an individual and that of a nation.
The sorrows and joys of Antonina Kashirina, a kolkhoz chairwoman,
and directly related to the progress of society as a whole.

NONE ARE BORN SOLDIERS — 1967 - Alexander Stolper (Mosfilm)
A sequel to Stolper's *The Living And The Dead*. An intelligent
psychological drama of men and officers during the Battle of Stalingrad.

NOT CAUGHT—NO THIEF — (See *Candidate For President*)

NOT TO BE FORGOTTEN — 1931 - D. Poznanski (Turkmenfilm)

THE OATH — 1937 - Alexander Usoltsev (Uzbekgoskino)
Story about resistance to land reform and collectivization in
Central Asia.

THE OATH OF THE YOUNG — 1944 - Dziga Vertov
War documentary.

OCCURRENCE IN THE STADIUM — 1928 - Alexander Ptushko
Animated film.

OCTOBER — 1927 - Sergei Eisenstein (Sovkino) — Also entitled *Ten
Days That Shook The World.*
The film was commissioned as part of the tenth anniversary cele-
brations of the 1917 October Revolution and loosely based on the book
by John Reed. The first version of the script had to be revised after
Party criticism. Eisenstein's editing and Eduard Tisse's photography
made the film memorable for its scenes of the destruction of the tsar's
statue and of Kerenski's first days of power. Despite the film's grand-
ness Eisenstein came under criticism for political reasons. In the first
version Eisenstein kept a scene of Trotsky despite the latter's fall into
disgrace. The original version of the film was reconstituted by Grigori
Alexandrov, Eisenstein's associate on the work, as part of the fiftieth
anniversary of the October Revolution.

OCTOBER AND THE BOURGEOIS WORLD — 1927 - G. Boltianski
(Belgoskino)
Feature cartoon film which was one of the first to show how
animation could be used for political films.

OCTOBER DAYS — 1958 - Sergei Vasiliev (Lenfilm)
Drama about the 1917 Revolution.

OCTOBER WITHOUT ILYICH — 1925 - Dziga Vertov (Sovkino)
Documentary about Lenin's life and death.

ODDBALL FROM 5B — 1972 - Ilya Frez (Maxim Gorki Studios)
Frez has long specialized in making films about and for children
which have always held a special appeal even for adult audiences. For
this work Frez received a special state prize and may well prove to be
his best work. Borya Zbanduto is an eccentric fifth grader who enjoys
entertaining his smaller, first grade schoolmates. His behavior is the object of scorn by his peers, but Borya prefers to stand by his smaller
comrades despite the taunts he must endure.

OH, THAT NASTYA! — 1973 - G. Pobedonostseva
(Maxim Gorki Studios)
   Nastya is the type of young girl that teachers around the world
have often met. Her energy, zest, and occasional antics are more than
her teachers can endure.

OILWORKERS OF THE CASPIAN SEA — 1953 - Roman Karmen
(Central Documentary Studios)

OKRAINA — 1933 - Boris Barnet (Mezhrabpomfilm) — Also entitled
Borderland and *Patriots.*
   Considered one of Barnet's best films by Soviet and Western film
critics. A drama about World War I and divided loyalties in a small
Russian town on the eve of revolution. The work had a blend of humor
and tragedy.

OKTIABRIUKOV AND DEKABRIUKOV — 1928 - A. Smirnov and
O. Iskander

THE OLD AND THE NEW — 1929 - Sergei Eisenstein
(Sovkino-Moscow) — Originally entitled *The General Line.*
   Production began in 1926, but completion was delayed by
Eisenstein's assignment to work on *October.* The film, dealing with
Russian agriculture, had to be extensively revised to keep abreast of
changing policies and strengthening of its antireligious theme. Despite
the changes neither Stalin nor the Party were happy with it. The film
was shot in many locales and wide use was made of nonprofessional
actors. For Eisenstein the film marked a change in editing style in which
he strove to evoke more emotion.

THE OLD BRIGANDS — 1971 - Eldar Ryazanov (Mosfilm)
   Comedy about elderly thieves and the planned theft of a
Rembrandt.

THE OLD GUARD — 1941 - Sergei Gerasimov
   Featurette, *Fighting Film Album No. 1.*

THE OLD JOCKEY — 1940 [1959] - Boris Barnet (Mosfilm)
   The reasons for the banning of this film until 1959 have never
been explained. A comedy about horse racing enthusiasts.

OLD WALLS — 1974 - Viktor Tregubovich (Lenfilm)
Based on the play *The Life Of A Career Woman* by Anatoli
Grebnev. The story revolves around the clash of differences between
older and younger workers at a textile factory. At the center of the
conflict is Anna Georgievna, the factory director, who must grapple
with these problems while continuing to strive for greater achievement.

OLESIA — 1972 - Boris Ivchenko (Alexander Dovzhenko Studios)

ON SIGNAL OF AIR ALARM — 1940 - M. Mustafayev (Azerfilm)
This documentary on civil air defense procedures reflects Soviet
concerns that involvement in World War II was a real possibility.

ON THE ASCENT — 1932 - L. Epelbaum (Sovetskaya Belarus)
Documentary on the development of the Belorussian industrial
center of Vitebsk.

ON THE BORDER — 1938 - Alexander Ivanov (Sovetskaya Belarus)
Action and intrigue thriller about a detachment of Soviet border
troops and their capture of foreign spies and domestic class enemies.
One of many of the "border" genre of Soviet film which stemmed
largely from Dovzhenko's *Aerograd*.

ON THE EVE OF IVAN KUPALA — 1967 - Yuri Ilyenko
(Alexander Dovzhenko Studios)

ON THE EVE OF THE THUNDERSTORM — 1925 -
Kote Mardzhanishvili (Goskinprom-Gruziya)

ON THE EVENTS IN SPAIN — 1937 - Roman Karmen
(Central Newsreel Studio)
Documentary on the Spanish Civil War.

ON THE RED FRONT — 1920 - Lev Kuleshov
(Film Section of the Moscow Soviet)
A semi-documentary film about espionage during the Russo-
Polish War of 1920. One of the first theatrical Soviet films. The film
was made at Lenin's suggestion and is now lost.

ON THE RUINS OF THE ESTATE — 1956 - Vladimir Skuibin
(Mosfilm)

ON THE SAME PLANET — 1965 - Ilya Olshvanger (Mosfilm)
A drama about Lenin in his last years after surviving an assassination attempt. The film emphasizes Lenin's contention that the United States can be trusted. Where Lenin appears as humane and tolerant, Stalin is depicted as a subordinate who is brooding and malevolent which is a sharp break from the manner in which he was portrayed in films prior to Khrushchev's de-Stalinization policy.

ONCE MORE ABOUT LOVE — 1969 - Georgi Natanson
Young love in contemporary times.

ONE FAMILY — 1943 - Girgori Alexandrov (Baku Studio)
Wartime comedy.

ONE HUNDRED PERCENT HOPE — 1975 - Ilya Frez
(Maxim Gorki Studios)
A light satire on Soviet school children and their teachers.

THE 102ND KILOMETER — 1942 - Vladimir Braun
Featurette, *Fighting Film Album No. 11.*

ONE NIGHT — 1945 - Boris Barnet (Erevan Studio)
A war drama based on the play by Fedor Knorr.

ONE OF MANY — 1931 - Ilya Kopalin (Sovkino)
An experimental sound documentary about life on a collective farm near Moscow.

ONE OF MANY — 1941 - Viktor Eisimont
Featurette, *Fighting Film Album No. 2.*

ONLY ONE LIFE — 1965 - Viktor Lisakovich
Popular science film about health.

THE ONLY ROAD — 1975 - Vladimir Pavlovic
(Mosfilm/Filmski Studio)
  Soviet-Yugoslav coproduction. Partly inspired by the wartime experiences of Pavlovic, who at 13 was one of Tito's partisans. The drama is about the planning and execution of a Yugoslav attack against a crucial supply road near Bihac.

OPENING OF THE RELIQUARY OF SERGEI RADONEISKI — 1919 - Dziga Vertov
  Documentary.

OPERATION LAUGHTER — 1965 - Leonid Gaidai (Gruziyafilm)
  Social comedy.

THE OPPENHEIM FAMILY — 1939 - Grigori Roshal (Mosfilm)
  The script was written by Lion Feuchtwanger and based on his novel *Die Geschwister Oppenheim*. One of the best and most remembered of the Soviet anti-Nazi films. Deals with the tragedy of a Jewish family as a result of Nazi terror.

AN OPTIMISTIC TRAGEDY — 1963 - Samson Samsonov (Mosfilm)
  Received a prize for best film on a revolutionary theme at the 1963 Cannes Film Festiva. Based on the play by Vsevolod Vishnevski. The story deals with a young woman commissar who is sent to gain the loyalty of a regiment of Baltic Fleet sailors during the Civil War at a critical period in the defense of Petrograd.

ORDER CARRIED OUT — 1941 - Ya. Aron
  Featurette, *Fighting Film Album No. 4.*

ORDER OF THE DAY OF OCTOBER 8TH — 1925 - Viktor Turin
(VUFKU)
  Revolutionary drama.

ORDINARY FASCISM — 1964 - Mikhail Romm (Mosfilm)
  Highly acclaimed historical documentary about the Nazi era and World War II. Romm spent a year in editing newsreels and archival films from several East European countries and from the former Nazi Ministry of Propaganda. The work is notable for the sharp contrasts of Nazi

childishness and raw brutality. The film ends on a strained note of propaganda by comparing contemporary East and West Germany with the implication that Fascism is the partner of capitalism.

OSTAP BANDURA — 1924 - Vladimir Gardin (VUFKU)
The film follows the youth and adulthood of the hero, Ostap, who becomes a dedicated revolutionary and Red Army commander following his suffering during the tsarist era. The film employed an all Ukrainian cast and was applauded for the way it caught the spirit of the revolutionary and Civil War eras. Critics, however, pointed up that Gardin at times slipped back to his tsarist era romanticism by injecting a romance between Ostap and a landowner's daughter.

OTAR'S WIDOW — 1958 - Mikhail Chiaureli

OTHELLO — 1955 - Sergei Yutkevich (Mosfilm)
Yutkevich had wanted to make this film as early as 1938. The work was a colorful spectacle and filmed on location in the Crimea. The script was written by Yutkevich and based on Boris Pasternak's translation of Shakespeare's work. Sergei Bondarchuk put in a distinguished performance as Othello, a tragic man in search of truth and faith in man.

OTHELLO-67 — 1967 - Fedor Khitruk (Soyuzmultfilm)
An animated adaptation of Shakespeare's drama.

THE OTHER WOMAN — 1929 - Ivan Pyriev (Mezhrabpomfilm)
Social satire which took a bemused stance towards archaic views about morality and marital fidelity. Later such films were discouraged as state policy changed toward encouragement of higher social morals and ethics.

OTTO YULEVICH SHMIDT — 1963 - Vladimir Shneiderov
Popular science and biographical film.

OUR COUNTRY'S YOUTH — 1946 - Sergei Yutkevich (Mosfilm)

OUR FATHER'S HOUSE — 1959 - Lev Kulidzhanov (Mosfilm)

OUR HEART — 1946 - Alexander Stolper (Mosfilm)

OUR LAD — 1930 - L. Frenkel
Story about a young boy who denounces his father as a former White officer and class enemy, and becomes a hero.

OUR MOSCOW — 1941 - Mikhail Slutski
Short documentary, *Fighting Film Album No. 5.*

OUR MUTUAL FRIEND — 1961 - Ivan Pyriev (Mosfilm)

OUR SPLENDID DOCTOR — 1958 - Shaken Aimanov (Kazakhfilm)

OUR YARD — 1957 - Revaz Chkeidze (Gruziyafilm)

OUR YOUTH — 1970 - Revaz Chkeidze (Gruziyafilm)
A drama about the era of World War II depicting young Georgians at home and at the front. Chkeidze skillfully avoided any concessions to sentimentality in this work.

OUT IN THE WORLD — 1939 - Mark Donskoi (Soyuzdetfilm) —
Also entitled *Among People.*
The second part of the *Maxim Gorki Trilogy.* The story traces Gorki's early working life (from age 9) until he leaves his grandparents to find new work and a life for himself. In this and in part I Gorki was played by Alexei Lyarski while Ya. Valbert played the role in part III. Both men died while serving in the Army in World War II. The trilogy is sometimes considered an excellent example of revolutionary romanticism.

OUT OF THE DARKNESS OF THE CENTURIES — 1931 -
A. Lemberg
Documentary on the life of the Chuvash people.

OUT OF THE WAY! — 1931 - Mikhail Chiaureli (Goskinprom-Gruziya)
Also known by its Georgian title *Khabarda.*
A revolutionary satire in which bourgeois, traditional localism was the obstruction to social progress. The story centered on the demolition of an old church that stood in the way of a planned housing development and the resulting social conflict.

THE OVERCOAT — 1926 - Grigori Kozintsev and Leonid Trąuberg (Leningradkino) — 1960 - Alexei Batalov (Lenfilm)
Based on Gogol's classical story of the same title. Both versions are highly regarded for the manner in which they evoke the mood and atmosphere of Gogol and the Russia he saw. The first film was highlighted by the FEKS eccentric style of acting and the expressionistic style of photography. In both films the overcoat itself becomes a character. When Batalov made his film he strove to recreate the atmosphere of Gogol and the style of Kozintsev and Trauberg.

PAGES OF A LIFE — 1948 - Boris Barnet and Alexander Macheret (Mosfilm)

PAGES OF IMMORTALITY — 1965 - Ilya Kopalin (Central Documentary Studios)

PAKHTA-OI — 1952 - Kamil Yarmatov (Uzbekfilm)

PALACE AND FORTRESS — 1924 - Alexander Ivanovski (Sevzapkino)
Historical drama about a tsarist officer who becomes disillusioned with the autocracy and joins the revolutionary movement. After participating in an attempt on the life of Alexander II he is imprisoned. The film portrays the tsar in an unfavorable light.

PAMIR — 1928 - Vladimir Shneiderov (Mezhrabpomfilm)
Popular science adventure.

PARADE OF ATHLETES — 1938 - Sergei Gerasimov (Mosfilm)
May Day documentary.

PARADISE WITHOUT ADAM — 1918 - Vyacheslav Turzhanski

PARIS COMMUNE — (See *People Of The Eleventh Legion*)

THE PARISIAN COBBLER — 1928 - Friedrich Ermler (Sovkino-Leningrad)
The script is reported to have been very closely studied by Party officials prior to production as it dealt with the sensitive theme of antisocial behavior of Young Communists. The hero, played by Fedor

Nikitin, is a deaf-mute shoemaker who comes to the aid of a young woman in trouble. The film was a great success and a scathing attack on dissolute behavior among Soviet youth.

PARTISANS IN THE STEPPES OF THE UKRAINE — 1942 - Igor Savchenko
    War drama about the heroism of Ukrainian partisans behind German lines. Based on a play by Korneichuk.

THE PARTY CARD — 1936 - Ivan Pyriev (Mezhrabpomfilm)
    A popular film, though melodramatic at times, about a young woman who is placed into difficulties because of her lost Party membership card. After a while she discovers her husband stole it and is a cynical spy whom she denounces to the authorities.

PASSING TRAINS — 1967 - Eduard Gavrilov (Mosfilm)
    A lyrical story about the life and problems of a young woman teacher in Siberia.

THE PASSIONATE PRINCE — 1928 - V. Shmidtgof
    Adventures of an indolent self-styled correspondent.

PASTYR — 1922 - V. Barski (Goskinprom-Gruziya)
    Melodrama about the tragic destiny of two young lovers. Based on the play by Alexander Kazbegi.

PATH OF A SHIP — 1937 - Yuri Tarich (Sovetskaya Belarus)

PATH TO TOMORROW — 1964 - Viktor Lisakovich
    Science documentary.

PATRIOT — 1941 - Vasili Pronin
    Featurette, *Fighting Film Album No. 4.*

PATRIOTS — (See *Okraina*)

PAVEL KORCHAGIN — 1957 - Alexander Alov and Vladimir Naumov (Kiev Studios)
    Based on N.A. Ostrovski's novel *How The Steel Was Tempered.*

The film differs from Donskoi's *How The Steel Was Tempered* in that Alov and Naumov used the whole novel while Donskoi used selected portions. Alov and Naumov portrayed the true hardships of the Russian Civil War while also evoking revolutionary romantic feelings.

PAVLINKA — 1952 - Alexander Zarkhi (Belarusfilm)
Filmed play.

PEACE TO HIM WHO ENTERS — (See *Peace To The Newcomer*)

PEACE TO THE COTTAGE, WAR TO THE PALACE — 1919 -
M. Bonch-Tomashevski (Film Section, War Commissariat)
A Civil War *agitka* about a soldier returning from the front during World War I and becomes a Bolshevik when he sees that only landowners and rich peasants are living well in his village.

PEACE TO THE NEWCOMER — 1961 - Alexander Alov and Vladimir Naumov (Mosfilm) — Also entitled *Peace To Him Who Enters*.
Took the prize for best direction at the 1961 Venice Film Festival. A compassionate and humanistic drama about the end of World War II that makes a strong anti-war statement. The story begins as three Soviet soldiers help a pregnant German woman to a hospital in order to give birth to her child — the newcomer in the world and the one, symbolically, who must have peace.

PEACE TO YOUR HOUSE — 1963 - Sergei Yutkevich (Mosfilm)
Animated film.

PEASANT WOMEN OF RYAZAN — 1927 - Olga Preobrazhenskaya (Sovkino) — Also entitled *Women of Ryazan*.
Long considered Preobrazhenskaya's best work. It is a poetic and lyrical ethnographical film which depicts social change in a Russian rural village. As a social document the film reveals, with sensitivity, the status of women in the old way of life which at times was demeaning.

PEASANTS — 1935 - Friedrich Ermler (Lenfilm)
A realistic drama about kolkhoz life in the early stages of collectivization and the bitterness of kulak resistance to state agricultural policies. The characters in the story are well and deeply drawn which provides an element of humanism to the tragic side of collectivization.

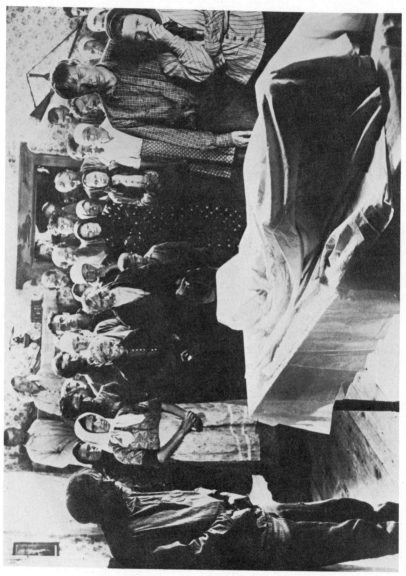

Peasants, Friedrich Ermler (Museum of Modern Art/Film Stills Archive)

PEASANTS — 1972 - I. Galin (Central Documentary Studios)
Documentary on contemporary Soviet farm life.

PECHORIN'S NOTES — 1967 - Stanislav Rostotski (Mosfilm)

A PEDAGOGICAL POEM — 1955 - I. Manevich and M. Mayevskaya
(Kiev Studios)
Based on the book of the Soviet educator Anton Makarenko. This drama about Soviet education did not quite measure up to Ekk's *The Road To Life.*

PEOPLE OF OUR COLLECTIVE FARM — 1940 - A. Ai-Artian
(Armenfilm)
A light comedy on social relationships that gave a light-hearted view of rural life.

PEOPLE OF THE BLUE FIRE — 1961 - Roman Grigoriev
(Central Documentary Studios)

PEOPLE OF THE CASPIAN — 1944 - Grigori Alexandrov (Baku Studio)
Semi-documentary.

PEOPLE OF THE ELEVENTH LEGION — 1937 - Grigori Roshal
(Mosfilm) — Also entitled *Paris Commune.*
A drama about the 1871 Paris Commune that is little remembered.

PEOPLE OF THE SUMBAR VALLEY — 1938 - N. Tikhonov
(Turkmenfilm)
A uninspired story about Soviet agronomists and their endeavors to turn Turkmenian deserts into productive farm land.

PEOPLE WITHOUT HANDS — 1931 - Igor Savchenko (Azerfilm)
A culture and popular science film that demonstrated the need for expanding technical education in the USSR.

THE PEOPLES' AVENGERS — 1943 - Vasili Belayev
(Central Newsreel Studio)
News film coverage about the operations of Soviet partisans.

PEPO — 1935 - Amo Bek-Nazarov (Armenfilm)

Considered as one of Bek-Nazarov's best works and a classic of Armenian cinema which was refurbished and reissued in 1964. Based on the play by Gabriel Sundukian. Through the life of Pepo, a simple fisherman, is seen the class struggles in Armenian society in the mid-19th century. A plain man, Pepo sets out to fight against the corruptive influence of money and bourgeois mentality. He is a man filled with optimism about the potential strength of common people. The film had a very moving musical score at the end which symbolized Caucasian solidarity.

PEREKOP — 1930 - Ivan Kavaleridze (Ukrainfilm)

A drama that centered around the Red Army's capture of Perekop in the Civil War and the ensuing social conflicts over land reform.

PERIOD, PERIOD, COMMA — 1973 - Alexander Mitta (Mosfilm)

An amusing story about Soviet school children, their antics, and their teachers. One of the most popular films with Soviet audiences in 1973-74.

PERSON NO. 217 — (See *Girl No. 217*)

A PERSONAL MATTER — 1932 - Georgi and Sergei Vasiliev

PETER AND ALEXIS — 1919 - Yuri Zheliabushski (Rus Studio) — Also entitled *Antichrist.*

Historical drama with an antireligious theme adapted from the play by Merezhkovski.

PETER THE GREAT — 1937, 1939 in two parts — Vladimir Petrov (Lenfilm)

One of the big historical films of the 1930s which however was not innovative in its style and was occasionally melodramatic. Petrov co-authored the script with Alexei Tolstoi and the film was several years in the making because of many changes. The final result was a portrayal of Russia's first, great tsar of modern times who struggled to make his country a great European power. The film had a strong patriotic bias. Widely exhibited abroad in a shorter version.

PETERSBURG NIGHT — 1934 - Grogori Roshal and Vera Stryeva (Soyuzfilm)
One of the best of the early sound films. Based on Dostoevski's stories "White Nights" and "Netochka Nezvarova," the film is about a Russian semi-tragic musician modelled after Apollon Grigoriev.

THE PINES RUSTLE — 1929 - L. Molchanov (Belgoskino)
An adventure drama about a Belorussian Robin Hood during the Civil War who makes life uncomfortable for the rich and the bureaucrats.

PIPELINE "FRIENDSHIP" — 1964 - Roman Grigoriev (Central Documentary Studios)
Documentary on the construction of the Soviet-East European gas and oil pipeline.

PIROGOV — 1947 - Grigori Kozintsev (Lenfilm)
Dramatized biography of the famous 19th-century Russian surgeon.

PIROSMANI — 1971 - Georgi Shengelaya (Gruziyafilm)
Won grand prize at the 1974 Chicago Film Festival. A sensitive and tender treatment of the life and work of the renowned Georgian primitive artist. Much admired for its humanism and naturalism.

PLAIN PEOPLE — 1946 [1956] - Grigori Kozintsev and Leonid Trauberg (Lenfilm)
The film was intended as a tribute to the labors of the home front during World War II, but was banned for what critics believed a distortion of reality. The story dealt with the difficulties of evacuating a factory because of poor leadership. The censoring of this film ended the long-time collaboration of its directors. The work was released only in 1956 in a highly edited version.

A PLAIN STORY — 1960 - Yuri Yegorov (Maxim Gorki Studios)
In theme the work is similar to *Member Of The Government.* Sasha Potapova, a soldier's widow, is a kolkhoz worker who is resigned at first to an aimless, lonely life. Half in jest she puts forth her own candidacy to be the new chairwoman of her kolkhoz. After her initial surprise in being elected, Potapova finds a new strength and purpose to her life.

PLAN FOR GREAT WORKS — 1930 - Abram Room
(Soyuzkino-Leningrad)
 A documentary about the First Five-Year Plan which incorporated footage from other film sources. An early, experimental sound film.

PLANET OF STORMS — 1962 - Pavel Klushantsev (Mosfilm)
 A fictional space drama about a Soviet expedition to Venus which was popular with Soviet audiences. The American export version was revised to include sexily-clad sirens.

POEM OF LOVE — 1954 - Shaken Aimanov (Kazakhfilm)

POEM OF THE SEA — 1957 - Yulia Solntseva (Mosfilm)
 Alexander Dovzhenko wrote the scenario but died only days before filming was to start. The story probed the lives of several people who were connected with the construction of a huge dam, the Kakhov Sea. Set primarily in postwar times, the film gives a fine portrayal of a cross-section of Soviet society that is very sensitive and not always flattering. Visually the film was lyrical and carried a strongly humanistic flavor.

POEM OF TWO HEARTS — 1967 - Kamil Yarmatov (Uzbekfilm)

POEM ON THE LIFE OF THE PEOPLE — 1958 - Mikhail Kaufman
(Central Documentary Studios)

POET AND TSAR — 1927 - Vladimir Gardin (Sovkino)
 A drama about the life of poet Alexander Pushkin which enjoyed a good deal of commercial success in its time. The film included some fine scenes of the Peterhof area. Critics at the time felt that the lustrous photography of the film tended to overwhelm the drama of Pushkin's life.

THE POET, WRESTLER AND CLOWN — 1957 - Boris Barnet and Konstantin Yudin (Mosfilm)

POISON — 1927 - Yevgeni Ivanov-Barkov
 Popular science film.

POLIKUSHKA — 1919 - Alexander Sanin (Rus Studio)
Considered to be the first true theatrical film of Soviet cinema and proved quite successful. The drama was about the poverty and social plight of Russian serfs and the demeaning results of the institution of serfdom. Based on a story by Lev Tolstoi, the film was made under the harshest conditions and the crew spent much time merely in search of precious film stock. Not officially released until 1922.

POST — 1929 - M. Tsekhanovski (Sovkino-Leningrad)
Animated film based on a children's book by Samuel Marshak.

THE POWER OF DARKNESS — 1918 - Cheslav Sabinski
Based on the play by Lev Tolstoi.

THE POWER OF LIFE — 1935 - Alexander Zguridi
Nature study documentary.

PRECIOUS GRAIN — 1948 - Iosif Heifitz and Alexander Zarkhi (Mosfilm)

THE PRESS OF TIME — 1932 - G. Krol (Sovetskaya Belarus)
A children's film which dealt with a group of adventurous youngsters who discover and expose a spy.

A PRICELESS HEAD — 1942 - Boris Barnet
Featurette, *Fighting Film Album No. 10.*

THE PRIEST AND THE GOAT — 1941 - Lev Atamanov (Armenfilm)
Cartoon based on folk stories.

PRIMA BALLERINA — 1946 - Alexander Ivanovski (Mosfilm)
A musical comedy that was banned for its cosmopolitanism, or similarity to American models.

PRINCE IGOR — 1971 - Roman Tikhomirov (Lenfilm)
Filmed musical performance by the Kirov Ballet and Opera Theater.

PRINCESS MARY — 1926 - V. Barski (Goskinprom-Gruziya)
1955 - Isidor Annenski (Mosfilm)
    Based in part on Lermontov's *Hero Of Our Time.*

THE PRIVATE LIFE OF PETER VINOGRADOV — 1935 -
Alexander Macheret (Mosfilm)
    An amusing situation comedy that indirectly encouraged greater
morality among youth. Vinogradov is a carefree Komsomol who is in-
fatuated with three girls at the same time. Keeping the girls apart leads
to amusing problems for Vinogradov, but in the end he receives poetic
justice when the girls leave him simultaneously.

PROFESSOR MAMLOCK — 1938 - Adolf Minkin and
Herbert Rappoport (Lenfilm)
    A forceful and realistic anti-Nazi film that is still considered one
of the best of its kind. Adapted from the play by Friedrich Wolf, who
collaborated on the script with Minkin and Rappoport. Wolf and
Rappoport were both German emigres and were able to give the film a
very accurate depiction of German realities. Mamlock, the hero of the
story, is a renowned German Jewish surgeon who finally takes a stand
against the Nazis and is assassinated. The film was briefly removed from
exhibition during the period of the Nazi-Soviet Nonaggression Pact. In
1961 Konrad Wolf who is the son of Friedrich Wolf made an East German version which failed to evoke the same stark strength of the
Soviet film.

THE PROJECT OF ENGINEER PRITE — 1918 - Lev Kuleshov
    Story about an engineer who plans an electrical station and be-
comes a victim of the intrigues of a corrupt company official.

PROLOGUE — 1956 - Yefim Dzigan (Mosfilm)
    Wide-screen color film about Lenin's life and the events leading
up to the October Revolution.

PROMETHEUS — 1936 - Ivan Kavaleridze (Ukrainfilm)
    Based on Taras Shevchenko's poems "The Dream" and "The
Caucasus." An epic historical drama about serfdom under Nicholas I
and especially the Russian conquest of the Caucasus. The film was
banned for so-called distortion of history, which meant that the film

contained a hint of nationalism. This was the second part of a trilogy that Kavaleridze envisioned to portray the liberation struggles of the various nationalities of the Russian Empire. Because of the severe criticism of this film Kavaleridze dropped his plans for the third film and concentrated on simpler, safer films.

PROSTITUTE — 1927 - Oleg Frelikh (Belgoskino)
    The script of this first Belorussian film was written by Mark Donskoi. Melodrama on the decadence and evil of commercial prostitution.

PRZHEVALSKI — 1953 - Sergei Yutkevich (Mosfilm)
    A dramatized and patriotic biography of the 19th-century Russian explorer of Central Asia.

THE PUBLIC PROSECUTOR — 1941 - Yevgeni Ivanov-Barkov (Turkmenfilm)
    Similar in theme to his earlier *Dursun,* but not as successful critically. The heroine of this women's emancipation drama is Yazgul who is sold as a child bride to Safar-bey. Later Yazgul runs away and remarries for love. Her child is then kidnapped by her former husband. This traumatic event leads her to a struggle for basic human rights for women in Turkmenia and in time becomes the procurator-general of the republic. At the end Yazgul succeeds in her struggle for women's rights and in being reunited with her son. Soviet critics felt Ivanov-Barkov lost an opportunity for a real triumph by relying too much on the schematics of a simple plot without probing more deeply into the motivations of the characters.

PUCK! PUCK! — 1964 - B. Dezhkin (Soyuzmultfilm)
    Animated film about hockey.

PUGACHEV — 1937 - P. Petrov-Bytov
    A historical drama about Emelyan Pugachev and his rebellion against Catherine II. The first scenario was written by Olga Forsh, but Petrov-Bytov had to revise it after criticism by Party censors.

THE PULKOVO MERIDIAN — (See *Blockade*)

PUNIN AND BABURIN — 1918 - Alexander Ivanovski
Based on a story by Turgenev.

PUPILS OF THE SEVENTH GRADE — 1938 - Yakov Protazanov
(Soyuzdetfilm)
     A film for and about children. The story focuses on seventh
grader Dima Roshchin who is rather independent and selfish in his
ways. In time his peers take him to task and teach him that the individual owes a higher obligation to the good of his collective [society].

QUIET FLOWS THE DON — 1931 - Olga Preobrazhenskaya and
Ivan Pravov (Soyuzkino) — 1957, 1958 in three parts —
Sergei Gerasimov (Maxim Gorki Studios)
     Based on the admired and controversial novel by Dmitri
Sholokhov, whose authorship of it has been questioned. The first film
version was originally made as a silent, but a limited sound track was
added later. Gerasimov's version is considered better and offering a
colorful and more emotional look at the era of the Russian Civil War.

RABA — 1927 - A. Yalovya (Armenfilm)
     Social drama about the upheavals in Armenian society as a result
of the Civil War.

RAIKHAN — 1940 - Moisei Levin (Lenfilm)
     Levin made this film immediately after *Amangeldi* and is praised
by Soviet film scholars for exhibiting a deeper understanding of the
Kazakh way of life. The drama is about a young Kazakh girl who, after
surfering humiliation as a child bride, sets out to win for herself a new,
liberated way of life under Soviet rule.

THE RAIKOM SECRETARY — 1942 - Ivan Pyriev
(Consolidated Studios, Alma-Ata) — Also entitled *Secretary Of The
Party Regional Committee.*
     One of the earliest feature theatrical films about World War II.
The film was made when Soviet victory was not a certainty and when
the partisan movement was much publicized. The main hero of this film
is Stepan Kochet, a Party official who organizes a band of partisans to
resist the Fascist invaders. Kochet instills the idea among his followers
that the Party will eventually lead the Soviet people to ultimate victory
and that Soviet power must be preserved.

THE RAINBOW — 1944 - Mark Donskoi (Kiev Studios)
One of Donskoi's best films and one that reflects the harsh, uncompromising Soviet hatred towards the Nazi invader. Donskoi spent much time in observing German prisoners of war prior to filming so that he could accurately portray the enemy. The work was based on the novel by Wanda Wasilewska, who also wrote the screenplay. The story focuses on the strength and courage of a woman partisan leader, Olena Kostiuk, and the plight of her young son, Maliuchiki. A moving and memorable scene in the film is Maliuchiki bringing bread to his mother who is freezing behind a barbed wire fence. The film was awarded a special Oscar by the U.S. Academy of Motion Picture Arts and Sciences, and made a deep impression on President Franklin D. Roosevelt when he saw it.

RAINIS — 1949 - Yuli Raizman (Riga Film Studio)

RAKHMANOV'S SISTERS — 1954 - Kamil Yarmatov (Uzbekfilm)

RAMAZAN — 1932 - Nabi Ganiev (Uzbekgoskino)
The story takes place during the collectivization campaigns and focuses on Timur, a poor Uzbek peasant who gradually realizes that the Uzbek mullahs and beys are really his class enemies.

RANKS AND PEOPLE: A CHEKHOV ALMANAC — 1929 - Yakov Protazanov (Mezhrabpomfilm)
Based on three stories by Chekhov: "Anna On The Neck," "Death Of A Petty Official," and "Chameleon." This was one of the first films to link three stories on a single theme, which in this case was "Russia — A Land Of Government." Striking, almost surrealistic photography highlighted the drama that probed the rank-conscious structure of tsarist society.

A REAL COMRADE — 1937 - A. Okunchikov and L. Bodik (Ukrainfilm)
A children's film that dealt with the problem of ethical education of Soviet youth. The story emphasized that mutual help and selflessness were virtues to be admired.

REAL HUNTERS — 1930 - N. Lebedev (Mezhrabpomfilm)
Children's film.

REAL LIFE IN THE FOREST — 1950 - Alexander Zguridi
(Central Documentary Studios)
    Nature study and popular science film.

A REAL PATRIOT — 1941 - Klimenti Mints
    Featurette, *Fighting Film Album No. 7.*

THE RECOVERER OF SIGHT — 1921 - L. Zamkovoi (VUFKU-Kiev)
    Drama about a White officer who decides to join the Bolsheviks
after observing the moral decay of his fellow Whites.

THE RED AND THE WHITE — 1968 - Miklos Jancso (Mafilm/Mosfilm)
    A Hungarian-Soviet coproduction which received wide acclaim.
Set in the time of the Russian Civil War, the story reveals the humiliation of people as they struggle for survival. One of the better Hungarian
films of the 1960s.

THE RED ARMY — 1925 - A. Stroyev (VUFKU/Political Section of
the Ukrainian Military District)
    An enacted film which did not advance technically beyond the
agitka about peacetime Red Army activities.

RED PARTISANS — 1924 - Vyacheslav Viskovski (Sevzapkino)
    Friedrich Ermler was featured in this Civil War drama about the
Bolshevik campaign against the White forces of Admiral Kolchak.

THE RED SNOWBALL TREE — 1974 - Vasili Shukshin (Mosfilm)
    A controversial film which, despite revision, became an out-
standing success in the USSR. This social film exposes some of the
negative aspects of Soviet bureaucracy and the evils of urban life. The
story is about a former convict who meets discrimination after his release from prison camp. At first he tries to avoid returning to his old
activities, but social pressures drive him back to his old gang and he is
murdered. This was the last film Shukshin made before his death and
reflected a strong Slavophile bent in contrasting the purer morality of
rural life with the pressures of urban life.

RED SQUARE — 1971 - Vasili Ordinski (Mosfilm)
    A drama that touched on Lenin's life.

THE RED TENT — 1969 - Mikhail Kalatozov (Mosfilm)
Italian-Soviet coproduction. Despite interesting photography and an international cast, this drama about the tragedy of Umberto Nobile's Arctic flight failed to stir much attention.

RELAY — 1967 - Daniil Khrabovitski (Tadzhikfilm)
The achievements in Tadzhik life since 1941 are traced through the lives and destinies of two generations of one family.

REMEMBER YOUR NAME — 1974 - Sergei Kolosov (Mosfilm/Illuzion)
Polish-Soviet coproduction. A moving and occasionally brutal drama about a Russian woman and her young son who are sent to a Nazi concentration camp in 1941. While in captivity the young boy is taken away from his mother, but survives the war because of the love and care of a Polish woman who becomes his mother. Twenty-five years later he is reunited with his Russian mother, largely because of the compassion of the Polish woman. Intended to illustrate the bonds of friendship that arose between Poles and Russians during the course of World War II.

RENDEZVOUS — 1963 - Elyer Ishmuhammedov

RENEWED LABOR — 1930 - Ilya Kopalin (Sovkino)
Documentary about agriculture at the beginning of collectivization.

REPORT BY COMRADE STALIN — 1937 - Grigori Alexandrov (Mosfilm)
Documentary.

REQUIEM FOR MOZART — 1966 - Vladimir Gorikker (Riga Film Studio)
Adapted from Pushkin's story "Mozart and Salieri."

RESTLESS YOUTH — 1954 - Alexander Alov and Vladimir Naumov (Kiev Studios)

RESURRECTION — 1962 - Mikhail Shveitser (Mosfilm)
Based on the novel by Lev Tolstoi.

THE RETURN OF MAXIM — 1937 - Grigori Kozintsev and
Leonid Trauberg (Lenfilm)
Part II of the *Maxim Trilogy*. The film is set in the time of World
War I when Maxim and his wife Natasha protest against the war and
dedicate themselves to the Bolshevik cause.

THE RETURN OF VASILI BORTNIKOV — 1952 - Vsevolod Pudovkin
(Mosfilm)
The film's hero, Bortnikov, returns unexpectedly after being
listed as missing in action for five years. He finds his wife, who believed
him dead, has remarried. The difficulties are eventually resolved by a
local Party official. The theme was to be dealt with more deeply in
films after Stalin's death. Pudovkin's last film.

RETURN TO EARTH — 1921 - Boris Glagolin

REVIVAL OF STALINGRAD — 1944 - I. Poselski (Central News
(Central Newsreel Studios)
Documentary on efforts at reconstructing the war-devastated city.

REVIZOR [The Inspector General] — 1953 - Vladimir Petrov
(Mosfilm)
A satire on social life in 19th-century Russia based on Gogol's
play of the same name.

REVOLT — 1928 - Semyon Timoshenko (VUFKU)
A Civil War drama set in Central Asia based on the novel by
Dmitri Furmanov.

REVOLT OF THE FISHERMEN — 1934 - Erwin Piscator
(Mezhrabpomfilm)
A drama about revolutionary class struggle in Germany based on
the novel by Anna Seghers. Piscator, who was then a recent emigre from
Nazi Germany, was more successful in depicting the realities of German
life than either Pudovkin in *The Deserter* or Pyriev in *Assembly Line
Of Death*.

REVOLT OF THE GRANDMOTHERS — 1929 - I. Galai
A group of Komsomols who campaign against anti-Semitism.

THE RICH BRIDE — 1938 - Ivan Pyriev (Ukrainfilm)
   A musical comedy and romance on a Ukrainian kolkhoz. The heroine is considered wealthy for the joy she derives from her work on the farm. Although simple and schematic in its plot, Soviet critics thought it was one of the better musical comedies.

THE RIDER WITH LIGHTNING IN HAND — 1975 - Khasan Khazhkasimov (Maxim Gorki Studios)
   A drama about the role of young Komsomol girls in the First Five-Year Plan. Inspired by the life of Vera Frelova, geologist.

RIDERS — 1939 - Igor Savchenko and A. Golovanov (Kiev Studios)
   Also entitled *Guerrilla Brigade*.
   An action Civil War drama about Red partisans based on the novel by Yu. Yanovski.

RIMSKI-KORSAKOV — 1953 - Grigori Roshal (Mosfilm)
   A biographical film, strong in patriotism and music, that paid tribute to the famous Russian composer who was one of the leaders of the so-called nationalist school of Russian music in the 19th century.

THE RISK — (See *A Degree Of Risk*)

THE ROAD — 1955 - Alexander Stolper (Mosfilm)

THE ROAD BEGINS AT MANGISHLAK — 1966 - Viktor Lisakovich

THE ROAD EAST — 1930 - A. Makovski (Azerfilm)
   A historical film chronicle on Soviet achievements in Azerbaidzhan. The work was commissioned to commemorate the tenth anniversary of the establishment of Soviet rule in Azerbaidzhan.

ROAD TO LIFE — 1931 - Nikolai Ekk (Mezhrabpomfilm)
   An immensely successful film that dealt honestly with a serious social problem. The drama focuses on the efforts of a government inspector to rehabilitate Civil War orphans who had become juvenile delinquents. The film was released at a time when the Soviet school system was undergoing a radical move away from the gross permissiveness of the 1920s. The story put great emphasis on group discipline.

The film's realism lay in part from the fact that Ekk spent much time at a labor training collective before shooting. When it was released in the United States the work was officially endorsed by the American Federation of Women's Clubs. The film enjoyed renewed popularity with Soviet audiences after Ekk reedited and refurbished it in the 1950s. Still considered one of the best films of Soviet cinema.

[See also *A Pedagogical Poem.*]

THE ROAD TO ORION — 1975 (Belarusfilm)
Short documentary about Major Pyotr Klimuk, commander of the Soviet spaceship Soyuz-13.

THE ROAD TO PEACE — 1929 - B. Shpis
An episodic historical drama about the Russian proletariat from 1901 to 1930 as seen through the life of one worker.

ROAD WITHOUT SLEEP — 1946 - Kamil Yarmatov (Tashkent Studio)

ROBINSON CRUSOE — 1945 - Alexander Andreevski
(Stereokino Studio)
A color three-dimensional film based on Defoe's novel.

ROLL CALL — 1965 - Daniil Khrabovitski (Mosfilm)

ROMANCE OF LOVERS — 1974 - Andrei Mikhalkov-Konchalovski
(Mosfilm)
A lyrical story about young love which has beautiful sentiment at the beginning only to end in trauma when the love dies.

ROMEO AND JULIET — 1955 - Lev Arnshtam (Mosfilm)
Color filmed ballet featuring the performance by prima ballerina Galina Ulanova.

ROTE FAHNE — (See *Shakir*)

THE ROUTE — 1975 - Vladlen Troshkin
(Central Documentary Studios)
Short color documentary on the construction of a gas pipeline in the Soviet Far North.

THE RUDOBELSKAYA REPUBLIC — 1971 - Nikolai Kalinin
(Belarusfilm)
A Belorussian village in 1918 is the focal point of this drama
about the Soviet struggle for power in Belorussia and against the Poles
and Germans.

THE RUMYANTSEV CASE — 1955 - Iosif Heifitz (Mosfilm)

THE RUNAWAY — 1919 - Boris Chaikovski

THE RUSSIA OF NIKOLAI II AND LEV TOLSTOI — 1928 -
Esther Shub (Sovkino)
A dramatic historical documentary on the era of 1897 to 1912.
The film incorporated rare and sparse footage of Tolstoi.

RUSSIAN ADVENTURE — 1966 - Leonid Kristy, Roman Karmen, and
Boris Dolin (Mosfilm)
English version narrated by Bing Crosby. Cinerama travel
documentary.

THE RUSSIAN QUESTION — 1948 - Mikhail Romm (Mosfilm)
Regarded as the first Soviet anti-American Cold War film and was
based on the novel by Konstantin Simonov. The drama concerns Harry
Smith an American reporter who is sent to Moscow in order to do research for a book exposing Soviet preparations for war against the
United States. While in the USSR Smith undergoes a change of view and
much inner turmoil. In the end he decides, at great risk, to give a true
account in which the real enemies of the American people are in Washington, D.C. Despite the political bias of the film some critics feel that
it had fine acting performances and indicated an attempt to avoid
typage.

RUSSIAN SOUVENIR — 1960 - Grigori Alexandrov (Mosfilm)

RUTS — 1928 - Abram Room (Sovkino-Moscow)
A probing psychological drama about the strains placed on a marriage by the birth of a child.

SABA — 1929 - Mikhail Chiaureli (Goskinprom-Gruziya)
Dealt with the social evils and human problems arising out of alcoholism. The film was partly satirical and included an amusing scene in which a lecture on alcoholism is disrupted by a fistfight and shows the erstwhile lecturer himself to be in a drunken stupor.

SADKO — 1951 - Alexander Ptushko (Mosfilm)
Based on the opera by Rimski-Korsakov. A colorful and admired film that conveyed the spirit of old Russian tales.

SAILOR FROM THE "AURORA" — (See *The Devil's Wheel*)

SALAMANDER — 1928 - Grigori Roshal (Mezhrabpom-Rus)
German-Soviet coproduction. A dramatization of the life of Austrian biologist Paul Kammerer which emphasized the struggle of science against Fascism and religion. Melodramatic.

SALAVAT YULAEV — 1941 - Yakov Protazanov (Soyuzdetfilm)
A depiction of revolutionary development in Central Asia as expressed through the life of a national hero.

SALT FOR SVANETIA — 1930 - Mikhail Kalatozov (Goskinprom-Gruziya)
Criticized when first released for its hyperbolism and naturalism, the film is now regarded as one of Kalatozov's best. Kalatozov employed a documentary style in this drama about a small, isolated Caucasian community as it struggles for survival. The camera itself becomes part of the story through dynamic movement, a characteristic seen in later films by Kalatozov. The French film historian Georges Sadoul considered the film similar to and as memorable as Luis Buñel's *Las Hurdes* in its photography.

SALTANAT — 1955 - Vasili Pronin (Mosfilm)
A story set in Kirghiziya.

SALUTE MARYA — 1970 - Iosif Heifitz (Mosfilm)
Tribute to and story about a Soviet woman who marries a Spaniard and loses both her husband and child during the Spanish Civil War. The film follows her turn to the USSR after 1939 and involvement in intelligence work.

SAR-PIGE [The Woman] — 1927 - I. Maksimov-Kashkinski
(Chuvashkino)
    Using nonprofessional actors the film depicts the life of Chuvash
women prior to 1917.

SAVUR'S GRAVE — 1926 - Ivan Perestiani (Goskinprom-Gruziya)
    Sequel to *Little Red Devils.*

SAVVA — 1919 - Cheslav Sabinski (Moscow Cinema Committee)

SAYAN DIARY — FIRST PAGES — 1975 - Eduard Kiselev
(Central Documentary Studios)
    A color documentary on the construction of the Sayan industrial
and power complex on the Yenisei River in Siberia.

SAYAT NOVAR — 1969 - Sergei Paradzhanov (Bek-Nazarov Studios)

THE SCARED BOURGEOISIE — 1919 - Mikhail Werner (VUFKU)
    Civil War *agitka.*

SCHOOL FOR SCANDAL — 1952 - Abram Room (Mosfilm)
    Film adaptation of the novel by Richard Sheridan.

SCHWEIK IN THE CONCENTRATION CAMP — 1941 -
Sergei Yutkevich
    Featurette, *Fighting Film Album No. 7.* A year later Yutkevich
expanded the material for a feature-length film.

[See also *The New Adventures Of Schweik.*]

THE SEAGULL — 1971 - Yuli Karasik (Mosfilm)
    A luxuriant color adaptation of Chekhov's play that has been
much admired and widely exported. Won Silver Hugo award at the
1973 Chicago Film Festival.

THE SECOND WIFE — 1927 - M. Doronin (Uzbekgoskino)
    Uzbek life is explored and examined through the life of the
heroine, Yunaya Adolyat, who as a young woman becomes the second
wife of a wealthy merchant. Yunaya's life is filled with drudgery and
sadness because she is the second wife. She attempts to run away, but is

brought back and beaten by her husband. The film was very popular and pointed up the lack of civil rights for women in the pre-Soviet era.

SECRET AGENT — (See *Feat Of A Scout*)

SECRET MISSION — 1950 - Mikhail Romm (Mosfilm)
An example of history recast in the political context of the Cold War. The drama takes place in January 1945 when an American Senator and intelligence agent attempt to effect a secret, separate peace with Hitler. The film ends with American attempts to prepare a new war against the Soviet Union.

SECRET OF BEAUTY — 1955 - Yakov Segel and Vasili Ordinski (Mosfilm)

THE SECRET OF KARA-TAU — 1933 - A. Dubrovski (Vostokfilm)
Adventure story about scientists searching for rubber plants.

SECRETARY OF THE PARTY REGIONAL COMMITTEE — (See *The Raikom Secretary*)

SECRETS OF NATURE — 1948 - Alexander Zguridi
Popular science and nature study film.

SEEKERS OF HAPPINESS — 1940 - Vladimir Korsh-Sablin (Sovetskaya Belarus)
Emphasized the theme of Jewish and Russian friendship. The story is about a group of industrious and cheerful Jews on a collective farm in Birobidzhan. The joy of communal labor is contrasted with one selfish individual. Enjoyed moderate success in its initial American exhibition.

SELF, SELF, SELF, SELF — 1966 - M. Zherebchevski (Soyuzmultfilm)
Cartoon feature film about animal life.

SERGEI LAZO — 1967 - Alexander Gordon (Moldovafilm)
Dramatization about the life and Civil War exploits of a legendary Red commander.

SERGEI YESENIN — 1970 - Sergei Urusevski and Gennadi Shpalikov (Mosfilm)
> Feature documentary on the poetry of the renowned Russian poet.

SERYOZHA — 1960 - Georgi Daneliya and Igor Talankin (Mosfilm)
> Life's complexities, growing up, and the world of adults are seen through the viewpoint of a young boy. A warm and tender story that was judiciously sprinkled with light humor. Sergei Bondarchuk gave a compassionate portrayal as the step-father to be of Seryozha. Won the Crystal Globe grand prize at the Karlovy Vary Film Festival.

THE SEVAN FISHERMEN — 1939 - A. Martirosian and G. Marinosian (Armenfilm)
> On the Civil War in Armenia.

SEVASTOPOL — 1944 - Vasili Belayev (Central Newsreel Studio)
> Documentary on the Soviet recapture of the famed Black Sea naval base which had fallen two years earlier.

SEVEN HEARTS — 1935 - M. Tikhonov and M. Mei (Turkmenfilm)
> An intrigue and sabotage thriller about a Komsomol oil prospecting expedition in the Kara Dzhube desert of Turkmenia.

SEVEN NURSEMAIDS — 1962 - Rolan Bykov (Mosfilm)

THE SEVENTH FELLOW TRAVELER — 1928 - V. Kasianov
> Drama about a former tsarist general who joins the Bolsheviks during the Civil War after undergoing inner turmoil.

SEVIL — 1929 - Amo Bek-Nazarov (Azerkino)
> Story about a young Azerbaidzhanian woman who frees herself from the old secludedness of feudal customs and becomes an independent and socially active person. Based on the play by Dzhafar Dzharbli.

SHACKLED BY FILM — 1918 - Nikandr Turkin
> Melodrama about a film actress.

SHADOWS OF OUR FORGOTTEN ANCESTORS — 1964 -
Sergei Paradzhanov (Alexander Dovzhenko Studios)
  Photography by Yuri Ilyenko and color art direction complemented this Carpathian Romeo and Juliet drama concerning love and hate. Widely acclaimed as one of the best Soviet films of the 1960s. Received prize for best film at the 1965 Mar del Plata Film Festival.

SHAKALY RAVATA — 1927 - K. Gertel (Uzbekgoskino)
  Civil War story about the Bolshevik campaign against bandits in Uzbekistan.

SHAKIR — 1932 - L. Eskiya (Goskinprom-Gruziya) — Also entitled *Rote Fahne.*
  Originally made as a silent with a sound track being added later by Lenfilm Studios. Internal class enemies and their intrigues within a group of German emigres as they establish the "Rote Fahne" collective farm in the northern Caucasus form the plot of this story.

SHAME — (See *Counterplan*)

SHANGHAI DOCUMENT — 1928 - Yakov Bliokh (Soyuzkino)
  Documentary on Chinese social and political affairs.

SHARIK AND SHURIK — 1960 - Leonid Makhnach
  Documentary.

SHCHORS — 1939 - Alexander Dovzhenko with Yulia Solntseva (Kiev Studios)
  A dramatized biography of the legendary Civil War Red commander in the Ukraine and made at Stalin's explicit suggestion. Work on the script took almost a year and filming extended over three years because of many changes in order to avoid any possible hint of Ukrainian nationalism. The key figure of Shchors bedevilled Dovzhenko and in the end emerged as a cold, god-like figure. Nevertheless, the film is impressive with strong battle scenes and the lyricism of the Ukrainian countryside. A Classical film despite Dovzhenko's uneasiness over it.

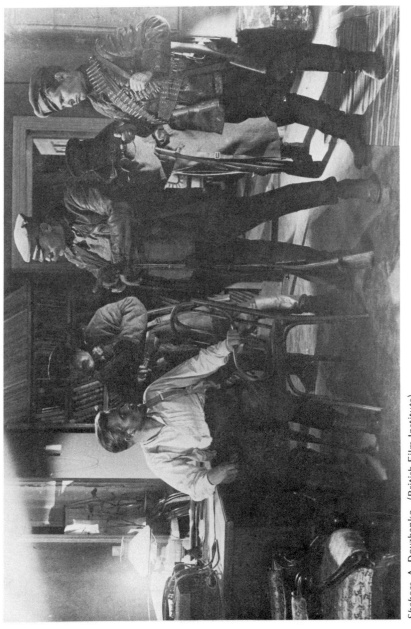

Shchors, A. Dovzhenko (British Film Institute)

SHE DEFENDS HER COUNTRY — 1943 - Friedrich Ermler
(Consolidated Studios, Alma-Ata) — Also entitled *No Greater Love.*
A Stalin Prize-winning film that was shown in the United States
with an English sound track. An angry film that portrayed human courage behind enemy lines. The drama centers on a peasant woman whose
family has been killed by the invading Germans. At first her grief is so
strong that she almost goes insane, but then recovers and becomes the
leader of a detachment of partisans under the codename of Comrade P.

SHIPS STORM THE BASTION — 1953 - Mikhail Romm (Mosfilm)
Part II of *Admiral Ushakov.* Colorful and sweeping battle scenes.

SHON AND SHER — 1974 - Kanimbek Kasimbekov (Kazakhfilm)
Children's film about the young generation of the 1970s.

SHOP WINDOW — 1955 - Samson Samsonov (Mosfilm)

SHOR AND SHORSHOR — 1926 - Amo Bek-Nazarov (Armenkino)
Script was written and filmed in less than three weeks. First
Armenian comedy about the zany mishaps that confront two drunken
peasants.

A SHOT IN THE MOUNTAINS — 1970 - Bolot Shamshiev
(Kazakhfilm)
Based on a novel by Mukhla Auezov. The story takes place on the
Kirghiz plains in 1910, when tsarist agents come to colonize the territory and drive off the nomadic Kirghiz and Kazakhs from their traditional lands. The drama focuses on a local prince who becomes torn
between helping his people and the desire for proferred wealth. The
prince decides to take the money, realizing it will cost him his life.
Contains scenes of dazzling Kazakh horsemanship.

SIBERIAN SINGING — 1961 - Leonid Makhnach
Ethnographical film.

THE SIBERIANS — 1940 - Lev Kuleshov (Soyuzdetfilm)
A successful film about Siberian hunters. The work marked
Kuleshov's return to film-making after a hiatus of several years
stemming from the banning of *The Great Consoler.*

SICKLE AND HAMMER — 1921 - Vladimir Gardin (Goskino)
Vsevolod Pudovkin acted in this film as well as serving as Gardin's assistant director. The story dealt with the fate of two peasant families, one poor and the other rich, during the Civil War. The semi-documentary style heightened the interest of the work and today it is regarded as a transitional work between the simple *agitka* and more complex feature theatrical film.

SIEGE OF LENINGRAD — 1942 - Roman Karmen
(Central Newsreel Studio)
Documentary.

SIGNAL — 1918 - Alexander Arkatov (Moscow Cinema Committee)
Civil War *agitka* based on the story by Vsevolod Garshin.

SILENCE — 1963 - Vladimir Basov (Mosfilm)
Won first prize at the 1964 Soviet All-Union Film Festival. An open and honest attempt to show the complexities of peacetime life for two demobilized Soviet war veterans. Emphasized the emotional readjustment on the part of veterans for whom peace was not idyllic.

THE SILENCE OF DOCTOR IVENS — 1973 - Budimir Metalnikov (Mosfilm)
Sergei Bondarchuk played the lead role in this science-fiction drama about three alien beings who come to an unhappy Earth.

SILVER DUST — 1953 - Abram Room (Mosfilm)
Based on *Jackals*, a play by Avgust Yakobson. Cold War drama about a Negro Communist and five others who are jailed on false charges in a small American town. They are secreted away for the purpose of being subjects in chemical warfare experiments, but are rescued by friends. The Communist vows that the jailers will answer one day to a people's court.

A SIMPLE CASE — 1932 - Vsevolod Pudovkin and Mikhail Doller (Mezhrabpomfilm) — Originally entitled *Life Is Beautiful*.
The film was to have been made with sound, but technical problems were unsolved and it was released as a silent. Despite many changes Pudovkin was unable to overcome the criticism of the film, which in

large part was because of its abstract style. The story dealt with a former Bolshevik commander who marries a woman during the Civil War. Later he meets another woman and leaves his wife, only to return to her after several years. The plot itself caused problems and criticism at a time when higher morality was being stressed. The film had a limited exhibition.

SING YOUR SONG, POET — 1973 - Sergei Urusevski (Mosfilm)
Dramatized biography of the poet Sergei Yesenin.

[See also *Sergei Yesenin.*]

THE SINGER — 1971 - Konstantin Voinov

THE SINGING THRUSH — 1970 - Otar Yoseliani (Gruziyafilm)
A somber story about a promising young musician who wastes his talent and time by focusing on mundane affairs. In a poignant ending he is killed accidentally and his life passes unnoticed.

A SINGULAR AFFAIR — 1934 - Ilya Trauberg

THE SISTERS — 1957 - Grigori Roshal (Mosfilm)
Part I of *The Way Of Sorrows Trilogy.*

THE SIXTEENTH — 1929 - P. Barkhudarian (Armenfilm)
A tale about the heroism and tragedy of a group of Red Army soldiers fighting in the rear of White forces.

THE SIXTH OF JULY — 1968 - Yuli Karasik (Mosfilm)
A historical drama about the events that led to the expulsion of the leftist Social Revolutionaries from the government in 1918 and eliminated a threat to Bolshevik power. Lenin is treated realistically as a political leader striving to keep control of the government.

A SIXTH PART OF THE EARTH — 1926 - Dziga Vertov (Goskino)
A documentary that was specially commissioned by the Soviet Ministry of Trade for foreign exhibition in order to publicize the vast potential wealth of Soviet resources and attract foreign investors.

SIXTY DAYS — 1940 - Konstantin Yudin — Also entitled *Commander Of The Reserve*.
This was a humorous, light comedy about a young man, played by Nikolai Cherkasov, who is called up for military training. In time he becomes serious and turns into a willing, talented junior officer. The film was removed from exhibition because its approach was considered inappropriate at a time when the Red Army was undergoing serious rearmament.

69TH PARALLEL — 1943 - Vasili Belayev (Central Newsreel Studio)
War documentary about the Soviet Navy's participation in the Allied convoys to Murmansk and Arkhangelsk.

SKALA ARSHAULA — 1935 - David Rondeli (Goskinprom-Gruziya)
First Georgian film to be made with a synchronized sound track. Dealt with problems of social change as a result of the industrialization in Georgia.

SKANDERBEG — 1954 - Sergei Yutkevich (Mosfilm)
Produced in cooperation with the Albanian Film Studio. An epic color historical drama about the great Albanian leader who fought against the Turkish domination over his people. A rich costume drama that has been well received.

SKARLATINA — 1924 - Friedrich Ermler
Culture film about health.

SKATING RINK — 1927 - Ivan Ivanov-Vano with Cherkes (Mezhrabpom-Rus)
Animated film.

THE SKATING RINK AND THE VIOLIN — 1959 - Andrei Mikhalkov-Konchalovski and Andrei Tarkovski (Mosfilm)

THE SKOTININS — 1926 - Grigori Roshal
Based on Fonvizin's comedy *Hobbledehoy*. A satire on an ignorant landowning family.

THE SKY — 1940 - Yuri Tarich (Sovetskaya Belarus)
Comedy about an old kolkhoz worker who is opposed to his daughter's marriage to a pilot because he fails to see the value of aviation to agriculture. Later, after being convinced of the potential of aviation he makes a parachute jump. Even Soviet film historians fail to see the humor in this one.

THE SKY OF OUR CHILDHOOD — 1967 - Tolomush Okeyev (Kirghizfilm)
A lyrical story about the Kirghiz people.

THE SKY-BLUE STEPPE — 1971 - Valei Lonski, V. Koltsov, and Oleg Bondarev

THE SLEEPING BEAUTY — 1930 - Georgi and Sergei Vasiliev (Sovkino-Moscow) — 1966 - Appolinari Dudko and Konstantin Sergeiev (Lenfilm)
The second work is a color film of the ballet performed by the Kiev Ballet.

SMOKE — 1925 - P. Sazonov (VUFKU)
Drama about the bitterness of class struggle in the Ukrainian countryside as shown in the murder of a Party official by kulaks.

SNATCHERS — (See *Happiness*)

SNIPER — 1931 - Semyon Timoshenko (VUFKU)
Civil War drama.

A SNOW FAIRY TALE — 1959 - Eldar Shengelaya and Alexei Sakharov

THE SNOW QUEEN — 1957 - Lev Atamanov (Soyuzmultfilm)
Animated children's film. Occasionally seen on American television with an English sound track.

SOKOLOVO — 1975 - Otakar Vavra (Mosfilm/Barrandov Studios)
Czechoslovak-Soviet coproduction. Based on the World War II memoirs of General Ludvik Svoboda, *From Buzuluk To Prague*. The film relates the story about the formation of Czechoslovak Army units in the USSR in 1942.

SOLARIS — 1971 - Andrei Tarkovski (Mosfilm)

A 70mm wide-screen color science-fiction drama that explores time and space on a strange planet. A psychologically complex film in which Tarkovski questions whether man is mentally resourceful enough to meet the unknown of space. Often regarded to be the Soviet response to Kubrick's *2001: A Space Odyssey,* but the two films differ markedly as Tarkovski had a definite theme. Won the special jury prize at the 1971 Cannes Film Festival.

THE SOLD APPETITE — 1928 - Nikolai Okhlopkov (VUFKU)

Based on "Un appetit vendu," a story by the French Marxist Paul Lafargue. A burlesque on capitalist society in which a young man is unable to afford the luxury of feeding his family and decides to sell his appetite to a wealthy, sated capitalist. French audiences at the time gave the bizarre film a cool, unamused reception.

A SOLDIER'S FATHER — 1965 - Revaz Chkeidze (Gruziyafilm)

The starring role in this film was played by the leading Georgian theater actor Sergo Zakariadze, who won the Lenin Prize and the prize for best male actor at the 1965 Moscow Film Festival for his performance. This World War II drama is about Georgi Makharashvili, an old Georgian peasant who finds himself compelled to find and see his son who is at the front. Through a blend of tragedy and comedy Makharashvili is caught up in the maelstrom of war and kills an enemy soldier, thereby becoming a soldier himself. One of the best films of the 1960s and well received abroad.

A SOLDIER'S SON — 1933 - N. Lebedev

A children's film about a young boy who must grow up rapidly and assume adult responsibilities during the revolutionary era.

SOLDIERS — 1957 - Alexander Ivanov (Lenfilm)

Based on the novel *In The Trenches Of Stalingrad* by V. Nekrasov, who also wrote the screenplay. A drama about simple soldiers whose inner character is hammered out on the anvil of war. In style and dramatic impact the work is comparable to *Ballad Of A Soldier.*

SOLDIERS ON THE MARCH — 1958 - Leonid Trauberg (Mosfilm)

War drama.

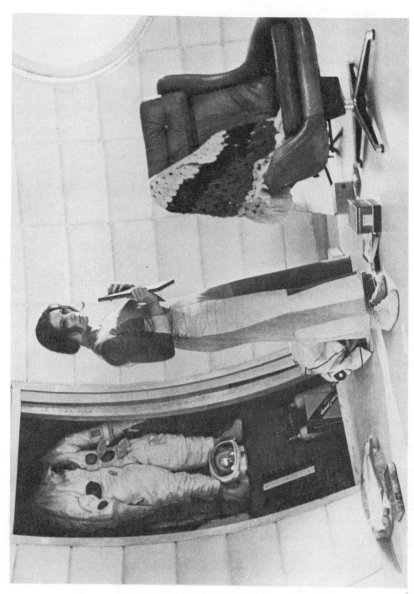

Solaris, Andrei Tarkovski (British Film Institute)

SOLDIERS ON THE MARCH — 1975 - Marina Babak
(Central Documentary Studios)
 Script written by Konstantin Simonov. The film took two years
to produce and features interviews with Soviet World War II veterans.
Newsreel footage was used from archival sources in the USSR, Poland,
and German Democratic Republic, and the emphasis lies on showing the
daily life of frontline soldiers. The film has no background music, only
the sound of artillery.

SOLDIERS' WIVES — 1974 - Yuri Marukhin (Belarusfilm)
 Documentary about the war years of 1941-45 as seen through the
reminiscences of women who lost their husbands and children.

SOMEBODY ELSE'S CHILDREN — 1959 - Tengiz Abuladze
(Gruziyafilm)

SON OF A CIRCASSIAN — 1939 - N. Dostal (Turkmenfilm)
 Espionage thriller about foreign spies and their capture on the
border area of Turkmenia.

SON OF A FIGHTER — 1942 - Vera Stroyeva
 Featurette, *Fighting Film Album No. 12.*

SON OF MONGOLIA — 1936 - Ilya Trauberg (Lenfilm)
 An exotic film shot on location in Buriat-Mongolia. The story
deals with a young Mongol shepherd and his adventures in Japanese-
occupied Manchuria.

SON OF TADZHIKISTAN — 1942 - Vasili Pronin, supervised by
Sergei Yutkevich
 Patriotic war drama about the heroism of a young Tadzhik Red
Army soldier.

SONA — (See *Gadzhi-Kara*)

SONG ABOUT FLOWERS — 1959 - Otar Yoseliani (Gruziyafilm)
 Love story.

A SONG ABOUT HAPPINESS — 1934 - Mark Donskoi and
Vladimir Legoshin (Vostokfilm)
A musical and humorous story about Soviet youth in the Volga
region, and Soviet education.

A SONG ABOUT HEROES — 1932 - Joris Ivens (Mezhrabpomfilm)
On the building of Magnitogorsk and Soviet heavy industry
during the First Five-Year Plan.

SONG OF ABAI — 1946 - Grigori Roshal (Kazakhfilm)
Dramatized portrayal of the life of a 19th-century Kazakh poet.

SONG OF MANSHUK — 1971 - Mazhit Begalin (Kazakhfilm)
Real life story of a World War II Kazakh heroine.

SONG OF THE FIRST GIRL — 1930 - Golub and Sadkovich
Based on the story "First Girl" by Nikolia Bogdanov. A Civil War
story about the work of Komsomols in the countryside.

SONS — 1946 - Alexander Ivanov (Lenfilm)
The tragedy and hardships of life in Nazi-occupied Latvia.

SONS AND MOTHERS — (See *Heart Of A Mother*)

SOROCHINSKI FAIR — 1927 - Grigori Grichin (VUFKU-Kiev)
1939 - Nikolai Ekk (Kiev Studios)
Based on Gogol's story of the same name. Grichin's work was
quite popular in its time while Ekk's sound remake proved unsuccessful.

THE SOUND OF LIFE — 1961 - R. Lukashevich (Mosfilm)
Based on the novel *The Blind Musician* by V.G. Korolenko.

SOVIET MEDICINE — 1921 - M. Verner (VUFKU-Kiev)
An agit-prop comedy about a bourgeois philistine, Nedoplyuev,
who suffers from obesity and is sated with life. However, after the
October Revolution he is "cured" by being drafted to the labor front.
Hard, honest labor soon makes a new man of Nedoplyuev, morally and
physically.

SOVIET PATRIOTS — 1939 - G. Lomidze (Turkmenfilm)
Spies and foreign agents are uncovered by vigilant workers in the kolkhozes along the Turkmenian border area.

SOVIET TOYS — 1923 - Ivan Ivanov-Vano and Bushkin (Kultkino)
First Soviet cartoon film.

SOZIA — 1967 - Mikhail Bogin (Mosfilm)

SPAIN — 1939 - Esther Shub (Mosfilm) — Also entitled *Spain In Flames.*
Edited newsreel compilation on the Spanish Civil War.

A SPECTER IS HAUNTING EUROPE — 1923 - Vladimir Gardin (VUFKU-Yalta Studio)
A symbolic, abstract allegory on the recent Russian revolutionary experience. Revolution is symbolized by a disease that threatens a monarchy in an unnamed European country. The royal family flees the country but is unable to avoid death while the citizens rebel and burn the palace. The use of abstract symbolism was attacked by critics who saw little need to use such a style to depict recent experiences.

SPIDER — 1942 - Ilya Trauberg and I. Zemgano
Featurette, *Fighting Film Album No. 11.*

SPORTING HONOR — 1951 - Mark Donskoi (Soyuzdetfilm)
Also entitled *Sporting Fame.*

SPRING — 1929 - Mikhail Kaufman (VUFKU)
A lyrical documentary film poem on the arrival of spring in Russia.

SPRING — 1946 - Grigori Alexandrov (Mosfilm)
A light social comedy which was revised many times and took four years to complete. A story which is a comedy of errors resulting from mistaken identity between two women, a teacher and an actress. Received an award at the Venice Film Festival.

SPRING IN MOSCOW — 1953 - Iosif Heifitz (Mosfilm)

SPRING ON ZARECHNAYA STREET — 1956 - Marlen Khutsiev and
F. Mironer (Odessa Studio)
Finely drawn characters with deep emotions made this love story
about a woman teacher and a factory worker one of the best films of
its time. The film was among those that breathed fresh life into Soviet
cinema after Stalin's death.

SPRING SONG — 1929 - Vladimir Gardin (Belgoskino)
A story about Komsomols in Belorussian village life and which
depicted changing social relationships under the Soviets. Based on a
play by Yakub Kolas. The film displeased critics who felt that Gardin
inaccurately portrayed the life of Belorussian peasants. Years later
Gardin admitted in his memoirs that he realized his errors only in the
final cutting of the film. However, until the Belorussian film industry
was physically based in Belorussia many of its films suffered from lack
of first hand observation of Belorussian life. Until 1939 the Belorussian
film studio was located in Leningrad because of the lack of proper
studio facilities and resources in Minsk.

SPRING SONG (1941) — (See *Anton Ivanovich Gets Mad*)

SPRINGTIME ON THE VOLGA — 1960 - V. Dorman and
G. Oganissian (Maxim Gorki Studios)
A musical romance with dances performed by the Beryozka
Dance Ensemble.

THE SPUTNIK SPEAKS — 1959 - Sergei Gerasimov with E. Volk,
V. Dorman, and G. Oganissian (Central Documentary Studios)
Documentary.

SQUADRON NO. 5 — 1939 - Abram Room (Mosfilm)
Soviet Air Force drama and its readiness to repel aggressors.

STALINGRAD — 1943 - Roman Karmen and L.V. Varlamov
(Central Newsreel Studio) — Also entitled *Heroic Stalingrad: The City
That Stopped Hitler.*
Documentary.

STALINGRAD (1970) — (See *Memory*)

THE STAR OF CAPTIVE GOOD FORTUNE — 1974 - Vladimir Motyl
(Mosfilm)

STARTING OUT — 1962 - Igor Talankin (Mosfilm)
A moving story about young love between Volodia and Valia
whose lives are disrupted by war. Received a special jury prize at the
1962 Venice Film Festival.

THE STARVING STEPPE REVIVES — 1925 - N. Shcherbakov
(Uzbekgoskino)
First Uzbek film which was made by a self-trained amateur.

THE STATIONMASTER — 1925 - Yuri Zheliabushski (Mezhrabpom-
Rus) — Also entitled *The Collegiate Registrar.*
Based on a story by Pushkin. This tale of an unscrupulous young
tsarist officer who rejects a girl who has fallen in love with him was
quite popular with Soviet audiences in its time. Much of the filming had
to be done at night and the cast of actors used the Stanislavski method.

STEEL ROAD — (See *Turksib*)

STELLAR BROTHERS — *FROM THE KREMLIN TO THE COSMOS* -
1962 - Dmitri Bogolepov (Central Documentary Studios)
Documentary on the space flights of cosmonauts Andrian
Nikolayev and Pavel Popovich.

STENKA RAZIN — 1937 - Olga Preobrazhenskaya and Ivan Pravov
The scenario for this historical drama about a popular uprising in
tsarist Russia was written by Alexei Chapygin, who was a blunt critic of
collectivization and a strong proponent of historical accuracy. The film
had to be revised prior to its release.

STEPAN KHALTURIN — 1925 - Alexander Ivanovski (Sevzapkino)
Revolutionary and biographical drama.

THE STEPMOTHER — 1973 - Oleg Bondaryev (Mosfilm)

THE STONE FLOWER — 1946 - Alexander Ptushko (Mosfilm)
Partly animated film that was shot partially in Prague with the

Agfacolor process acquired from Germany. Stalin Prize winner based on Russian legends.

STORIES ABOUT LENIN — 1958 - Sergei Yutkevich (Mosfilm)
A personal drama about Lenin and his wife Nadezhda Krupskaya. A color film.

STORM OVER ASIA (1928) — (See *Descendant Of Genghis Khan*)

STORM OVER ASIA — 1965 - Kamil Yarmatov (Uzbekfilm)
A historical drama about the 1917 Revolution in Turkestan. The story emphasized class conflict and social tensions of the period.

STORMY NIGHTS — 1931 - Ivan Kavaleridze (Kiev Studios)
Story about a poor peasant who decides to take a temporary job in construction work in order to save money to buy a cow. In the end he decides to give up his pastoral way of life and remains in industry.

STORY OF A CRIME — 1962 - Fedor Khitruk (Soyuzmultfilm)
Feature cartoon.

STORY OF A FOREST GIANT — 1954 - Alexander Zguridi
Nature study film.

STORY OF A GIRL — 1960 - Mikhail Chiaureli

STORY OF A MOTHER — 1963 - A. Karpov (Kazakhfilm)
For her feature role in this film Amina Umurzakova received the prize for best actress at the 1964 Soviet All-Union Film Festival. Widely exported to African and Asian nations. A simple, moving story set in Kazakhstan in the first autumn of war of 1941. An illiterate woman who, as a mother has her own tragedies, takes on the task of delivering mail from the front. Through her eyes is experienced the bitterness of women losing their sons and husbands in war.

STORY OF A REAL MAN — 1948 - Alexander Stolper (Mosfilm)
A dramatization of the real life story of Soviet fighter pilot Maresiev, based on **Boris** Polevoi's novel. After being shot down and having both legs crushed, the pilot crawled his way back to Soviet lines

over a period of eighteen days. Maresiev later returned to duty with artificial legs. One of Stolper's best films.

THE STORY OF ASYA KLIACHINA, WHO LOVED BUT DID NOT MARRY — 1966 - Andrei Mikhalkov-Konchalovski (Mosfilm)
Release was delayed so that the film could be revised because of its controversial social theme.

STORY OF SEVEN WHO WERE HANGED — 1920 - Pyotr Chardynin (VUFKU)
Agitka based on an actual execution.

STORY OF THE FLAMING YEARS — 1961 - Yulia Solntseva (Mosfilm)
The original script for this epic story of World War II was written by Alexander Dovzhenko in 1945. Solntseva modified the script and received the prize for best direction at the 1961 Cannes Film Festival for this film. A 70mm color film that focuses on the Ukraine and the wartime odyssey of a gallant soldier who survives the war and returns home to marry.

STRANGE PEOPLE — 1970 - Vasili Shukshin (Mosfilm)

A STRICT YOUTH — 1936 - Abram Room
Banned from exhibition despite a cost of two million rubles. Room was suspended from directing for a time while Yuri Olesha, the scenarist, was arrested. The film suggested that an advanced intellectual elite might well be treated with more privilege in a future classless society. The Komsomols in this story were seen by critics as weak and without Communist fervor.

STRIDE, SOVIET — 1926 - Dziga Vertov (Goskino)
Commissioned by the Moscow Soviet as a documentary and information film for th citizens of Moscow prior to municipal elections. The film offered a tableau of Soviet life and achievements in the period of reconstruction following the Civil War.

STRIKE — 1925 - Sergei Eisenstein (Goskino/Proletkult)
The film that brought Eisenstein to the forefront of Soviet

cinema and influenced many of his contemporaires in film-making. The work was produced to celebrate the 20th anniversary of the 1905 Revolution and dealt with the suppression of a workers' strike by tsarist police. Eisenstein succeeded in glorifying the heroic masses rather than the individual. Through rearrangement of certain sequences Eisenstein made this an example of the art of the masses.

THE STRUGGLE CONTINUES — 1939 - V. Zhuravlev
(Sovetskaya Belarus)
An anti-Nazi drama about the workers' resistance movement in Germany.

THE STRUGGLE FOR PEACE — 1921 - Eduard Tisse and
G. Boltianski
A historical revolutionary film chronicle that was not preserved for long. Esther Shub utilized fragments of the remaining film for her *The Great Road.*

STRUGGLE FOR THE "ULTIMATUM" FACTORY — 1923 -
Dmitri Bassaligo (Proletkino)
One of the early big films of the revolutionary era. A drama of intrigue and workers' struggle against tsarist police.

STRUGGLE OF THE GIANTS — 1926 - Viktor Turin (VUFKU)
Turin attempted to create a grand, almost epic, story about the Communist-led revolutionary movement in an unnamed Western country. Class struggle between monopolists and workers was the main theme, but the film failed to please critics who saw little character conflict or development. Enjoyed only a modest commercial success.

SUBJECT FOR A SHORT STORY — 1969 - Sergei Yutkevich
(Mosfilm)
Based on a fragment of Anton Chekhov's life which revolved around the first, poor showing of his *The Seagull.* Visually delightful and striking.

SUBMARINE T-9 — 1943 - Alexander Ivanov
War drama about the heroism of a Soviet submarine crew.

A SUMMER TO REMEMBER — 1959 - Ivan Pyriev (Mosfilm)

SUN, RAIN AND SMILES — 1962 - Leonid Makhnach

A SUNNY CAMPAIGN — 1931 - Vladimir Korsh-Sablin
(Sovetskaya Belarus)
    A group of middle peasants *(seredniaki)* are skeptical about the
benefits to be gained from joining the kolkhozes. They choose one of
their number, Filimon, to investigate the collective farms. Filimon then
goes off and visits various kolkhozes and is pleasantly surprised by what
he sees.

SUNNY TADZHIKISTAN — 1937 - N. Dostal (Tadzhik-kino)
    Documentary on the achievements of Tadzhikistan after twenty
years of Soviet power.

SUSPICIOUS LUGGAGE — 1926 - Girgori Grichin (VUFKU)
    A light satire on the West. While in the United States a Soviet
traveller becomes ill and is told to eat oranges. The bourgeois police become suspicious of the man and are embarrassed when they mistake a
box of oranges for a container of poison gas.

SUVOROV — 1940 - Vsevolod Pudovkin and Mikhail Doller (Mosfilm)
    A big historical film that paid tribute to the patriotism and gener-
alship of the tsarist general who saved his Russian army by crossing the
Alps. A second part to the film was planned but never realized because
of the Soviet Union's war with Germany. Filmed on location in the
Caucasian mountains. Suvorov was played by Nikolai Cherkasov-
Sergeiev.

SVANETIA — 1927 - Yuri Zheliabushski (Sovkino)
    An ethnographical film about the medieval society in the
Caucasus that was to be made famous by Kalatozov's *Salt For Svanetia*.

S.V.D. [Soyuz Velikogo Dela-Union of a Great Cause] — 1927 -
Grigori Kozintsev and Leonid Trauberg (Sovkino-Leningrad)
    An adventure and romantic drama based on selected episodes of
the Decembrist Uprising of 1825.

SWAMP SOLDIERS — 1938 - Alexander Macheret (Mosfilm)
An anti-Nazi drama that was occasionally gruesome in depicting the treatment of German Communists in a Nazi concentration camp. Along with *The Oppenheim Family* and *Professor Mamlock* it was considered one of the better Soviet anti-Nazi films of the 1930s.

SWAN LAKE — 1957 - Z. Tulubyeva (Central Documentary Studios)
1971 - Apollinari Dudko and Konstantin Sergeiev (Mosfilm)
Both filmed ballet performed by the Bolshoi Ballet in color.

THE SWINEHERD GIRL AND THE SHEPHERD — 1941 -
Ivan Pyriev (Mosfilm) — Also entitled *They Met In Moscow*.
An unpretentious, light musical comedy and romance which was very popular with Soviet audiences. Most critics regard it as one of the most successful of its genre. The film emphasized the strength of multinational friendship in the USSR.

SWORD AND SHIELD — 1969 - Vladimir Basov (Mosfilm)
Espionage drama about a Soviet agent in Nazi Germany.

SYLVIA — 1944 - Alexander Ivanovski (Mosfilm)
A musical based on a Viennese operetta by Kalman.

SYMPHONY OF OIL — 1934 - B. Pumnyanski (Azerfilm)
A documentary depicting the tempo and rhythm of the Soviet Caucasian petroleum industry.

TADZHIKISTAN — 1946 - L. Stepanova
(Central Documentary Studios)

TAHIR AND ZUHRA — 1945 - Nabi Ganiev (Uzbekfilm)
Romance based on an Uzbek folk legend.

TAILOR FROM TORZHOK — 1925 - Yakov Protazanov
(Mezhrabpom-Rus)
A social satire about the Soviet state lottery loan.

TAKING OFF — 1973 - R. Raamat (Tallinfilm)
Animated film.

TALE OF A BIG SPOON — 1932 - Alexander Medvedkin (Soyuzkino)
Short comedy.

TALE OF A WHITE CALF — 1933 - Lev Atamanov and V. Sutsev
(Mezhrabpomfilm)
Cartoon allegory on disarmament moves in the League of Nations.

A TALE OF PRIEST PANKRATI — 1918 - Alexander Arkatov and
Preobrazhenski (Moscow Cinema Committee)
Antireligious *agitka* based on a fable by D. Biednyi.

TALE OF THE SIBERIAN LAND — 1948 - Ivan Pyriev (Mosfilm)
In this color film a young pianist returns from the war with crippled hands. After arriving in a Siberian village, the young man becomes
heartened and inspired by the simple life of the people around him. He
again turns to composing music. One of the better films of the immediate postwar era because propaganda was so muted.

TALE OF TSAR DURANDA — 1934 - Ivan Ivanov-Vano with
Valentina and Zenaeda Brumberg (Mezhrabpomfilm)
Animated feature film based on folk legends.

THE TALE OF TSAR SULTAN — 1967 - Alexander Ptushko (Mosfilm)
A highly colorful adaptation of the fairy tale by Alexander
Pushkin.

THE TAMING OF THE FIRE — 1972 - Daniil Khrabovitski (Mosfilm)
Major prize winner at 1972 Soviet All-Union Film Festival. A
large time scale film that ranges from the period of the construction of
Magnitogorsk to present day missile engineering. The life of a rocket
designer is the focal point of this drama about the ethical problems that
confront a society at different stages of national development. Contains
good, interesting scenes of the Baikonur cosmodrome.

TANYA — (See *Bright Road*)

TARAS SHEVCHENKO — 1925, in two parts - Pyotr Chardynin
(VUFKU) — 1951 - Igor Savchenko (Kiev Studios)
Of the two films on the life of the renowned Ukrainian poet

Savchenko's is the better known of the two and had a greater time scale. Chardynin's film focused on Shevchenko's middle years and the events surrounding them. The main part was played by the famed Ukrainian actor Amvrosi Buchma who was applauded for the way he probed into and revealed Shevchenko's character. Buchma projected the poet as a revolutionary leader and this made the film very controversial when it was shown in Polish-occupied Ukraine. Prior to actual filming Chardynin spent a good deal of time in research in order to give an accurate portrayal of Shevchenko's Ukraine.

Savchenko, who died just before the film's completion, managed to convey the essence of the poet's spirit and life. The film was a highlight of the 1951 Karlovy Vary Film Festival, earning the prize for best direction and the prize for best male actor which went to Sergei Bondarchuk.

TARAS TRYASILO — 1926 - Pyotr Chardynin (VUFKU)
Chardynin made this film immediately after his very successful *Taras Shevchenko*, but was unable to score a critical triumph. Amvrosi Buchma played the lead role of the legendary Ukrainian hero, who along with the Zaporozhian Cossacks struggled against class domination. Filmed on location in Kiev, Zhitomir, Dnepropetrovsk and Uman.

THE TARDY FIANCE — 1940 - K. Mikaberidze (Goskinprom-Gruziya)
Love and comedy on a collective farm.

THE TEACHER — 1939 - Sergei Gerasimov (Lenfilm) — Also entitled *The New Teacher.*
No less than 1,000 teachers were surveyed for comments on the screenplay prior to filming. The result produced a polished, critical and strong film about the Soviet educational system and its problems as seen through the experiences of a teacher on a collective farm.

TEDDY BEAR — 1964 - Fedor Khitruk (Soyuzmultfilm)
Animated film.

THE TELEGRAM — 1972 - Rolan Bykov (Mosfilm)
A comedy about two youngsters who come upon an old wartime telegram and decide to have a little fun with it.

TELL ME ABOUT YOURSELF — 1972 - S. Mikaelian (Lenfilm)

TEN DAYS THAT SHOOK THE WORLD — (See *October*)

TENDERNESS — 1966 - Elyer Ishmuhammedov (Uzbekfilm)
A contemporary love story about the dreams and hopes of Soviet youth in Tashkent. Fine photography.

TENI BELVEDERA — 1927 - A. Anoshchenko (VUFKU)
Suspense melodrama about class struggle in bourgeois Poland.

TEST OF FIDELITY — 1954 - Ivan Pyriev (Mosfilm)

THAT SUMMER LONG AGO — 1975 - Nikolai Lebedev (Lenfilm)
A film made primarily for children about the first days of the German invasion of June 1941.

THAT SWEET WORD — LIBERTY — 1973 - Vitautas Zalakevicius (Mosfilm)
Grand prize winner at the 1973 Moscow Film Festival. A revolutionary drama set in contemporary Latin America. The hero, Francisco, commands a group of determined revolutionaries who decide to dig a tunnel to rescue their imprisoned leader. A commercial and critical success.

THAW — 1931 - Boris Barnet (Mezhrabpomfilm)

THERE ARE ALSO PEOPLE — 1960 - Georgi Daneliya and Igor Talankin (Mosfilm)

THERE CAME A SOLDIER FROM THE FRONT — 1972 - Nikolai Gubienko (Mosfilm)
World War II drama.

THERE LIVES SUCH A FELLOW — 1964 - Vasili Shukshin (Maxim Gorki Studios) — Also entitled *There Was A Lad*.
Won prize for best comedy at the 1964 Soviet All-Union Film Festival and the Golden Lion award at the 1964 Venice Youth Film Festival. Pashka Kolokolnikov is the hero of this story. He is a man

with a good heart and can bring a smile to anyone's face, although he is not free of his own troubles.

THERE ONCE LIVED A YOUNG GIRL — 1944 - Viktor Eisimont (Soyuzdetfilm)
    A sensitive, tender and intelligent story about the hardships of children during the blockade and siege of Leningrad in World War II. The film had a muted criticism of Party officials who lacked leadership at a crucial time.

THERE SERVED TWO COMRADES — 1968 - Karelov (Lenfilm)
    Story about two friends and their involvement in the Battle of Perekop during the Civil War.

THERE WAS A LAD — (See *There Lives Such A Fellow*)

THERE WAS AN OLD MAN AND AN OLD WOMAN — 1964 - Grigori Chukhrai (Mosfilm)

THERE WILL BE NO LEAVE TODAY — 1959 - Andrei Tarkovski (Mosfilm)

THERE WILL BE WORK FOR YOU — 1932 - Ilya Trauberg (Sovkino)

THERE ARE HORSES — 1965 - Tolomush Okeyev (Kirghizfilm)

THESE WON'T GIVE UP — 1932 - Mikhail Kaufman
    Documentary about shock workers at a Leningrad tractor plant.

THEY AND WE — 1933 - B. Antonovski
    Animated film.

THEY ARE NEIGHBORS — 1968 - Grigori Roshal (Mosfilm)

THEY DIDN'T TEACH US THAT — 1975 - Ilya Frez (Maxim Gorki Studios)
    Story about Soviet school teachers and their problems.

THEY FOUGHT FOR THEIR MOTHERLAND — 1975 -
Sergei Bondarchuk (Mosfilm)
    A two-part 70mm color film based on the novel by Mikhail
Sholokhov. A sweeping psychological World War II story about 117
Soviet soldiers, all that is left of a regiment, who are ordered to hold a
low hill against heavy German forces. Set in the early period of the
Soviet-German conflict, the story reveals a shift in the mentality of the
men, from defensive to offensive. The film features Vasili Shukshin in
one of his last roles prior to his death.

THEY HAVE A NATIVE LAND — 1950 - Alexander Faintsimmer
(Mosfilm)
    A harsh Cold War film that depicted the Americans as no better
than the Nazis in their treatment of Soviet children in Germany after
World War II. The story is about Soviet efforts to effect the return of
children who had been deported during the war. The Anglo-Americans
treat the youngsters as little more than captives. At the end, after some
of the children have been returned, one mother makes a strong emotional plea for the return of the rest.

THEY MET IN MOSCOW — (See *The Swineherd Girl And The
Shepherd*)

THIEVING MAGPIE [Soroka vorovka] — 1920 - Alexander Sanin
(VFKO/Rus Studio)
    Tragic melodrama about a woman and her life.

THE THIRD BLOW — 1948 - Igor Savchenko (Kiev Studios)
    One of the big films about World War II that dramatized the of-
fensive period of Soviet operations against Germany. The story extols
the military genius of Stalin.

THE THIRD PHILISTINE — (See *Bed And Sofa*)

THE THIRTEEN — 1937 - Mikhail Romm (Mosfilm)
    A story about the Civil War in Central Asia, where a Red Army
unit is cut off and annihilated except for one man. The film was made
at the suggestion of Boris Shumyatski, who had been much impressed
by John Ford's *Lost Patrol*. Although Romm experienced difficulties in

making the film it was a popular and critical triumph. Some critics and film historians have credited the work as the inspiration for the American film *Sahara*.

THIRTEEN DAYS — 1931 - I. Poselski
Documentary and day by day account of the show trial of Soviet industrial saboteurs.

THIRTY-THREE — 1965 - Georgi Daneliya (Mosfilm)
Autobiographical story and look at Daneliya's generation.

THIS HAPPENED IN THE DONBAS — 1945 - Leonid Lukov (Soyuzdetfilm)
Drama about the Soviet partisan resistance against German occupation forces on the Donets Basin.

THIS HAPPENED TO POLYNIN — 1971 - Alexei Sakharov (Mosfilm)
A World War II love story about a Soviet Air Force officer and an actress.

THOSE WHO RECOVERED THEIR SIGHT — 1930 - V. Kasianov (Mezhrabpomfilm)
A Civil War drama about a Hungarian's search for revolutionary truth and his friendship with a Bolshevik soldier.

A THOUGHT ABOUT COSSACK GOLOTU — 1937 - Igor Savchenko (Soyuzdetfilm)
A children's film about the Civil War.

THREE COMRADES — 1935 - Semyon Timoshenko (Ukrainfilm)
A comedy about three Civil War veterans who, as plant directors, face problems as a result of conflicts arising between the currents of socialist industrialization and the remnants of NEP.

THREE DAYS OF VIKTOR CHERNISHEV — 1968 - Mark Ossepian (Maxim Gorki Studios)
Another film of the 1960s that reflects changes in social outlook by examining society's responsibility to the individual rather than vice versa. The story, with occasional chilling scenes, delves into the life of a

teen age delinquent who drifts aimlessly into a brutal street fight and goes to jail.

THREE FAT MEN — 1963 - Valentina and Zenaeda Brumberg (Soyuzmultfilm)
Animated film.
1966 - Alexei Batalov and Iosif Shapiro (Lenfilm)
Theatrical feature film.

THREE HEROINES — 1938 - Dziga Vertov
Film poem.

300 YEARS AGO — 1956 - Vladimir Petrov (Mosfilm)

THREE IN A SHELL HOLE — 1941 - I. Mutanov and Alexei Olenin
Featurette, *Fighting Film Album No. 1.*

THREE IN A TANK — 1942 - N. Sadkovich
Featurette, *Fighting Film Album No. 8.*

THREE LIVES — 1925 - Ivan Perestiani (Goskinprom-Gruziya)
Based on the novel *The First Step* by Georgi Tsereteli. The drama is about the onset of capitalism in Georgia during the late 19th century. The film explored changing social relationships and their complexities as a result of the growth of a bourgeois-merchant class.

THREE MEETINGS — 1948 - Sergei Yutkevich, with Vsevolod Pudovkin and Alexander Ptushko (Mosfilm)
Political drama in color.

THREE NEIGHBORS — 1966 - V. Bakhtadze (Gruziyafilm)
Animated fairy tale about animals and their relationships.

THREE POPLARS IN PLYUSHIKHA STREET — 1969 - Tatiana Lioznova (Mosfilm)
A contemporary love story.

THREE PORTRAITS — 1918 - Alexander Ivanovski
Based on stories by Turgenev.

THE THREE SISTERS — 1969 - Samson Samsonov (Mosfilm)
Film adaptation of a play by Anton Chekhov.

THREE SONGS OF LENIN — 1934 - Dziga Vertov (Mezhrabpomfilm)
Vertov spent three years in working on this film, which included archival film footage and is considered by some critics his best work. A lyrical film poem about Lenin's work on behalf of the women of Central Asia.

THREE SPRINGS OF LENIN — 1964 - Leonid Kristi
(Central Documentary Studios)
Documentary about Lenin's life.

THE THUNDERSTORM — 1934 - Vladimir Petrov
(Soyuzfilm-Leningrad)
Based on the play by A.N. Ostrovski. A moving drama about the difficult life of women in tsarist Russia as seen through the eyes of Katerina, the heroine. Well received at the 1934 Venice Film Exhibition.

TIMUR AND HIS COMMAND — 1940 - Alexander Razumni
(Soyuzdetfilm)
A very popular children's film on the theme of national preparedness for possible war. The story was about a group of youngsters and their vigilance against foreign spies. The film's popularity proved so large that a whole Timur cult and movement was started and lasted until the 1950s.

TIMUR'S OATH — 1943 - Lev Kuleshov

TO THE DANUBE — 1940 - Ilya Kopalin and I. Poselski
(Central and Ukrainian Newsreel Studios)
Documentary about the Soviet reannexation of western borderlands in 1940.

TO LOVE A MAN — 1973 - Sergei Gerasimov (Maxim Gorki Studios)
A contemporary story of love and trust. In polls among Soviet movie goers this work proved one of the most popular in 1973-74.

TODAY — 1930 - Esther Shub (Soyuzkino-Moscow)
 One of Shub's most admired and dramatic documentaries that depicted social and political life of the USSR and the West. Interesting editing developed political viewpoint as in a sequence of Western churchmen followed by a shot of penguins.

TOGETHER WITH OUR FATHERS — 1932 - L. Frenkel (Kiev Studios)
 A drama about youngsters who join their elders in the Russian revolutionary struggles of 1917.

TOM CANTY — 1942 - E. Garin with Lokshina
 An adaptation of Mark Twain's *The Prince and The Pauper*.

TOMMY — 1931 - Yakov Protazanov (Mezhrabpomfilm)
 Based on the play *Armored Train* 14-69 by Ivanov. A drama about the Civil War and Allied Foreign intervention as experienced by a British soldier. A related film is *Jimmie Higgins*.

TORN SHOES — 1933 - Margarita Barskaya (Mezhrabpomfilm)
 Child labor and its role in the class struggles in Germany of the 1920s-30s.

TOWARDS AN ARMISTICE WITH FINLAND — 1944 - Yuli Raizman (Central Documentary Studios)
 Documentary on Finland's cessation of hostilities with the USSR.

TRACTOR DRIVERS — 1939 - Ivan Pyriev (Mosfilm/Kiev Studios)
 A light hearted musical comedy in which the heroine falls in love with and marries the outstanding tractor driver of her collective farm. Despite the film's simple plot it proved popular with audiences and was liked by critics.

TRAGEDY AT TRIPOLYE — 1926 - A. Anoshchenko (VUFKU)
 The cast of this film included many veterans of the actual events depicted. The story was about a detachment of young Red soldiers in the Ukraine that was nearly annihilated by the Whites during the Civil War.

THE TRAIN GOES EAST — 1948 - Yuli Raizman (Mosfilm)
A comedy that had only a limited run because of criticism that Raizman had patterned the work after Western models.

THE TRAITOR — 1926 - Abram Room (Goskino)
The work was criticized so badly for its drawing room, melo-dramatic manner that many who worked on it disavowed it. The story dealt with an *agent-provocateur* who betrayed a group of revolutionary Russian sailors to the tsarist police prior to the October Revolution.

TRANSPORT OF FIRE — 1929 - Alexander Ivanov (Belgoskino)
An adventure story about a group of underground revolutionaries who surreptitiously take a train loaded with weapons from a small border village to Moscow on the eve of the 1905 Revolution.

TRAVELLER WITH LUGGAGE — 1966 - Ilya Frez
(Maxim Gorki Studios)
Children's film.

TREASURE ISLAND — 1938 - V. Vainshtok
Based on the novel by Robert Louis Stevenson. An expensive film for its time; Vainshtok exceeded his budget by one-half million rubles. The work was banned because of Party criticism.

THE TRIAL — 1963 - Vladimir Skuibin (Mosfilm)

THE TRIAL MUST CONTINUE — 1931 - Yefim Dzigan (Belgoskino)
The legal rights of women in the new Soviet society was the theme of this drama about a woman worker who is verbally abused by a hooligan. The man is then tried, but the trial then focuses on society and its morals.

TRIAL OF THE SOCIAL REVOLUTIONARIES — 1922 - Dziga Vertov
Film report on the trial of several members of the Social Revolutionaries who were treated as enemies of the state by the Bolsheviks.

THE TRIANGLE — 1968 - Genrikh Malian (Bek-Nazarov Studio)
A story about the relationships of five blacksmiths against the background of social life in an Armenian village in the 1930s.

TRIANGLE LOVE — (See *Bed And Sofa*)

TRIO — 1919 [1922] - M. Narokov (VFKO and Neptun Studio)

TRIPLE CHECK — 1971 - Alois Brench (Riga Film Studio)
World War II espionage drama based on an actual episode.

THE TROTTER'S GAIT — (See *The Ambler's Race*)

TRUBACHEV'S UNIT IN BATTLE — 1957 - Ilya Frez
(Maxim Gorki Studios)
Children's film; sequel to *Vasek Trubachev and His Comrades.*

THE TSAR WANTS TO SLEEP — (See *Lieutenant Kije*)

THE TSAR'S BRIDE — 1964 - Vladimir Gorikker (Mosfilm)
Filmed opera performed by the Bolshoi Opera based on the work
by Rimski-Korsakov. Rich in costume and color.

TURKSIB — 1929 - Viktor Turin (Vostok-kino) — Also entitled
Steel Road.
Still considered by film historians as one of the outstanding documentaries of world cinema. The film was the highlight of Turin's
directorial career. Lean photography was a hallmark of this work which
depicted the building of the Turkestan-Siberian Railway and symbolized the industrialization of the USSR.

THE TWELVE CHAIRS — 1971 - Leonid Gaidai (Gruziyafilm)
A Georgian comedy based on the novel by Ilf and Yevgeni Petrov.

XXTH SPRING — 1940 - M. Mikhailov (Azerfilm)
Documentary celebrating twenty years of Soviet achievements in
Azerbaidzhan.

THE 26 BAKU COMMISSARS — 1966 - A. Ibragimov
(Mosfilm/Azerbaidzhanfilm)
A remake of Shengelaya's classic 1932 film (see next page) which
according to Soviet writers is an artistic highlight of the 1960s. Sharp,
interesting photography.

TWENTY-SIX COMMISSARS — 1932 - Nikolai Shengelaya (Azerfilm)
Shengelaya's best film which depicts the execution of twenty-six
Communist leaders in 1918 by the British in Baku. The actual event
continues to have a special place as a heroic episode in the history of
the Communist Party and the Civil War. Shengelaya's direction gave the
characters of the commissars a distinct humanistic aspect by combining
elements of humor with tragedy.

TWENTY-TWO MISFORTUNES — 1930 - Sergei Gerasimov and
S. Bartenev

TWENTY YEARS OF CINEMA — 1940 - Vsevolod Pudovkin and
Esther Shub
A documentary chronicle of the artistic achievements and devel-
opment of Soviet cinema.

TWICE BORN — 1934 - Eduard Arshanski (Sovetskaya Belarus)
Melodrama about the life of a poor Belorussian peasant who concludes that despite the material poverty of his life he has a place in the
world around him.

THE TWO — 1965 - Mikhail Bogin (Mosfilm)
A contemporary love story.

TWO ARMORED CARS — 1928 - Semyon Timoshenko (VUFKU)
Drama about the events of the 1917 October Revolution and how
Russian soldiers decided to join the Bolshevik cause.

TWO-BULDI-TWO — 1929 - Lev Kuleshov
A provincial circus forms the arena for the struggle of Red and
White forces during the Civil War. Soviet historians now contend the
film was unfairly criticized at the time of its release.

TWO CAPTAINS — 1956 - Vladimir Vengerov (Mosfilm)

TWO DAYS — 1927 - Georgi Stabovoi (VUFKU)
One of the better Ukrainian films of its time because of the depth
of character portrayal and revelation of a man who decides his true
feelings lie with the revolutionaries during the Civil War.

TWO FEDORS — 1958 - Marlen Khutsiev (Maxim Gorki Studios)

TWO FRIENDS — 1937 - Ivan Perestiani (Goskinprom-Gruziya)

TWO FRIENDS, A MODEL AND A GIRL — 1927 - Alexei Popov
(Sovkino)
A highlight of Soviet cinema of the NEP period when satire was
strong. The story is about two young inventors and their girl friend who
are confounded and frustrated by bureaucrats and private industrialists
when they attempt to have their invention tried out.

TWO NIGHTS — 1933 - P. Barkhudarian (Armenfilm)
Drama about the revolutionary movement in Armenia.

TWO SOLDIERS — 1943 - Leonid Lukov (Tashkent Studio)
Adapted from the novel *My Land* by Lev Slavin. A simple, but
very popular film about the frontline friendship between two soldiers
during the defense of Leningrad in 1941. The song "Dark Night", sung
by Ivan Kozlovski, proved immensely popular during the war and provided the backdrop for a very moving sequence in the film.

TWO WOMEN — 1929 - Grigori Roshal (VUFKU-Odessa Studio)
A social film about contrasting moral currents during the NEP
period. The story concerns the style of life of two women, one a devoted, heroic Communist while the other a symbol of decaying rem-
nant of the bourgeois NEPmen.

UGUBZIARA — 1930 - David Rondeli (Goskinprom-Gruziya)
Class struggle and collectivization in the Georgian countryside.

UKRAINE IN FLAMES — (See *Victory In The Ukraine*)

UKRAINIAN RHAPSODY — 1961 - Sergei Paradzhanov
(Alexander Dovzhenko Studios)

UKRAZIYA — 1926 - Pyotr Chardynin (VUFKU)
Espionage thriller about a Bolshevik agent known as "Seven Plus
Two" operating in Odessa during the Civil War.

UMBAR — 1937 - A. Makovski (Turkmenfilm)
First theatrical sound film of the Turkmenian cinema, but with little dialog. Umbar is a young Komsomol who goes through the furnace of the Civil War.

THE UMBRELLA — 1966 - Mikhail Kobakhidze (Gruziyafilm)

UMKA — 1969 - V. Pekar and V. Popov (Soyuzmultfilm)
Animated film about the adventures and misadventures of a young polar bear.

UNCLE VANYA — 1971 - Andrei Mikhalkov-Konchalovski (Mosfilm)
Based on the play by Anton Chekhov. The film is regarded as a critical success for Mikhalkov-Konchalovski and has been widely exhibited internationally. Won the Special Silver Seashell prize at the 1971 San Sebastian Film Festival and prize for best art direction at the 1973 Cork Film Festival.

THE UNCLE'S DREAM — 1967 - Konstantin Voinov (Mosfilm)
Based on Dostoevski's story about life and social relationships in a rural Russian village in the 19th century.

THE UNCONQUERED — 1945 - Mark Donskoi (Kiev Studios)
A war film that did not enjoy the same success as Donskoi's earlier *The Rainbow*. The story dealt with the Soviet partisan resistance to German occupation in the Donets Basin. Based on the novel by Boris Gorbatov. The film gives a larger role and credit to the Party and Komsomol members which signalled a return of tighter censorship.

UNDER A SKY OF STONE — 1974 - Knut Anderssen and Igor Maslennikov (Lenfilm/Timfilm)
Norwegian-Soviet coproduction. This drama about World War II centers on an episode in October 1944 when the Soviet Army was advancing on Kirkenes and the Norwegian province of Finmarken. Two thousand Norwegians took refuge in the Benwarten mine to avoid being deported by the retreating Germans. The film depicts the operation of a Soviet unit with the help of Norwegian partisans to rescue the beleaguered people before the Germans can blow up the mine.

UNDER ANCIENT DESERT SKIES — 1961 - Vladimir Shnęiderov
Popular science film.

UNDERGROUND — 1918 - Vladimir Kasianov
Civil War *agitka.*

UNFINISHED STORY — 1955 - Friedrich Ermler (Lenfilm)
Drama about a woman doctor (Yelina Bystritskaya) who breaks
from a selfish suitor only to fall in love with her crippled patient (Sergei
Bondarchuk). At first he tries to reject her love, but as he regains the
use of his legs he returns the doctor's love. Largely credited with good
direction and acting, the film offered little in the way of social comment which had long been Ermler's hallmark as a film-maker.

UNFORGETTABLE — 1969 - Yulia Solntseva
(Alexander Dovzhenko Studios)

UNFORGETTABLE 1919 — 1952 - Mikhail Chiaureli (Mosfilm)
Stalin is reported to have liked this film very much. The drama
concerns the crucial Bolshevik defense of Petrograd in 1919 and por-
trays Stalin in a larger historical role than Lenin. This film, along with
The Fall Of Berlin, was cited by Khrushchev as one of the evils of
Stalinism in the distortion of history during his speech at the 1956
Party Congress.

THE UNFORGETTABLE YEARS — 1957 - Ilya Kopalin
(Central Documentary Studios)
World War II documentary.

UNINVITED LOVE — 1964 - Vladimir Monakhov (Mosfilm)

UNLIKELY BUT TRUE — 1928 - Georgi Vasiliev (Sovkino)

UNREPEATABLE SPRING — 1957 - Alexander Stolper (Mosfilm)

THE UNRULY BAND — 1938 - Alexei Popov (Azerfilm)
Story about an ungovernable, individualistic young boy whose behavior is finally set straight by his fellow students. The film emphasized
the theme of the individual's responsibility to the collective.

UNTIL MONDAY — (See *Let's Live Until Monday*)

UNTIL TOMORROW — 1929 - Yuri Tarich (Belgoskino)
   A political drama which concerned, at least in Soviet eyes, the unjust division of Belorussia between Poland and the USSR. The story revolves around an anti-Pilsudski revolutionary movement in Polish-controlled western Belorussia.

UNTIL WE MEET AGAIN SOON — 1934 - Georgi Makarov
(Goskinprom-Gruziya)
   A silent social comedy of errors that proved so popular that the film was technically restored and a sound track added in 1964 when it was rereleased.

THE UNTIMELY MAN — 1973 - Abram Room (Mosfilm)

THE UNVANQUISHED — 1927 - A. Kordium (VUFKU)
   A drama about class struggle and the workers' movement in the United States. The film was roughly handled by critics who felt that neither Kordium nor the scenarist, L. Kniazhinski, showed any knowledge of American realities.

THE UNWILLING INSPECTORS — 1954 - Yulia Solntseva
(Kiev Studios)

UPRISING — 1918 - Alexander Razumni and Vladimir Karin
   Civil War and revolutionary *agitka*.

THE URALS FORGE VICTORY — 1943 - V. Boikov
(Central Newsreel Studio)
   Documentary on Soviet military production efforts.

USSR-AMERICA, THE GREATEST HOPE OF THE PEOPLE — 1959 -
Leonid Makhnach (Central Documentary Studios)
   Political documentary on US-Soviet relations.

VALERI CHKALOV — 1941 - Mikhail Kalatozov (Lenfilm) — Also
entitled *Wings Of Victory*.
   A dramatized story about the temperamental Soviet aviator who

flew from the USSR to the United States across the North Pole. Very popular in its time and contained interesting aerial sequences. The film probed deeply into the character of Chkalov, who was a man always happiest when alone in the air.

THE VALUE OF LIFE — 1940 - N. Tikhonov (Turkmenfilm)
The script was written by V. Skripitski and A. Konstantinov and was to have originally been filmed by another studio before it was given to Turkmenfilm. The story, simple in its structure, dealt with an old surgeon, Yastrebov, who is an implacable enemy of parachuting and forbids his daughter to engage in it. In the end Yastrebov himself must parachute down into a remote area to save the life of a dying child. The film came out at a time when aviation and parachuting were much publicized in the USSR.

THE VALUE OF MAN — 1928 - Mark Donskoi and Mikhail Averbakh (Belgoskino)

VANKA — 1942 - Herbert Rappoport
Featurette, *Fighting Fi lm Album No. 12.*

VASEK TRUBACHEV AND HIS COMRADES — 1955 - Ilya Frez (Maxim Gorki Studios)
Children's film.

[See also sequel *Trubachev's Unit In Battle.*]

VASYA THE REFORMER — 1926 - Alexander Dovzhenko (VUFKU-Odessa Studio)
An eccentric comedy about a devilish little boy, Vasya, who causes a good deal of commotion in his Ukrainian village. Despite his odd ways Vasya does good, such as saving a drunkard from drowning. The film gives a good portrayal of Ukrainian rural life.

VENDETTA — 1924 - Les Kurbas (VUFKU-Odessa Studio)
Antireligious comedy about the bitter differences that erupt between a priest and deacon over ownership of a cherry tree situated on the border of their respective houses.

THE VICTORS — 1932 - Eduard Arshanski (Sovetskaya Belarus)
A children's film about a group of city youngsters who go to the countryside to help their rural counterparts. Emphasized the solidarity between rural and urban elements of Soviet society.

VICTORY — 1938 - Vsevolod Pudovkin and Mikhail Doller (Mosfilm/Mezhrabpomfilm)
The film was originally to have been entitled *The Happiest One,* and later *Mother and Sons* before its title was finally decided. The filming was long delayed by the scenarist Natan Zarkhi's death in a car accident in which Pudovkin was the driver. The story was about a mother whose first son suddenly disappears while on an exploratory flight over the Arctic. The woman's youngest son then goes to find and rescue his brother. In the end the family is happily reunited. Filmed during a Soviet Arctic expedition.

VICTORY IN THE UKRAINE — 1945 - Alexander Dovzhenko and Yulia Solntseva (Central Newsreel and Kiev Studios)
Feature documentary about the Soviet liberation of the Ukraine in 1944. One of Dovzhenko's best efforts in documentary film-making.

VIENNA — I. Poselski (Central Newsreel Studio)
Record of the Soviet entry into the Austrian capital in 1945.

VIETNAM — 1954 - Roman Karmen (Central Newsreel Studio)
Film report on the victory of the Viet Minh over French forces and the political moves in Vietnam.

THE VILLAGE — 1930 - Ilya Kopalin (Sovkino)
Documentary on agriculture that emphasized need for collectivization.

A VILLAGE AT THE TURNING POINT — 1920 - Cheslav Sabinski (Slonfilm)
Civil War *agitka* about agitation in the countryside.

THE VILLAGE OBSERVED — 1935 - Ilya Kopalin
Documentary on kolkhoz life that was more lyrical and softer in style than Kopalin's earlier *Village Trilogy.*

THE VILLAGE TEACHER — (See *The Country Teacher*)

VIRGIN SOIL UPTURNED — 1939 - Yuli Raizman (Mosfilm)
Considered a classic adaptation of Mikhail Sholokhov's novel about the Russian countryside.

VIRINEYA — 1968 - Vladimir Fetin (Lenfilm)
A tale about a lusty, high-spirited peasant girl against a background of wretched poverty in the years prior to the Revolution. Politically naive, Virineya, is drawn to revolutionary forces out of emotion. Her defiance and strength of will are firm even as she is executed by a firing squad.

THE VODKA CHASE — 1924 - Abram Room (Goskino)
Short eccentric comedy about illegal spirit distillation.

VOICES OF SPRING — 1955 - Eldar Ryazanov (Mosfilm)

THE VOLGA IS FLOWING — 1964 - Yakov Segel (Mosfilm)

VOLGA REBELS — 1926 - P. Petrov-Bytov (Chuvashkino)
Drama about the revolutionary struggle of the Chuvash people.

VOLGA-VOLGA — 1938 - Grigori Alexandrov (Mosfilm)
A light musical comedy which also poked fun at bureaucratic mentality. The film was very popular in its time and featured many non-nonprofessional actors. Considered as one of Alexandrov's most successful films. Once used at the U.S. Army Language School as an instructional film because of its rich, sparkling dialog.

VOLOCHAEVKA DAYS — 1937 - Georgi and Sergei Vasiliev (Lenfilm)
Drama about the struggle of Bolshevik partisans against Japanese interventionist forces in the Far East during the Civil War. The scene of the wintry battle for Emelkin's hill was one of the most dramatic photographically. This film failed to bring the Vasilievs the same critical triumph as their earlier *Chapayev*.

THE VOW — 1946 - Mikhail Chiaureli (Tbilisi Studio)
Set at the time of Lenin's death the story deals with the pledge

made by Stalin to carry on Lenin's work. In the film Stalin makes his vow at Lenin's bier in a very dramatic scene whereas in reality he made it at the Bolshoi Theater. This was another of Chiaureli's heroic, monumental Stalin films which were later to be so severely attacked after 1953. Received Stalin Prize.

THE VYBORG SIDE — 1938 - Grigori Kozintsev and Leonid Trauberg (Lenfilm)

The third part of the *Maxim Trilogy*. Along with the first two parts this film is still regarded as among the best of Soviet cinema of the 1930s. In this film is traced Maxim's final political maturation and achievement as a people's commissar of the Soviet state bank. The action is set in the time from the capture of the Winter Palace to the Bolshevik dispersal of the Constitutent Assembly. Maxim is seen in meetings with Lenin, played by Maxim Shtraukh, and Stalin, played by Mikhail Gelovani. The character of Maxim was to reappear in other films, including Ermler's *The Great Citizen*.

WAIT A MOMENT! — 1969-71, in three parts — V. Konetochin (Soyuzmultfilm)

Animated film story about the hectic adventures of a wolf and a hare.

WAIT FOR ME — 1944 - Alexander Stolper and Boris Ivanov (Consolidated Studios, Alma-Ata)

Adapted from the play by Konstantin Simonov, who also wrote the film scenario. The warmth and tenderness reflected in this story about a wartime romance made this one of the most popular war films. The story delves into the problem of fidelity under the stress of war, a theme Soviet film-makers had not explored in the first few years of war.

WAITING FOR LETTERS — 1960 - Yuli Karasik (Mosfilm)

WAITING FOR VICTORY — 1941 - Ilya Trauberg (Mosfilm)

WAKE MUKHIN UP! — 1965 - Yakov Segel (Maxim Gorki Studios)

A light social satire about contemporary society.

WALKING AROUND MOSCOW — 1964 - Georgi Daneliya (Mosfilm)
A Soviet "new wave" comedy that was well received at the 1964 Cannes Film Festival because of its youthful, refreshing style. The story involves Soviet youth and amusing incidents in Moscow.

WANDERING STARS — 1926 - Grigori Grichen (VUFKU)
Based on the story by Sholem Aleichem. A drama and bitter satire about the persecution of Jews in the tsarist era.

WAR AND PEACE — 1964 - Sergei Bondarchuk (Mosfilm)
Soviet version is in four parts, eight hours running time while American version is in two parts and fewer hours. 70mm color film which took five years and 40 million dollars to make. Bondarchuk played the role of Pierre in this colossal and extravagant adaptation of Tolstoi's work. Bondarchuk's work is faithful to Tolstoi but is tedious. Voted Best Foreign Language Film by American Academy of Motion Picture Arts and Sciences in 1968.

THE WARMTH OF YOUR HANDS — 1970 - Shota and Nodar Managadze (Gruziyafilm)
A political and social drama about the development of Georgia from 1914 to contemporary times as witnessed and experienced by a peasant woman.

WARRIORS OF THE STEPPES — 1943 - Vera Stroyeva
War drama about Soviet partisans.

WARSHIPS BLOW UP IN THE PORT — 1966 - Anton Timonishin (Alexander Dovzhenko Studios)
Story about Soviet forces in combat along the Black Sea coast in World War II.

WATERCOLOR — 1958 - Otar Yoseliani (Gruziyafilm)

WATERLOO — 1970 - Sergei Bondarchuk (Mosfilm/Dino De Laurentis)
Italian-Soviet coproduction. Historical spectacle about Napoleon's defeat which is so grand in scale that acting performances are almost dwarfed. The international cast was headed by Rod Steiger.

THE WAY OF ENTHUSIASTS — 1930 - Nikolai Okhlopkov (Sovkino-Moscow)

Not released as a result of criticism that Okhlopkov had been too formalistic and intellectual in his approach to satire. The story dealt with the mutual suspicions between peasants and city workers, a theme that was politically uncomfortable as a result of the bitter resistance to Stalin's agricultural collectivization drive.

THE WAY OF SORROWS [Trilogy] — 1957-59, three parts - Grigori Roshal (Mosfilm)

The three parts are individually entitled *The Sisters, The Eighteenth Year,* and *Gloomy Morning* and are based on the novel by Alexei Tolstoi. An epic sage of the destiny of the Bulavin family from the October Revolution to the first years of the Soviet state.

THE WAY TO THE WHARF — 1962 - Georgi Daneliya (Mosfilm)

WE ARE FOR PEACE — 1951 - Ivan Pyriev and Joris Ivens (Mosfilm)

WE ARE FROM KRONSTADT — 1936 - Yefim Dzigan (Mosfilm)

A story about the Bolshevik defense of Petrograd in 1919 against the White forces of General Yudenich. Visually the film had panoramic battle and naval scenes. The drama initially reveals the poor morale of the Baltic sailors whose spirits undergo a change to strong determination. The final tragedy which is the highlight of the film is the capture and execution of several of the Baltic sailors. Adapted from the novel *An Optimistic Tragedy* by Vsevolod Vishnevski who wrote the screenplay and is today given as much credit for the film as Dzigan.

[See also *An Optimistic Tragedy.*]

WE ARE FROM THE URALS — 1944 - Lev Kuleshov

WE ARE WAITING FOR YOU, LAD! — 1973 - Pavel Batyrov (Uzbekfilm)

Script by Andrei Mikhalkov-Konchalovski. Dealt with Soviet adolescents and their inner conflicts as they come upon the threshold of adulthood.

WE LIVE HERE — 1957 - Shaken Aimanov (Kazakhfilm)

WE SEARCH FOR LITTLE BLOT — 1969 - V. Polkovnikov
(Soyuzmultfilm)
  Animated fantasy about two youngsters who find themselves in a
fairy tale land while visiting the workshop of a cartoonist.

THE WEDDING — 1944 - Isidor Annenski (Mosfilm)
  Based on the comedy by Anton Chekhov.

THE WEDDING — 1965 - Mikhail Kobakhidze (Gruziyafilm)
  Comedy on a Georgian theme.

WELCOME! — 1964 - Elem Klimov (Mosfilm)
  A light comedy about life at a camp for Young Pioneers which is
run by Comrade Dynin. The camp director is a strange man who is at
the same time concerned for the welfare of his charges and a strict observer of rules in the manner of all petty bureaucrats. His life changes
and becomes confused when Kostia Inochkin, one of the Pioneers, leads
a revolt against Dynin.

WHAT IF IT IS LOVE? — 1961 - Yuli Raizman (Mosfilm)
  A controversial film in which Raizman explored contemporary
morals against the background of social hypocrisy. The love story
emphasized the clash of old and new views about human relationships.

WHAT WERE YOU? — 1919 - Yuri Zheliabushski
  Civil War *agitka*.

WHEN EMIRS DIE — 1932 (Tadzhik-kino)
  First enacted Tadzhik film which dealt with the disruption of the
class system as a result of agricultural collectivization in Tadzhikistan.

WHEN I WAS YOUNG — 1970 - Algirdas Araminas
(Lithuanian Film Studio)
  A retrospective look at childhood.

WHEN ROSES BLOOM — 1959 - Kamil Yarmatov (Uzbekfilm)

WHEN THE DEAD AWAKE — 1928 - Viktor Turin (VUFKU)
Comedy.

WHEN THE TREES GREW TALL — 1961 - Lev Kulidzhanov
(Maxim Gorki Studios)
    A contemporary story of love which stressed the theme of man's faith in man.

WHEN WILL WE, THE DEAD, AWAKEN? — 1918 - Yakov Poselski
(Literfilm)
    Based on a play by Ibsen.

THE WHIRLPOOL — 1927 - P. Petrov-Bytov
    Drama about the resistance of rich peasants to land reform.

WHISTLE STOP — 1963 - Boris Barnet (Mosfilm)

WHITE BIRD WITH A BLACK MARK — 1971 - Yuri Ilyenko
(Alexander Dovzhenko Studios)
    Awarded Gold Medal at the 1971 Moscow Film Festival. A love story set against the background of peasant life in Transcarpathia during 1937-45 and traces the destiny of a family scattered by war. Ilyenko's training in cinematography made the film visually lyrical.

WHITE CARAVAN — 1964 - Eldar Shengelaya (Gruziyafilm)

THE WHITE EAGLE — 1928 - Yakov Protazanov (Mezhrabpomfilm)
    Based on the story "The Governor" by Andreev. The film proved successful abroad, but was attacked by Soviet critics for violating Party guidelines which has since been viewed by Soviet film historians as unfair. The drama is set in the time of the 1905 Revolution and the hero is the tsarist governor who broke up a workers' protest. He then becomes the target for assassination and while he awaits his death he experiences great inner turmoil. The sympathetic and compassionate portrayal of a tsarist official was the reason the film was severely criticized. Anna Sten was featured in the cast and emigrated to Hollywood after completing the film.

WHITE FANG — 1946 - Alexander Zguridi
Nature study film.

WHITE HORSEMAN — (See *God Of War*)

WHITE NIGHTS — 1959 - Ivan Pyriev (Mosfilm)

THE WHITE RAVEN — 1941 - Sergei Yutkevich
Featurette, *Fighting Film Album No. 7.*

THE WHITE SEA CANAL — 1933 - Viktor Turin (Sovkino)
Documentary on the building of the then so-called Stalin Canal.

WHITE SUN OVER THE DESERT — 1971 - Vladimir Motyl (Mosfilm)
A comedy about the confused adventures of a Red Army soldier while on his way home after the Civil War.

A WHITE, WHITE DAY — 1974 - Andrei Tarkovski (Mosfilm)

WHO IS YOUR FRIEND? — 1934 - Mikhail Averbakh
(Sovetskaya Belarus) — Also entitled *Zhulik.*
Suspense and intrigue mark this story about young workers unmasking a foreign agent in Soviet industry.

WHY THE ROOSTER HAS SHORT PANTS — 1966 - Yu. Batitski
(Kievnauchfilm)
Feature cartoon.

WHY THE SWALLOW HAS A TAIL WITH FEELERS — 1967 -
A. Khaidarov (Kazakhfilm)
Cartoon based on a Kazakh folk tale.

WILD DOG DINGO — 1963 - Yuli Karasik (Mosfilm)

WIND FROM THE EAST — 1940 - Abram Room (Ukrainfilm)
Filmed on location in Peremysl after the Soviet annexation of the Western Ukraine in 1939. The story was intended to show the hard life of landless peasants as reflected in the life of Khoma Gabrysia (played by Amvrosi Buchma).

A WIND FROM THE RAPIDS — 1930 - A. Kordium (VUFKU)
   Social change arising from industrial development is the theme of this story about an old river pilot who has guided vessels across the Dnieper River. With the building of the Dneprostroi Dam the pilot's work is no longer needed and he must find a new way of life for himself. There is inner turmoil and initial bitterness on his part as he watches his own sons join the construction project that will eventually alter his life.

WIND OF FREEDOM — 1961 - Leonid Trauberg

THE WINGED PAINTER — 1937 - Leo Esakiya (Goskinprom-Gruziya)
   Comedy about Soviet youth and aviation.

WINGS — 1969 - Larissa Shepitko (Mosfilm)
   Drama about a Soviet woman veteran combat flyer who finds herself coping with the problems of readjusting to peacetime, civilian life. The individual's role and problems with society are often found in Shepitko's films and this was one of her best.

WINGS OF A SERF — 1926 - Yuri Tarich (Sovkino-Moscow) —
Exhibited abroad under the title *Ivan the Terrible.*
   Now considered Tarich's best film, which was edited by Esther Shub and enjoyed much success abroad. The film was intended to depict the theme of class struggle in Russian history by focusing on the efforts of a serf to invent a flying machine. The tsar, convinced the machine is the work of the devil, has the serf executed for his troubles.

WINGS OF A SONG — 1966 - Shaken Aimanov (Kazakhfilm)

WINGS OF VICTORY — (See *Valeri Chkalov*)

WITH REGARDS — 1974 - Yuri Ilyenko
(Alexander Dovzhenko Studios)

WITH YOU AND WITHOUT YOU — 1973 - Rodion Nakhapetov
(Mosfilm)
   This film, which brought Nakhapetov international attention, dealt rather honestly with the bitter social and personal struggles brought on by the agricultural collectivization of the 1930s.

Wings, Larissa Shepitko   (British Film Institute)

WITHOUT DOWRY — (See *The Dowerless*)

WITHOUT FEAR AND REPROACH — 1964 - Alexander Mitta
(Mosfilm)

A WOLF, A BEAR AND A MOTORCYCLE WITH SIDECAR — 1969 -
P. Nosov (Soyuzmultfilm)
     A cartoon film about the crazy adventures of two animal friends
and their mechanical conveyance.

WOMAN — 1932 - Yefim Dzigan (Belgoskino)
     Mashka, the heroine of this story, is a young peasant woman who
desires to become a tractor driver, an occupation thought only for men.
Her dream runs into opposition with the old, male-oriented views of her
husband and others on the collective farm. Mashka decides to struggle
on and in the end wins her dreams while the men give growing respect.

WOMAN FROM THE FAIR — 1928 - G. Makarov
     Film was later banned. Drama about the Italian revolutionary
movement based on Eugene O'Neill's *Desire Under The Elms*.

THE WOMAN WHO INVENTED LOVE — 1918 - Vyacheslav Viskovski

A WOMAN'S VICTORY — 1927 - Yuri Zheliabushski
(Mezhrabpom-Rus)
     Based on N.S. Leskov's story "The Old Years in Plodomasov Vil-
lage." A historical costume drama which was heavily criticized for its
lack of social significance.

WOMEN OF RYAZAN — (See *Peasant Women Of Ryazan*)

THE WOODPECKER'S HEAD DOES NOT HURT — 1975 - D. Asanova
(Lenfilm)

A WORDLY MAN — 1972 - Yu. Dubrovin (Belarusfilm)

YAKOV SVERDLOV — 1940 - Sergei Yutkevich (Soyuzdetfilm)
     Based on the play *Bolshevik* by B. Levin and Pyotr Pavlenko. A
dramatization and idealization of the life and work of the first chairman

of the Party's Central Executive Committee. Considered one of the more successful films about Party history.

YAKUTIA — 1952 - Roman Grigoriev (Central Documentary Studios)
Ethnographical and geographical documentary.

THE YEAR 1919 — 1939 - Leonid Trauberg (Mosfilm)
Civil War drama about the underground work of Sergei Kirov in Baku when that city was under British occupation.

YEGIT — 1936 - Nabi Ganiev (Uzbekgoskino)
Silent film drama about the Civil War in Uzbekistan.

YELLOW PASSPORT — (See *Earth In Chains*)

YESTERDAY, TODAY, TOMORROW — 1923 - Dziga Vertov
Political and social documentary.

YOU AND I — 1972 - Larissa Shepitko (Mosfilm)
A somewhat controversial film in which Shepitko probes the theme man vs. society. The story deals with a doctor who questions the usefulness of his own existence and that of his own needs in relation to society's. Seeking isolation, he goes to Siberia, leaving behind his family. In Siberia he meets and falls in love with a young, carefree woman, but their affair ends as they realize that they are incompatible. He finally returns to Moscow and his family after deciding where his true interests lie.

YOU ARE A CRIMINAL, OBERLANDER! — 1960 - Leonid Makhnach
Documentary.

YOUNG GIRLS — 1961 - Yuri Chulukin (Mosfilm)
A further story of development of Chulukin's *Nadya's Charges.*

THE YOUNG GUARD — 1948 - Sergei Gerasimov
(Maxim Gorki Studios)
Based on the novel by Alexander Fadeev. The initial version was screened in 1947, but had to be remade because of ideological shortcomings. The story was about the struggle of Komsomols against Nazi

forces near Krasnodon. In the first version the Komsomols are seen fighting almost without Party leadership and included scenes of panic before the German advance. In revising the film Gerasimov changed the tone to bombastic patriotism and thereby won the Stalin Prize. The film gave rise to a whole new, postwar generation of actors and directors, including Sergei Bondarchuk and Samson Samsonov.

THE YOUNG LADY AND THE HOOLIGAN — 1918 - Yevgeni Slavinski

YOUNG PEOPLE — 1972 - Nikolai Moskalenko (Mosfilm)
A social comedy adapted from A. Andreev's novel *Settle Our Dispute, People.*

YOUNG WINE — 1942 - Ya. Aron
Featurette, *Fighting Film Album No. 10.*

YOUR ACQUAINTANCE — (See *The Journalist Girl*)

YOUR CONTEMPORARY — 1967 - Yuli Raizman (Mosfilm)
Social drama about changing social outlook as represented in the moral and psychological differences between older and younger generations of Soviet society. Nikolai Plotnikov who played the lead role received the award for best actor at the 1968 Karlovy Vary Film Festival.

YOUR SON AND BROTHER — 1966 - Vasili Shukshin (Mosfilm)

YOUTH — 1935 - Leonid Lukov (Ukrainfilm)
Story about Komsomols and their vigilance against saboteurs.

YOUTH CONQUERS — 1929 - Mikhail Gelovani (Goskinprom-Gruziya)
Comedy of errors about warring families in an isolated, feudal part of Georgia.

THE YOUTH OF MAXIM — 1934 - Grigori Kozintsev and L Leonid Trauberg (Lenfilm)
First part of the *Maxim Trilogy* (see also *The Return Of Maxim* and *The Vyborg Side*). All three parts were conceived as a whole project, which Kozintsev and Trauberg made based on their research of

memoirs of old Bolsheviks. In this first part Maxim is a young worker in the years prior to the First World War. Using a judicious mixture of seriousness and light humor the film reveals Maxim's depth of character and his growing awareness of the need for political change. Received a first prize at the 1935 Moscow Film Festival.

THE YOUTH OF OUR FATHERS — 1958 - Moisei Kalik with Ritsarev (Mosfilm)

THE YOUTH OF THE POET — 1937 - I. Naroditski
Drama about the early years in the life of Alexander Pushkin while he was a student at the lyceum at Tsarskoe Selo.

YUGOSLAVIA — 1946 - L.V. Varlamov (Central Newsreel Studio)
Documentary on the last year of war in Yugoslavia and Tito's partisans.

YVES MONTAND SINGS — 1957 - Sergei Yutkevich (Mosfilm)
Semi-documentary.

ZAMALLU — 1930 - Ivan Perestiani (Armenfilm)
First Armenian film to deal with the history of the Communist Party of Armenia. A dramatization of real events of 1920-21 and based on the activities of the Bolshevik Artashes Stepanian.

ZANGEZUR — 1938 - Amo Bek-Nazarov (Armenfilm)
Historical drama about the Civil War in Central Asia depicting the operations of the Red Army in capturing a mountain stronghold of the Whites.

ZARE — 1926 - Amo Bek-Nazarov (Armenkino)
An ethnographic film about the Kurds and their life under the tsars. The story's hero is Saido who becomes socially aware of the plight of his people and leads the anti-tsarist resistance movement. Considered to be the precursor of better revolutionary films of the sound period of Armenian cinema.

ZHUKOVSKI — 1950 - Vsevolod Pudovkin (Mosfilm)
A patriotic film biography of the pioneer of Russian aviation.

ZHULIK — (See *Who Is Your Friend?*)

ZHUZHUNA'S DOWRY — 1934 - S. Palavandishvili
(Goskinprom-Gruziya)
 A silent social comedy which was popular for so many years that it was technically refurbished with a sound track and rereleased in 1964.

ZIGZAG OF FORTUNE — 1969 - Eldar Ryazanov (Mosfilm)
 Social satire.

ZOYA — 1944 - Lev Arnshtam (Soyuzdetfilm)
 One of Arnshtam's best films which has been much acclaimed. This expressionistic wartime film depicts the true-life story of Zoya Kosmodemianskaya, an eighteen-year old Komsomol who worked behind German lines. She was brutally tortured before being hanged in 1941. Received 1946 Stalin Prize.

ZUMRAD — 1962 - A. Rakhimov and A. Davidson (Tadzhikfilm)
 A contemporary social drama about a young Tadzhik woman who struggles for her social rights. Zumrad, the heroine, is pitted against her husband who wants to preserve the old custom of secluding women in Central Asian society. The film illustrates the known fact that even in the 1960s Soviet Central Asian society continues to hold on to its old ways and customs.

ZVENIGORA — 1927 - Alexander Dovzhenko (VUFKU-Odessa Studio)
 Dovzhenko's stature as an important director was established with this film, which was admired by Eisenstein and Pudovkin. A surrealistic and heavily symbolic work that dealt with buried treasure from the time of the Vikings through the Civil War. The film is filled with poetic images of Red Army horsemen amid war-torn fields and phantoms from the Ukrainian past. The complex symbolism was given high marks by critics, but displeased audiences who could not understand it. The work was produced in a hundred days but filming was marred by a series of illnesses among the cast.

ZYGMUNT KOLOSSOWSKI — 1946 - L.S. Navrotski
 Made during the last stages of World War II, the film revealed

how much film censorship had been relaxed. The drama was a tribute to the Polish resistance movement during the Nazi occupation of Poland. Catholic priests are portrayed in near heroic roles for their cooperation with the partisans.

SOVIET FILM STUDIOS

Since the late 1960s the Soviet film industry has undertaken a long-range and extensive program of modernization and expansion of studio production facilities. Moscow and Leningrad continue to remain the leading film production centers, but their qualitative primacy has been effectively challenged by the national republican studios. A noticeable trend in the Soviet film industry is the growing number of co-productions undertaken with communist and capitalist countries. Annual film production averages 125 feature theatrical films, 25 feature documentaries, 30 animated or cartoon films, and almost 1,000 shorts, educational, popular science, and nature films. Film studios are also engaged in the production of films for Soviet television. Soviet films exported abroad increase yearly, especially to Third World countries. The exhibition of Soviet films in the United States is done primarily through Artkino Pictures, Inc. of New York and has shown steady growth since the late 1950s following the surprise of *The Cranes Are Flying*. Below are the major film studios:

MOSCOW, RSFSR:

Mosfilm (feature theatrical films)

Maxim Gorki Children and Youth Films Studios (formerly Soyuzdet-film and Mezhrabpomfilm; produces feature theatrical films for young people)

Tsentrnauchfilm [Central Popular Science Films Studios] (educational and popular science films)

Central Documentary Films Studios (newsreels, documentaries, educational, and nature films)

Soyuzmultfilm (cartoon and animated films)

LENINGRAD, RSFSR:

Lenfilm (feature theatrical films)

Lennauchfilm [Leningrad Popular Science Films Studios] (cartoon, popular science, educational, and documentary films)

KIEV, UKRAINIAN SSR:

Alexander Dovzhenko Studios (formerly Kiev Film Studios; feature theatrical films)

Kievnauchfilm [Kiev Popular Science Films Studios] (cartoon, popular science, and educational films)

Ukrainian Documentary Films Studios (documentary films)

ODESSA, UKRAINIAN SSR:
Odessa Film Studio (feature theatrical films)

MINSK, BELORUSSIAN SSR:
Belarusfilm (formerly Belgoskino and Sovetskaya Belarus; theatrical, documentary, cartoon, popular science, and educational films)

TBILISI, GEORGIAN SSR:
Gruziyafilm (formerly Goskinprom-Gruziya; theatrical and cartoon films)
Georgian Studios of Popular Science and Documentary Films (educational, popular science, and documentary films)

EREVAN, ARMENIAN SSR:
Amo Bek-Nazarov Studios — Armenfilm (theatrical, cartoon, and documentary films)

BAKU, AZERBAIDZHANIAN SSR:
Dzhafar Dzharbli Studios — Azerfilm (theatrical, cartoon, and documentary films)

ALMA-ATA, KAZAKH SSR:
Kazakhfilm (theatrical, cartoon, and documentary films)

TASHKENT, UZBEK SSR:
Uzbekfilm (theatrical and cartoon films)
Uzbek Popular Science and Documentary Films Studios (educational, popular science, and documentary films)

ASHKHABAD, TURKMENIAN SSR:
Turkmenfilm (theatrical, cartoon, and documentary films)

VILNIUS, LITHUANIAN SSR:
Lithuanian Film Studio (theatrical, cartoon, popular science, and documentary films)

RIGA, LATVIAN SSR:
Riga Film Studio (theatrical, cartoon, popular science, and documentary films)

FRUNZE, KIRGHIZ SSR:
Kirghizfilm (theatrical, cartoon, popular science, and documentary films)

KISHINEV, MOLDAVIAN SSR:
Moldovafilm (theatrical, cartoon, popular science, and documentary films)

TALLIN, ESTONIAN SSR:
Tallinfilm (theatrical, cartoon, popular science, and documentary films)

DUSHANBE, TADZHIK SSR:
Tadzhikfilm (theatrical, cartoon, popular science, and documentary films)

Documentary films are also produced in Rostov and Sverdlovsk.

GENERAL SELECTED BIBLIOGRAPHY

The works listed below are those of a general and comparative nature dealing with the development of Soviet and world cinema. Books or articles about a specific director have been listed at the end of relevant biographic entries.

Babitsky, Paul, and John Rimberg. *The Soviet Film Industry.* New York: Praeger, 1955. Traces the social and industry development of Soviet cinema to 1954. Throughout the book the authors approach the subject from political and sociological viewpoints. Babitsky himself worked in the Soviet film industry in the 1930s and gives a good glimpse of the problems that confronted film-makers.

Beaumont, Roger A. "Images of War: Films as Documentary History," *Military Affairs,* 1971 (Spring, vol. 35, no. 1, p. 5. Although written for the professional historian, serious film enthusiasts can gain ideas of how to look at war films in a different perspective.

Bleiman, M. *O kino-svidetelskie pokazaniya* [About the Cinema: Eyewitness Accounts]. Moscow: Iskusstvo, 1973. Brief reminiscences of Soviet film development by cinema personnel.

Cowie, Peter, ed. *International Film Guide.* New York: A.S. Barnes & Co., 1963-   . Annual reference guide to new films and developments around the world. Very useful for the film aficionado.

Crowther, Bosley. *The Great Films: Fifty Golden Years of Motion Pictures.* New York: Putnam, 1967. Illustrated, informative critical essays about key films from world cinema, including *Battleship Potemkin* and *Ivan the Terrible.*

Dickinson, Thorold, and Catherine de la Roche. *Soviet Cinema.* New York: Arno Press, 1972 [1948]. A comprehensive, succinct survey of thematic trends in Soviet films and organizational development of the film industry from 1917 to the immediate post-World War II period.

Furhammar, Leif, and Folke Isaksson. *Politics and Film.* New York:

Praeger, 1971. An historical analysis of film as a medium for political propaganda from around the world. Good critical analysis of several Soviet films.

Hibbin, Nina. *Eastern Europe: An Illustrated Guide.* Screen Series. New York: A.S. Barnes & Co., 1969. Anyone seriously interested in the East European and Soviet film scene will find this work an excellent reference. Hibbin is a contributing editor of the *International Film Guide* and long time observer of the Communist cinema. Contains hundreds of biographic profiles of actors, actresses, directors, scriptwriters, and cinematographers from all of the East European nations. Brief essays on the organization, thematic, and production developments of each country since 1945.

Istoriya Sovetskogo kino [History of the Soviet Cinema]. 4 vols. Moscow: Iskusstvo, 1969, 1973. A projected four-volume comprehensive history of the aesthetic development of Soviet cinema since 1918. Written by several film scholars under the auspices of the Soviet Institute of the History of Arts, Ministry of Culture. The two volumes published to date cover 1918 to 1940 and survey developments by each of the republican cinemas. The authors often point up what they consider to have been unfair criticism of films and directors in earlier years.

Kalashnikov, Ya. S., *et al. Ocherki istorii Sovetskogo kino* [Outline of the History of Soviet Cinema]. Moscow: Iskusstvo, 1959. A comprehensive, one-volume survey that is now dated by the above work.

Knight, Arthur. *The Liveliest Art: A Panoramic History of the Movies.* New York: Macmilland, 1957. Brief survey of Soviet film art in the context of world cinema written by foremost film critic.

Leyda, Jay. *Kino: A History of the Russian and Soviet Film.* New York: Macmillan, 1960. Still the indispensable source for anyone interested in the aesthetic development of tsarist and Soviet cinema down to 1958. Leyda is one of the foremost scholars and critics of Soviet film and had first-hand experience as a student in the USSR in the 1930s.

Macdonald, Dwight. *Dwight Macdonald On Movies*. Englewood Cliffs: Prentice-Hall, Inc., 1969. Bright wit and a sharp style mark this work by a respected critic. Macdonald provides a brief survey of Soviet cinema of the 1920s but his reviews of recent Soviet films do not provide much insight into the political context in which they were made.

Manchel, Frank. *Film Study: A Resource Guide*. Rutherford, Madison, Teaneck: Fairleigh Dickinson University Press, 1973. Written primarily for teachers and serious students of film. Many of the essays can provide the film enthusiasts with information and tips about looking at films in a new perspective.

Manvell, Roger. *Films and The Second World War*. South Bunrswick and New York: A.S. Barnes & Co., 1974. On themes and trends in films about World War II from the late 1930s through the early 1970s. Manvell, respected film scholar, writes in an eminently readable style and analyzes the work of film-makers from each of the countries involved in the war.

_____, and Lewis Jacobs, eds. *International Encyclopedia of Film*. New York: Crown, 1972. This comprehensive reference was prepared by an international group of film scholars and covers everything the serious film enthusiast might want to know regarding filmmaking. The work includes biographic profiles, explanations of technical processes, and surveys of the development of national cinemas.

Pisarevski, D. *Sto filmov Sovetskogo kino* [One hundred Films of Soviet Cinema]. Moscow: Iskusstvo, 1967. Profusely illustrated with analytical essays and filmography of 100 noteworthy films produced from the 1920s through the mid-1960s. The films are arranged in four periods and the thematic trends for each are covered in introductory essays.

Robinson, David. *The History of World Cinema*. New York: Stein & Day, 1973. For any serious film-goer or student Robinson's work provides a thorough survey of film history from a comparative international viewpoint.

Sadoul, Georges. *Dictionary of Films.* trans. and ed. by Peter Morris. Berkeley and Los Angeles: University of California Press, 1972. Synopses and filmography of hundreds of films from around the world.

Selezneva, T. *Kino-mysl 1920-x godov* [Cinema Theory of The 1920s]. Leningrad: Iskusstvo, 1972. A theoretical treatise written largely for the film scholar about the ideas that guided Soviet film-makers during their Golden Age.

Salisbury, Harrison E. "Theater: The Naked Truth" in *The Soviet Union: The Fifty Years,* edited by Harrison E. Salisbury. New York: Harcourt, Brace & World, 1967. A pessimistic look at Soviet cinema fifty years after the October Revolution.

Schnitzer, Luda, *et al,* eds. *The Cinema in Revolution: Twelve Witnesses of the Heroic Era of the Soviet Film.* New York: Hill & Wang, 1973. Contains interviews, reminiscences, and essays by twelve major film directors who began work in the 1920s. The various writings offer a lively and immediate glimpse of what it was like to be a young film artist in those materially poor, but intellectually challenging years of Soviet cinema's Golden Age.

Tyler, Parker. *Classics of the Foreign Film.* New York: Citadel, 1962. Critical, illustrated essays on *Battleship Potemkin, Descendant of Genghis Khan, Earth, Que Viva Mexico!, The Childhood of Maxim Gorki, Alexander Nevski,* and *Ivan the Terrible.*

Voronov, B., ed. *Filmy-skazki* [Film Tales]. Moscow: Iskusstvo, 1972. Stories adapted from the scenarios of animated feature films.

Yurenev, R. *Sovetskaya kinokomediya* [Soviet cine-comedy]. Moscow: Nauka, 1964. Discusses the start and themes of Soviet film humor and satire.